The Sense of Sound

THE NEW CULTURAL HISTORY OF MUSIC

SERIES EDITOR **Jane F. Fulcher**

SERIES BOARD Celia Applegate
Philip Bohlman
Kate van Orden
Michael P. Steinberg

The Sense of Sound

Musical Meaning in France, 1260–1330

EMMA DILLON

OXFORD
UNIVERSITY PRESS

OXFORD
UNIVERSITY PRESS

Oxford University Press, Inc., publishes works that further
Oxford University's objective of excellence
in research, scholarship, and education.

Oxford New York
Auckland   Cape Town   Dar es Salaam   Hong Kong   Karachi
Kuala Lumpur   Madrid   Melbourne   Mexico City   Nairobi
New Delhi   Shanghai   Taipei   Toronto

With offices in
Argentina   Austria   Brazil   Chile   Czech Republic   France   Greece
Guatemala   Hungary   Italy   Japan   Poland   Portugal   Singapore
South Korea   Switzerland   Thailand   Turkey   Ukraine   Vietnam

Published by Oxford University Press, Inc.
198 Madison Avenue, New York, New York 10016

www.oup.com

Oxford is a registered trademark of Oxford University Press

Library of Congress Cataloging-in-Publication Data
Dillon, Emma.
    The sense of sound : musical meaning in France, 1260-1330 / Emma Dillon.
       p. cm. — (The new cultural history of music series)
    Includes bibliographical references.
    ISBN 978-0-19-973295-1 (hardcover : alk. paper) 1. Music—Philosophy and aesthetics.
2. Music—France—500-1400—History and criticism. 3. Music and literature.
4. Auditory perception. 5. Listening. I. Title.
    ML3877.D37   2011
    780.944'09022—dc23   2011022191

Publication of this book was supported by the Margarita Hanson Endowment of the American
Musicological Society.

1 3 5 7 9 8 6 4 2
Printed in the United States of America
on acid-free paper

For my brother,

Charles Dillon

ACKNOWLEDGMENTS

I began this project in 2003–2004 when I was a Member of the School of Historical Studies at the Institute for Advanced Study in Princeton. I thank the Director, Faculty, and Andrew Mellon Foundation for their generous support. My time at the Institute changed the way I think about music in medieval culture, due in large part to the many stimulating interactions with scholars across a range of fields. I benefited tremendously from conversations with Jane Fulcher, Ellen Harris, Irving Lavin, and Heinrich von Staden. I am especially indebted to Giles Constable, Cynthia Hahn, Tia Kolbaba, and other participants in the weekly "medieval table." Above all, my thanks to Caroline Walker Bynum, who has been a profound inspiration to me in many facets of my life, academic and personal. I am indebted to Sir Timothy Lankaster and the Fellows of Corpus Christi College, Oxford, and thank them for welcoming me as a visiting scholar in Hilary and Trinity terms of 2005. I am grateful to the University of Pennsylvania Research Foundation for their generous support towards the costs for research in France and the website that accompanies this book.

My work would have been impossible without the cooperation and expertise of many librarians. My thanks to the librarians of the Bibliothèque nationale de France, the British Library, Cambridge University Library, and the Bodleian Library in Oxford. I am particularly grateful to William Noel at the Walters Art Museum, who as well as allowing me easy access to the manuscript collection, drew my attention to several manuscripts relevant to my research. The librarians of Van Pelt Library at the University of Pennsylvania have helped me out above and beyond the call of duty more times than I can remember. I am particularly grateful to Nancy Shawcross, Amey Hutchins, and John Pollock in the Rare Book and Manuscript Library, and to Richard Griscom and his team on the fourth floor.

I am fortunate to have such wonderful people to work with in the Music Department at the University of Pennsylvania. Every one of my colleagues, past and present, has made a difference to the way I think about music, and I am glad to have the opportunity to thank them: Carolyn Abbate, Lawrence Bernstein, Mark Butler, Emily Dolan, Christopher Hasty, Cristle Collins Judd, Jeffrey Kallberg, Jairo Moreno, Carol Ann Muller, Eugene Narmour, James Primosch, Guthrie Ramsey, Jay Reise, Timothy Rommen, Gary Tomlinson, and Anna Weesner. Warm thanks to Margaret Smith Deeney, Alfreda Frazier, and Maryellen Malek for their good-natured professionalism and support, and to Eugene Lew for bringing calm to so many technological storms. I am grateful to the many generations of Penn graduates who worked through the materials and ideas in this book with me in seminar. I must pay special tribute to my talented Ph.D. students: Jennifer Saltzstein, Anna Grau, Elizabeth Mellon, Lauren Jennings, and Emily Zazulia; and also Daniel DiCenso and Sean Curran, who happily joined our community from the remote. Beyond the Music Department, many other colleagues at Penn have enriched my understanding of medieval culture and books. I am especially indebted to Ann Matter, Rita Copeland, Peter Stallybrass, and David Wallace. Kevin Brownlee has been a generous collaborator on many projects, and his influence is felt on many pages of this book.

Over the years of research and writing, I have presented my work at conferences and colloquia, and am grateful for all the feedback and suggestions I have received from patient audiences. I am particularly grateful to Bruce Holsinger and members of the Music Department at the University of Virginia; Anne Stone and students of the CUNY Graduate Center; and to members of the History of Material Texts Seminar at the University of Pennsylvania, where I received very helpful comments on earlier versions of the material in this book. Bill Burgwinkle and Sylvia Huot and other members of the Old French Seminar at Cambridge University gave me invaluable suggestions on my chapters relating to Adam de la Halle.

Several people have read and commented on portions of the book. I am especially grateful to Bojan Bujic, Suzannah Clark, Joel Kaye, and Judith Peraino for their thoughtful feedback on portions of the book. Gary Tomlinson read sections along the way, and has been a careful listener and generous critic as my ideas have taken shape. Beth Williamson read the complete manuscript, and in addition to her useful comments, I am grateful to her for the many years of fruitful conversation and collaboration on matters medieval. Roger Parker has continued to read what I write with enormous care and insight. As I have assumed the role of advisor with my own students, I see ever more clearly the extraordinary gift of his patient and brilliant mentoring, and I continue to learn so much from him. Special thanks must go to Shane Butler. As our friendship has taken shape, so has this book, and our constant thread of conversation has helped me to make sense of sound, and so much more. I am grateful to the anonymous reader for OUP who offered very helpful comments on the final draft of the manuscript. Particular thanks to Bonnie Blackburn for her meticulous attention to detail during the copyediting process, to Norman Hirschy for his expert help designing the website that accompanies this book, and to Jeanne Roberts for her beautiful work on the musical examples. Warm thanks are due to Suzanne Bratt for her exceptional work in preparing the index. Suzanne Ryan has been a most accommodating and encouraging editor, and I thank her, Adam Cohen, Apurupa Mallik, and Erica Woods for the professionalism with which they have seen my book through to completion. I finished the draft of the book in early 2010. Since then, a number of excellent studies have appeared that I have been unable to incorporate into my argument. However, where possible, I have indicated recent publications in the footnotes and bibliography.

My work would be impossible without the support and community of friends and family. They have all sustained me through the highs and lows of writing with wisdom, kindness, and humor. It is therefore with great pleasure and gratitude that I acknowledge Suhnne Ahn, Bill Bell, Shane Butler and Leo Proietti, Shehra, Ethan, Gladia, and Cyrus Boldt, Vahni Capildeo, Alex Colvin, Denise Dillenbeck, Emily Dolan, Patricia Furlan, Cordula Grewe and Warren Breckman, Karen Henson, Sara Mitchell, Fiona, Francisco, Patrick, and Naomi Soria, Anna Weesner, and Beth Williamson. Some debts go back a very long way. My friend Claire Dixon has been a constant source of inspiration and comfort across the years, and I am grateful to her and Alex and their beautiful girls, my goddaughters, Sophie, Jessica, and Isabelle, for always keeping a place for me at their table. I thank my father for his generous enthusiasm for what I do. My mother has lovingly helped me with intellectual insight as well as with unwavering belief in my endeavors. This book is dedicated with great affection to my brother, Charles Dillon.

CONTENTS

LIST OF TABLES

LIST OF MUSIC EXAMPLES

Ba	Bamberg, Staatsbibliothek, Lit. 115 (*olim* Ed.IV.6)
Cl	Paris, Bibliothèque nationale de France, nouv. ac. f. fr. 13521 (La Clayette)
Da	Darmstadt, Hessische Landes- und Hochschulbibliothek, 3471
F	Florence, Biblioteca Medicea Laurenziana, Pluteus 29.1
Fauv	Paris, Bibliothèque nationale de France, f. fr. 146
Ma	Madrid, Biblioteca Nacional, 20486
Mo	Montpellier, Bibliothèque Interuniversitaire, Section Médecine, H 196 (Montpellier Codex)
MuB	Munich, Bayerische Staatsbibliothek, lat. 16444
MuC	Munich, Bayerische Staatsbibliothek, lat. 5539
St.V	Paris, Bibliothèque nationale de France, lat. 15139 (St. Victor manuscript)
Tu	Turin, Biblioteca Reale, MS varia 42
V	Paris, Bibliothèque nationale de France, f. fr. 24406 (Chansonnier de la Vallière)
W₁	Wolfenbüttel, Herzog August Bibliothek, 628
W₂	Wolfenbüttel, Herzog August Bibliothek, 1099 (*olim* Helmst. 1206)
X	Paris, Bibliothèque nationale de France, nouv. ac. f. fr. 1050 (Chansonnier de Clairambault)

A NOTE TO THE READER

Ars antiqua motet texts are numbered according to the system assigned in Ludwig's *Repertorium*. In the case of tenors, the letter preceding the number "O," "M," or "BD" refers to the chant's liturgical source in the Office, Mass, or *Benedicamus Domino* setting. Chant texts are quoted from Tischler, *The Style and Evolution of the Earliest Motets* and the *Corpus antiphonalium officii*. Trouvère songs are numbered according to the system assigned in Spanke's revision of Reynaud's catalogue (RS). Refrains follow the numbering of van den Boogaard's *Rondeaux et refrains* (R). Biblical citations are from the Vulgate, and translations from the Douay–Rheims version. In other cases, I cite English translations where good ones are available; all other translations are my own.

Although the music examples cited exist in excellent editions, I have provided my own transcriptions in all cases. Most examples of motets are edited from versions extant in *Mo*, the largest of the motet compendia. This has allowed me to reflect and maintain notational consistencies in the original source. I include full concordances and directives to modern editions should readers wish to pursue issues of transmission and reworkings of individual pieces. There is just one editorial convention that may be unfamiliar. Notation in many of the sources of this period makes use of the plica (a small stroke ascending or descending from a note, indicating a decorative inflection of the voice up or down). Most modern editions realize that as a grace note, above or below the main note depending on the direction of the stroke in the original notation. However, this introduces an independent note shape where there is none in the original. I therefore realize plicas as small arrows above the note they inflect.

ABOUT THE COMPANION WEBSITE

The Companion Website to *The Sense of Sound*, at www.oup.com/us/thesense ofsound, offers digital color images of many of the images reproduced in black and white in the book, which are signaled with an additional call-out number in the main text. I have thus far opted to reproduce images on the website from manuscripts that are not readily available in color facsimile or in library databases, with a view to giving the reader a more vivid sense of the original manuscripts. Images not included on the website are available in color reproduction, and the reader may pursue these with reference to my footnotes and bibliography.

User Name: Music2   Password: Book4416   📖

The Sense of Sound

Exeter High Street is much like that of any other West Country town in England. Cutting through the center of the city, it is host to the usual busy scenes of commerce and people. You can also depend on a musical presence. Somewhere in the arcades around Marks & Spencer, within sight of the fifteenth-century Guildhall and the Norman towers of the cathedral, street musicians take up their pitch. These days, it is likely to be the comic turn of the man accompanied by his "wonder" dog who barks on cue; or the suave, professional busker, strumming an amplified guitar. And on any shopping day, you may find all of them. They settle at corners of the shop front, in competition and oblivious to cacophony forgiven in the city context, where all sounds are in free exchange. Indeed, song, guitar, and barking intermingle with other sonic fixtures: the white-noise of chatter and feet, the uneven roll of bus wheels on cobbles, the cry of seagulls; and, on the hour, the resonances of the cathedral bell. If the scene is familiar the country over, it is the distinctive elements in the conversation—musical, verbal, avian, mechanical—that make Exeter sound unique, that make it sound like Exeter. It is by listening to this colloquy—and music's place within it—that I want to explain the project that has become this book.

Walking the streets and writing have long been entwined: the blocked take a turn round the block; and throughout history, from Plato to de Certeau, the city has been a constant cipher for interior landscapes, a template for moral codes, or a model for complex critical practice. For now, though, Exeter is no metaphor. The story of the High Street is necessarily literal. Its reality is a sensual presence that exemplifies how music can be in and of the world. As such, my turn around the city in all its messy actuality is a reaction against the past, where the sense of real-time experience seems remote and unattainable, and often incidental, in the musicologist's effort to make the notes sing again. I begin in Exeter because it seems so unlike the musical past I study, for the uncontrived sense of the real often missing in accounts of medieval song. And to be in a place where sound is vividly and unavoidably of the world, where even as you encounter the street musician, physical space forces you to rub shoulders with a living, breathing humanity at the edge of the performance. To preface my journey into the medieval past in this most mundane of musical contexts is not just a moment of ethnographic envy. It became an opportunity to reframe the sense of sound in the Middle Age, and to engage music once again in the elusive worlds in which it once existed.

So, let's walk.

First a tiny temporal leap. Nowadays on Exeter High Street I catch myself listening past the street music for the strains of a musician long since departed. In my childhood, one particular spot outside M & S was the site of the city's most notorious music man: an accordion player. He appeared there sometime in the late 1970s, tweed jacket, jaunty hat, squeezing tunes out of a dinosaur of an instrument fringed with Morris-man tassles. He had a repertory of folk songs and sea shanties like "Bobby Shaftoe" and "What shall we do with the drunken sailor?". During December, as holiday lights appeared, he expanded his canon to a medley of carols that included "Hark the Herald Angels Sing," and a lugubrious version of "Silent Night." He was hardly virtuosic: to foreign ears he was downright unmusical, puffing out a limited harmonic repertory under his tunes. Depending on a capricious alternation of tonic and dominant, he took unabashed delight in grandiose cadences that extended indefinitely— at least, as long as the air lasted. But time and familiarity tuned out wonky harmonization, indeed rewrote it as ordinary and usual—simply as the way those tunes sounded in that particular place, in those particular hands, and for that particular period of High Street history. In the years I lived there, the accordion player's presence was as predictable as my own; and in the years after, his music was a reassurance of continuity. When he vanished a few years ago (I hope to a new pitch, in a new town), to be replaced by the fiasco of barking and crooning, his memory provoked something more complicated than nostalgia: a kind of heightened aural awareness, attentive listening made acute by absence.

In that silent place of memory I have found not only a metaphor for music's quintessential condition—Isidore of Seville said it perished the instant it sounds—but also a reenactment of the project of historical musicology: held captive in sound's wake, listening for something that cannot be recuperated. But on the streets of Exeter, it was possible to inject into that affective sensation of loss a unique sense of the familiar, a move impossible in my medieval scholarship: to call on the living to help explain the sounding past. Picking up the threads of schooldays, I asked old friends to recast themselves into the

High Street of the 1980s and 1990s.[1] In many cases, this was the first time we had spoken of the accordion player: my enduring companion on the High Street recalled him in as vivid detail as I did, but our teenage agendas had rarely allowed much room for discussion of him. A startling theme in the recollections was not just the precise detail with which people recalled his melodies, sometimes prompting (one conjured the forgotten strain of "English Country Garden"), but also delight in being asked to summon into conversation an old experience—one so taken for granted back then that it rarely enjoyed much scrutiny. While some recalled the musician's shaky harmonies with the language of their subsequent musical training, others remembered him in more forgiving (and less theoretical) terms, as "lost in the music." People heard him in different ways, yet all recollections situated *him*. Where he had played was at least as memorable as what came out of the accordion. His M & S pitch was seconded with another hot-spot, just across the street down near the Ship Inn, a fifteenth-century pub in cramped Martin's Lane, an alley from the High Street to the Cathedral. Common to all my conversations, many conducted in emails across continents and time zones, was a pleasure both in revisiting Exeter in the virtual realm, and in the fleeting reassembly of a past community. My friends thought back on the sound as an icon or relic of younger times, not of great events, but of a time mundanely regular. What emerged from this brief venture is that "Harmonizing Harry," as one family knew him, was for a pocket of Exeter society of the 1980s and 1990s no less sturdy a monument than the cathedral itself. His music, now long departed, was in its absence a kind of tape-recorder, not for its own memorialization, but rather of its once powerful, shared sense of home and communal identity.

The lessons of the accordion player have become pertinent to the ways I want to listen to the musical repertories that are the subject of this book. They invite reflection on listening; on what musical sound can mean; on the very ontology of music. Even the primitive ethnographic gesture to situate a lost musician is a reminder of the limits of medieval evidence: limits that have inevitably shaped the agenda for a history of musical experience. The absence of a living constituency of listeners, or of many traces of first-hand listening experiences in the Middle Ages, is reflected in a tendency away from questions of song's affect, its relationship to the people around it and those who perform it, its potential to shape experiences. Instead, focused more on music's material traces, efforts to recover pieces for performance, study of notational technology and performerly improvisation, and analytical investigation of the processes of music's makers, have necessarily led much musicological inquiry. Subsequently, medieval song

---

1 This was in no sense a scientific survey. I am especially grateful to Paul and Thomas Yates, Philip Fairweather, Claire Dixon, John Wase, Rosemary Garnham, and to my family, who all shared their memories of this musician with me.

is often bounded by later notions of the musical work, and of music's rarified place in the world. That classification is sometimes reinforced by cultural historians who, perhaps cautious in the face of the notational and analytical dimensions of music, have treated musical experience as separate from other kinds of experience, and listening and performing as activities set apart.

However, as the exemplum of Exeter reminds us, categories of music and sound, and the borders between listening and other kinds of social experience, are more complicated. Even my earlier moment of comparative reflection— glancing across the disciplinary boundaries—is a simple reminder of music's capacity to participate in a landscape of human experience, one not limited to the purely musical, but connected in various ways to a more worldly environment. In fact, the accordion player's sound was part of a wider sonority of the city so that it is hard to know where musical experience ends and soundscape begins: folded into the hubbub of city sound, music takes its place as one sonority among many, all of which are imbued with social, emotional, even ethical meanings unique to the people and place they inhabit. To unsettle the category of musical listening is not to deny music any of the expertise necessary for its creation or performance. Rather, it allows for the inclusion of other kinds of sounds and environments as contexts to inform musical experience, and welcomes in a more holistic mode of listening to music. Above all, I wish to take from this brief excursion in Exeter (one overlaid, after all, on the terrain of a medieval city) the simple reminder of how, situated in that broader context of place and people, music has a powerful role in shaping the sense of its surroundings; and how in turn that world imbues music with meaning.

Using the real-time experience of the present as a prompt, *The Sense of Sound* is an experiment in listening to a medieval repertory whose wider sonic environment is now almost completely silent. Although it risks dealing in a currency of faint echoes, my hope is to revive around some familiar music, fragments a listening environment every bit as noisy and meaningful as was the Exonian scene. To broaden that listening environment is, moreover, a response to where the music has led me: for a few decades at the end of the thirteenth century and beginning of the fourteenth in northern France, it seems that musicians, in collaboration with artists, intellectuals, poets, painters, and manuscript makers, were experimenting with the possibilities of sound, and the range of meanings it could convey. Theirs was not a deliberate agenda. Through a strange alchemy of circumstances—creative, economic, intellectual, and technological—these years marked a moment at which music not only sounded different in some quarters, but also began to shape new meanings.

My primary witness and touchstone in this book to the changing nature of musical sound is the polytextual motet, a genre notorious in its own time, and more so in our own scholarly moment, for its extraordinary effect: a distinctive sound of words lost in the mêlée of music, a strange musicality brought about through a surplus of language. It is a genre that magnifies a tension heard across music's history (and that of language also): between sense and sound, meaning and effect. While the motet will be my main reference point, in pursuing the question of what such a soundworld signified to its listeners, it has become apparent that the genre was part of a much larger cultural contemplation of sound around 1260 to 1330. In music, the play on a musical sound wrought through verbal excess—what I term the supermusical—is evident in genres other than the motet: in other polyphonic repertories such as the early rondeaux; in experimentation with semi-lyric forms; in genres premised on verbal nonsense such as *fatras* and *fatrasie*; and in representations of singing in genres like the *pastourelle*.

But the experimentation with sound is not limited to music alone: poets and artists are complicit, too, in the play with sound's sense, and interested in the ways it could disrupt, edify, and upset. And it is here that the lost sonorities or sounding realities of the medieval environment begin to encroach on its more durable records. For the range of sounds folded into the arts of this period extends well beyond the musical, and among the sonorities referenced are those more worldly and quotidian—the cityscape, charivaric protest, prayerful voices, and the strange sounds of a host of outcasts (the dispossessed and possessed), to name but a few. In inscribing such soundworlds, sounds by their nature elusive and resistant to reproduction, artists seem concerned not just with the creative challenge to find an aural equivalence for the "real" sound of their originary model, but also to demonstrate and utilize its social meanings and effects. That distinction between acoustic reality and cultural meaning reflects in turn a distinction historians of sound see in the conception of soundscapes of more recent epochs. In her groundbreaking account of cultures of listening in modern America, Emily Thompson offers eloquent summary of that relation: "a soundscape is simultaneously a physical environment and a way of perceiving that environment; it is both a world and a culture constructed to make sense of that world."[2] While we shall look more deeply into theories of soundscape in later chapters, for now this distinction is a pertinent *vade mecum* for the nature of the medieval evidence I shall attend to. While Thompson's soundscapes are often fully acoustically available—sounding realities—the material evidence of medieval soundscapes of prayer, the city, and so forth is in most instances the only record extant. The absence of technologies by which to record sounding reality means we can never fully determine its authenticity. The status of the surviving records as representations of sounding realities will inevitably be a theme in what follows. However, while I hope to show how we

---

2 Emily Thompson, *The Soundscape of Modernity: Architectural Acoustics and the Culture of Listening in America, 1900–1933* (Cambridge, MA: MIT Press, 2002), 1. Thompson here draws on the work of R. Murray Schafer and Alain Corbin.

may "listen through" them, in dialogue with other sorts of evidence, to hear some fragment of the sounding past, their relationship to processes by which the acoustic is simultaneously a "culture constructed to make sense of the world" is, I believe, more vividly accessible, and often articulated, through the sounds made or implied by the words, music, or images used to render the world beyond. Thus, although surviving at the remove of a system of representation, such sonic evidence offers remarkable insight into a reality where sound was imbued with meaning and power. It is with those meanings, as well as with their originary sounding source, that I shall be concerned. That those concerned with inscribing soundscapes had recourse in their constructions to aural effects consonant with the supermusical will be especially revealing.

Such materials relate to music in a number of ways, and not least because musicians, too, sometimes attempt to represent music's other: in motets filled with city cries, for example, or in the musicalization of charivaric noise. But all these materials are connected by their environments of production: in manuscripts, where songs sit alongside poetic representation of the mad; in libraries, where chansonniers share a shelf with books illuminated with noisy marginalia; and in the artistic constituency of cities such as Arras or Paris. I do not suggest there was any deliberate or contrived attempt to codify sound in these creative and listening communities; nor do I want to impose a new paradigm for listening. Rather, I will argue that the consonances between different sorts of sonic evidence offer precious insights into a sense of musical sound in this period. My book is thus an attempt to restore to music a lost interlocutor: a world captured in words, images, and music, in which sounds of all kinds shaped human experience, and which also shaped musical listening.

The first chapter will take these themes up more fully. As well as introducing the musical repertories at the heart of the project, it makes the case for an alternate mode of musical listening, drawing on a range of materials from a broad base of medieval and modern critical evidence. The succeeding chapters 2–8 are organized as a series of conversations, in which I relocate the supermusical in a range of sonorities, the two kinds of sound bound in dialogue by a common community of makers and listeners. These spheres of conversation are organized loosely around the worldly, physical realm of the city, charivari, and madness (chapters 2–4), with a turn to the more spiritual realm of prayer (chapters 5–8). In each case, as well as illuminating what these records may have to say about the sensation, power, and meaning of sounds normally left out of historical inquiry, I strive to rehear familiar music in light of the alternate sonic setting.

*

Before we begin, though, I wish to look briefly behind the scenes of this book's production. For in experimenting with modes of listening to medieval song,

I have been inspired to expand and deepen my foundation of medieval evidence in part by concerns that are rather more contemporary. The desire to focus attention on the embodied and experiential dimensions of sound, to widen its spheres of reference and meaning, and to reassemble it within a wider listening community echoes a growing chorus in various quarters of musicology and among medievalists of many stripes, scholars whose commitment is to what might be termed the "humanness" of the past. Indeed, I am fortunate to be writing at a moment where scholars of many disciplines and styles are newly sensitive to the currency of liveness that illuminates the materials and people that are the focus of study. There are such strong resonances between the disciplines of musicology and medieval studies in this regard that, born at the intersection of those fields, my book's concerns with the contextually broad, humanizing approach to song have sometimes felt like a foregone conclusion.

Within the field of medieval studies, an increased emphasis on human experience has manifest itself in numerous studies about issues of identity, community, emotion, sensation, and memory. Having led the way in early groundbreaking studies of female spirituality and the physicality of devotion,[3] Caroline Walker Bynum's more recent work on the theme of metamorphosis, hybridity, and monstrosity—a trope among medieval writers of many cultural spheres—offers new paths into how people understood themselves, and particularly so in relation to the sacred.[4] Her monograph *Wonderful Blood* exploring the cults and theology surrounding the phenomenon of holy blood, underscores a pervasive paradox in medieval believers of the fourteenth and fifteenth centuries: their committed, often violent, devotion to a religious symbol that itself remembers the pain and violence at the core of Christian tenets of faith.[5] In all cases, such work emphasizes how formations of selfhood occur, and how they are different from the modern idea of identity; it also underscores the vital importance of the body—of things felt through the senses—as a mode of expression. In a different context, in her exploration of the workings of medieval memory, meditation, and writing, Mary Carruthers

3 See in particular Caroline Walker Bynum, *Holy Feast and Holy Fast: The Religious Significance of Food to Medieval Women* (Berkeley: University of California Press, 1987), and *Resurrection of the Body in Western Christianity, 200–1336* (New York: Columbia University Press, 1995).

4 Caroline Walker Bynum, *Metamorphosis and Identity* (New York: Zone Books, 2001).

5 Caroline Walker Bynum, *Wonderful Blood: Theology and Practice in Late Medieval Northern Germany and Beyond* (Philadelphia: University of Pennsylvania Press, 2007), and Mary Carruthers, "Sweetness," *Speculum* 81 (2006): 999–1013.

has likewise emphasized the importance of sensual experience as the starting point of thought and learning.[6]

Related to the experiential theme of such work, scholars such as Carl Morrison and Rachel Fulton have suggested that in excavating the somatics and belief systems of medieval people, we too, as feeling, bodied people, may identity with our subjects. They call for a relationship founded on empathy: a sense of connection forged by shared humanness, but one also mindful of fundamental cultural differences.[7] In their research, this emerges in a commitment to the deepest possible contextualization of materials, in an effort to illuminate how the textual, musical, and visual traces were expressive of individual or collective feelings and beliefs. Fulton's study of medieval attitudes to Mary, and to Christ's Passion, operates by a pattern of accumulation, layering close readings of texts upon one another, in the belief that however fragile, it is "not only possible but necessary to read . . . texts 'on their own terms,' if, that is, we are to recover something of the power that they had for their original authors and audiences."[8] In a recent collaboration with Bruce Holsinger, both authors reflect on the need also to historicize the notion of individuality and selfhood, using the model of community as a more appropriate means to explore identity.[9] Vigilant, again, about imposing a universal standard on the notion of individuality, their essay collection rather investigates the "category of person . . . in relation to community: the forms of mediation, materiality, incarnation, representation, and transcendence that go into the making of the medieval human being in all its individual and collective complexity," and asks: "What are the boundaries of person at particular moments, and how are these boundaries imagined and negotiated in particular circumstances?"[10]

Community is also a unit of investigation in another flourishing area devoted to human experience, namely emotion and feeling, what Barbara Rosenwein has termed one of the "invisible" topics of medieval studies.[11] In the last decade or so, the history of emotions has blossomed in a range of

---

6 See her *The Book of Memory: A Study of Memory in Medieval Culture* (Cambridge: Cambridge University Press, 1990, repr. 1996) and *The Craft of Thought: Meditation, Rhetoric, and the Making of Images, 400–1200* (Cambridge: Cambridge University Press, 1998).

7 Rachel Fulton, *From Judgment to Passion: Devotion to Christ and the Virgin Mary, 800–1200* (New York: Columbia University Press, 2002), and Karl Morrison, *I Am You: The Hermeneutics of Empathy in Western Literature, Theology, and Art* (Princeton: Princeton University Press, 1988).

8 Fulton, *From Judgment to Passion*, 6.

9 *History in the Comic Mode: Medieval Communities and the Matter of Person*, ed. Rachel Fulton and Bruce Holsinger (New York: Columbia University Press, 2007).

10 Fulton and Holsinger, "Introduction," ibid., 5.

11 Barbara Rosenwein, *Emotional Communities in the Early Middle Ages* (Ithaca: Cornell University Press, 2006), 1.

disciplinary contexts, and nowhere more so than within medieval studies, with various new methods of historicizing the complex area of feeling emerging.[12] Some have tackled feelings as they manifest in social behavior. C. Stephen Jaeger's work on courtliness, love, and friendship has been pioneering in that regard: exploring those feelings through the lens of literary and visual traces, designed for specific court and school environments, Jaeger's work shows clearly how feelings translated into highly complex ritual and social acts and behavior patterns.[13] Barbara Rosenwein has taken up the idea of feeling as social action in her recent work on the emotion of anger, and more recently she has emphasized emotion's communal dimensions: "emotional communities," she argues, are "groups in which people adhere to the same norms of emotional expression and value—or devalue—the same or related emotions."[14] In all these cases, the emotion of the past is traced via its social effects, through its representations in language (literary and visual), representations which naturally speak of, and to, a collective.

Closer to home, recent studies on the specific terrain of medieval song and poetry have offered fresh incentive to think about song in this more communal manner. Ardis Butterfield's and Carol Symes's explorations of song and poetic production in northern France, and in Symes's case especially in the city of Arras, both offer insightful new ways in which to situate artistic productivity as bound to the social environment of its locale.[15] In the case of Arras, partly owing to the unusually rich archival records of that region, it has been possible to situate song-makers and performers in their civic setting, and to see not just the extent to which artistic creativity was a collective endeavor (manifest in the

---

12 See in particular *Representing Emotions: New Connections in the Histories of Art, Music, and Medicine*, ed. Penelope Gouk and Helen Hills (Aldershot: Ashgate, 2005), and with particular focus on ancient and medieval evidence, see Simo Knuuttila, *Emotions in Ancient and Medieval Philosophy* (Oxford: Clarendon Press, 2004), and *Anger's Past: The Social Uses of an Emotion in the Middle Ages*, ed. Barbara Rosenwein (Ithaca: Cornell University Press, 1998). For an excellent account of the relationship of historical, anthropological, and cognitive approaches to the investigation of emotion, see William Reddy, *The Navigation of Feeling: A Framework for the History of Emotions* (New York: Cambridge University Press, 2001).

13 See in particular his *The Origins of Courtliness: Civilizing Trends and the Formation of Courtly Ideals, 939–1210* (Philadelphia: University of Pennsylvania Press, 1985) and *The Envy of Angels: Cathedral Schools and Social Ideals in Medieval Europe, 950–1200* (Philadelphia: University of Pennsylvania Press, 1994).

14 Rosenwein, *Emotional Communities*, 2; see her "Introduction," 1–31 for a detailed account of recent work on medieval emotion.

15 Ardis Butterfield, *Poetry and Music in Medieval France: From Jean Renart to Guillaume de Machaut* (Cambridge: Cambridge University Press, 2002), and Carol Symes, *A Common Stage: Theater and Public Life in Medieval Arras* (Ithaca: Cornell University Press, 2007).

sharing of citations, in the *jeux-partis* dialogues), but also woven into the fabric of city life (in the confraternity of jongleurs, for example). Butterfield's balance of close analysis of texts and music, with deep understanding of the social mechanisms of their production, offers particularly rich critical models for my own engagement with musical material, much of which overlaps with the repertorial base of her investigation.

Holsinger's work on the somatics of medieval devotional song, a vital model for my own thinking about the French song, brings evidence of personal, embodied representations of musical experience into dialogue with musical artifacts, offering new models, then, for how our musical evidence might have been felt and experienced by those who sang, listened, or played.[16] His "musicology of empathy" seeks new ways for "musicologists and performers to forge new identifications with those whose musical remains we enliven and study, to invent new ways of merging and blending the musical cultures of our time with the musical cultures of the dead."[17] In reinstating somatic evidence as a topic of research, Holsinger also invites reflection on more ontological issues. His attention to literary accounts of the feeling and effect of music, and its connection to revelation, fear, pain, desire, and so forth, argues that what we may take to be "secondary" evidence is itself musical performance of a sort.

Musical ontology and issues of music's expressivity are also at the heart of Elizabeth Eva Leach's groundbreaking study of the topic of birdsong in music, theory, and poetry of the Middle Ages.[18] A constant source of debate in thinking about the nature of musical sound, birdsong's alluring sweetness was on the one hand a foil to the rational nature of human-made song (a way, then, of defining music), and on the other a means of articulating the sometimes disturbing aspect of music's expressive quality. Through painstaking excavation of medieval attitudes to birdsong, and especially the question of whether their songs counted as music, Leach not only illuminates new evidence of medieval definitions of music; her work also demonstrates the value for a more comparative approach to musical listening. Although my evidence often falls outside the theoretical discourses of song Leach has traced, the ideas of music uncovered in her research, and especially those relating to the meaning of non-verbal sound, have been an important point of reference.

All these approaches have been instrumental to my thinking about the invisible, and to us largely inaudible, trace of medieval musical experience. In putting musical evidence into dialogue with other accounts of sounding

---

16 Bruce Holsinger, *Music, Body, and Desire in Medieval Culture: Hildegard of Bingen to Chaucer* (Stanford: Stanford University Press, 2001).

17 Holsinger, *Music, Body, and Desire*, 348.

18 Elizabeth Eva Leach, *Sung Birds: Music, Nature, and Poetry in the Later Middle Ages* (Ithaca: Cornell University Press, 2007).

experience, my intention is not just to reconstitute members of a listening community in northern France, but also to use the representational aspect of sound in literary, visual, and sometimes musical evidence, to begin to recuperate a palette of sonic "feelings" or effects. That is to say, putting music back together with representations of sounds that are highly stylized in their meaning and effect invites and facilitates an interesting exercise: the fragments of a lexicon of sonic meaning that may help account for the sense musical sounds made within that same community of listeners.

While pursuit of these "invisible topics" of humanness within medieval studies has thus inspired and shaped my endeavor to understand musical sound, those scholarly priorities are also congruent with musicology's current attention to music's live, performed incarnation. Particularly influential in focusing attention on the actuality of musical experience has been Carolyn Abbate's essay on what she calls the drastic versus gnostic dilemma.[19] Indeed, the debate stirred by her call to the sonic is evidence of a contemporary fascination with performance and issues relating to musical "liveness." The binary of Abbate's essay title points to the often limited space allowed for the things that happen in the moment of performance or listening in the established disciplinary modes for writing and thinking about music, which tend towards a textual, analytical ("gnostic") focus. Her encouragement that we attend to the "drastic," then, is simultaneously a call to reassess the tactics and methods of making sense of music that characterize most musicological enterprises: "While musicology's business involves reflecting upon musical works, describing their configurations either in technical terms or as signs, this is, I decided, almost impossible and generally uninteresting as long as real music is present—while one is caught up in its temporal wake and its physical demands or effects."[20] Pursuit of the drastic is borne out in a number of subdisciplines, particularly those dealing with living performance traditions. The field of ethnomusicology in particular offers inviting exempla of scholarship alive to the actuality of music, to music's embodied effects, and its invisible power.[21] In popular music studies, too, questions of liveness and mediation are established

---

19 Carolyn Abbate, "Music—Drastic or Gnostic?" *Critical Inquiry* 30 (2004): 505–36.
20 Ibid., 511.
21 Music's and sound's role in the creation of a sense of space has been eloquently explored in *Senses of Place*, ed. Steven Feld and Keith Basso (Santa Fe, NM: School of American Research Press, 1996), and especially in Feld's essay in that collection: "Waterfalls of Song: An Acoustemology of Place Resounding in Bosavi, Papua New Guinea," 91–135. Carol Ann Muller's *Musical Echoes: South African Women Thinking in Jazz*, with Sathima Sea Benjamin (Durham: Duke University Press, 2011) offers a powerful and moving contemporary case study of the relationship between musical memory and a sense of home.

concepts, bringing current work in media and performance studies into dialogue with musical inquiry.[22]

For historians, however, especially those working with broken transmission histories, technologies of only partial prescription of sound, and gaping absences in evidence of the human experience of music, the possibility of recovering the living pulse of musical sound can seem more out of reach: to historicize the moment of performance is, after all, seemingly at odds with the very essence of music—its vanishing quality. Yet here, too, in recent years, a number of scholars have turned attention in their musical analyses to the now-immaterial experiences of performers, audiences, and composers. In the field of medieval song, Bruce Holsinger's eloquent account of a somatic history of musical experience (mentioned above) has reinstated the human subject in the evidence. Sound and the performing body are also at the centre of Elizabeth Le Guin's exploration of the music of Luigi Boccherini. Here, the instrument and the performer are the locus of musical meaning, and Le Guin develops a new interpretive model, pairing critical theory of performance with musical analysis that creates room for invisible traces of performerly traits—signs of virtuosity, dynamic range, timbre are read as symptoms of the lost performer.[23] Her case for what she has termed a "carnal musicology," in which the sonorous body is the centre of meaning, is furthermore underscored with the inclusion of a CD (of her own performances), an imaginative and experimental gesture of "empathy," perhaps, that encourages her readers to keep listening and sound in the air as we engage with her critiques. Meanwhile, among opera scholars, the long-standing fascination with the voice has burgeoned into new studies that use a range of evidence—descriptions of performance, autobiography, early recordings, philology, and musical analysis—seeking to inject into the history of the operatic repertories the agency of the singer, and what Karen Henson describes as the "presentification" of past performances.[24]

22 As in the work of Philip Auslander. See in particular his *Liveness: Performance in a Mediatized Culture* (London: Routledge, 1999). Auslander has also edited and co-edited several useful compilations of essays relating to performance theory. See in particular his *Theory for Performance Studies: A Student's Guide* (London: Routledge, 2008) and *Performance: Critical Concepts in Literary and Cultural Studies*, 4 vols. (London: Routledge, 2003).

23 Elisabeth Le Guin, *Boccherini's Body: An Essay in Carnal Musicology* (Berkeley: University of California Press, 2006).

24 See, for example, Mary Ann Smart's work on gesture and music in opera in her *Mimomania: Music and Gesture in Nineteenth-Century Opera* (Berkeley: University of California Press, 2004). Karen Henson's work on nineteenth-century singers engages theories of presence and performance to reanimate familiar works by composers such as Verdi with the sense of a living past. See in particular her "Verdi, Victor Maurel and Fin-de-siècle Operatic Performance," *Cambridge Opera Journal* 19 (2007): 59–84. Meanwhile, Roger Freitas's work on Verdi's singers exemplifies the usefulness of the evidence of early

All these debates and approaches have been a further invitation to think again about medieval song in the melting pot of philosophical and methodological innovation in our field—indeed, there has never been a more appealing moment to engage in an effort to recover listening practices. *The Sense of Sound* is thus an experiment in listening, undertaken in a vein of optimism in the face of a past that seems so often muted. Through an unusual alchemy of evidence and methodologies, it has been possible to reassemble some portions of a world alive with sound, and to initiate fresh ways to eavesdrop on the multiple effects and meanings of music. Now, then, it is time to turn our ears to the matter of song.

---

recordings in deciphering accounts of singing before technologies of reproduction. See in particular his "Towards a Verdian Ideal of Singing: Emancipation from Modern Orthodoxy," *Journal of the Royal Musical Association* 127 (2002): 226–57. Henson's use of the concept of "presentification" here alludes to Hans Gumbrecht's influential monograph, *Production of Presence: What Meaning Cannot Convey* (Stanford: Stanford University Press, 2004), also an important reference in Abbate's essay.

1 | Listening to the Past, Listening in the Past

Song's Embrace

Let us begin by listening.

The three witnesses to be summoned are eloquent representatives of their tradition. Exemplifying standard postures of the northern French love songs of the thirteenth century (unrequited love; daring voyeurism of protagonists in pursuit), the three songs also strike another, rather more self-conscious pose. For not only does each speak with uncanny directness to—and therefore of—a listener; each voice also enacts or activates situations of listening. Do not be surprised, then, if the songs seem to turn their reflective gaze outward, and if the boundary between sounding object and reality wavers, to make space in the song's cast for another, exterior persona.

First, the most familiar of all lyric productions: the "I" who speaks to "you" (see example 1.1). Here, the raison d'être of the poem is to speak to the absent lover, the one whose imagined presence is the inspiration for the poem: dying for love, the "I" can do nothing but entreat the beloved to listen. It is not just the repetition of "voz" throughout that implies another. The closing rhetorical question (inviting response) writes into the poem a living—listening—presence:

> *Je ne puis plus durer sanz voz,*
> *fins cuers savoreurs et douz,*
> se n'avés merci de moi,
> pour voz sui en grant effroi
> et ai esté longuement.
> A mains jointes humlement

EXAMPLE I.I. *Je ne puis plus durer sanz voz*

merci vous proi.
Je vous serf, si com je doi,
loiaument en bone foi;
si que quant je ne vous voi,
je me muir tous
com fins loiaus amourous.
Et sans moi,
coment durez vouz?[1]

1 The text of this and the ensuing examples is also edited and translated in *The Montpellier Codex*, ed. Hans Tischler, with translations by Susan Stakel and Joel Relihan, 4 vols., Recent Researches in the Music of the Middle Ages and Early Renaissance 5–8 (Madison: A-R Editions, 1978–85), 4: 9.

I cannot endure any longer without you, true heart delicious and sweet, if you do not have mercy on me. For you I live in great fear and have for a long time. With hands joined, I humbly beg you for mercy. I serve you just as I should, loyally in good faith; so when I do not see you, I die exactly like a true, loyal lover. And without me, how do you endure?

Presence is emphasized not only by the implication of hearing and listening bound into the direct address, but also by the suggestion of visible vessels—embodied voices. The lover is made fleetingly tangible through blurring of secular and sacred symbols as he devotes himself to the lady as if at prayer ("mains jointes humlement"). It is an act so quotidian, and so constantly visualized in this period, from the margins of books of hours, to carved wood panels of bourgeois homes and church pews, as to make him instantly, humanly credible. The beloved is a no less physical presence, conjured through verbs of sight: the lover dies "quant je ne vous *voi.*" Insofar as this song is about anything, then, it is about the desire to be heard, and the longing for a listener. More fundamentally, it is about the constant reach into an elsewhere, beyond the world of the song.

Our second song exemplifies a strand of the tradition much more explicitly about listening (see example 1.2). The song, a classic *pastourelle*, is a vignette told from the perspective of a wandering eavesdropper, caught in an act of voyeurism common in the landscape of thirteenth-century lyric. The engine of the poem is the sound—and sight—of another's voice:

Par un matin me leva[i];
por deduire et pour moi alegier
delés Blangi m'en alai.
Si trovai, seant en un vergier,
tose chantant de cuer gai
et legier;
chapel de mai
fesoit et eglentier.

I got up one morning and went out near Blangi to divert and comfort myself. There I found a girl seated in an orchard singing with a gay and light heart; she was making a May wreath of eglantine.

The lady is so compelling a spectacle that after watching (listening?) for a while, our peeping tom cannot resist trying his luck. In the brief "he said" "she said" that ensues, the narrator turns ventriloquist, repeating the exchange verbatim:

Je l'esgardai,
pres de li m'acointai.
Si la saluai

EXAMPLE 1.2. *Par un matin me leva{i}*

Par un ma-tin me le-va[i], por de-duire et pour
moi a-le-gier de-lés Blan-gi m'en a-lai. Si tro-vai, se-ant
en un ver-gier, to-se chan-tant de cuer gai et le-gier;
cha-pel de mai fe-soit et d'e-glen-tier. Je l'es-gar-dai, pres de
li m'a-coin-tai. Si la sa-lu-ai et li dis bo-ne-ment:
"Bele au cors gent de moi voz fas pre-sent; a voz me rent et mon
cuer voz o-troi. Fe-sons que doi d'un trop bel es-ban-oi,
te-nés par foi, ja mes ne voz fau-drai." "Foi que vous doi," dit, "Si-
-re, non fe-rai; ains a-me-rai qui j'aim de cuer vrai."

et li dis bonement:
"Bele au cors gent,
de moi voz fas present;
a voz me rent
et mon cuer voz otroi.
Fesons que doi
d'un trop bel esbanoi,
tenés par foi,
ja mes ne voz faudrai."
"Foi que vous doi,"

dit, "Sire, non ferai;
ains amerai,
qui j'aim de cuer vrai."

I watched her and edged near to her. I greeted her and said graciously:
"Fair beauty, I make a gift of myself to you; to you I surrender myself
and offer you my heart. Let us do what we should with ever so great joy;
you have me in faith, I will never fail you." "By the faith which I owe
you, my lord," she said, "I will not; rather will I love him whom I love
with a true heart."

As with the previous example, visual emphasis ("je l'esgardai") makes embodied the personalities of the song, while seeing and singing are elided to keep us
wondering whether it is the song, or the sight of the singer, that holds the
protagonist entranced before he advances. The effect is to sharpen the sense of
literal performance, as something issuing from, and received by, living beings.
At the same time that the world within the lyric becomes more plausible, a
certain amount of tension begins to emerge: it makes us ask not only "what did
he say, what did she say?" but also, "how did they say it?" For the mixing of
verbs of articulation (singing, when he first comes upon the lady; speaking, as
he narrates their conversation) prompts us to wonder about the vocal registers
in this amorous scene.

Uncertainty about how the voice sounds (singing or speaking) persists in
our third witness as awareness of the real time of performance intrudes into
the illusory world of the song's interior: the fourth wall of the lyric starts to
crumble (see example 1.3).

Le premier jor de mai
acordai
cest quadruple renvoisié,
car en cest tans
sunt amant
cointe et lié.
Mes je me truis
d'amours desconseillié
n'onques confort n'i trovai
ne ja pour ce ne m'en partirai,
quar j'encontrai
celui, dont dolour ai.
S'ele n'a de moi merci,
ja n'avrai mes
nul jour mon cuer joli!
Por ce li pri
et salu par cest nouviau chant ici:

EXAMPLE 1.3. *Le premier jor de mai*

Le pre - mier jor de mai a - cor - dai cest qua - dru - ple ren - voi - sié, car en cest tans sunt a - mant cointe et lié. Mes je me truis d'a - mours des - con - seil - lié n'on - ques con - fort n'i tro - vai ne ja pour ce ne m'en par - ti - rai, quar j'en - con - trai ce - lui, dont do - lour ai. S'e - le n'a de moi mer - ci, ja n'a - vrai mes nul jour mon cuer jo - li! Por ce li pri et sa - lu par cest nou - viau chant i - ci: "Qui se lui pleiz, a a - mi, qu'au - cun con - fort ai - e pro - chein de li."

"Que se lui pleiz, a ami,
qu'aucun confort aie prochein de li."

On the first day of May I finished this cheerful quadruplum for, in this season, lovers are elegant and joyful. But I found myself distressed in love, I never found comfort; yet never on account of this shall I leave off loving, for I met the one from whom my pain comes. If she does not have mercy on me, I will never again have a joyful heart! Thus I beg her and greet her with this new song: "If I pleased her as a sweetheart, let me have some comfort close to her."

Once again, the poem narrates a performance. This time, one that appears to happen in real time, as the narrator, his own *compère*, introduces "a new song" ("cest nouviau chant ici") he has written to woo his lady. "Nouviau" could be a pun: the lines that follow may be a refrain (that is, not new at all but chosen from a pre-existent lyric context): in this repertory, reported speech is often an opportunity to import preexistent voices. Or it could serve to authenticate desire: novelty here is testament to the depth of his love; as borne out by countless other lyrics, true feeling inspires fresh creativity. But in this particular context, "nouviau" may signify something that "comes after": new in the context of something older. We can be in no doubt as to the speaker's ability to make songs, for we hear his little creation within another creative act—the song that is host to his performance. In the first lines, he introduces himself retroactively, making the very quadruplum (an ostentatiously technical, compositional term, implying polyphony) we are actively engaged in listening to, and in which he thus reports his contrastively spontaneous "chant."

What are we to make of this intricate network of performance cues in this lyric hall of mirrors? In the first instance, it magnifies the blurring of speech and song we have seen elsewhere. If speaking and singing seem distinguishable in the previous lyrics, if singing can be set apart from a "real" world of spoken exchange, in this song all the world sings: the medium of reportage of the new lyric is itself explicitly named as singing. Far from distancing the medium from reality, this suspension of registral distinction contributes to an illusion that the lover is real—or, put another way, suggests that the act of singing is no longer separable from the reality conception in which people communicate with song rather than speech. And there is no more intense moment in this fiction of lyric spontaneity than when love presses our protagonist to break into his "nouviau chant."

But there is a more potent connection between this song and the reality at its fringes. For those listening are no longer eavesdroppers on a lonesome soliloquy, detached observers of the "I" longing for the "you"; indeed, the lady herself barely registers, distanced, now, as the "ele" displaces her as addressee, and when the protagonist does sing to her, his song is not a direct address but a song about her. Yet this entire song (and the song within it) assumes— indeed commands—an audience. It objectifies itself by means of two demonstrative pronouns: it is "*cest* quadruple," "*cest* nouviau chant *ici*." These small directives deliver the songs into reality, no longer products of the interior imagination, but things, now, for others to behold. It is nothing less than an apostrophic embrace to those in its vicinity, enticing them to complete the lyric dialogue.

*

So far, my engagement has taken these songs at their word. In treating them to so literal a gloss, my purpose is to illuminate a self-conscious performativity that characterizes the medieval French vernacular song tradition. Echoing their Southern ancestors of the twelfth century, these songs stage a familiar topos: The bond of loving and singing, of an interior lyric "I" singing outwards to an exterior "You" was, by the middle of the thirteenth century when these songs were copied down, so commonplace that we may be forgiven for tuning it out as cliché.[2] Perhaps because of its conventionality, the real-time implications of singing subject and exterior listener are often curiously muted in scholarly engagement with the repertory. While modern writers have fruitfully devoted energy to signs of subjective presence in and outside song, attention has focused more on issues of identity, transmission, and autobiography than on an actual moment of vocal realization. Some have treated performative cues either as unmediated autobiographical evidence,[3] or as evidence of song's social environment.[4] At the other extreme, much influenced by Paul Zumthor's *Essai de poétique médiévale*,[5] another approach treats signs of

2 On the use of topoi in troubadour lyrics, see Elisabeth Schulze-Busacker's "Topoi," in *A Handbook of the Troubadours*, ed. Frank Akehurst and Judith Davis (Berkeley: University of California Press, 1995), 421, where she notes that read abstracted from a wider sense of the poetics of the period, and in light of its aesthetic reliance on rhetoric (especially on topoi), "it is easy to feel a sense of lassitude [when reading twelfth- and thirteenth-century song]: such useless repetition, especially of so many well-known motifs and so many overused themes."

3 Sarah Kay traces what she terms the "autobiographical assumption" in treatment of the troubadour lyric in her "Rhetoric and Subjectivity in Troubadour Poetry," in *The Troubadours and the Epic: Essays in Memory of W. Mary Hackett*, ed. Linda Patterson and Simon Gaunt (Warwick: University of Warwick Press, 1987), 102–42.

4 An alternative approach to the "historical reality" of troubadour and trouvère song may be found in the more explicitly archival investigation of audience and performance venues in work by Christopher Page and Fredric Cheyette. See, for example, Fredric Cheyette, "Women, Poets, and Politics in Occitania," in *Aristocratic Women in Medieval France*, ed. Theodore Evergates (Philadelphia: University of Pennsylvania Press, 1999), 138–77, with notes at 225–33, and his *Ermengard of Narbonne and the World of the Troubadours* (Ithaca: Cornell University Press, 2001), and Christopher Page, "Listening to the Trouvères," *Early Music* 24 (1997): 38–59.

5 Paul Zumthor, *Essai de poétique médiévale* (Paris: Seuil, 1972). In Zumthor's linguistic-led approach, and his focus on composition and transmission in an oral environment characterized by "mouvance," the "je" of the lyric was removed from a real human agent, and seen rather as product of a closed "grammatical" system. There is thus a rupture between the system of identification and self-identification in song and external reality, locating meaning more in the internal forms and structures of language than in a text's literal meaning and effect: "poetic discourse is determined more by its verbal and rhythmic organization than by its conceptual and affective matter" ("Le discours poétique est davantage déterminé par son agencement verbal et rythmique que par sa substance conceptuelle et affective"), quoting from his *Essai*, 109. Thus, as Sarah Kay observes in a critique of Zumthor, "the human circumstances of its [song's] production . . . [seem] irrecuperably lost"; see her "Desire and Subjectivity," in *The Troubadours: An Introduction*,

subjectivity as removed from reality and performance, and rather as the product of the closed system of poetic language.[6]

Some other accounts, however, treat performance rather more literally. While performance is largely an abstract concept in the linguistic-driven approach to the lyric, work on troubadour lyrics by Sarah Kay, for example, suggests ways that interpretation may take into account real-time performance.[7] Meanwhile, the rich vein of scholarship devoted to topics of transmission or "mouvance" in troubadour and trouvère song deploys philology as a tool to recuperate the oral dimension of song.[8] Through attention to melodic and textual variance, it is possible to recover a sense of performance-driven composition, and to see in the physical trace hints of song's "live" quality. More often, though, the evidence of song's transmission is a lens through which to contemplate compositional processes that are tied to performance, improvisation, and memory, and to the singer—and sometimes the scribe—as agents of creative

---

ed. Simon Gaunt and Sarah Kay (Cambridge: Cambridge University Press, 1999), 212–27, at 212.

6 Zumthor's influence is perhaps most deeply felt in troubadour studies, particularly in attention to themes of rhetoric and topoi in the repertory. For useful introductions to these fields see the essays by Elisabeth Schulze-Busacker on topoi, Frede Jensen on language, Nathaniel Smith on rhetoric, and Eliza Miruna Ghil on imagery and vocabulary in *A Handbook of the Troubadours*, ed. Akehurst and Davis. See also Sarah Spence, "Rhetoric and Hermeneutics," in *The Troubadours*, ed. Gaunt and Kay, 164–80.

7 Kay's groundbreaking work on gender and subjectivity in the troubadour lyric devotes a chapter to issues of performance: Sarah Kay, *Subjectivity in Troubadour Poetry* (Cambridge: Cambridge University Press, 1990), 132–170, notes 245–50. With obvious echoes of the Zumthorian model, Kay detects a tension between song experienced as literary convention and as "historical reality": "the songs addressed to female patrons present the first-person singer as composer and lover, anchoring both roles in the historically real. But their ambiguity also releases the 'love plot' into playfulness, fantasy, or linguistic solipsism. Both object and subject (*qua* lover) belong in the domain of rhetoric and tradition as such as of historical reality" (p. 161). In performance, she argues, the singer may enact the role of the protagonist of the song—the boundaries between the poetic and physical self blurred for a moment—and may sing the song as if for the first time, while at the same time he "represents the traditional to the audience. . . The 'old' becomes 'new' as he sings it, makes it present, and bears witness to it. The 'newness' of song marks the importance of performance as process of interaction between singer and his audience, and between the poet and his literary inheritance" (170).

8 On the troubadour repertories see especially Simon Gaunt, "Orality and Writing: The Text of the Troubadour Poem," in *The Troubadours*, ed. Gaunt and Kay, 228–45, and Hendrick van der Werf, *The Extant Troubadour Melodies: Transcriptions and Essays for Performers and Scholars* (Rochester, NY: Author's Publication, 1984). On transmission of the trouvère repertories see Mary O'Neill, *Courtly Love Songs of Medieval France: Transmission and Style in the Trouvère Repertoire* (Oxford: Oxford University Press, 2006).

remaking of songs; or more practically, as support for modern editorial agendas. Amelia Van Vleck offers an interesting exception, folding philological understanding of troubadour song into more theory-led critique. Arguing for awareness of the changeability of a song in performance, she suggests that poets frequently questioned the stability of their own voices, and were sensitive to the external agents who might have had the power subsequently to alter their text: " 'She,' the feminine Other in many songs, is not just the autobiographical object of affections but represents all potentially benevolent alterity, particularly the alterity of the audience that will challenge the song and transform it."[9]

Even where orality and performance are central, questions of vocality—whether the voice of the words sings or speaks; the effect of a singing voice on words—remain largely unexplored. In Zumthor's conception, "voix" is essentially synonymous with "performance" and "orality," as the living opposite to writing, while its sonorous registers are reduced to a simple monotone. What would it mean to understand the outward reach of song in more literal terms, as having to do with—indeed, relying upon—a singing voice, tangible listeners, and an environment that surpasses the boundaries of poetic production? What would be at stake in bringing song's geography back into a critical reading, and in accounting for the vocality of the performance? What role might that exterior place of reception have had in the process of generating meaning and significance in the experience of song? In short, what would it mean to make listening and sound the center of investigation, and to take song up on its most basic apostrophic invitation?

I wish to use the performative dimension of the medieval vernacular lyric as entry into a more localized aspect of song emerging around the mid-thirteenth century. This coincides with the first written records of unprecedented transformations in song-making, which rearticulate the apostrophic, outward-directed dimension of song, such that musical sound started to have a different kind of currency. Simply put, the musical voice of song asserts itself in new ways: as a kind of supermusicality. At its most transparent, this alternate musicality announces itself through—and beyond—the omnipresent texts in the practice of music, and it is audibly evident in certain compositional innovations. A more heightened musicality is not only audible, but also visible. It is signaled by the growing cultural appetite to compile and keep music—not just recently composed, but also traditions dating back much earlier (in the troubadour chansonniers; and collation of the Notre Dame repertories). It is not just the greater presence of musical notation that reminds readers of song's special voice. Singerly gestures—"audio-visual cues"—fill these books: from

9 Amelia Van Vleck, *Memory and Re-Creation in Troubadour Lyric* (Berkeley: University of California Press, 1991), 198–99.

author portraits to the *vidas* and *razos* prefacing troubadour song, all recreating in material form the moment of performance.[10] The later thirteenth century also sees an expansion of the technologies of notation, for making visible, permanent, and independent of texts voices that were otherwise hidden in the memory. Finally, it is around this time that a revolution in the practice of writing about music occurs: writers such as Johannes de Grocheio and Jacques de Liège offer a new sociology of music, a new way of writing about a musical sound as moral effect, tucked into the more traditional framework of theoretical explanation.

What was the nature of this supermusicality? I should like now to summon its sound through perhaps its most strident representative. For that, we need to return to the songs with which we opened. Restoring a singing voice to these texts, an uncanny transformation of meaning occurs. Despite their narrative promise to engage their audience to play a role in their scene, when sung, these poems cease to make sense. In performance, these voices were intended to sound simultaneously, joined by a fourth line, a chant tenor "Iustus" from an antiphon for the Common of a Confessor,[11] to form a polytextual motet.

Listen again (see example 1.4).

What do we hear? It is little wonder that the genre came to be known by the designation "motez." *Le premier jor* (521)/*Par un matin* (522)/Je ne puis plus (523)/*Iustus* (M53) offers sound that is simultaneously verbal and non-verbal; a plenitude of semantic possibility that slips just beyond the reach of the ear. It would be tempting to categorize the sound as confusing or complex—terms often used in evocation of this sonorous effect. But that would be to suggest something is lacking, that something more is striving to be heard. There is

---

10 Sylvia Huot, *From Song to Book: The Poetics of Writing in Old French Lyric and Lyrical Narrative Poetry* (Ithaca: Cornell University Press, 1987) remains the most influential and comprehensive treatment of the material aspect of Old French song and poetry. For more localized studies see for example Elizabeth Poe, Compilatio: *Lyric Texts and Prose Commentaries in Troubadour Manuscript H (Vat. Lat. 3207)* (Lexington, KY: French Forum, 2000) and Olivia Holmes, *Assembling the Lyric Self: Authorship from Troubadour Song to Italian Poetry Books* (Minneapolis: University of Minnesota Press, 2000) for treatment of troubadour chansonniers; *Gautier de Coinci: Miracles, Music, and Manuscripts*, ed. Kathy Krause and Alison Stones, Medieval Texts and Cultures of Northern Europe 13 (Turnhout: Brepols, 2006) for a recent assessment of the manuscript tradition of Gautier de Coinci's *Miracles de Nostre Dame*; and my *Medieval Music-Making and the* Roman de Fauvel (Cambridge: Cambridge University Press, 2002) for an exploration of music's visual meanings in the *Fauvel* manuscript. For a more general account of the range of audio-visual cues in medieval manuscripts, see Michael Camille, "Seeing and Reading: Some Visual Implications of Medieval Literacy and Illiteracy," *Art History* 8 (1985): 26–49.

11 "The just man will sprout like the lily and flower in eternity" ("Iustus germinabit sicut lilium et florebit in eternum").

EXAMPLE 1.4. *Le premier jor de mai/Par un matin me leva{i}/*Je ne puis plus durer sanz voz/*Iustus* (*Mo*, fols. 49ᵛ–52ʳ)

EXAMPLE I.4. (continued)

EXAMPLE 1.4. (continued)

another sense in this sound, though. While the immediate meaning of the single voices is lost in the moment of delivery, something else steps into that communicative space: a presence that is expressive, evanescent, and unavoidably audible—the supermusical.

Playing around the hinge of sense and sound, the motet makes apparent the verbal source of its effect. Like many of its kind, it plays back and forth between verbal address and supermusical presence on account of the ebb and flow of phrases. The tenor largely follows a simple repeating mode 2 pattern, by which each ligature (here transcribed as a measure) culminates in a rest. This enforces a constant pace of silence within the piece, which allows the upper voices to momentarily reveal and conceal themselves. Sometimes, they all sing through the space; and other times, they all cease, opening up a moment of unison silence in the fabric of the piece (as at m. 3); and sometimes a single voice is left exposed to smooth the gap (for example, mm. 7, 9, 11, 14, and so on). The effect, then, is a constantly shifting aural spotlight, and moment by moment the piece sounds more or less verbal, more or less musical.

The issue of audibility and comprehension of text in motets of this kind has preoccupied audiences almost from the genre's inception. To the modern ear, the sinuous texture of musical lines that are in constant and competing motion appears contrived to obscure, more than to articulate, the words each voice sings. That those voices may be singing different texts, often in different languages, contributes to the impression that verbal clarity was a low priority and fuels the sense that the genre was an esoteric puzzle, inviting expert, rational contemplation by a learned audience to reveal its semantic secrets.[12]

12 Such a view may be traced back to the earliest surveys of medieval polyphony, for example Friedrich Ludwig, "Die Quellen der Motette ältesten Stils," *Archiv für Musikwissenschaft* 5 (1923): 185–222 and 273–315, and "Musik des Mittelalters bis zum Anfang des 15. Jahrhunderts," in *Handbuch der Musikgeschichte*, ed. Guido Adler (Frankfurt: Frankfurter Verlags-Anstalt, 1924), 157–295; Heinrich Besseler, *Die Musik des Mittelalters und der Renaissance*, Handbuch der Musikwissenschaft (Potsdam: Akademische Verlagsgesellschaft Athenaion, 1931–34). The tendency towards monumentalist and esoteric narratives in these accounts may, as Daniel Leech-Wilkinson suggests, be understood within the broader pioneering goals of their authors: to survey, synthesize, and demarcate the major repertories of the period. For more on the context for these works, and later medieval survey texts, see Leech-Wilkinson, *The Modern Invention of Medieval Music: Scholarship, Ideology, Performance* (Cambridge: Cambridge University Press, 2002), esp. 70–82. Later accounts often amplified the characterization of the motet as intellectual, esoteric, and monumental. See, for example, Ernest Sanders's seminal survey of the genre in the Middle Ages, "The Medieval Motet," in *Gattungen der Musik in Einzeldarstellungen: Gedenkschrift Leo Schrade*, ed. Wulf Arlt et al. (Berne: Francke Verlag, 1973), 497–573. There, he famously likened the motet to the summative structure of a

The few contemporary commentaries have often been marshaled as reassuring support of the modern musical intuition. Johannes de Grocheio's *De musica* (ca. 1300) and Jacques de Liège's *Speculum musicae* (ca. 1330), both approaching the *ars antiqua* motet from a position of hindsight, appear to situate the genre among an elite audience of active listeners, highly educated and thus primed to crack its codes and extrapolate meaning from its texts. Grocheio's references to a lettered audience ("literati"), well-versed in subtleties ("qui subtilitates artium sunt quaerentes"), excluding the vulgar (typically read as non-clerical) populus ("non debet coram vulgaribus propinari, eo quod eius subtilitatem non advertunt"),[13] and Liège's society of skilled singers and discerning laymen (". . . in quadam societate, in qua congregati erant, valentes cantores et laici sapientes"),[14] have, until recently, been read as confirmation of the modern critique: that the motet was a demanding form requiring a specialized listener. Their imagined colloquia are frequently summoned as endorsement for modern analyses that emphasize the allusive, allegorical, and symbolic content of the texts, and the complexity of the text–music relationship.[15] Finally, persuaded,

---

Gothic cathedral—both as complex, and as laden with invisible meaning. The "cathedralism" syndrome in accounts of the medieval motet is thoroughly contextualized, with reference to parallel trends in other medieval disciplines, in Christopher Page, *Discarding Images: Reflections on Music and Culture in Medieval France* (Oxford: Clarendon Press, 1993), 1–42.

13 *Die Quellenhandschriften zum Musiktraktat des Johannes de Grocheio*, ed. Ernest Rohloff (Leipzig: Deutscher Verlag für Musik, 1972), 144 for discussion of the motet. Christopher Page has published a new edition and translation of key passages from the treatise, including the ones discussed here: see Christopher Page, "Johannes de Grocheio on Secular Music: A Corrected Text and a New Translation," *Plainsong and Medieval Music* 2 (1993): 17–41.

14 *Jacobi Leodiensis Speculum musicae*, ed. Roger Bragard, Corpus scriptorum de musica 3, vol. 7 (Rome: American Institute of Musicology, 1973), Book VII, ch. 48, pp. 93–95. The passage is translated in *Strunk's Source Readings in Music History, Revised Edition*, vol. 2: *The Early Christian Period and the Latin Middle Ages*, ed. James McKinnon (New York: Norton, 1998), 166–68.

15 There is a growing bibliography in this field. Some key studies in which textual analysis and the argument for non-sounding meanings dominate, often citing Grocheio and Liège as justification for such an approach, include: Dolores Pesce, "The Significance of Text in Thirteenth-Century Latin Motets," *Acta Musicologica* 58 (1986): 91–117, and "Beyond Glossing: The Old Made New in *Mout me grief/Robin m'aime/Portare*," in *Hearing the Motet: Essays on the Motet in the Middle Ages and Renaissance*, ed. Dolores Pesce (New York: Oxford University Press, 1997), 28–51; Beverly Jean Evans, "The Textual Function of the Refrain Cento in a Thirteenth-Century French Motet," *Music & Letters* 46 (1993): 295–305, and Anne Walters Robertson, "Remembering the Annunciation in Medieval Polyphony," *Speculum* 70 (1995): 275–304. Such analytical approaches are taken even further in recent work on the early *ars nova* motet, where numerological meaning

perhaps, by Jacques de Liège's nostalgic retrospective, which portrayed the *ars antiqua* as venerable parent to the *ars nova* that was his main subject, the progress of history towards the ever-greater subtly and virtuosity in the fourteenth century has encouraged the game of stylistic hindsight: surely the template for the motet's conceptual challenges was present at its thirteenth-century inception?

In recent years the genre has been subject to reevaluation, in part prompted by Christopher Page's revisionist readings of the two theorists in question. Revealing different semantic resonances in the audience categories in *De musica*, Page argues that Grocheio may have had a less specialized audience in mind. By the thirteenth century, "literati" had a "broader constituency," and could refer not just to someone versed in Latin learning (traditionally associated with clerics), but could encompass a more "secularized concept of 'learning'," including children studying grammar, curates, canons, parish priests, as well as those who read only the vernacular.[16] He reminds us that Liège's society, referenced in the treatise as authority for the comments he transmits, had, by that very function, to have impeccable intellectual and critical qualifications: "Jacques naturally wishes to establish the credentials of such allies beyond doubt."[17]

Page's aim to throw into question the intellectual, elitist context of the motet was part of a larger project, a reaction to what he felt to be an overly analytically, and essentially unmusical, approach to the form. The standard emphasis on the esoteric, verbally complex aspects of the motet, encouraged by the older readings of the treatises, overshadowed and discouraged other, more musically or aurally oriented approaches. Within the polemics of *Discarding Images*, Page presented a new reading of the motet, arguing that the pure sensual, sonic experience surpassed the conceptual readings proposed by literary

---

generated by the tenor organization, length of the motet, and even the number of words in each text is now emphasized as having a symbolic meaning, or acting as a kind of signpost lending emphasis to particular key words or melodic motifs. A crucial model for that approach is set out in Margaret Bent, "Polyphony of Texts and Music in the Fourteenth-Century Motet: *Tribum que non abhorruit/Quoniam secta latronum/Merito hec patimur* and its Quotations," in *Hearing the Motet*, ed. Pesce, 82–103.

16 See Page, *Discarding Images*, 81–84, for the full discussion of "literati." For a more recent investigation of pedagogical and intellectual categories in the Middle Ages, see Mariken Teeuwen, *The Vocabulary of Intellectual Life in the Middle Ages* (Turnhout: Brepols, 2003); for the account of "litteratus" and "illiteratus," see 92–94. While reinforcing Page's reading, Teeuwen notes, too, that in certain contexts, for example Cistercian writings, "litteratus" could also have a virtuous undertone, as counterpoint to "simplex," "idiota," as well as "illiterates," emphasizing, then, the moral efficacy of reading and writing.

17 Page, *Discarding Images*, 70.

and musical scholars. The motet, he argues, is a genre that "most candidly acknowledges the importance of verbal sound over verbal sense."[18]

Page famously prompted lively responses, some characterizing his approach as anti-intellectual for appearing to silence the textual meanings of the form, an outcome, perhaps, of his position as performer and recorder of the music.[19] Page's unequivocal emphasis on sound has served as a useful corrective to the idea of an approach premised on non-sounding meaning. However, in the years since *Discarding Images*, as the literary and musical understanding of the genre has deepened, so has the conviction of the genre's meaning-laden premise intensified, especially in studies by Sylvia Huot, Lisa Coulton, Ardis Butterfield, Suzannah Clark, to name but a few. In the face of the sheer quantity of motets that are receptive to the model of reading best exemplified in Huot's *Allegorical Play*, it is hard to dispute that complex literary messages were a vital part of the experience. Some have sought to bridge the gap between how a motet sounds and what it means, as Suzannah Clark does, arguing that "medieval composers . . . seem to tackle the problem of comprehension, by using the music to bring out the meaning of the words in performance."[20] Her analyses, like those of Ardis Butterfield, Dolores Pesce, and Jennifer Saltzstein,[21] are virtuosic in demonstrating how the melodic reference or positioning of syllables and sounds can contribute to a literary interpretation—how sound can be an exegetical tool, helping the listener fathom literary meaning.

What of our motet's "meaning"? It seems no less inviting to interpretation. Like its contemporaries, it exhibits magpie-like tendencies—it is what Pierre Bec likened to a "véritable conservatoire" of its surrounding traditions—curating pre-existent materials and citing from an array of literary genres, thus

18 Ibid., 85.

19 Margaret Bent, "Reflections on Christopher Page's *Reflections*," *Early Music* 21 (1993): 625–33; Christopher Page, "A Reply to Margaret Bent," *Early Music* 22 (1994): 127–32; Reinhard Strohm, "How to Make Medieval Music our Own: A Response to Christopher Page and Margaret Bent," *Early Music* 22 (1994): 715–92; Rob Wegman, "Reviewing Images," *Music & Letters* 76 (1995): 256–273, and Philip Weller, "Frames and Images: Locating Music in Cultural Histories of the Middle Ages," *Journal of the American Musicological Society* 50 (1997): 7–54.

20 Suzannah Clark, " 'S'en dirai chançonete': Hearing Text and Music in a Medieval Motet," *Plainsong and Medieval Music* 16 (2007): 31–59, at 34.

21 See especially Ardis Butterfield, "The Language of Medieval Music: Two Thirteenth-Century Motets," *Plainsong and Medieval Music* 2 (1993): 1–16; Pesce, "The Significance of Text"; Jennifer Saltzstein, "Wandering Voices: Refrain Citation in Thirteenth-Century French Music and Poetry" (Ph.D. diss., University of Pennsylvania, 2007); and her "Relocating the Thirteenth-Century Refrain: Intertextuality, Authority, and Origins," *Journal of the Royal Musical Association* 135 (2010): 245–79.

adding intertextual resonances to all its texts.[22] In the spirit of that quadru-plum text's self-styling as "nouviau," it is premised on prior traditions: it comes out of genres including *pastourelle* (triplum), *grand chant* (motetus), and, of course, liturgy (tenor). Meanwhile, its use of direct speech implies the presence of refrains—short citations of other songs. It would be easy to get caught up in a game of chase, and to take these texts' apostrophic narrative as an inter-textual invitation. For example, the refrain that frames the motetus text, enté style (the preexistent refrain spliced with new material), *"Je ne puis plus durer sanz voz/et sans moi, coment durez voz?"* (R1009), opens out to a network that includes, among others, an anonymous *Salut d'amour*. That context, a semi-lyric form whereby each strophe of poetry is concluded with a different musical refrain, offers context for the suffering lover of the motetus, amplifying his anguish with a chorus of the lovesick.[23]

We might also resolve the aural obfuscation innate to its texture via philo-logical means. The material evidence may suggest that medieval listeners experienced the piece as we did at the opening: voice by voice. A philological approach shows it appears in various formulations, including as a two-part motet, in which the single-texted voice (motetus) would have been easily com-prehensible.[24] Its subsequent copying in three- and four-part form suggests the possibility of performances with the successive addition of voices, allowing for multiple listenings to extrapolate meaning.[25] The characteristic format in parts illustrates how the motet's physical manifestation invites voice-by-voice com-prehension. Motets, like other *cum littera* polyphony, were copied in parts rather

22 Pierre Bec, *La Lyrique française au Moyen Age (XIIe–XIIIe siècles): Contribution à une typologie des genres poétiques médiévaux. Études et textes*, 2 vols. (Paris: A. and J. Picard, 1977–78), 1:219.

23 For an excellent discussion of the genre, and in particular its use of refrains, see Butterfield, *Poetry and Music in Medieval France*, 237–39. For the classic overview of the tradition, see Paul Meyer, "Le *Salut d'amour* dans les littératures provençale et française," *Bibliothèque de l'Ecole des chartes* 28 (1867): 24–170. The *Salut* in which R1009 is quoted is edited in *Nouveau recueil de contes, dits, fabliaux et autres pièces inédites des XIIIe, XIVe et XVe siècles*, ed. Achille Jubinal (Geneva: Slatkin Reprints, 1975; first published 1842), 235.

24 *Le premier jor/Par un matin/Je ne puis plus durer/Iustus* survives in various forms in the following manuscripts: in four and two parts (motetus and tenor) in *W2*, fols. 209ᵛ–210ᵛ and 240ʳ–240ᵛ; in four parts in *Cl* 751–52 (fol. 380ʳ⁻ᵛ); in four parts in *Mo*, fols. 49ᵛ–52ʳ; Paris, Bibliothèque nationale de France, f. fr. 12615 (*Chansonnier de Noailles*), fol. 182ʳ⁻ᵛ; portions of a three-part Latin double version of the motet are extant in *MuB*, fol. Ib; and in three parts (triplum, motetus, and tenor) in Leuven, Universiteitsbibliotheek, frag. Herenthals, 1ʳ⁻ᵛ.

25 This is a strategy adopted by many modern performers, including recordings by Anonymous 4 and Gothic Voices.

than in score; in the later chansonniers, they were often in column format, aligned almost as mutual gloss.

The juxtaposition of voices might also provoke an allegorical reading. Reading the upper voices against the Christological implications of the tenor, Sylvia Huot argues that the motet "invites—indeed, forces—the audience to choose among the possible readings."[26] These include, for example, a reading taking up the "flowering" connotations of the tenor's fuller context, "Iustus germinabit." The florid topos draws from the upper voices' multiple ruminations on love more erotic suggestions of sexual desire and procreation, and, argues Huot, "valorizes erotic love as a source of poetic inspiration."[27]

We could continue in such a vein to piece together from the motet a range of viable readings. Yet valuable and plausible as such investigations are, I wish to resist the route of decipherment and resolution. In pursuing the motet's sound as agent of meaning, as linked to the verbal semantics of the genre, we may miss a more immediate, if unfamiliar possibility. Of a sense of sound apart from semantic resolution—a musical sound that is imbued with a range of meanings perhaps at odds with, or supplemental to, the meaning of its words. In the case of Le premier jor de mai/Par un matin/Je ne puis plus durer/Iustus, we may offer a different interpretation of what its sonic surface "means," but one more fitting for the expressive intentions of the three upper voices. In the moment of singing it conjures an uncanny and engulfing musical presence, the human voices themselves the purest mimesis of the abiding theme of the French lyrics with which we began this chapter: "I love, therefore I sing," an interior subject singing to an exterior realm. Thus, one might say that the sound itself, in all its semantic evasion, is a narration of its texts—the "I" reaches to the "You" clear of language altogether, in a vibrating realm of voice resonating in the world outside the bodies that produce it.

As we take up the invitation of the supermusical, new questions present themselves. To the ears and intellects of listeners and makers, not just of the motet, but of any song of this period, what was at stake in finding oneself in the presence of a vocal sound so distanced from verbal articulation, in the presence, then, of the supermusical? What was the meaning of such an entanglement of sound and word, the association of its effect? In the next part of this chapter, I wish to initiate some new ways to frame the sense of such sound, to make space in the modern hermeneutics of the music for the supermusical. I offer a model born of two very different contexts, a hybrid of medieval and modern ways to think about how we might grant such sound a currency. The first is a necessarily detailed context for the supermusical, and one that will be

26 Sylvia Huot, *Allegorical Play and the Old French Motet* (Stanford: Stanford University Press, 1997), 72.

27 Ibid., 71. See 69–72 for her full reading of this motet.

a constant reference point in this book: a quintessentially medieval preoccupation with the relationship between sound and words. The second explores more recent initiatives to pursue sound outside the boundaries of theoretical definition, to seek interpretive frameworks born of contexts less systematic or deliberate in their production and use of sound.

Contexts for the Sense of Sound
WORDS AND MUSIC

To evoke binaries such as "words" and "music" or "sound" and "meaning" in discussion of song is to summon some of musicology's most savored old chestnuts. But precisely because of their later eminence, it is important to reclaim and reframe such distinctions. Long before the likes of Rousseau, throngs of writers from Augustine, Priscian, Isidore of Seville, through to Dante and Eustache Deschamps, observed a fascination with the origins of language, and familiar among the topics of linguistic genealogy was the relationship between sound and word.

The most explicit example of how sound is implicated in meaning can be found in music's sister in the quadrivium: grammar. In her recent account of medieval ontologies of music and birdsong, Elizabeth Leach offers the important reminder that for most of the Middle Ages, music theory was in essence a branch of grammar.[28] Her painstaking work to trace the links between the two disciplines reveals just how deeply engrained musical sound is with verbal meaning. The starting point of grammar was none other than a genealogy of words that begins with sound, which, as Leach explains, included musical sound. In grammars such as Donatus's *Ars minor* and *Ars maior*, or Priscian's *Institutiones grammaticae*, texts much studied and glossed by generations of medieval students and grammarians, the foundations of language are explained as a chain of events grounded in aural experience: beginning with sound ("vox"), then syllable, word, and finally complete communication. Here, reiterated by etymologists and music theorists alike, "vox" is taken to signify both sound and letter, to be both potentially semantically articulate ("articulata") and meaningless ("confusa").[29] That "vox" could exist devoid of semantic

28 Leach, *Sung Birds*, esp. ch. 1, 11–54, where she traces the relationship of music and grammar through definitions of "vox." Another fascinating exploration of themes of language and nature in medieval thought, including discussion of "vox," is Christopher Cannon, "The Owl and the Nightingale and the Meaning of Life," *Journal of Medieval and Early Modern Studies* 34 (2004): 251–78.

29 The *Ars maior* opens thus: "*Vox* is struck air perceptible to hearing, insofar as it is in itself. *Vox* is either articulate or confused. Articulate is that which can be comprehended;

content is also apparent through common oppositions of "vox" against "dictio," which signifies a word "as an entity having both form and meaning,"[30] while the later use of "verbum" signifies just meaning or semantic content. These nuances of the language of language betray an inherent orality at the heart of words. At the same time, it is words that make music music: that lend it reason and meaning apart from pure sound. Here Leach's exploration of medieval comparisons between birdsong and music is revealing. For while a bird may sing, and may even mimic words, their sounds are produced without intention to mean something, and are thus "vox confusa"—without reason: "only human singing is singing since only humans can mean."[31] How, then, are we to explain music that seems deliberately to confuse the sense of words? In the grammatical context, such an act would result in confusion, indeed in some quarters would be understood as non-musical.

The science of words, so much a part of the lively discourse of theory and music, was just one component in a complex understanding of language. Around the consideration of the properties of words appeared historiographies and genealogies of language. Indeed, another "origins of language" might take a historical approach, imagining the earliest utterances as described in Genesis; the cataclysm of the fall of Babel; the desire to hear Hebrew as the earliest language, and to hear in it traces of the lost language of creation, of the voice of God himself.[32] Theories of signs and symbolism were also deeply rooted in linguistics, as writings such as Isidore's *Etymologies* suggest: writers consistently pondered a word's ability to express the actual property of the thing indicated, or its "stand-in" quality (famously debated in Augustine's *De doctrina Christiana*).[33] Such contexts remind us that any consideration of medieval words must take account of powerful streams of philosophical, ethical, and

---

confused is that which cannot be written" ("Vox est aer ictus sensibilis auditu, quantum in ipso est. omnis vox aut articulata est aut confusa. articulata est, quae litteris conprehendi potest; confusa quae scribi non potest"). Quoted from Louis Holtz, *Donat et la tradition de l'enseignement grammatical: Étude sur l'*Ars Donati *et sa diffusion (IVe–IXe siècle) et édition critique* (Paris: CNRS, 1981), 603; my translation. Louis Kelly offers a detailed account of the treatment of "vox" across a range of medieval writers in his *The Mirror of Grammar: Theology, Philosophy and the* Modistae (Amsterdam: J. Benjamins, 2002), 11–38.

30 Vivian Law, *Grammar and the Grammarians in the Early Middle Ages* (London: Longman, 1997), 262. See 260–69 for further context on the terminology of grammar.

31 Leach, *Sung Birds*, 43.

32 For an account of the relationship between medieval linguistics and genealogy, see R. Howard Bloch's excellent *Etymologies and Genealogies: A Literary Anthropology of the French Middle Ages* (Chicago: University of Chicago Press, 1983).

33 See especially Book II, chs. 1–4. For an edition with English translation see Augustine, *De doctrina Christiana*, ed. Roger Green, Oxford Early Christian Texts (Oxford: Clarendon Press, 1995).

theological meaning bound into language. At the same time we must heed the importance of sound within such a discourse. While the tension of sense and sound shifts across the Middle Ages, writers of our period concerned with issues of linguistics demonstrate how entwined the scientific and historiographical understandings of language were. There is no more pertinent testimony to this grammatical/genealogical idea of language than Dante's *De vulgari eloquentia*, written in the early years of the fourteenth century.[34] In an effort to authorize his vernacular mother tongue, Dante turns to linguistic genealogy as a tactic of proof. He takes language back to its primary moment, before the bliss of Eden, before Eve's words of betrayal in the garden (a woman, after all, cannot be the source of language), to a time before sound's solidification into signs, letters, and articulate meaning. The first human utterance, Dante imagines, must have been Adam pronouncing the word—or sound— "El" in recognition of God his creator: and because no one but God can name himself, Adam's sound is neither a name, nor a question, nor an answer to God. It is a meaningful cry of joy, hovering, then, somewhere between "vox" and "dictio": "it is reasonable that he who existed before should have begun with a cry of joy" ("rationabile est quod ante qui fuit inciperet a gaudio").[35] As R. Howard Bloch explains, "this primal moment of signification and of origin is thus removed from all semantic function. Meaning everything and excluding nothing, it is both divine presence and a potential mirror of the created world—an undifferentiated utterance whose subsequent division into syllables, words, parts of speech, languages, regional tongues, city dialects, and intramunicipal patois serves as a reminder that language breeds and that its history parallels that of humanity."[36]

It is within this context of medieval linguistics that we may situate a current in discourses of musical sound. While grammar and *musica* are entwined through their mutual concern to define "vox" and "sonus," linguistics also accounts for a much better-known theme: the concern with the complicated relationship between "cantus" and "verbum," and "sonus" and "sensus." It will be useful to revisit these concerns about sense and sound through one of the most eloquent and heartfelt witnesses to music's effects. The anxiety about what singing did to the sound and sense of words is most famously articulated by Augustine, in passages in *Confessions* and *Enarrationes in Psalmos*, texts frequently cited and paraphrased across the Middle Ages. Augustine's fretful dilemma at giving in to the pleasurable sonorities of psalm singing is

34 Dante, *De vulgari eloquentia*, ed. and transl. Steven Botterill, Cambridge Medieval Classics 5 (Cambridge: Cambridge University Press, 1996).

35 Dante, *De vulgari eloquentia*, Book I, ch. 4, 4. Quoting from Botterill's edition, 8–9.

36 Bloch, *Etymologies and Genealogies*, 43.

pertinent. It establishes a standard for musical sound in relation to verbal sound and meaning; but when resituated in the larger medieval discourse of words, it reminds us of the high ethical stakes of effecting a rift between sense and sound. In Book 10, chapter 33 of *Confessions* Augustine contemplates the moment when sound surpasses sense:

> voluptates aurium tenacius me implicaverant et subiugaverant, sed resolvisti et liberasti me. nunc in sonis quos animant eloquia tua cum suavi et artificiosa voce cantantur, fateor, aliquantulum adquiesco, non quidem ut haeream, sed ut surgam cum volo. . . . sed delectatio carnis meae, cui mentem enervandam non oportet dari, saepe me fallit, dum rationi sensus non ita comitatur ut patienter sit posterioir, sed tantum, quia propter illam meruit admitti, etiam praecurrere ac ducere conatur.
>
> verum tamen cum reminiscor lacrimas meas quas fudi ad cantus ecclesiae in primordiis recuperatae fidei meae, et nunc ipsum cum moveor non cantu sed rebus quae cantantur, cum liquida voce et conve-nientissima modulatione cantantur, magnam instituti huius utilitatem rursus agnosco. ita fluctuo inter periculum voluptatis et experimentum salubritatis magisque adducor, non quidem inretractabilem sententiam proferens, cantandi consuetudinem approbare in ecclesia, ut per oblecta-menta aurium infirmior animus in affectum pietatis adsurgat. tamen cum mihi accidit ut me amplius cantus quam res quae canitur moveat, poenaliter me peccare confiteor et tunc mallem non audire cantantem.

The pleasures of the ear had a more tenacious hold on me, and had sub-jugated me; but you set me free and liberated me. As things now stand, I confess that I have some sense of restful contentment in sounds whose soul is your words, when they are sung by a pleasant and well-trained voice. Not that I am riveted by them, for I can rise up and go when I wish. . . . But my physical delight, which has to be checked from ener-vating the mind, often deceives me when the perception of the senses is unaccompanied by reason, and is not patiently content to be in a subor-dinate place. It tries to be first and to be in the leading role, though it deserves to be allowed only as secondary to reason.

Nevertheless, when I remember the tears which I poured out at the time when I was first recovering my faith, and now that I am moved not by the chant but by the words being sung, when they are sung with a clear voice and entirely recognize the great utility of music in worship. Thus I fluctuate between the danger of pleasure and the experience of the beneficent effect, and I am more led to put forward the opinion (not as an irrevocable view) that the custom of singing in Church is to be approved, so that through the delight of the ear the weaker mind may rise up towards the devotion of worship. Yet when it happens to me that the music moves me more than the subject [meaning or truth] of the song, I confess myself to commit a sin deserving of punishment, and then I would prefer not to have heard the singer.[37]

Augustine here expresses a fundamental tension between the sensuality of singing—the "pleasure of the ear" ("voluptates aurium")—and the "truth" or "meaning" of the words sung (in this case, Psalms), expressed in the second part of the passage as a contrast between "song" and "meaning" ("cantus, quam res") and echoing a binary inherent in the unit of "vox." But Augustine also pinpoints a second important dynamic of that gap between sense and sound: the possibility that departure from "res" is potentially revelatory, softening the listener for devotion—for feelings greater than the normal or everyday. At the same time, it is also potentially sinful, so much so that he wishes he had never heard the singer.

Singing, then, can leave performer and listener alike poised between the revelatory pleasures of "cantus," as free of meaning ("res"), and the peril of sin—again, because of song's ability to transcend the sense (or "res") of the song. At the very hinge of this dilemma is language: the words the singing voice is intended to communicate, both practically (to make audible) but also semantically (communicating the "res" of the words). In Augustine's commentary on the word "iubilus" from Psalm 94 (*Enarrationes in Psalmos*), that "cantus–verbum" dichotomy is even more explicit, as he articulates a mode of singing that surpasses words altogether, this time nominating such unfettered vocality as the ideal voice for communicating praise for God:

qui iubilat, non verba dicit, sed sonus quidam est laetitiae sine verbis: vox est enim animi diffusi laetitia, quantum potest, exprimentis affectum, non sensum comprehendentis.

One who jubilates does not utter words [express sense], but it is rather a kind of sound of joy without words; for the voice is thus the soul dispersed out in joy, demonstrating as much as it is able the feeling without grasping the sense.[38]

Bruce Holsinger's interpretations of these passage in Augustine and other Church Fathers lead him to conclude that "Augustine seems to sense something innately non- or even prelinguistic in music's flow through the

---

37 Augustine, *Confessions*, Book X, ch. 33 (§§49 and 50). For the Latin edition see *Confessions*, ed. with an English commentary by James O'Donnell, vol. 1 (Oxford: Clarendon Press, 1992), and for the English translation see *St. Augustine: Confessions*, transl. Henry Chadwick (Oxford: Oxford University Press, 1991, repr. 1998).

38 Augustine, *Enarrationes in Psalmos*, commentary on Psalm 94. Cited from *Enarrationes in psalmos*, ed. Eligius Dekkers and Johannes Fraipon, Corpus Christianorum series Latina 38–40 (Turnhout: Brepols, 1990).

human body."[39] Perhaps, though, the real potency of music's flow is in the uneasy yet exhilarating tension that comes about in its relationship to words, a tension that goes back to the roots of language itself, the word poised between sonority and sense.

Augustine thus articulates tensions between words and their sound, and music's particular ability to complicate the sound–sense relationship, which clearly has roots in a broader linguistic theory. While we will never know precisely what kinds of musical sounds gave the saint such treacherous pleasures, he put his finger on something essential about music's capacity to unsettle words: something that generations of listeners and writers would uphold in the centuries following. As we edge closer to our period of concern, we see subtle adjustments and transformations of Augustine's original "res"/"cantus" distinction, shifts that themselves seem to pick up audible changes in the nature of musical sound, and which make the connections to linguistics and grammar more precise. For two Cistercian commentators of the twelfth century, quotation and paraphrases of *Confessions* involve a few small adjustments: "res"/"cantus" is changed to "verbum"/"cantus," and opened out with a second distinction, "sonus"/"sensus"—sound and sense (or meaning). Both Bernard of Clairvaux (likely author of these amendments) and his follower Aelred of Rievaulx had occasion to cite Augustine's *Confessions* in their invectives against polyphony. Consider this passage from Aelred's *Speculum caritatis* (ca. 1142):

> sic quod sancti Patres instituerunt, ut infirmi excitarentur ad affectum pietatis, in usum assumitur illicitae voluptatis. non enim sensui praeferendus est sonus, sed sonus cum sensu ad incitamentum majoris affectus plerumque admittendus. . . . ideoque talis debet esse sonus, tam moderatus, tam gravis, ut non totum animum ad sui rapiat oblectationem, sed sensui majorem relinquat portionem. ait nempe beatissimus Augustinus: "movetur animus ad affectum pietatis divino cantico audito: sed si magis sonum quam sensum libido audiendi desideret, improbatur." et alias: "cum me, inquit, magis cantus quam verba delectant, poenaliter me peccasse confiteor, et mallem non audire cantantem."

What the holy fathers instituted to excite the weak to an attachment of devotion is seized for illicit pleasure. Sound ("sonus") should not be given preference over sense ("sensui"), but wound up with sense should generally be allowed to incite greater attachment. Therefore, the sound should be so restrained, so dignified, that it does not ravish the whole soul to delighting in itself, but leaves the greater part to the sense. As the most blessed Augustine said: "The soul is moved to a disposition of piety on hearing sacred song. But if the longing to hear desires the song

---

39 Holsinger, *Music, Body, and Desire*, 77.

("cantus") more than the sense of the words ("verba"), it should be censured." And elsewhere he says: "When the singing delights me more than the words, I acknowledge that I have sinned through my fault, and I would prefer not to listen to the singer."[40]

On the one hand, the small changes here draw the passage closer to discourses of linguistics. On the other, they resonate with an emerging musicality in which words are, quite literally, less audible in the moment of performance, tucked within multiple voices, sometimes stretched out in melismatic luxury. That much more practical invasion of "sensus" by "sonus" is brought out in these new inflections: in keeping with the records of the Aquitanian repertories, for instance, where musical sound is increasingly distinguishable from and independent of words. In the century that followed, the great *organa* of Notre Dame would test the listener's hold on words with textures that staged chant as grossly extended syllables in a swirl of multi-voice vocalization. Even if the familiarity of the chant, and the sheer force of memory and devotional habit, kept the listener anchored in verbal sense, the motet would sever that connection of 'sensus' and 'sonus' in ways that, heard against this linguistic topos, were quite simply radical.

Finally to a commentary on polytextuality in our period. As we have seen, Jacques de Liège offered rare reaction to the genre of the motet. His complaints about the *ars nova* are many and complex, but it is through the medium of verbal sound that he makes his most compelling case for the falsity and failure of the new art. Throughout his attack on the *moderni*, he leans on the binary of sense and sound, now brought specifically into alignment with the reality of the musical sounds assaulting his senses (and sensibilities). The nebulous "verbum" is now concretely "littera"—the word for word—as he attributes the "lasciviousness" of the motets in part to a loss of words: "ad quid tantum placet cantandi lascivia, curiositas in qua, ut aliquibus videtur, littera perditur . . ." ("Wherein does this lasciviousness of singing so greatly please, this excessive refinement, by which, some think, words are lost?"). Warming to his theme, he takes the *moderni* to task through a reformulation of Augustianian rhetoric, pitting "cantus" against "dictamina" (another specific reference to texts) and seeing this loss of the word as an absence of intelligibility: "sic Moderni, licet multa pulchra et bona in suis cantibus faciant dictamina, in modo tamen suo cantandi, cum non intelligantur, perdunt ea." ("Thus, although the moderns

---

40 Quoting from Book II, ch. 23 of the *Speculum caritatis*, in vol. 1 of Aelred of Rievaulx, *Opera omnia*, ed. Anselm Hoste and Charles Talbot, Corpus Christianorum, continuatio mediaevalis 1–2B, 2D (Turnholt: Brepols, 1971). The Latin is reproduced with an English translation by Randall Rosenfeld in Timothy McGee, *The Sound of Medieval Song: Ornamentation and Vocal Style according to the Treatises* (Oxford: Clarendon Press, 1998), translation on 23–24.

compose good and beautiful texts for their songs, they waste them by their manner of singing, since they are not understood.")[41] There are competing agendas in these passages—Jacques's scholastic background accounts for certain themes in the diatribe; in addition, he leaves open the question of whether the loss of sense experienced in the fourteenth-century motets was also a concern for his predecessors. Nevertheless, these lines are a vivid example of how entwined were the practices of music and the practices of words. It will now be apparent that linguistics formed a familiar part of Jacques's listening apparatus, and also that for some it was well-near impossible to listen without the filter of linguistics and all its baggage.

Medieval discourses of language thus offer a specific framework for thinking about the supermusical in French repertories from the era of the first great chansonniers around 1260 to roughly 1330, the period when Jacques was writing. But the lesson of linguistics extends beyond the suggestion of a broad cultural context for music, and I do not want to impose on the material a single schematic for musical ontology, one determined by theory alone. Jacques, after all, was just one kind of listener. The context evoked here illustrates one way in which we might recover some sense of that supermusical effect. It demonstrates how engaging music with other kinds of sonorous evidence—in this case with theory of linguistic sound—we may inject meaning into musical effect. Hearing a genre such as the motet in dialogue with that broader environment of words, we catch overtones of sonic sense: philosophical, ethical, theological. We start to imagine a context where musical effect was charged with emotive, inspiring, and perhaps sometimes worrying suggestion. Although music of the late thirteenth century is hardly unique in carrying such cultural meanings at its sonorous surface, to attempt to recuperate traces of sound's sense is a departure from the questions more often asked of these repertories. It invites an experiment in a much more contextually entrenched form of listening, and a form of listening more holistic and dialogic. In the next section, I therefore wish to offer some models that theorize an approach for situated listening, ones derived from some much more recent thinking about the nature of texts and their reception.

SENSE THROUGH DIALOGIC LISTENING

In her study of thirteenth-century French poetry and music, Ardis Butterfield offers a fascinating portrait for a mode of social listening to song.[42] Echoing older models that approached French medieval song from a sociological

41 Jacques de Liège, *Speculum musicae*, Book VII, ch. 48, from p. 95. Translation from *Strunk's Source Readings*, 167–68.

42 Butterfield, *Poetry and Music*.

perspective, notably those of Alfred Jeanroy and Pierre Bec with their emphasis on the registral aspect of the repertory, Butterfield's proposition of how song may relate to its social environment nonetheless marks a radical departure. In a section entitled "The Location of Culture," the agenda to hear registers within French song as related to a specific social context is set out in the locale of thirteenth-century Arras, a major center for literary and musical production.[43] Butterfield's definition of song's sociability is thus grounded in the documented reality of place. At the same time, her reading of song is rooted in the analytical—that is, it attempts to understand what sonic or literary components of a song generate a sense of social register and association. In this instance, it is refrains that serve as Butterfield's window into song's outward reach, and for the development of a hypothesis for how the exterior environment invited in by a citation can create meaning in song.

For Butterfield, the presence of a refrain citation represents a moment of rupture—one that is inherently registral. In determining precisely how citations communicate a sense of "elsewhere," she turns to a very specific critical model. Drawing on Bakhtin's theory of dialogue and utterance, she argues that the medieval composition's use of refrain engineers a moment of "dialogic contact" "between distinct languages and genres." In fact, the refrain does not so much come from a popular social context outside a song or poem (an old assumption, dating back to Jeanroy), but rather inhabits a space somewhere between the two: "In its wandering existence as a recurrent citation, the refrain reflects a fluidity about generic definition which is at the heart of many types of compositional procedure in the thirteenth century. One of the reasons for this is that (in Bakhtinian terms) refrains are inherently difficult to perceive as being either internal or external to a work."[44] That liminal status invites not only investigation of how making and breaking generic function shapes compositional choices in a given work; Butterfield pushes this further, and an opportunity opens up to explore the relationship between "form, register, and social expectation."[45] It is a social expectation grounded in a real place and at a real time. In the ensuing two chapters, Arras's highly charged social boundaries become backdrop for reading a cluster of works connected in some cases by their locus of production and performance (Arras), and by their shared corpus of refrains. The starting point is two lyric-interpolated romances, *Renart le nouvel* and *Le tournoi de Chauvency*, and a collection of songs, all connected to Arras. Building on this core of works by tracing author connections, the work of copyists, and literary and generic themes, Butterfield recreates a family of literary and musical works likely consumed by an Artesian audience.

43 Ibid., 125–68.
44 Ibid., 131.
45 Ibid.

Paying attention to the migration of refrains in and out of the collection, Butterfield examines how the refrain's capacity to disrupt and transform register may operate in ways that resonated with the social confrontations and dynamics of Arras itself. As she writes:

> A rewriting of register takes place throughout the thirteenth century in romance. Refrains play a key part in this gradual relocation of registral boundaries. Their inherent mobility of register . . . allows them to create liaisons between the different worlds of the aristocrat and the peasant, the sacred and the secular, or the animal and the human. Neither exactly external nor internal to a work in which they occur, refrains play out the polymorphous clerical procedures by which the courtly and the popular in the thirteenth century at once collide and are mutually absorbed.[46]

Butterfield's model of social listening offers an approach that is at once engaged in critical and analytical understanding of musical and poetic works, and also in a deeply documentary sense of the Artesian world in which these works were written. Her evocation of the political landscape of the city and attempts to understand social nuance in the city as backdrop to registeral distinctions in the works, is one of the few accounts of medieval song that position it in a "thick" cultural context. At the same time, the social Arras is also a world of literary production—it is a "literary centre." In other words, it is a vision of culture—and of the social—that is ultimately defined by literary and musical production. As well as suggesting a more integrated relationship between artistic production and the social, ritual life of the Middle Ages, it also throws into question the very notion of "social reality." Butterfield's interpretations encourage us to consider the possibility of a kind of musical sound that is neither the literal call heard on the street of Arras, nor ultimately bound up in the rarified context of "music." It is, in a sense, a sound in between, and implies a social reality that is simultaneously transforming itself into representations that can be deployed in artistic production.

Such an approach may also be applicable to and desirable for thinking about the supermusical. It offers a model for a holistic mode of listening: a way of listening to song that places as central its presence as audible, felt, experience; a form of sound produced by, and made sense of in, its audible environment. In defining such an approach to listening, I wish to conclude with a closer look at the inspiration for Butterfield's approach, for it is in the dialogic model proposed by Bakhtin that I have found the most feasible and productive tools for situating the supermusical, and for developing ways to make sense of sound.

46 Ibid., 147.

Bakhtin's theory of the novel offers perhaps the most famous exemplum of ways in which works of art may be understood as written by and constantly engaging with their worldly surroundings. In the anti-generic—or perhaps poly-generic—dimensions of the novel, a form of constant direct and indirect speech, in which Bakhtin identified a mode of writing where all languages, all styles, and all registers could come into constant dialogue: "the novel can be defined as a diversity of social speech types (sometimes even diversity of languages) and a diversity of individual voices, artistically organized."[47] The novel not only conversed with itself internally, in the frame of the work, but also constantly communicated externally, with the inflections, registers, and meanings of the different utterances that made up the work, contingent in myriad ways on reality. It was the constant mobility and organicism of the novel, its movement and change determined by the changing external realities, that made Bakhtin so resistant to modes of stylistic analysis, which in essence freeze the register of a particular voice at a single moment and "lock every stylistic phenomenon into the monologic context of a given self-sufficient and hermetic utterance, imprisoning it, as it were, in the dungeon of a single context; it is not able to exchange messages with other utterances; it is not able to realize its own stylistic implications in relation with them; it is obliged to exhaust itself in its own single hermetic context."[48] Freed from such a prison, the dialogic is born, and so begins the constant conversation, internal and external, central to Bakhtin's poetics. In the concept of heteroglossia—that is, the "primacy of context over text"—the novel comes to life, and breathes in a reality without the boundaries of "art." Works are understood as being in a process of "living interaction" with environments that constantly shift and inflect the meaning of language.[49] He writes: "The living utterance, having taken meaning and shape at a particular historical moment in a socially specific environment, cannot fail to brush up against thousands of living dialogic threads, woven by socio-ideological consciousness around the given object of an utterance; it cannot fail to become an active participant in social dialogue."[50] To apply such a viewpoint to the study of historically distant works is not only to link work to world: to recover those moments of dialogue is in a strange way to resuscitate a moment where one breathes life into the other, where the work, according to Bakhtin, is truly organic and transformative.

47 Mikail Bakhtin, "Discourse in the Novel," in *The Dialogic Imagination: Four Essays*, ed. Michael Holquist, transl. Caryl Emerson and Michael Holquist (Austin: University of Texas Press, 1981, repr. 2004), 262.

48 Ibid., 274.

49 Ibid., 276.

50 Ibid., 267.

The novel was Bakhtin's shorthand for a more general idea about writing, one characterized by works that were anti-generic or hybrid in nature: " 'Novel' is the name Bakhtin gives to whatever force is at work within a given literary system to reveal the limits, the artificial constraints of that system. Literary systems are comprised of canons, and 'novelization' is fundamentally anticanonical. . . . Always it will insist on the dialogue between what a given system will admit as literature and those texts that are otherwise excluded from such a definition of literature."[51] It is not hard to see how such an idea resonates not only with the verbal content of thirteenth-century song repertories, the motet in particular, but also with the sonorous dimensions of that medium: the polyphonic structures of the motet make active the dialogic relationship between different textual and musical registers. It is surely telling that when medieval musicologists turn to contemporary theory to illuminate their materials, it is Bakhtin who is most commonly summoned.[52]

However, there is a more direct correlation between Bakhtin's dialogic model and thirteenth-century song. Grounded in medieval studies, Bakhtin turned time and again to the French Middle Ages, evoking the thirteenth century as a prehistory for the modes of writing his was primarily concerned with. Among the essays on the dialogic is one entirely devoted to the "prehistory" of novelistic discourse, and central in his quest for ancient precursors to the modern novel are the French literary forms of the thirteenth century.[53] Touching on a wide spectrum of literature, from the Feast of Fools, the bilingual farcies, cento forms, and many others, Bakhtin characterized the French Middle Ages as a moment of intense hybridity—of languages, genres, and registers. The constant play on mixing high and low styles in the literature he selected, reminiscent of the more extensive exploration of mixing in his vision of the carnivalesque, was for Bakthin nothing less than evidence of "a complex and centuries-long struggle with cultures and languages" that would result in the novel writ large.[54] For my purposes, Bakhtin's consistent revelation of the dialogic in the parodic structures in the literary tradition opens new directions for reconsidering music. He points to obvious ways in which the dialogic potentiality in medieval writing was, as with the later novelistic form, an impulse "that reaches out beyond it" into the social.[55] In accounting for the traditions of *parodia sacra* (including Feast of Fools), he sought to hear words

51 Michael Holquist, "Introduction," in *The Dialogic Imagination*, xxxi.

52 See, for example, Page, *Discarding Images*, 49–51 for discussion of the carnivalesque in relation to the motet.

53 Bakhtin, "From the Prehistory of Novelistic Discourse," in *The Dialogic Imagination*, 41–83.

54 Ibid., 83.

55 Bakhtin, "Discourse," 292.

against and as emerging from lived social rites: "the great parodic literature of the Middle Ages was created in an atmosphere of holidays and festivals. There was no genre, no text, no prayer, no saying that did not receive its parodic equivalent."[56]

While the dialogic vision seems fitting as a way of understanding the hybridity of thirteenth-century genres, and extendable to musical repertories, it is the possibility of putting song into dialogue with sounding environments external to itself that interests me here. Heteroglossia works through a kind of constant conversation between the fixity of a work and the social worlds around it that alter and inflect the meaning through time. A work is, then, complete only by being understood as being in conversation not only within itself, but with alternate environments outside itself.

Such a mode of thinking about song seems especially inviting, particularly if boundaries between song and other sonorities were flexible, with song not necessarily understood as being rarified or separate from other sorts of experiences. There is much to encourage us to think about song's participation in—conversation with—the environments at its fringes: it is time, in other words, to turn our gaze out, like the longing protagonists of the songs with which we began this chapter, to contemplate what form such sonic interactions might take, what that tug, in and out of song, in and out of a performance and its worldly exterior, could mean for those song sought to embrace.

Listening to the Supermusical: Spheres of Conversation

Let us now take the sound of medieval song up on its apostrophic invitation—and follow its reach outwards, trace its paths to other sonorous interlocutors. Into what spheres of medieval culture shall we listen in? While theories of words traced earlier will be an essential reference point, the desire to catch echoes of cultural meanings in sound opens the way to a quite different body of evidence. A musicologist might be forgiven for overlooking it, for by their very clamorous and unpredictable nature, these soundscapes will seem the very antithesis to what we think of as musical. Such sonorities originate far outside the frame of textual, visual, or musical representation: they are audible in the environments of the people, places, and experiences that were host to the artistic matter of song—from the hubbub of city life, to the murmur of devotion, from the ravings of the insane to, most terrifying of all, the soundtrack of the imagination, conjuring the sonorities of the metaphysical and otherworldly.

56 Bakhtin, "From the Prehistory," 74.

A word, too, about a sonority that we shall be less concerned with here, namely that of birdsong, music's most ostentatious opposite. As noted above, the relationship of music to birdsong (and other kinds of animal sound) have been admirably researched in Elizabeth Leach's monograph. Part of what makes birdsong so fascinating an interlocutor to music is its constant and systematic treatment in theory as well as practice. While it thus offers major insights into medieval ontological explorations of song, I strive in my account to explore musical sound in sonic contexts that were perhaps less clearly theorized, and where as a result we can catch traces of a broader range of sound's meanings, and for constituencies of listeners perhaps less versed in theory. The picture is in many respects messier and less systematic. However, it hopes to recover contexts for listening that might include those less steeped in discourses of music and poetry.

Nor is my purpose to attempt an archival excavation of the acoustic past, or to recuperate sound as ambient backdrop to music. As set out in the Prologue, more so than music, what characterizes this historical sonority is its elusive and unpredictable quality: sounds that were produced without the kind of design and intent we associate with music; sound born of the spontaneity of everyday circumstance. To recall Emily Thompson, these acoustic realities formed soundscapes that were "both a world and a culture constructed to make sense of that world."[57] We will focus, then, on how this broader spectrum of sound found its way into the productions of artists (poets, illuminators, manuscript-makers, musicians)—those who in a way constructed sense for sound in the act of representing it—working in precisely the same cultural and creative communities as those producing and listening to the musical repertories at the centre of my investigation. Time and again, a short step beyond musical production (sometimes a mere turn beyond the folios of the musical portion of a manuscript) has opened out onto a rich array of artistic effort to represent a range of real life situations, of places and people bursting with all manner of sounds. These materials are a precious resource for the perception of sound ca. 1260–1330. While we may catch echoes here and there of the actual sonic source of these representations, their artistic rendering is more consistent in recording and prescribing the range of effects—emotional, ethical, revelatory. These sounds are, then, also imbued with sense, and are rife with meaning: a fascinating and productive counterpoint to supermusical production.

To bring such materials together is thus to reassemble members of a lost creative and listening community of the late thirteenth and early fourteenth centuries, and to hear snatches of conversation between different sorts of people in different kinds of social contexts, conversations made audible through a range of sonorities. It is, moreover, a community for whom these noisy and

57 Thompson, *Soundscape of Modernity*, 1.

melodic materials had meaning, perhaps even ethical imperatives, where musical sound and other kinds of sounds were mutually defining. In this more socially and sonorously holistic environment, I hope to offer not just new ways to rehear the extant evidence of sound from this period, but also to recover some fragile sense of how the sounds that once resonated in the originary medieval moment were felt, understood, and acted upon.

We will begin with perhaps the loudest of all sonic environments: the sound of the city, in this case, the largest urban center of the Middle Ages—Paris.

2 | Sound and the City

A Song at the Bridge

We begin with a rare snapshot of singers in Paris in the second decade of the fourteenth century (see figure 2.1). The image of three singing clerics in a boat, ferried down the Seine by two taciturn rowers, appears in the borders of a royal manuscript produced not far from the city represented throughout its luxurious folios. Made in the *scriptorium* of the abbey of Saint-Denis for the accession of Philip V in the early months of 1317, and emphatically fit for a king, it is a pictorial and textual account of the life of the city's first bishop, St. Denis.[1] However, in an unusual twist, the *vita* (told in Latin and Old French) is simultaneously visualized in a program that shows the city's patron in a clearly recognizable urban frame. Staged amid the symmetries of Paris's walls, bridges, and river, the saint is literally—as well as metaphorically—the city's heart. By so binding saint with city, the manuscript is doubly exemplary. Its didactic intent is to enlighten the royal dedicatee with lessons of a saintly life; but it also demonstrates, folio by folio, the laudable city over which king—as saint—presided. The book is as much *encomium* as Mirror of Princes, suggesting that the real city is a glorious embodiment of desirable sanctity.[2]

---

1 Paris, Bibliothèque nationale de France, f. fr. 2090–2092, fol. 99ʳ. Images from the manuscript are reproduced in *Légende de Saint Denis: Reproduction des miniatures du manuscrit original présenté en 1317 au Roi Philippe le Long*, ed. Henry Martin (Paris: Honoré Champion, 1908). See also Virginia Wylie Egbert, *On the Bridges of Mediaeval Paris: A Record of Early Fourteenth-Century Life* (Princeton: Princeton University Press, 1974).

2 Charlotte Lacaze first suggested the book's connection to the tradition of Mirror of Princes. See her "*Parisius–paradisus*: An Aspect of the *Vie de Saint Denis* Manuscript of 1317," *Marsyas* 16 (1972–73): 60–66.

FIGURE 2.1. Paris, Bibliothèque nationale de France, f. fr. 2090–2092, fol. 99ʳ. By permission of the Bibliothèque nationale de France

What place do rotulus-wielding singers have in so solemn a didactic program? Dwarfed by the saintly narrative, is their meaning proportionally marginal? Are they mere soundtrack to the central narrative? For today's musicological viewer these questions are inflected by the image's iconicity. While the *Vie de Saint Denis* has long been a fixture in the historiography of the city, the image of song accrued a special currency in the late 1980s when it was the cover to Christopher Page's monograph on medieval French song. It was a fitting entry-point to its deep cultural contextualization of music.[3]

3 Christopher Page, *The Owl and the Nightingale: Musical Life and Ideas in France 1100–1300* (London: Dent, 1989).

Like the boat song, cast against the backdrop of the medieval city, music according to Page's account emerged from vibrant urban and court cultures of northern France: as product of a burgeoning manuscript economy, of intellectual revolutions in the schools and universities, of an ever-expanding vernacular poetic tradition.

In one sense, then, the song at the bridge is a reminder that music was a prestigious and pleasurable part of the cultural economy of Paris around 1317. Imbued with such value, it functions in the scene to reflect, perhaps even to make audible, a different kind of economy: the lofty values of the saint and his idealized city. From the modern vantage point, the image also reinforces a familiar historiographical mode: a lesson in "context," showing how music is born of, and is reflective of, its environment. But that does not entirely explain how the sighting of song here signified in its own historical and material terms. A closer look suggests a more complex relationship between music and its environment, and specifically between musical sound and other sounds of the city. Situated in their material context, the musicians are one group in a vast, noisy populus. On this folio alone, the bridge is home to another kind of sound: the hammering of a latter-day Tubal Cain, a goldsmith at his anvil. He competes with clattering hooves; the animated chit-chat of the money-changer to the left and the purse-seller to the right; with the shouts of the man at the parapet, mouth open and finger pointing. The presence of sound in this scene is enhanced by the visible sign of its interlocutor: the swirl of speech scrolls in the centre scene signals authoritative (and audible) locution of the saintly caste.

These remarkable attempts at realism embedded in the city structure—what Camille Serchuk has called "naturalistic representations of the urban environment"[4]—were radical for the time. Folio by folio, the city comes to life as the architectural frame is animated through constantly shifting scenes on the bridges and river. With each turn, so does the impression of sound change, as people, carts, cattle, and boats bustle back and forth, oblivious to the saintly epic unfolding within. In figure 2.2 (fol. 125^r), coaches of visitors enter on the left; to the right a man receives a urine consultation from the resident doctor. The Seine, the means by which so much produce entered and exited the city, teems with boats: with fisherman, and a convoy carrying barrels. Elsewhere, in figure 2.3 (fol. 30^r), a wine-peddler enters the gates carrying a chalice and jug aloft to the sounds of the goldsmith; meanwhile, a boatman takes a siesta.

In these examples, sound participates in announcing a division between the real (a city of known spaces and humdrum activity), and the symbolic

4 Camille Serchuk, "Paris and the Rhetoric of Town Praise in the *Vie de St. Denis* Manuscript (Paris, Bibliothèque nationale de France, ms fr. 2090–2)," *Journal of the Walters Art Gallery* 57 (1999): 35–47, at 35.

FIGURE 2.2. Paris, Bibliothèque nationale de France, f. fr. 2090–2092, fol. 125ʳ.
By permission of the Bibliothèque nationale de France

(the sacred city that stages St. Denis). The medium of painting permits dialogue between the two registers: mutually reinforcing, they collaborate on a
vision of the city that was, according to one fourteenth-century visitor,
a "paradisus mundi," a paradise on earth: the sublime in an earthly reality.[5]
Such a binary resonates with some pervasive ideas of the city. From Augustine

5 Richard of Bury, *Philobiblon*, Book VIII. See Richard of Bury, *The Love of Books: The
Philobiblon of Richard of Bury*, transl. Ernest Thomas (London: A. Moring, 1902),
reprinted with a foreword by Michael Maclagan (Oxford: Blackwell, 1960), 56.

FIGURE 2.3. Paris, Bibliothèque nationale de France, f. fr. 2090–2092, fol. 30ʳ.
By permission of the Bibliothèque nationale de France

to de Certeau, the city has offered writers with an inexhaustible cipher for
philosophical and theological values, and was a template for the exploration of
ideals of social conduct, and later for the nature of writing itself.[6] In such

6 As modern theologian of the city Graham Ward notes, the link between writing
and urbanism reaches across history, from ancient theology to the present day. See his
Cities of God (London: Routledge, 2000), 4. For an alternative interpretation of the manuscript imagery, see Cornelia Logemann, *Heilige Ordungen: Die Bild-Räume der Vie de Saint
Denis (1317) und die französische Buchmalerei des 14. Jahrhunderts* (Cologne: Böhlau, 2009),
who proposes an allegorical reading of the bridge imagery. Joel Kaye proposes another
interpretation, and reads the design of the imagery within contemporary discourse

accounts, the realistic elements of the city, including its sound, appear at the fault line between the actual place (what de Certeau characterized as the "practice" of the city) and its hermeneutic potential brought about through writing.

We will hear more about ideas of the city presently. For now, though, sound's place in the *Vie*, caught up in discourses of the real and symbolic, the everyday and the sublime, invites new ways of thinking aurally about the city, and about music's relationship to its sonorous environment. It suggests fresh ways to listen to the evidence of the past: for as well as signifying the prestige of Paris's musical traditions, the scenes situate song in a world of contingent clamor that seems to be music's very opposite. Yet, as this brief excursion has suggested, the very act of representation imbues the everyday with value and function. In the world of this book, and within the wider conventions of civic representation and *Encomium*, the seemingly incidental soundtrack of the city is no longer simply ambient effect. It transforms into an urban *magnificat*. It becomes thus not merely an audible foil and counterpoint to musical sound, but also potentially a hermeneutic one.

It is on those terms of "urban magnificat" that I wish in the rest of this chapter to turn up the volume on the quiet parchment, to listen more closely to the city. Taking my cue from the *Vie*, I will explore an idea of the urban soundscape as magnificent, within the medieval framework of that term. A concept synonymous with civic values, magnificence may best be understood through its Latin roots: *magnum facere*, an act of enlarging, making great, expanding.[7] We can also situate magnificence in an older Aristotelian sense as expressed through wealth; demonstrated in acts of material excess and surplus, which could in turn reflect virtues such as magnanimity or benevolence.[8] There is also an interesting correspondence between magnificence as a virtue or ideal, and as a process of accountability: that is, as related to acts of enumeration, quantification, and proliferation, all efforts at containment of a thing

---

relating to economic and ethical equilibrium and political thought. This material will be part of his forthcoming book: *A History of Balance, 1250–1375* and I am grateful to him for sharing drafts of a chapter entitled "The Model of Equilibrium in Medieval Political Thought" and for extremely helpful feedback on this chapter.

7 Medieval magnificence is subjected to a new interdisciplinary treatment in *Magnificence and the Sublime: The Aesthetics of Grandeur in Medieval Art, Architecture, Literature and Music*, ed. Stephen Jaeger (New York: Palgrave Macmillan, 2010).

8 On Aristotle's ideas of wealth and magnificence in his *Ethics*, and its reiteration in the Middle Ages with in relation to consumerism, see Richard Goldthwaite, *Wealth and the Demand for Art in Italy, 1300–1600* (Baltimore: Johns Hopkins University Press, 1993), 176–255. I am grateful to Beth Williamson and Stephen Jaeger, and other contributors to *Magnificence and the Sublime*, for fruitful and stimulating discussion of ideas relating to magnificence.

enlarging to infinity. Like the very roots of the word, magnificence thus operates in superlatives whose ultimate expression is one of *excessus*. As we shall see, such terms find uncanny correspondence with the Parisian soundscape, both in its aural substance and in the cultural meanings ascribed to it by contemporaries. I propose, too, that such sound also intersects with another kind of sonic superabundance: the supermusical effect of contemporary music, and particularly that of the motet.

In what follows, we shall thus attune to the sound of the city about its everyday affairs. The intent is not one of urban archeology. While there have been fruitful attempts to excavate the archive of urban sound, and to explore the regulatory and revelatory meanings of sound in the experience of medieval city life, my interest is with a specific moment of its reception.[9] We shall be concerned with a group of artists, thinkers, musicians, and manuscript-makers who not only listened carefully to their city in all its hybrid mix of unpredictable noise and planned musical performance; they also turned their city—and its sounds—into writing. In the decades around the creation of the *Vie de Saint Denis*, Paris became a topic for creative rumination as never before. And little wonder. The explosion of artistic representations mirrored the city's own dramatic transformations in the thirteenth and fourteenth centuries, when it expanded beyond the scale of other cities, and when the lure of its university, royal palaces, and marketplace swelled its population into one of the largest and most diverse in Europe.[10] As one historian describes it, Paris was "une exception, un monstre démographique."[11] We will focus on an eclectic array of materials dating from the death of St. Louis (Louis IX, d. 1270) to the

9 For recent work on the medieval city see Keith Lilley, *Urban Life in the Middle Ages, 1000–1450* (Houndmills: Palgrave, 2002); for a selection of medieval writings about the urban experience see *Medieval Towns: A Reader*, ed. Maryanne Kowaleski, Readings in Medieval Civilizations and Cultures 11 (Toronto: Higher Education University of Toronto Press, 2008).

10 The following samples the most frequently cited accounts of Paris, including the city's expansions during the thirteenth and fourteenth centuries: Jean Favier, *Paris: Deux mille ans d'histoire* (Paris: Fayard, 1997); Pierre Lavedan, *Nouvelle histoire de Paris: Histoire de l'urbanisme à Paris* (Paris: Hachette, 1993); and Raymond Cazelles, *Nouvelle histoire de Paris: De la fin du règne de Philippe Auguste à la mort de Charles V, 1223–1380* (Paris: Hachette, 1972, repr. 1994), esp. 13–31 for a summary of the expansions of the city limits, and changes to the parish boundaries within.

11 Favier, *Paris*, 38. Historians estimate a doubling of the population, during Philippe Auguste's reign, from 25,000 to 50,000. Based on the evidence of the Paris *tailles* of the early fourteenth century, it is possible that in the early decades of that century the population had exploded to in excess of 200,000. Such numbers made Paris not only one of the largest cities in Europe, but also the most densely populated: according to Favier, the largest cities in Italy (including Florence) stretched only to 100,000 occupants.

coronation of his great-grandson, Philip V (in 1317)—a period important for architectural developments on the Ile-de-la-Cité, and no less for its burgeoning musical traditions. These materials include vernacular poetry, Latin *encomia*, dictionaries, images, and music: all united in a mission to memorialize the city. Departing from the scopic focus of modern analyses of civic representation, we shall attend to the elusive, yet pervasive, presence of sound in these texts: as we shall see, their sonorous dimensions are no less communicative than their attempts at visualization. Not only that, the very elusive consistency of sound—a feature that so preoccupied medieval writers and theoreticians—is precisely what seems to lend it agency in these aggrandizing accounts. In locating traces of this soundworld, we shall consider what such accounts suggest about the sense of urban sound. How do the properties of sound differ from other symbols of the everyday, and how is such effect put to use in the idealization of place? By what artistic means is contingent sound transformed into lasting record? As we shall see, there is an eerie consonance between the rational, contrived medium of song and the seemingly random effect of the sound of the city.

*

First, a word about some recent contexts. In the last few years sound has become a fascination to constituencies of scholars often far outside musicology.[12] As reaction to a perceived visual bias, disciplines such as anthropology and history have become more sensitive to the lessons of the "ethnographic ear."[13] Theoretical discussions surrounding this growing interest will be useful to the exploration of my more localized materials. Particularly relevant is the priority

---

For further detailed evidence of the Parisian population expansion, see Lavedan, *Nouvelle histoire*, 129–31.

12 For an excellent introduction to the field see *The Auditory Culture Reader*, ed. Michael Bull and Les Back (Oxford: Berg, 2003); *Hearing Cultures: Essays on Sound, Listening and Modernity*, ed. Veit Erlmann (Oxford: Berg, 2004); and *Hearing History: A Reader*, ed. Mark Smith (Athens: University of Georgia Press, 2004). Other influential monographs include Jonathan Sterne, *The Audible Past: Cultural Origins of Sound Reproduction* (Durham, NC: Duke University Press, 2003); Penelope Gouk, *Music, Science, and Natural Magic in Seventeenth-Century England* (New Haven: Yale University Press, 1999); Bruce Smith, *The Acoustic World of Early Modern England: Attending to the O-Factor* (Chicago: University of Chicago Press, 1999).

13 The term "ethnographic ear" was first used by anthropologist James Clifford in the introduction to *Writing Culture: The Poetics and Politics of Ethnography*, ed. James Clifford and George Marcus (Berkeley: University of California Press, 1986), and was taken up by Veit Erlmann in his introduction to *Hearing Cultures*. Erlmann's essay, "But What of the Ethnographic Ear? Anthropology, Sound, and the Senses," 1–20, offers an excellent overview of some of the major and recurring themes in the field.

of sound studies to greatly expand the types of sounds to be considered a field of investigation. That expansion owes a debt to pioneering writers like R. Murray Schafer and Jacques Attali.[14] Schafer's foundational lexicon for sound studies reflected a broadening of the sound spectrum beyond the musical. His concept of "soundscape," denoting "any portion of the sonic environment regarded as a field of study,"[15] and of "keynote," which "in soundscape studies . . . are those [sounds] heard by a particular society continuously or frequently enough to form a background against which other sounds are perceived,"[16] both commonplace today, illustrate that any sonority has potential for meaning and effect.[17] These influential ideas animate the current generation of sound scholarship, both by encouraging the definition of new soundscapes for investigation, and by inviting theorization of how these sonorous fields carry and shape meaning both in real terms (as heard) and metaphorically (as reconstituted in writings of various kinds). There is also a subset within the field devoted to a history of sound. The communal space of cities and villages have featured prominently: from Bruce Smith's attempt to recuperate the historical sonority of early-modern England;[18] to Alain Corbin's work on nineteenth-century bells;[19] to several accounts of the sonic experience of modern cities.[20]

The urban soundscape has also garnered attention as part of a sustained interest in the "everyday" as a window into the mentalities of the past, one that defined a generation of Annales School historians. In pioneering writings by Jacques Le Goff, George Duby, and others, interest in the history of human experience led to fresh sensitivity to aural evidence.[21] The clamorous

14 R. Murray Schafer, *The Soundscape: Our Sonic Environment and the Tuning of the World* (Rochester: Inner Traditions International, 1993; reissue of New York: Knopf, 1977) and Jacques Attali, *Noise: The Political Economy of Music*, transl. Brian Massumi (Minneapolis: University of Minnesota Press, 1985).

15 Schafer, *The Soundscape*, 274.

16 Ibid., 272.

17 On the influence of Schafer and Attali on the current field of sound studies, see Mark Smith, "Introduction: Onward to Audible Pasts," in *Hearing History*, ed. Smith, ix–xxii, esp. x–xii.

18 Smith, *The Acoustic World*.

19 Alain Corbin, *Village Bells: Sound and Meaning in the Nineteenth-Century French Countryside*, transl. Martin Thom (New York: Columbia University Press, 1998).

20 Michael Bull and Les Back devote a section of their *Auditory Reader* to "Sounds in the City," including an essay by Jean-Paul Thibaud on the "musicalization" of the city.

21 Le Goff's path-breaking essays on medieval ideas of time illustrate the ways sound served historians of this generation. See especially his "Merchant's Time and Church's Time in the Middle Ages" and "Labor Time in the 'Crisis' of the Fourteenth Century: From Medieval Time to Modern Time," both in Jacques Le Goff, *Time, Work, and Culture in the Middle Ages*, transl. Arthur Goldhammer (Chicago: University of Chciago Press, 1980),

soundscape is also opening to one of the most famous evocations of the Middle Ages, Johan Huizinga's *Autumn of the Middle Ages*.[22] Spilling over into a genre of "city studies," sounds of bells, merchants, clocks, and general urban clatter remain part of the modern imagining of the medieval city.[23] Today, medievalists are increasingly well attuned to sound, and many accounts of architectural spaces, literature, geography, politics, and government attend to sounding experience.[24]

All these approaches raise stimulating questions about the nature of sound, and about sound's potential for meaning. At the same time, they invite new questions. While writers like Bruce Smith, Penelope Gouk, and Alain Corbin illustrate the value and problems of historicizing sound, few accounts stray so far back as we shall here.[25] Building on such work, the present chapter thus also offers another sample of the ways medieval people construed their aural environment. By exploring the meaning of urban sound at so precise a moment, and in such a specific body of texts, we have the opportunity to contribute a new perspective to the sense of sound: both as concept and as lived experience.

29–42 and 43–52, with footnotes at 289–93 and 293–96. Both essays appeared previously in French in 1960 and 1963, respectively.

22 Johan Huizinga's 1919 *Waning of the Middle Ages* was issued in a new edition and translation as *The Autumn of the Middle Ages*, transl. Rodney Payton and Ulrich Mammitzsch (Chicago: University of Chicago Press, 1996). Huizinga was later the inspiration for musicological treatment in the opening of Reinhard Strohm's monograph, *Music in Late Medieval Bruges* (Oxford: Clarendon Press, 1985).

23 The imagined ambient sounds of the medieval city were a feature of nineteenth-century fantasies of the Middle Ages, most famously Victor Hugo's *Notre Dame de Paris*. In the twentieth century, sound was a fixture in a number of scholarly portraits of the medieval city. Aimed often at a more popular audience, such accounts use sound to add color and authenticity to the imagined reality of the medieval past. See, for example, Goronwy Tidy Salusbury-Jones, *Street Life in Medieval England* (Oxford: Pen-in-Hand, 1948); Joseph and Frances Gies, *Life in a Medieval City* (New York: Harper Row, 1981); Chiara Frugoni, *A Day in a Medieval City*, transl. William McCuaig with an introduction by Arsenio Frugoni (Chicago: University of Chicago Press, 2005).

24 Examples include Paul Binski, *Becket's Crown: Art and Imagination in Gothic England, 1170–1300* (New Haven: Yale University Press, 2004); David Wallace, *Premodern Places: Calais to Surinam, Chaucer to Aphra Behn* (Malden, MA: Blackwell, 2004); and Miri Rubin, *Mother of God: A History of the Virgin Mary* (London: Penguin, 2009).

25 An exception is Charles Burnett, "Sound and its Perception in the Middle Ages," in *The Second Sense: Studies in Hearing and Musical Judgement from Antiquity to the Seventeenth Century*, ed. Charles Burnett, Michael Fend, and Penelope Gouk (London: The Warburg Institute, 1991), 43–69. An abridged version appears as "Perceiving Sound in the Middle Ages," in *Hearing History*, ed. Smith, 69–84. Burnett's trajectory is less anthropological than the others cited, and explores sound through the filter of medieval theory and philosophy.

More pressing is the desire to complicate a distinction that still haunts accounts of the sounding past: that between musical sound and other categories; and by extension, between different kinds of listening. While we shall see that musical performance can be quite unlike other, more contingent sonorities, I wish to suggest that the one experience of sound can inflect and shape the other; that musical listening had a context not just in an intellectual, literary, or political environment of Paris, but also in the city's uncontrived hubbub. Remote though the audible sonorities of medieval Paris may be, the sense of proximity of different kinds of sound speaks loudly in the sources we shall visit.

Now, though, it is time to step into the Paris of the *Vie de Saint Denis*. Let us turn our attention downwards, to the street, to the hum of the everyday, and to a pair of aching feet.

A Walk in Paris

Some time around 1300 Guillot de Paris took a walk. As he set off into his city, little could he have known what resonance history would lend his feet: his journey spawned the earliest vernacular poetic representation of Paris, and thus a landmark in the long tradition of writing about the metropolis. Although the original terrain of his constitutional would later fade, overlaid by the groove of nineteenth-century boulevards and architectural symmetries intended to inscribe the city's grandeur into every turn and vista, Guillot's walk nonetheless resonates with the shape of today's city: it, too, was a monument of sorts. For in transforming walking into writing, Guillot was concerned to make his city memorable, to translate his route—and all the things he witnessed—into a literary map.

What remains of Guillot's Parisian outing, and of Guillot himself, is a poem, the *Dit des rues de Paris*, preserved in a fourteenth-century compilation manuscript.[26] Written from the first-person perspective, the poem is a tour de force of the art of naming. In around 550 lines of rhyming couplets, it presents

26 Paris, Bibliothèque nationale de France, f. fr. 24432, fols. 257ᵛ–260ᵛ. Partial and complete editions of the poem were made in the nineteenth century. I shall refer to the following in this chapter: *Le Dit des rues de Paris par Guillot: Manuscrit du quatorzième siècle, vers l'an 1300*, compiled in a collection of essays by Louis Lazare (Paris, n.d.); *Les Rues de Paris mises en vers à la fin du 13ᵉ siècle par Guillot publiées d'après un manuscrit du 14ᵉ siècle* (Paris: Baillieu, 1866); and *Le Dit des rues de Paris (1300) par Guillot (de Paris) avec préface, notes et glossaire par Edgar Mareuse, suivi d'un plan de Paris sous Philippe-le-Bel* (Paris: Librairie générale, 1875). All citations from the poem are taken from the 1875 edition; translations are my own.

a whistle-stop tour of the city streets, its sole premise to record every one of their names. Organized around the three major areas of the city, beginning on the Left Bank, moving to the Cité, and concluding on the Right Bank, the poem depicts the narrator hurtling through the city in a frenzy of enumeration. Told in real time, Guillot's excursion comprises little more than a string of names, tenuously held together by the tug of rhyme.

A few examples will illustrate the abbreviating effects of poem's topographical priority. In a brief prologue, Guillot makes clear an intention to "put into rhyme" the streets of his city:

> Maint dit a fait de roys, de conte;
> Guillot de Paris en son conte
> Les rues de Paris briément
> A mis en rime. Oiez comment.[27]

Many a poem has told the tale of kings; Guillot, in his, has briefly put into rhyme the streets of Paris. Listen how.

On the Left Bank, enumeration is reinforced by the directives of prepositions "près," "après," and "puis":

> A rue de la Huchete à Paris
> Première, dont pas n'a mespris.
> Ases tost trouva Sacalie,
> Et la petite Bouclerie,
> Et la grant Bouclerie après,
> Et Hérondale tout en près.[28]

First of all rue de la Huchete à Paris, from whence the path is not mistaken. Quite soon you will find Sacalie, and Petite Bouclerie, and Grant Bouclerie after, and Hérondale close by.

The purpose is not only to name but also to quantify. At the end of his tour of the Cité, Guillot alights on the bridge to reckon up the thirty-six streets ("il n'a que trente-sis/Rues constables en Cité").[29]

At first sight, the city of the poem seems far removed from the monumentalizing rhetoric of the *Vie de Saint Denis*. That vision of Paris is tinged with admiration, while Guillot's city is decidedly makeshift—little more than a series of networks. However, there is an important correspondence. As Guillot's city flies by, an uncanny and unpredictable array of sounds and sights cram into the tiny gaps between streets and lines. Like the bridges of the *Vie*,

27 *Dit des rues*, 1.
28 Ibid., 3–5.
29 Ibid., 35–36.

Guillot's city clamors in a fiction of real time—the living is layered over the fixed pattern of streets. A few examples will illustrate:

Une femme vi batre lin
Par la rue Saint-Mathelin.[30]

At Rue Saint-Mathelin I see a woman beating her linen.

Et puis la rue du Noier,
Où pluseurs dames pour louier
Font souvent batre leur cartiers.[31]

And then there is rue du Noier, where several prostitutes often beat their bounds.

En la rue du Marmouset
Trouvai i homme qui mu fet
Une muse corne bellourde.[32]

On rue du Marmouset I find a mute who plays a beastly bagpipe.

Mès par la crois de Tiroüer
Ving en la rue de Neele
N'avoie tabour de viele:
En la rue Raoul Menuicet
Trouvai un homme qui mucet
Une femme en terre et en siet.[33]

But by the Crois de Tiroüer comes rue de Neele which has neither tabour nor vielle. On the rue Raoul Menuicet I find a man who buried a woman and who sits on the spot.

Un homs a granz ongles locus
Demanda: Guillot, que fes-tu?
Droitemet la Chastiau Festu
M'en ving à la rue Prouvoires.[34]

A man with grubby nails asks : "Guillot, what are you up to?" Right by Chastiau Festu I come to rue à Prouvoires.

30 Ibid., 11.
31 Ibid., 18.
32 Ibid., 33.
33 Ibid., 49.
34 Ibid., 50.

Une dame vi sus un seil
Qui moult se portoit noblement;
Je la saluai simplement,
Et elle moi, par Saint Loys!
Par la saint rue Saint-Denis,
Ving en la rue As Ouës droit,
Pris mon chemin et mon adroit
Droit en la rue Saint-Martin,
Où j'oï chanter en latin
De Nostre-Dame un si dous chans.[35]

I spy a woman in a doorway who carries herself very nobly; I greet her simply, and she me, by St. Louis! By way of the holy rue Saint-Denis I come right to rue As Ouës, take my path nimbly right to rue Saint-Martin, where I hear sung in Latin from Nostre-Dame such a sweet chant.

Reference to a dirty-nailed man lurking on a street corner sits side by side with sightings of a man perched on the burial site of a woman; meanwhile, Guillot's report of greetings exchanged between himself and a noblewoman is one of an abundance of female sightings, and a reminder that we see the city through male eyes. The voices mingling in these bizarre scenes are also part of a more pervasive and chaotic textual soundtrack. The salutations of Guillot and the citizens of Paris mix with a woman beating her laundry, the clamor of prostitutes, a man and his bagpipes, and, just once, the sound of Latin song seeping from a church interior. It is impossible to single any sound out as contrived or deliberate. Rather, the sheer pressure for Guillot to keep moving adds to the impression of random spontaneity. Indeed, squeezed between street names, these extra descriptions of the city are so brief and fortuitous that we might be forgiven for paying them no attention at all.

What, then, is the purpose of such a map, and the meaning of such a peculiar soundworld? At first glance, the poem reads like an embellished A–Z of medieval Paris, its purpose indexical more than literary, and seemingly casual as a representation of the city's status and value.[36] Yet for some, the *Dit des rues*

---

35 Ibid., 58–59.

36 It was largely treated as an archeological resource by its earliest nineteenth-century editors. Even Edgard Mereuse, the poem's greatest champion, characterized the poem as "naive." See *Dit des rues*, xi. It has received almost no treatment in modern scholarship. An exception is Michelle Chilcoat's unpublished conference paper, " 'Walking Rhetorics': Articulations of Daily Life in Paris in Some Thirteenth-Century Old French *dits*," available on the web at http://www.georgetown.edu/labyrinth/e-center/chilcoat.html. I am grateful to Professor Chilcoat for permission to cite this work.

was anything but a literary anomaly. It survives in a bulging compendium of some of the most highly prized Old French poetry of the thirteenth and fourteenth centuries: the likes of Rutebeuf, Gautier de Coinci, translations of Aristotle, collections of chansons are companions to the *Dit des rues*, by association assimilating it into a mainstream tradition. Read in that context, the poem invites us to contemplate "naivety" and realism as part of agendas less causal, and perhaps more authoritative.

We may better understand those agendas by situating the poem in the tradition of civic representation and mapping. Created at a time when there were no street maps, the poem's navigational impulse is simply radical. World and city maps of this period were intended to do almost anything but serve their users as practical tools to get from A to B, and had little to do with representing spaces as they actually were.[37] The task of genres such as the *mappa mundi* was rather to map ideologies and religious and political views, and to cope with the unknown.[38] If this is so, then what might Guillot have been writing about, and what purpose did sonic realism serve?

Easy though it is to be distracted by the quasi-science of relentless street-listing, Guillot's text does indeed have a story to tell, one contingent on the haphazard effect of sound and sight at the interstices of streets. To help articulate that meaning, we will turn briefly to one of the few modern critiques of the poem. In her unpublished paper on the *Dit des rues*, Michelle Chilcoat makes an illuminating connection between the poem and Michel de Certeau's famous essay "Walking in the City," in which the latter memorably deploys the city as a metaphor for exploring distinctions between speech and writing.[39] A recurring theme is the affinity of speech to walking; writing to mapping. The walker is engaged in the "practice" of the city, in opposition to those with a "scopic" vision, such as the urban planner, who is "seeing-the-whole." These perspectives mimic modes of communication: the city-as-practice akin to the

37 Evelyn Edson, *Mapping Time and Space: How Medieval Map-Makers Viewed their World* (London: British Library, 1997). On the ideological contexts for spatial conceptualization see *Regions and Landscapes: Reality and Imagination in Late Medieval and Early Modern Europe*, ed. Peter Ainsworth and Tom Scott (Oxford: Peter Lang, 1998), and *Text and Territory: Geographical Imagination in the European Middle Ages*, ed. Sylvia Tomasch and Sealy Gilles (Philadelphia: University of Pennsylvania Press, 1998).

38 On the *mappa mundi* see Jocelyn Wogan-Brown, "Reading the World: The Hereford *mappa mundi*," *Parergon* 9 (1991): 117–35; Paul Harvey, Mappa mundi: *The Hereford World Map* (Toronto: University of Toronto Press, 1996); and Paul Zumthor, "*Mappa mundi* et performance: La cartographie médiévale," in *Le Moyen Age dans la modernité: Mélanges offerts à Roger Dragonetti*, ed. Jean Scheidegger, Sabine Girardet, and Eric Hicks (Paris: Honoré Champion, 1996), 459–71.

39 Michel de Certeau, "Walking in the City," in *The Practice of Everyday Life*, transl. Steven Rendall (Berkeley: University of California Press, 1984), 91–114.

speech act; the city-as-whole closer in its totalization to the act of writing. Reading through the lens of de Certeau, Chilcoat likens Guillot to de Certeau's "street walker": "the narrator is caught up in the 'acte de marcher' within [the urban] system." She goes on: "the narrator makes no attempt to interpret what he sees," and thus creates a text which is, in essence, "unreadable."

We can take the analogy further. Guillot's poem may be better understood as occupying a middle ground. For implicit in de Certeau's distinction between walker and planner—between practice and concept of the city—is a distinction between the experiential, reality-effect of place, and the monumentalizing, all-time perspective of its representation. In the *Dit des rues*, both aspects are in play simultaneously. For, as Chilcoat senses, Guillot's city is both effect (a rushed, real-time progression of the walker); but also, as we have seen, literary contrivance (a network of streets made whole through writing). And perhaps more than any other aspect of the city, it is the soundscape that mediates the two realms. The poem harnesses the sounding, vanishing, aspect of the city for more writerly or hermeneutic purposes. The story it tells is one of the city's immensity, of the vastness and magnitude of the place. Indeed, Guillot is forced to stop here and there, to snatch a drink, to catch his breath, before running on and on, through a network it is easy as a reader to get lost in. That readerly effect is all-important: in that intersection of the experiential and monumental is a sense of the city that chimes with the magnificent city of more familiar civic representation. Although the Paris of the *Dit des rues* seems remote from the aggrandizing imagery of the *Vie*, it has its own lexicon of the sublime. Strange though it may seem, there is no better emblem of Paris's magnificence than its most invisible, intangible, and unreadable aspect: its sound.

Situated in the language of medieval magnificence, grandeur, and the sublime, Guillot's Paris finally comes into visual and sonic focus. His is a city of sonic *excessus*, speaking to an idea of magnificence that expresses itself through aggrandizement, and ultimately through the sublime. Situated within such discourse, this poem succeeds in communicating a sense of place that is almost too vast to quantify, despite Guillot's best efforts to count the streets. Within such a model, the strange sights and sounds picked up en route are just as important a part of the process of aggrandizement. As we twist and turn through Guillot's conception, there is no knowing what we will see and hear next: no sense of their being a final limit to how this city sounds and looks. The very nature of sound, as construed by theologians, etymologists, and theorists of this period, is especially congruent with the superlative aspect of the magnificent. For sound's perishing and invisible aspect—literally beyond permanent record—as much as the overwhelming effect of its clamor, is another version of *magnum facere*.

In the next part of this chapter we shall use Guillot as *cicerone*, pursuing the sense of city sound as magnificent and sublime in a text that seems the very antithesis to the *Dit des rues*.

A Scholastic's Turn

Our next view of Paris is as systematic and contained as Guillot's is frenetically unpredictable: a city of familiar landmarks and clearly-defined locales. While Guillot's poem defied easy classification, Jean de Jandun's *Tractatus de laudibus Parisius*, dated 1323, is conspicuously aware of its literary tradition.[40] It follows the conventions of Latin civic praise poems, or *encomia*, a medium given to lauding cities in grandiloquent literary expression, reinforced by a genealogy that stretched back to Antiquity. Nor is it simply genre that lends authority to the poem. Jandun was a university man, better known for the erudition of his writings on Aristotle and Averroes. He was first recorded as a member of the Faculty of Arts in 1307, and by 1315 was a professor at the College of Navarre. In 1316 he was also made a canon of Senlis, a position he maintained while teaching in Paris, and a connection relevant to the genesis of the poem.[41] The *Tractatus* is product of these intellectual environments, and with every echo of prior models, every rhetorical trope and literary turn, Paris is reconstituted as an admirable ideal. In contrast with the *Dit des rues*, the discourse of the magnificent city is explicit. The *Tractatus* is so steeped in the language of laudation that Paris could be *any* wonderful city—the real place lost in the forest of rhetorical formulas. However, there is a twist. Part of Jandun's intention was to break to mold of the genre, and he did so by trumping literary expectations of *encomia* with an agenda of realism.

Written in four parts with a Prologue, the *Tractatus* follows basic conventions almost to the letter. Part I celebrates the city's University, Part II the places, people, and natural phenomena that signal Paris's excellence in the world. These include unprecedented descriptions of the churches and palace of the Cité, and of the market of Les Halles on the Right Bank, followed by more familiar tributes to the merchants, the city's river, the temperament of the citizens, the natural world, the climate, and concludes with celebration of the king. The two remaining parts, recording a scholarly dispute between Jandun and an adversary, mark the departure from convention. As Erik Inglis explains,

40 Published with a parallel French translation in *Paris et ses historiens aux XIVᵉ et XVᵉ siècles*, ed. Le Roux de Lincy and Lazare Maurice Tisserand (Paris: Imprimerie Impériale, 1867), 3–79. For English translations of extracts of the poem see Erik Inglis, "Gothic Architecture and a Scholastic: Jean de Jandun's *Tractatus de laudibus Parisius* (1323)," *Gesta* 42 (2003): 63–85, and *In Old Paris: An Anthology of Source Descriptions, 1323–1790*, ed. and transl. Robert Berger (New York: Italica Press, 2002), 7–17. Translations from Inglis, "Gothic Architecture," unless otherwise stated.

41 Inglis, "Gothic Architecture," 63–65. For additional discussion of Jandun's intellectual context see also Paul Binski, "'Reflections on the 'Wonderful Height and Size' of Gothic Great Churches'," in *Magnificence and the Sublime*, ed. Jaeger, 147.

they document the genesis of the *Tractatus*—as prompted by an attack on Jandun for having earlier praised Senlis at the expense of Paris.[42] His now-anonymous detractor had written a defense of Paris as the city of all cities: a defense so bland that Jandun had taken up his pen again, to answer the criticism, this time with a lavish celebration of Paris, and also with a swipe at shoddy rhetoric. As set out in the *Prologue*, his Paris was not to be lost in the predictable literary conventions that characterized his critic's efforts, which dealt only in rhetorical "generalities" and leaned on literary "commonplaces."[43]

The move beyond "commonplaces" was not merely literary. As is well known to art historians, Jandun extended the scope of *the genre* by including accounts of particular locales, gestures largely unheard of in earlier *encomia*. He focused attention specifically on the Ile-de-la-Cité, notably Notre Dame, the Sainte-Chapelle, and the royal palace.[44] A closer look at the famous description of the Sainte-Chapelle will illustrate the heady rhetoric at play in relaying not just the appearance of the real spaces, but also their effect and meaning:

> Sed et illa formosissima capellarum, capella regis, infra menia mansionis regie decentissime situata, integerrimis et indissolubilibis solidissimo-rum lapidum gaudet structuris. Picturarum colores electissimi, ymaginum deauratio preciosa, vitrearum circumquaque rutilantium decora pervietas, altarium venustissima paramenta, sanctuariorum virtutes mirifice, capsularum figurationes extranee gemmis adornate fulgentibus, tantam utique illi orationis domui largiuntur decoris yberbolem, ut, in eam subingrediens, quasi raptus ad celum, se non immerito unam de Paradisi potissimis cameris putet intrare.

> But also that most beautiful of chapels, the chapel of the king, most fittingly situated within the walls of the king's house, enjoys a complete and indissoluble structure of most solid stone. The most select colors of the pictures, the precious gilding of the images, the beautiful transparency of the gleaming windows on all sides, the most beautiful cloths of the altars, the wondrous merits of the sanctuaries, the figured work on the reliquaries externally adorned with dazzling gems, bestow such a hyperbolic beauty on that house of prayer, that, in going into it from

42 Inglis, "Gothic Architecture," 65.

43 Jandun, *Tractatus*, Prologue, 32: ". . . ad enarrandum gratiam Parisius, ad cujus descriptionem non sufficerent omnes lingue, nonnisi ex quibusdam universalibus que nichil movent aut modicum, et ex aliquibus similitudinibus metaphorisque, etsi aliqualiter oblectant animum, paucis tamen aut nullis quietant certitudinibus intellectum; et rursus ex nonnullis verbis communibus aliunde collectis constituit suum opus."

44 Ibid., Part II, chs. 1–2, pp. 44–49.

below, one understandably believes oneself, as if rapt to heaven, to be entering one of the best chambers of Paradise.[45]

Here, the tension detected in Guillot's poem—between the real-time city and the city-as-meaning—is considerably more pronounced. The precise and realistic elements that would have made this passage so startling to Jandun's original readers—the windows, reliquaries, stone, and so forth—are swathed in rhetoric that simultaneously imbues them with sense and effect. The superlatives and amplifications situate us in a moment of writerly virtuosity that offers equivalence to the staggering effects of the actual spaces. While it illustrates how place transforms into meaning, I am particularly interested in what sense the spaces have, and especially with what rhetorical techniques Jandun coaxes meaning from the effects of reality.

In discussion of the passage, Paul Binski notes Jandun's use of asyndeton (absence of conjunctions), arguing that the device "has the effect of speeding up a series of dislocated impressions in its onward and upward rush to Paradise."[46] It is thus as if the reader reexperiences the spindly upward effects of the chapel space. No less important is the use of hyperbole ("decoris yberbolem"). This trope is concerned with magnification, with a sense of surpassing the limits of the quantifiable. For a classic formulation, we may evoke *Ad Herennium*: "Hyperbole is a manner of speech exaggerating the truth, whether for the sake of magnifying or minifying something."[47] In Geoffrey of Vinsauf's *Poetria nova* we also have the conjunction with excess: "This manner can marvelously increase or lessen praise; and that excess is pleasing which both ear and custom approve."[48] The way in which Jandun lists attributes of the chapel (the gilded images, the gleaming windows, the altar cloths, and so on), exaggerated through asyndeton, embodies the meaning of hyperbole: in counting out the things that make the chapel beautiful, he draws attention to the notion of quantification. That suggests both the actual wealth of things and the possibility for infinitude—of there being more "stuff" than can ever be quantified. In hyperbole, then, there is a fascinating conjunction between excess, magnification, and laudation itself.

---

45 Ibid., Part II, ch. 1, pp. 46–47.

46 Binski, "Reflections," 147.

47 "Superlatio est oratio superans veritatem alicuius augendi minuendive causa." Cicero, *Ad C. Herennium de ratione dicendi (Rhetorica ad Herennium)*, ed. and transl. Harry Kaplan (London: Heinemann, 1954), 4. 43, quoting from pp. 338–39.

48 "mirifice laudes minuit modus iste vel auget; / et placet excessus, quem laudat et auris et usus." Geoffrey of Vinsauf, *The* Poetria nova *and its Sources in Early Rhetorical Doctrine*, ed. and transl. Ernest Gallo (The Hague: Mouton, 1971), lines 1023–25; 68–69.

Through literary means that emphasize plenitude, excess, and quantity, Jandun's description thus situates the reality of the chapel in discourses of the magnificent and the sublime. The "rush" through this description, like the eye moving through space, or overwhelmed by numerous elements that make the chapel beautiful, is transporting, effecting a kind of rapturous movement to Paradise. It is within these terms that we will now turn our ear to Jandun's city and explore ways he imbues its sonority with sublime potential and on terms as rhetorically virtuosic as the chapel description.

*

We will begin on the Ile-de-la-Cité: it is here, in the thick of the most vivid architectural descriptions, that the author furnishes a template for sound's role in the construction of the sublime city. Given the Ile's place as the city's spiritual and royal heart, it is not surprising that its sounds are the most orthodox: voices doing their work of praying and chanting. At the climax of the description of the Sainte-Chapelle (seen above), the text breaks off for short laudations on three aspects of ceremony that communicate the sublimity of the space:

> O quam salubres in illis oratoriis Deo potentissimo preces fundunt, cum spirituales et interne puritates ipsorum precantium corporalibus et externis oratoriorum munditiis proportionaliter correspondent!

> O quam placide piissimo Deo in illis tabernaculis laudes canuntur, cum ipsorum corda canentium sunt amenis tabernaculorum picturis analogice virtutibus venustata!

> O quam acceptabilia gloriosissimo Deo super hec altaria holocausta parantur, cum ipsorum sacrificantium vita, correspondente deaurationi altarium claritate, resplendet!

> O how salutary the prayers to the all-powerful God that pour out in these oratories, when the internal and spiritual purities of those praying correspond proportionally to the external and physical elegance of the oratory!

> O how peacefully are praises sung to the most holy God in these tabernacles, when the hearts of the singers are anagogically beautified with the virtues through the pleasing pictures of the tabernacle!

> O how acceptable to the most glorious God appear the offerings on these altars, when the life of those sacrificing shines in correspondence with the gilded light of the altars![49]

49 Jandun, *Tractatus*, Part II, ch. 1, p. 46.

Each act—prayer, singing, and altar offerings—is linked by a common theme: its anagogic or corresponding role. They are sensual or embodied equivalents to the virtue and divinity expressed through the architectural spaces in which they occur. Thus the outpouring of prayer embodies a connection between the inner purity of the prayerful and the outer elegance of the chapel; the singers' hearts are made more beautiful by analogy to images of their surroundings; and the celebrants are radiant in proportion to the gleam of their altars. Jandun thus ascribes to these performing bodies the role of translation: these are the living, outward testament to the ineffable meaning of the space itself.[50]

Sound's analogical and revelatory function also applies to less ecstatic sonorities. On the Left Bank, the senses are again brought into service, now as the vehicle to make the presence of knowledge felt. The liberal arts radiate their truth, while Philosophy is scented like nectar and "delights the noses

---

50 There are echoes here of Abbot Suger's accounts of Saint-Denis from the twelfth century. *De administratione* describes the analogical effects of the abbey's superabundant ornaments, which transport those present from the material to the immaterial realm. See *Abbot Suger on the Abbey Church of St. Denis and its Art Treasures*, ed. and transl. Erwin Panofsky (Princeton: Princeton University Press, 1946; repr. 1979), 62–64, from the *De administratione*, ch. 33: "Thus, when—out of my delight in the beauty of the house of God—the loveliness of the many-colored gems has called me away from the external cares, and worthy meditation has induced me to reflect, transferring that which is material to that which is immaterial, on the diversity of the sacred virtues: then it seems to me that I see myself dwelling, as it were, in some strange region of the universe which neither exists entirely in the slime of the earth nor entirely in the purity of Heaven; and that, by the grace of God, I can be transported from this inferior to that higher world in an anagogical manner" ("unde, cum ex dilectione decoris domus Dei aliquando multicolor, gemmarum speciositas ab exintrinsecis me curis devocaret, sanctarum etiam diversitatem virtutum, de materialibus ad immaterialia transferendo, honesta meditatio insistere persuaderet, videor videre me quasi sub aliqua extranea orbis terrarum plaga, quae nec tota sit in terrarum faece nec tota in coeli puritate, demorari, ab hac etiam inferiori ad illam superiorem anagogico more Deo donante posse transferri"). In *De consecratione*, there is overt reference to sound's sublime meaning. The description culminates in the deployment of twenty dignitaries to the many altars of the church, and the simultaneous celebration of mass at these stations. The effect is a heavenly "keynote," the cacophony a form of superlative harmony. See *De consacratione*, ch. 7; quoting from *Abbot Suger on the Abbey Church*, 118–21: "[celebrated] so festively, so solemnly, so different and yet so concordantly, so close [to one another] and so joyfully that their song, delightful by its consonance and unified harmony, was deemed a symphony angelic rather than human" ("qui omnes tam festive, tam solemniter, tam diversi, tam concorditer, tam propinqui, tam hilariter ipsam altarium consecratione missarum solemnem celebrationem superius inferiusque peragebant, ut ex ipsa sui consonantia et cohaerente harmoniae grata melodia potius angelicus quam humanus concentus aestimaretur").

susceptible to such delicate emanations."[51] The connection between intellectual truth and the senses is recast a few lines later, as Jandun explains that the marvels of philosophy and mathematics express themselves across a range of situations—from the science of number to "celestial magnificence, harmonious sounds, and in visual rays."[52] With echoes here of his other writings on Aristotle and Averroes, he posits again that multi-sensory reality serves as experiential proof of the ineffable truth of intellect.

In elaborating the theme, Jandun calls too on sound. On the rue de Sorbonne, home to the Theology Faculty, the health-giving truth of the Scriptures is apparent through oral/aural practice—lecturing, debating, and devout preaching—while the proponents of such practice, the clergy and seigneurs, are fashioned as sublime.[53] Just streets away, the details of the law are unraveled through reading to the masses.[54] Voices thus indicate the presence of the virtuous work of elucidation. Sound is the aural equivalent to the sweet scent of nectar and bright lights that emanate from the intellect, and the vocal hum of the voices-at-work are reassurance that divine knowledge is present.

---

51 "in vico vocato Straminum, non solum septem artes liberales exercitantur, sed et totius philosophici luminis jocundissima claritas, veritatis sincere diffusis radiis, animas sui capaces illustrat. ibidem quoque philosophici nectaris suavissima fragrantia tam subtilis diffusionis susceptivos olfactus oblectat." Jandun, *Tractatus*, Part I, ch. 1, p. 34.

52 "amplius, nonne dogmatizatur in vico philosophie infallibilis et incontradicibilis doctrine mathematice certitudo, per quam numerorum et figurarum, tam secundum se quam per celestes magnitudines, sonos armonicos ac visuales radios contractorum, mirabilia accidentia indicantur." Ibid., 36.

53 "one may admire most venerable fathers and seigneurs, who, like celestial and divine satraps, happily exalted to the summits of human perfection, to the extent that intellect joined with magnificence is able to achieve that, illuminate the most sacred texts of the Old and New Testaments with solemnity, by the frequent practice of lecturing and debating, they work, by continuous pronouncement of devoted preaching, to fasten in the hearts of the faithful the most life-bringing revelations of divine law, revelations which they too confirm, in their very beings, through the evidence of holy works" ("admirari poteris reverendissimos patres et dominos qui, velut celestes et divini satrape, ad apices humane perfectionis, prout intellectus magnitudini conjunctus accipere potest, feliciter sublimati, sacratissimas Veteris et Novi Testamenti scripturas lecturarum ac disputationum frequentibus exercitiis solemniter elucidant, ac saluberrima divine legis oracula, que et ipsi per sanctorum operum evidentiam verificant in se ipsis, crebro devote predicationis eloquio in cordibus fidelium radicare laborant"). Ibid., ch. 2, p. 38. My thanks to Shane Butler for help translating this passage.

54 "In the street named Clos-Bruneau, the proficient lecturers on decrees and decretals put forth their doctrines before a vast multitude of witnesses" ("in vico quem nominant Clausum Brunelli, decretorum et decretalium lectores proficui in multitudine numerosa sua jura proponunt"). Jandun, *Tractatus*, Part I, ch. 3, p. 40; my translation.

The final locale is the hubbub of the market around Les Halles and the Grand Pont. With a kaleidoscopic swirl of the eye, Jandun captures its multiplicity of products and the diversity of merchants, cramming his account with vivid quantifying description. Although the visible dominates, sound also surfaces, and not merely as descriptive, but also as instructive. The noise in question emerges on the Grand Pont, among a collection of artisans. There, Jandun spies the metal workers, whose noisy hammering fills the air:

in super metallicorum vasorum, precipue de auro et argento, stanno et cupro, figuratores optimi supra Pontem vocatum Magnum, atque in ceteris, prout unicuique suppetit, pluribus locis, malleos super incudes, quasi armonice concurrentibus ictibus, faciunt resonare.

Also to be found on the Grand Pont, and in many other locations, are excellent sculptors of metal vases, mainly of gold and silver, tin and copper, according to the facility of each, making the hammers resound on the anvils, forming as it were a harmonious concord.[55]

The sound may be authentic enough (we have seen such scenes on the bridge of the *Vie*). But the sound here does double service. In addition to cuing association with street sound, there is an unmistakable Pythagorean allusion, recalling a founding myth of the speculative tradition of music. The earlier allusion to the "harmonious sound" of mathematics on the Right Bank similarly evokes "musica" and the ancient idea of sounding number. Just like the voices of the university, or the songs of the Cité, "pure" urban sound here acts as an outward sign of the city's "truth," while the Pythagorean associations elevate the status of the workmen to that of lofty myth-makers.

However, the sound on the bridge is not just symbolic. We can linger a little longer, for it is here that the quotidian city takes on its most eloquent meaning. Seemingly far removed from the heady philosophical world of the university, or the architectural glories of the Ile-de-la-Cité, the market description descends into voracious material excess. It includes lavish lists of clothes, from animal skins to softest silks, as well as eclectic accessories ranging from ivory combs to sparkly crowns. As the text describes the work of the city's artisans, more tempting and tasty things appear on the conveyer-belt of the text: javelins, swords, shields rush by, mixed in with bread, parchment, and book-making accoutrements, gold, and so on.

The turn to listing is reminiscent of Guillot de Paris's enumerating impulse. It resonates, too, with the kind of detailed quantifying of precious ornaments and objects in Jandun's account of the Sainte-Chapelle. There is thus a connection here between enumeration and quantification and magnificence.

---

55 Ibid., Part II, ch. 4, p. 54; translation from Berger, *In Old Paris*, 13–14.

Most obviously, enumeration is a means of marking material wealth. The enumeration of ecclesiastical ornament in Jandun's *Tractatus* recalls standard accounting procedure for quantifying and archiving the collateral of a particular institution.[56] At the same time, as in Guillot's street-counting, counting things out seems to signal a kind of proliferation that again resonates with concepts associated with magnificence and the sublime. Specifically, the enumerative style offers another version of hyperbole—a practical means of "magnifying" or "minifying" things, a way of signaling limits that are to be broken. As we shall presently see, there comes a point at which the market surpasses quantification altogether. It is precisely the shift into the enumerative style here that signals the intent to be one of laudation or magnification. The market signals the city's success in obvious ways. It is first of all a place where people buy by desire more than necessity. Everything listed is surplus to requirement: luxuries, fripperies, signs of conspicuous consumption:

> ibi namque, si facultates tibi suppetunt et voluntas, emere poteris omnia genera ornamentorum, que sagacissima factive rationis industria, ut lacune desideria compleantur, deproperat excogitare.

> There, if you have the desire and the means, you will be able to buy all types of ornaments that most practiced industry and the most inventive spirit hasten to imagine to gratify all your desires.[57]

Extravagant excess, then, is the ideal sign of the city's economic success.[58]

The success of the marketplace is also expressed through language itself: or rather, through a transcendence of words. Twice in the following account the narrator claims the impossibility of naming all the city's goods. As he reels off the range of products on sale, Jandun encounters a variety that is literally beyond his knowledge: not just foreign, but entirely beyond his language:

> hoc tamen prorsus nolo tacere quod, in quibusdam inferiorum partium illius foralis domus, offeruntur, quasi sub innumeris congeriebus et cumulis, panni pulcri, pulcriores et pulcherrimi; in aliis autem forrature decentes, hec quidem ex animalium pellibus, ille vero ex sindalis

---

56 On the practices of monastic administration and the connections between the archiving of institutions and power in French Benedictine monasteries of the Middle Ages, see Robert Berkhofer III, *Day of Reckoning: Power and Accountability in Medieval France* (Philadelphia: University of Pennsylvania Press, 2004).

57 Jandun, *Tractatus*, Part II, ch. 3, p. 50; translation from Berger, *In Old Paris*, 11.

58 As Sharon Farmer's work on the poor of Paris reminds us, sustaining a class of the poverty-stricken, reliant on charitable giving, is the best indicator of a city's prosperity and wealth. See Sharon Farmer, *Surviving Poverty in Medieval Paris: Gender, Ideology, and the Lives of the Poor* (Ithaca: Cornell University Press, 2002).

constitute; alie quoque ex ceteris delicatis et extraneis materiebus facte sunt, quarum propria nomina latini ydiomatis michi fateor esse ignota. in superioribus vero illius edis partibus, que ad modum unius vici mirabilis longitudinis ordinate sunt, pretenduntur specialia particularum humani corporis paramenta; pro capite quidem corone, serta et mitre; discriminalia quoque eburnea pro capillis . . . ceteraque talia de quibus nominum latinorum penuria, magis quam visive cognitionis defectus, me tacere compellit.

I do not wish, however, to omit entirely to say that, in some places amid the lower parts of this market, and as it were beneath some heaps, some piles of other merchandise, are found draperies, one more beautiful than the other; in others, some superb pelisses, some made of animal skins, others of silk materials, others, finally, composed of delicate and foreign materials, whose Latin names I confess I do not know. In the upper part of the building, which is formed like a street of an astonishing length, are displayed all the objects that serve to adorn the various parts of the human body: for the head, crowns, braids, caps; ivory combs for the hair . . . and other things of this sort that I cannot name, because of the penury of Latin words rather than not having actually seen them.[59]

It is possible—indeed likely—that Jandun's claim was based in reality: in this center for international trade, with goods from all across Europe finding their way into the city's economy, fourteenth-century residents would certainly have encountered objects they had never seen before. But to run out of words is also, in the arena of writing, the ultimate accolade: it defines a kind of limit of language, the boundary of excess, or a hyperbole of sorts—a coming-to-the-end of the currency of language that mirrors the success of the market it seeks to represent. It is as eloquent an expression of the sublime as Jandun's rapturous account of the Sainte-Chapelle or the university. It is precisely at that limit of words that another kind of sound steps in.

For as the text looks off to the horizon of this cornucopia, there is something else that may elude the power of representation. Hinted at in the hammering metalworkers on the Grant Pont, what Jandun's bursting market also implies is sonic excess. Just as knowledge hums with lecturing voices, or sacred spaces resonate with song, so do the goods and chattels on sale, and in manufacture, have a voice. To bring sound to this scene, we shall step sideways, to texts circulating in Jandun's sphere, and covering almost identical ground.

---

59 Jandun, *Tractatus*, Part II, ch. 3, p. 50; translation from Berger, *In Old Paris*, 11–12.

Street Cries and the Economy of Hubbub

John of Garland's Latin *Dictionarius*, written around 1230 and circulating with a lively commentary tradition well into the fourteenth century, seems designed for exactly the wordless moment of the *Tractatus*.[60] As explained in the *Prologue*, it was a Latin word-list for Parisian university students, providing terms for all manner of things: parts of the body, flowers and fauna of royal gardens, sites of pilgrimage, and paraphernalia of the city. While the *Dictionarius* claims a utilitarian function, offering vocabulary for spoken rather than written Latin,[61] the encyclopedic scope and latent scholasticism of its etymological approach reveals that to be a disingenuous claim. Nowhere is this more so than in the words for the city. In the act of translation, the *Dictionarius* Latinizes—and therefore authorizes—commonplace realities, making the everyday city available for scholastic discourse.

As in the *Tractatus*, Paris is a city of flourishing economy, and among the commonplaces are lists of consumables—from delectable foods to handy gadgets, the sorts of things student readers might see on their turn through the city. But these are not just visible "things"; the *Dictionarius* creates its wordlists via short anecdotes or sketches of their actual context, presenting them as things seen on a walk in the city: "things will be called by the names that I have noted down as I wandered through the city of Paris" ("nominabuntur res quas, eundo per civitatem Parisius, denotavi").[62] In some instances, it is the voices of vendors and hawkers, crying out their wares and services, that offer John his living crib-sheet. The "voice" of the stuff of the city is heard, for instance, in the description of cloak-makers and repairers: "Some hawkers run through the city streets calling for fur cloaks to be repaired, and they repair the fur linings of their overcoats and cloaks mostly by thieving" ("quidam clamatores peliciorum reparandorum discurrunt per plateas civitatis, et reparant furraturas epitogiorum eorum et palliorum, partim furando").[63] Or in the cries of goblet-makers: "Repairers of goblets call out for cups to be repaired with copper and silver wires. They also repair goblets made of tree

---

60 John of Garland, *The Dictionarius of John de Garlande*, transl. Barbara Blatt Rubin (Lawrence, KS: Coronado Press, 1981).

61 Ibid., 10–11: "This little book entitled 'Dictionarius' from the most necessary words which each and every student needs to keep, not so much in his wooden letter-case, but in the little cupboard of his heart in order to obtain an easier command of speech" ("dictionarius dicitur libellus iste a dictionibus magis necessaries, quas tenetur quilibet scolaris, non tantum in scribio de lignis facto, sed in cordis amariolo firmiter retinere, ut ad faciliorem oracionis constructionem perveniat").

62 Ibid., 16–17.

63 Ibid., 30–31.

burls, of wood from plane trees, of boxwood, of maple wood, and of aspen" ("reparatores ciphorum exclamant ciphos reparandos cum filo ereo et argenteo. ciphos autem reparant de murinis, et planis, et brucis, de acere, et tremulo").[64] Then there are the wine-vendors who shout out to thirsty throats: "To the gaping gullets wine peddlers loudly offer wine diluted in the tavern" ("precones vini clamant gula yante vinum ataminatum in tabernis").[65] Finally, the students' favorite cry might be that of the roaming waffle-vendors: "Street-cries of wafers and waffles call out through the night, selling waffles and wafers and meat pies in baskets covered with a white towel; and the baskets are often hung by the windows of clerks who are damned by dice" ("precones nebularum et gafrarum pronunciant de nocte grafras et nebulas et artocreas vendendas in calatis velatis albo manutergio; et calati suspendentur frequenter ad fenestras clericorum, senione perditi").[66]

John's *Dictionarius* reminds us of the city's most obvious soundtrack: the street cry. While the presence of these sounds and associated vocabulary in the dictionary endows them with value, the text has little more to say about their meaning. For further insight, we may turn to Guillaume de Villeneuve's *Crieries de Paris*, the earliest vernacular representation of the cries. Surviving in a large compendium of northern French poetry and chansons, the poem con-figures the market's economy in a manner similar to Jandun's *Tractatus*: through abundance, representing the city as being full of temptations out of reach for the narrator. It is also reminiscent of the *Dictionarius*, and of Guillot de Paris's *Dit des rues*, in the erratically pedantic way in which it enumerates the city's contents.[67] However, explicitly focused on the sound of commerce, the *Crieries* is organized not as a collection of things but as a medley of merchant cries.

The poem comprises 194 lines of rhyming couplets. It is told from the first-person perspective of Guillaume, who identifies himself in the poem as a pov-erty-stricken citizen, looking and listening longingly to his city's bursting marketplace:

> Un noviau dit ici nous trueve
> Guillaume de la Vilenueve
> puisque povretez le justice.
> Or, vous dirai en quele guise
> et en quele manière vont

64 Ibid.

65 Ibid., 30–33.

66 Ibid., 32–33.

67 Bibliothèque nationale de France, f. fr. 837. The poem is edited with a partial translation in *Proverbes et dictons populaires avec les dits du mercier et des marchands, et les crier-ies de Paris aux xiiiᵉ et xivᵉ siècles*, ed. Charles Crapelet (Paris: Imprimerie de Crapelet, 1831), 137–46.

cil qui denrées à vendre ont,
et qui penssent de lor preu fère,
que jà ne fineront de brère,
parmi Paris jusqu'à la nuit.
Ne cuidiez-vous qu'il lor anuit,
que j'à ne seront à sejor;
oiez con crie au point du jor.[68]

Guillaume de Villeneuve here discloses to us a new poem, since he is
punished by poverty. Now I will tell you about the form and manner of
those who have goods to sell, and who think of the value of their profit,
so that they never cease to cry out throughout Paris until nightfall. Do
not imagine that they sleep, for they will never rest; hear how they cry
at the break of day.

It proceeds as vivid enumeration of all the edible things available (and out of
Guillaume's reach), presented not simply as a catalogue, but as a record of the
cries that invite their acquisition. Reminiscent of Guillot de Paris's *Dit des rues*,
the poem moves without narrative logic from cry to cry, and food to food, and
depicts a world groaning with produce of every kind from cherries to cheese;
oils to breads; fish to nuts; and goods coming from all corners of the country.
The effect of the whole poem is one of dizzying excess, a kind of sensory
overload—of sounds, sights, tastes, smells—that leaves the reader reeling
and disorientated. A few excerpts suggest a sense of hubbub in this urban
delicatessen:

J'ai bon frommage de Champaingne,
or i a frommage de Brie;
au burre frès n'oublie mie.
. . .
huile de nois or au cerniaus:
vin aigre qui est bons et biaus,
vin aigre de moustarde i a.
. . .
J'ai cerises, or au verjus![69]

I have good cheese from Champangne! Now I have cheese from Brie!
Don't forget my fresh butter! . . . Nut oil and green walnuts! Vinegar
which is good and tasty, I've mustard vinegar! . . . I've cherries and
verjuice!

---

68 "Les Crieries," in *Proverbes et dictons populaires*, 137.
69 Ibid., 139.

Not surprisingly, the poem's refrain-like patchwork of edible aphorisms has often been interpreted as authentic records of the voices of Paris's merchants. The *Crieries* even appears in one of the most famous accounts of street cries: Bakhtin's *Rabelais and his World*. Bakhtin, who characterized the author as "compiler" of the street,[70] in a tradition that included Janequin's famous chansons, here echoed the work of nineteenth-century historian George Kastner, who positioned the poem in a tradition of realistic reportage.[71] Like Kastner, Bakhtin took the description at face value, and assumed that Villeneuve's poeticization of the cries reflected a reality in which the cries were an artistic contrivance. Thus, Bakhtin designates them as a "genre": "the *cris* were loud advertisements called out by the Paris street vendors and composed according to a certain versified form: each cry had four lines offering and praising a certain merchandise."[72] Questions about the authenticity of poetic and musical records of street cries persist to this day. However, while we cannot recuperate the sounding reality of the streets, there is danger in the assumption that contrivance and artistry were the defining aspect of the cries: it subdues another way of listening to these records, one that conveys a sense of sound much more unpredictable and unruly.

For an alternative model for listening, we may take a cue from Bakhtin himself. Elsewhere, he characterized the carnivalesque world—of which the market is a microcosm—in terms more dynamic and uncontrived: as poised between a state of life and death, between praise and abuse. It is a world that is "eternally unfinished; a world dying and being born at the same time."[73] Bakhtin's conception of the market is a fitting model for the city of our texts. Its sublime economy is contingent on the coming-and-going quality of the market: on perishable and consumable produce, ever to be replenished. While such evanescence expressed itself in Jandun's market as a bankruptcy of language, in the *Crieries* it defines another boundary: between sense and sound, between the voices of the cries and the things they seek to sell. There is no more apt marker of economic success than its sound: the ultimate perishable. If we now lend an ear to the *Crieries*, listening less for the artifice or authenticity

70 Mikhail Bakhtin, *Rabelais and his World*, transl. Hélène Iswolsky (Bloomington: Indiana University Press, 1984), 181.

71 Georges Kastner, *Les Voix de Paris: Essai d'une histoire littéraire et musicale des cris populaires de la capitale depuis le Moyen Age jusqu'à nos jours* (Paris: Brandus, 1857). See p. 23 for his citation of *Les Crieries*. Part of Kastner's desire to hear the medieval evidence as authentic was shaped by the larger goal to propose continuity with the street of his own day and the voices of history. For another early history of the cries see Victor Fournel, *Les Cris de Paris: Types et physiognomies d'autrefois* (Paris: Firmin-Didot, 1887).

72 Bakhtin, *Rabelais and his World*, 181.

73 Ibid., 166.

and allow the poem its performative voice, the "eternally unfinished" world begins to yield a remarkable keynote.

The theme of Guillaume's poverty is the first clue of the market's audible magnitude. We learn that Guillaume is not simply poor, but that the scale of potential acquisition is so vast as to be unattainable: even the wealthiest would be destitute, faced with the scope of the market. Thus, even purchase of the tiniest portions of everything available would render him bankrupt:

Tant i a denrées à vendre,
tenir ne me puis de despendre;
que se j'avoie grant avoir
et de chascun vouisse avoir
de son mestier une denrée,
il auroit moult courte durée.[74]

There is so much merchandise for sale that I cannot hold back from spending; and if I had plenty, so as to buy one penny's worth from each merchant, it would soon run short.

Plenitude thus results in annihilation, while elsewhere recourse to hyperbole, listing, and quantification reinforce the sense of excess. Elsewhere, echoing Jandun's linguistic limits, the narrator gives up his attempt to recall all the cries, noting:

Et autres choses assez crie,
que raconter ne vous sai mie.[75]

And there are so many other things cried out, that I do not know how to recount it to you.

The most powerful marker of plenitude is the sound of the poem itself, of the cries as wrought through performance, communicating their ubiquity and the hubbub of their pervasive presence in the city. Throughout, Guillaume shifts between description of the cries and the things they offer, to quotation of the cries themselves, a slippage resulting in unmediated immediacy, reminiscent of the unpredictable "realism" of Guillot's Paris in the *Dit des rues*. Meanwhile, reeling through items echoes the rush of description in Jean de Jandun's Sainte-Chapelle. The effect is haphazard tumult, and in performance this makes for a discombobulating sense of "voice," capturing the vocal multitude of the world Guillaume seeks to convey. The shift from first person to third person implies a change of voice, and the reader is encouraged to "put on" the voices of the marketers. The overwhelming volume and cacophony of the

74 Ibid., 145.
75 Ibid.

marketplace—the sonic equivalent for the material abundance of the stuff—is evident in the vocabulary of the cries: they become "bruit," while reference to "haute voix" reminds us of the human agents of the sounds. Finally, there is precise attention to locale and temporalities. The street cries run all through Paris, all day long and even into the night. It is not merely the superabundance of things being advertised, pressed past us through the speed of rhyme, that gives this poem the same frenetic feel as the *Dit des rues de Paris*. It is also scattered with temporal and spatial reminders that these cries are ubiquitous. They are heard in every corner of the city, and they are constant; finally they are also multiple, as suggested by the string of "et puis . . . et puis . . . et puis" and "aussi" in the reportage.

The sound of the market emerges in the poem as excess and surplus; of multiple voices, clamoring against one another; as a hectic sense of movement, replenishment, and finally of decay (as emphasized at the end of the day, when vendors make pitiful efforts to sell their remaining produce). At times, as the poet abandons narrative to report the different cries, the poem loosens from the semantic impulse of poetry. Like the cries themselves, it allows non-verbal sound to communicate the sense of place. I suggest that in evoking the cries of the street, the writer of this poem also communicated the city's magnificence. For these sounds, like the things they sell, are ultimately perishable, unpredictable, mobile, and spontaneous. For the city to be successful, the sound of the streets should be exactly as Guillot originally suggested—surprising and constantly changing; dissonant with the multiplicity of cries in order to be consonant, just as the noisy hammering of the goldsmiths was "harmonious." In the economy of civic sound, it would appear that nonsensical hubbub is the most precious and desirable commodity of all.

The Musicality of City Sound

At the beginning of this chapter, I suggested that the proximity of song to urban hubbub in the *Vie de Saint Denis* illuminations echoed a context in which these two sound types were more integrated. Having explored some of the meanings ascribed to city sound in texts and images of the late thirteenth century, I now return to song, considering how the sense of city sound might contribute to an understanding of music's supermusical effect. Are there commonalities between these seemingly unrelated realms of sound? Is there the possibility of productive and harmonious dialogue in their amplification of the city?

One intersection occurs in the idealization of the city. Non-musical sound is imbued with meaning in accounts of the city. The cries and hubbub of Guillot de Paris or Guillaume de Villeneuve are entwined with ideas of superlative wealth; in Jean de Jandun, sound participates in metaphors of the sublime city. Thus, the outward clamor of the city enshrines the inaudible *musica mundana*: it is the sonority of "paradisus mundi."

Such ideas of sound signal the most obvious connection to music. Namely, the familiar and ancient idea of music's relationship to civic concord reaching back to Plato's *Republic*: that music could have an efficacious, moderating, even medicinal effect on the body politic, as well as the potential to incite the soul to extreme and unruly behavior. Civic *harmonia* was much reiterated in the Middle Ages. In the twelfth century John of Salisbury examined music's effect on government in his *Policraticus*, while in the fourteenth century Lorenzetti's frescos of Good Government on the walls of Siena's Palazzo Pubblico included citizens dancing in a circle (the perfect embodiment of music's potential to coordinate civic unity).[76]

In most accounts, it was a theoretical idea of music—as taught in the quadrivium—that served metaphors of civic *harmonia*. However, at the time of our Parisian representations, there was a shift in its configuration. If the quotidian sounds of Paris could have utility, so too could its living song tradition. The "idea" of music was supplemented by something radically more particular and practical—of music grounded in the actual repertories of the day. One attempt at a musical sociology is Grocheio's *De musica*, dated ca. 1300 and cast as a reflection on the musical habitat of Paris. While Grocheio opens with a virtuosic display of intellectual credentials regarding the theoretical ideas of *musica*, he is not ultimately concerned with the silent lessons of *musica mundana*. He grounds theory in Parisian practice, one constantly reinforced by citing contemporary songs as proof.

> partes autem musicae plures sunt et diversae secundum diversos usus, diversa idiomata vel diversas linguas in civitatibus vel regionibus diversis. Si tamen eam diviserimus, secundum quod homines Parisiis ea utuntur et prout ad usum vel convictum civium est necessaria, et eius membra, ut oportet, pertractemus, videbitur sufficienter nostra intentio terminari, eo quod diebus nostris principia cuiuslibet artis liberalis diligenter Parisiis inquiruntur et usus earum et fere omnium mechanicarum inveniuntur. dicamus igitur, quod musica, qua utuntur homines Parisiis, potest, ut videtur, ad tria membra generalia reduci. . .[77]

There are many elements of music according to diverse usages, diverse dialects and diverse languages in different cities and regions. But if we divide it according to the usage of the Parisians, and if we treat the elements of music, as is fitting, according to how they are necessary for the

---

76 John of Salisbury, *Policraticus*, ed. Katharine Keats-Rohan, Corpus Christianorum 118 (Turnhout: Brepols, 1993).

77 *Die Quellenhandschriften zum Musiktraktat*, ed. Rohloff, 124.

entertainment and use of Parisian citizens, our intention will be seen to be adequately accomplished because in our day the Parisians diligently enquire into the fundamentals of every liberal art and ascertain the practice of them and of virtually every skill. We declare therefore that the music that is employed by the Parisians can be divided, as may be seen, into three categories. . .'[78]

The ensuing classifications not only subject living practice to rigorous intellectual procedure, aligning music with the heady topics of the university; they also use social effect as a diagnostic of genre. Some songs encourage benevolence while others temper passions. Interestingly, as Christopher Page has shown, other Parisian intellectuals of this era sought to suggest a "constructive pleasure in secular music."[79] As they translated writers like Aristotle, inflected through gloss and commentaries staple texts like Peter Lombard's *Sentences*, so they deployed their city—and its music—as a topic pertaining to ethical living or *utilitas* (usefulness).[80] Influenced by the city they inhabited, and by the "circumstances of urban living," writers such as Robert Grosseteste or Pierre de Tarentaise argued for virtuous *exempla* closer to home: "the good of the city or urban community was increasingly recognized as the supreme criterion for judging usefulness."[81] In turn, as reflected in Grocheio, musical entertainment—the very songs we might imagine on the rotulus of the boatmen in the *Vie de Saint Denis* manuscript—was as never before a model for virtuous living. In that subtle shift towards the living city as template for philosophical problems of *utilitas* and virtue, there emerges another possibility. Namely, that the audible reality of the city was *materia* of sorts: a body of evidence from which philosophical proof might be sought. What we hear in these accounts is a curious congruence of meaning: between song and the urban keynote, one not simply grounded in ideas or silent discourses, but rooted in sound itself.

There is thus the possibility that the artists and thinkers of the city recognized a compatibility of urban, everyday, contingent sound of the city and the more enduring, artful sound of song. There is the potential, moreover, that they might even have been understood to sound alike in some essential way. I mean not just that the surface aurality of these two sorts of sound shared a kinship, but also that the meaning, associations, and sensations each defined shared common ground.

78 Translation from Page, "Johannes de Grocheio on Secular Music," 20.
79 Page, *The Owl and the Nightingale*, 40.
80 Ibid., 33–41.
81 Ibid., 35.

Is it possible to go further, to suggest what aspects of musical sound had affinity with urban hubbub? What can the song repertory reveal about its relationship to the sonorous city? If we imagine for a moment that the makers of the *Vie de Saint Denis* manuscript inscribed something more precise than "fake" notation on the rotulus, it is possible they might have chosen from a small corpus of songs that refer explicitly to Paris. While the majority of monophonic and motet repertories inhabit fictional landscapes of religious expression or lush naturalism associated with lyric love, on occasion reality intrudes as authors took explicit care to locate their songs. Among such songs, Paris has a particular place in the musical imaginary.

Paris sometimes serves as a default locus: the city associated with the social and economic circumstances necessary for love, creativity, and therefore for the creation of song itself. It is backdrop for *Je chevauchoie l'autrier* (RS 1255), a classic *chanson de rencontre* by Moniot de Paris, a monk-turned-trouvère active in the city in the third quarter of the thirteenth century.[82] It opens with the formulaic narration of a horseback chevalier, but with a twist, as he locates himself not in a generic pastoral setting, but trotting by the banks of the Seine:

> Je chevauchoie l'autrier
> seur la rive de Seine.[83]

I was riding along the banks of the Seine the other day.

He goes on, predictably, to encounter a woman alone and singing, in this case cursing her boorish husband. Her song forms the refrain of the song:

> J'aim mult melz un poi de joie a demener
> que mil mars d'argent avoir et puis plorer.[84]

I would much rather have a little joy than get a thousand silver marks and then weep.

The contrast of two kinds of value—joyous feeling and money—is heightened by the Parisian setting. The city is stage for the affair, its presence rooting the heightened currency of love within a more mundane economy. The wicked husband inhabits the Grand Pont—the scene of commerce we saw in the *Vie de Saint Denis*—and the wife recounts how she was "sold" into marriage, again

---

82 See *Songs of the Troubadours and Trouvères: An Anthology of Poems and Melodies* ed. Samuel Rosenberg, Margaret Switten, and Gérard Le Vot (New York: Garland Publishing, 1998), 348–49.

83 Strophe 1, lines 1–2.

84 Strophe 1, lines 9–10, and ensuing strophes.

exaggerating the contrast between the different economies of the song.[85] At the lady's inevitable capitulation to the chevalier, she becomes the "Dame de Paris."[86] In this case, Paris is a useful narrative device to stage two competing currencies of love.

In other examples the city has a more complex function, and its economy becomes the pretext for love and song-making, spilling into the audible impression of the music. Paris is a feature too in the Old French motet repertory, especially in a group that emphasizes a theme of "bons compaignons" in which one of the voices begins with an evocation of a group of friends at play. One such piece, *Entre Copin et Bourg{e}ois* (866)/*Je me cuidoie tenir* (867)/Bele Ysabelos, appearing in three manuscripts from the turn of the fourteenth century,[87] illustrates how song-making and civic ideology become entwined. The triplum begins with a formula of community found in other contemporary motets:

> Entre Copin et Bourg[e]ois, Hanicot et Charlot et Pierron
> sunt a Paris demourant mout loial compaignon.[88]

> Copin and Bourgeois, Hanicot and Charlot and Pierron are all great companions living in Paris.

The concept of "loial compaignon," reinforced by the call-sheet of friends, embodies a loftier civic virtue of "communitas" on account of the motet's locus: Paris. As we shall see, other motets of this category develop the theme of companionship by narrating the friends at play—dancing, making music, feasting—echoing tropes of civic unity and concord. In this motet, the "play" takes the form of the lyric premise of love. One among the friends is smitten with a lady, the 'bele Ysabelot":

> Il n'a en autre riens mise s'entencion
> fors en la bele Ysabelot
> a cui il a du tout son cuer fait don.[89]

> He has his attention set on nothing else but the fair Isabel, to whom he has made a gift of his whole heart.

---

85 Strophe 3, lines 3–4: "My husband lives on the Grand Pont, of the bad he is the worst" ("Seur Grant-Pont maint mes maris, / Des mauves tot le pire"), and strophe 4, lines 1–2: "Curse on the one who had me married! Same to the priest!" ("Mal ait qui me maria! / Tant en ait or le prestre").

86 Strophe 5, line 7.

87 *Mo*, fols. 277v–279r. For an edition see *The Montpellier Codex*, ed. Tischler, no. 256.

88 Triplum, lines 1–2.

89 Triplum, lines 9–11.

The remaining two voices enact a progression from love to communal song. The motetus is sung from the perspective of the amorous (and anonymous) lover of the triplum, who reels through a classic qualification for his need to turn love into song:

Je me cuidoie tenir
de[s]oremais de chanter;
mes Amours, a qui je sui,
me fait cest chant trouver.[90]

I thought I would hold back from now on from singing; but Love, who owns me, made me compose this song.

The tenor presents the song itself: it is a virelai, its refrain the memorialization of Isabel:

Bele Ysabelos m'a mort,
Bele Ysabelos![91]

Fair Isabel has killed me, fair Isabel!

The tenor song accrues a special value here, occupying the place usually reserved for liturgical chant.[92] By usurping the position of greatest musical authority, the motet creates the means to endow vernacular song with high value. It is a form of commodification of song, elevating its worth via the musical means available, and according to an urban economy steeped in values of community and love. Those values too find audible voice in the motet. The love-song is audible in the musical texture, reinforced by the repetition of the refrain at beginning and end of the tenor, and also, as Mark Everist has shown, by mirroring those refrains in the motetus voice.[93] But the genre itself animates the virtue of "loial compaignon" by its essential characteristic: a collective of voices singing as one. The supermusical effect—superabundance of words, collectivity of voices, and the audible "authority" of love in the tenor—are akin to the sonority of the city's own superlative keynote.

I have reserved for last a piece in which we may best hear the productive conversation between the supermusical and urban sounds. As with *Entre Copin/ Je me cuidoie*/Bele Ysabelos, it appears in the Montpellier Codex (*Mo*) and is thus contemporary with many of the other civic representations explored in

---

90 Motetus, lines 1–4.

91 Tenor, lines 1–2 and 11–12.

92 On the use of French tenors in the *ars antiqua* repertory, see Mark Everist, "Motets, French Tenors, and Polyphonic Chanson ca. 1300," *Journal of Musicology* 24 (2007): 365–406.

93 Ibid., 383.

this chapter. *On parole de batre* (904)/*A Paris soir et matin* (905)/*Frese nouvele* offers us a rare instance where the city itself is the topic of the motet (see example 2.1).[94] This piece makes Paris the subject of every one of its voices. The triplum celebrates the pleasures of the city—wine, women, and once again the playful camaraderie of "bons compaignons":

Triplum

On parole de batre et de vanner
et de foïr et de haner;
mais ces deduis trop me desplaisent,
car il n'est si bone vie que d'estre a aise
de bon cler vin et de chapons,
et d'estre aveuc bons compaignons,
liés et joiaus,
chantans, truffans et amorous,
et d'avoir, quant c'on a mestier,
pour solacier,
beles dames a devis:
et tout ce truev[e] on a Paris.

One speaks of threshing and winnowing, of digging and cultivating; but these pleasures quite displease me, for the only good life is to take one's ease with good, clear wine and capon, and to be with good friends, happy and joyful, singing and joking and loving, and to have for comfort, when in need, one's fill of beautiful ladies: and all this you can find in Paris.

The motetus enumerates the tasty delights of the city and, with echoes of Guillaume de Villeneuve, emphasizes the perpetual nature of the market, where things are available "soir et matin," as well as the economic realities of cost and availability:

Motetus

A Paris soir et matin
truev' on bon pain et bon cler vin,
bone char et bon poisson,
de toutes guises compaignons,
sens soutie, grant baudour,
biaus joiaus dames d'ounour;

---

94 The piece is extant in *Mo*, fols. 368ᵛ–369ᵛ; it is edited in *The Montpellier Codex*, ed. Tischler, no. 319.

EXAMPLE 2.1. *On parole de batre/A Paris soir et matin/Frese nouvelle* (Mo, fols. 368ᵛ–369ᵛ)

EXAMPLE 2.1. (continued)

et si truev[e] on bien entredeus
de menre feur pour homes desiteus.

In Paris, morning and evening, you can find good bread and good, clear
wine, good meat and good fish, every sort of friend, clever wits, great
merriment, beautiful, joyous noblewomen; and, in the middle of it all,
you can find it all at the lowest price for the man short of funds.

The tenor, however, appears to bypass representation altogether. As it announces
the juicy produce of the city, it offers us the unthinkable—an audible trace of
the lost reality of the streets:

Tenor

Frese nouvele, muere france, muere, muere france!
Frese nouvele, muere france, muere, muere france! (etc.)

New strawberry, noble mulberry, mulberry, noble mulberry!
New strawberry, noble mulberry, mulberry, noble mulberry!

It is tempting to hear in this melody a vocal counterpart to the cries of the
Crieries de Paris. The rhythmic variety of the tenor and the simplicity and circumscribed range (just a fifth) sound wholly unlike the usual pattern of chant
tenors. Yet the question of authenticity is again secondary. Divorced from the
produce it advertises, and from the crowd of competing cries, the line is at best
little more than an echo of reality, transformed into the memento of a world
that in order to be worth preserving must be turning itself over, constantly
moving out of reach. However, as with the *Crieries*, there may be another way
to listen to the city through this piece, and to hear how musical sound com-
municates something of the sense of the urban soundscape. The very location
of the street cry in the musical texture imbues it with import: as with the
previous example, in occupying the place normally allocated to plainchant, the
cry assumes the authority normally designated to the tenor. But there are more
audible ways that the motet musicalizes its sonic subject. For in harnessing an
emphatically contrived musical effect, the motet finds an ideal equivalent to
civic hubbub. We rehear the chaos and cacophony of the magnificent market
within the tightly controlled framework of polyphony, which here contrives
words to clash and cancel out their semantic content. As words spin past
the ear, just out of semantic reach, the piece offers us another version of hyperbole, another version of a city whose unpredictable vitality is the hallmark of
its glory.

As we saw in the previous chapter, the question of musical sense was of
pressing concern for listeners of this epoch, and nowhere more so than in the
motet. What I have hoped to show in this chapter is that this entanglement of
musical and civic soundworlds itself illuminated meaning. It suggests that the

sense of musical sound had to some ears and minds an affinity with the sound of the city: that the semantic no man's land of the motet and other genres that stretched their words to a limit could accrue meaning by audible analogy with other kinds of sounds—a city alive with the bustle of people; a market clamorous with merchants; a chapel vibrating with holy revelation. It is possible that in the "paradisus mundi," the very experience of urban sound—of the city's audible economy—felt something like the supermusical: like the uneasy and exhilarating possibility that song could surpass the semantic potential of words in the flight of sound. That authors of poems like the *Tractatus* or *Crieries* represented urban glory in terms so superlative as to surpass language is a further clue of the potential congruence of the musical and non-musical realms. In these strange likenesses and analogies there was potential for both experiences, in conversation with one another, to imbue sound with a rich lexicon of meaning, meaning with productive potential: to negotiate sonorous experience and through it to make sense of the world beyond.

3 | Charivari

Among the most overwhelming sounds experienced in the cities and villages of the Middle Ages was the noise associated with the ritual of charivari. While records of urban hubbub stress the spontaneous and unplanned nature of sonic events, in the practice of charivari we encounter sonorities no less unruly, but which were produced as part of defined ritual—as intentional as a musical performance. The earliest records of the term "charivari," "charavaria," or "chelevelet" date from the late thirteenth century, from cities such as Paris, Lyons, Avignon, and Bourges, recounting aggressive and sometimes violent outbursts of civic protest around marriages;[1] threads of the tradition persist in chronicles, dictionaries, literary and, later, photographic records, right up to the present day. Outside France, comparable traditions appear from the fourteenth century in Scotland and England, where "charivari" is supplemented or replaced with terms like "rough music" or "ridings,"[2] and

1 The bibliography for charivari is extensive. The most comprehensive study of the history and practice of charivari remains *Le Charivari: Actes de la table ronde organisée à Paris (25–27 avril 1977) par l'Ecole des Hautes Etudes en Sciences Sociales et le Centre National de la Recherche Scientifique*, ed. Jacques Le Goff and Jean-Claude Schmitt (Paris: Mouton, 1981).

2 An early account of charivaric behavior, including the use of "rough music," was during events reported to have taken place in 1390, in the months following the accession of Robert III as king of Scotland. In efforts to compel the new king to compensate them for damage to their crops by the crowds attending his coronation, farm workers staged a noisy procession. For a detailed account, see John McGavin, "Robert III's 'Rough Music': Charivari and Diplomacy in a Medieval Scottish Court," *Scottish Historical Review* 74 (1995): 144–58. For further accounts of charivari and its connections to English traditions of "ridings" and "rough music" in the later Middle Ages and early modern periods,

components of charivari migrated as far afield as America, in the practice of shivaree.[3]

While charivari could signify in a variety of ways, its meaning changing dramatically over time and space, and shaped too by the medium of its recording, there is consensus regarding its social provocations and forms in its early history. Records reflect rituals of planned civic disturbances, often by self-designated groups of local young men, traditionally in protest of second marriages, or marriages between people of significantly different ages.[4] The frenzy normally erupted on the eve of the nuptials: participants would don masks and grotesque costumes and take to the streets in what one commentator calls "an ordered representation of disorder."[5] Participants ran amok, hurling dung, smashing down doors, and polluting wells with salt; and it is hardly surprising that a consistent theme in the reportage was the excessive, abrasive noisiness of the rite. That it was intended to be productive is suggested by a common culmination: the confrontation between couple and charivari, and the exchange of money in a symbolic admittance of the couple's sin.

It is, however, hard to be sure precisely what charivari's original function was, particularly as its emphasis appears so mobile, ranging from seemingly aggressive responses to marital upset in many early cases, to later traditions

---

see in particular Martin Ingram, "Ridings, Rough Music and Mocking Rhymes in Early Modern England," in *Popular Culture in Seventeenth-Century England*, ed. Barry Reay (New York: St. Martin's Press, 1985), 166–97; Richard Moll, "Staging Disorder: Charivari in the *N-Town* Cycle," *Comparative Drama* 35 (2001): 145–61; and Tom Pettit, "Protesting Inversions: Charivari as Folk Pageantry and Folk-Law," *Medieval English Theatre* 21 (1999): 21–51.

3 The alteration of the term charivari into "shivaree" is addressed in Alva Davis and Raven McDavid, " 'Shivaree': An Example of Cultural Diffusion," *American Speech* 24 (1949): 249–55.

4 Noted by François Lebrun, "Le Charivari à travers les condemnations des autorités ecclésiastiques en France du XIVe au XVIIIe siècle," in *Le Charivari*, ed. Le Goff and Schmitt, 222–23. He cites synodal statutes from Tréguier in 1365, pinpointing the motive for charivari thus: "si vir et mulier ad secunda vota vel ulteriora transierit"; see n. 12, at 223. On the connection of charivari to "youth groups," see Natalie Zemon Davis's foundational essay "The Reason for a Misrule, Youth Groups, and Charivari in 16th-Century France," *Past and Present* 50 (1971), reprinted in her *Society and Culture in Early Modern France* (Oxford: Polity Press, 1987), 97–123. See esp. 104–10 for the emergence of youth groups in relation to charivari from the thirteenth century. For further discussion see also Claude Gauvard and Altan Gokalp, "Les Conduites de bruit et leur signification à la fin du Moyen Age: Le charivari," *Annales: Economies, Sociétés, Civilisations* 29 (1974): 693–704, and esp. 698–701 for documentation of sources relating to "compagnons," "varlets," and "varlets jeunes hommes" associated with charivari.

5 Claude Karnoouh, "Le Charivari ou l'hypothèse de la monogamie," in *Le Charivari*, ed. Le Goff and Schmitt, 38.

that were festive celebrations more than divisive responses to nuptials. In its medieval history, charivari's association with nuptial concerns, particularly second marriages, has been persuasively explained as a fear both of the noisy retributions of the dead spouses,[6] and in cases of marriages involving older members of a society, also of anxiety among the youth about access through marriage to the economic and social security of family.[7] Interpretations of charivari are enriched, if complicated, by the ritual's appropriation in modern critiques of social unrest, most famously in Bakhtin's reading of carnival. Absorbing medieval evidence of charivari into discussion of other popular rites, Bakhtin understood charivari as a symptom of universal tendencies to test authority and assert identity. In the "carnivalesque," rituals such as charivari surpassed the role of complaint against social transgression, functioning as an arena for a purely subversive, free voice of the populus.[8] That the earliest

6 Paul Fortier-Beaulieu was among the first to argue for the quasi-magical dimensions of the ritual as a living representation of the anger of the dead. See his "Le Charivari dans le *Roman de Fauvel*," *Revue de folklore français* 11 (1940): 1–16. While that view is more prevalent in later sources of charivari in France, at least two earlier medieval representations allude to the tradition of Hellequin, a figure associated with the "chasses fantastiques" or "chasses sauvages," legends in which the souls of the dead made themselves heard in a terrifying clamor. For a useful exploration of the symbolic meanings of charivari, including a critique of Fortier-Beaulieu's approach, see Nicole Belmont, "Fonction de la dérision et symbolisme du bruit dans le charivari,'" in *Le Charivari*, ed. Le Goff and Schmitt, 15–21, esp. 18–20. For connections between charivari and the "chasses fantastiques," including a comprehensive survey of the literature on the deathly component of charivari, see Margherita Lecco, "Lo *charivari* del *Roman de Fauvel* e la tradizione della *Mesnie Hellequin*," *Mediaevistik* 13 (2000): 55–85, and on the particular history of Hellequin, see Otto Driesen, *Der Ursprung des Harlekin: Ein kulturgeschichtliches Problem* (Hildesheim: Gertsenberg, 1977, first ed. 1904). For further on the wider contexts of ghosts in medieval folklore and their relationship to charivari see Jean-Claude Schmitt, *Ghosts in the Middle Ages: The Living and the Dead in Medieval Society*, transl. Teresa Fagan (Chicago: University of Chicago Press, 1998), and esp. 93–121 for the Hellequin tradition, and 164–69 for its relationship to charivari.

7 According to Natalie Zemon Davis, those who remarried "jeopardized the chances of the village young to find a mate of a seemly age." See her *Society and Culture*, 106–7 for further discussion.

8 Bakhtin makes numerous references to charivari in *Rabelais and his World*. In discussion of the role of images of the body in medieval popular spectacles, he explicitly connects charivari with other forms of social and poetic subversion: "This image of the body acquired a considerable and substantial development in the popular, festive, and spectacle forms of the Middle Ages: in the feast of the fool, in charivari and carnival, in the popular side show of Corpus Christi, in the diableries of the mystery plays, the *soties*, and farces." Bakhtin, *Rabelais and his World*, 27. Elsewhere, he hinted at the problem of generic distinctions between charivari and carnival: the demonic associations of carnival

records of charivari are ecclesiastical prohibitions, trying to curb and proscribe behavior,[9] seems to support Bakhtin's reading, suggesting that the very mechanism that sought to uphold "official" values was simultaneously an opportunity to transgress them. More recent critics to follow the Bakhtinian model argue that charivari was never primarily concerned with social justice, but was rather "a transgression on transgression," using the occasion of a second marriage as "excuse for breaking out in riotous behavior."[10]

While the ambiguity and scarcity of the evidence means that charivari's true meaning and practice may be lost for good, Bakhtin's aligning of charivari with other kinds of medieval ritual may nonetheless be useful in other ways. It is a reminder of the important role played by sound in rituals of social dissent. Although never explicitly theorizing the place of derisive sound, *Rabelais and his World* resounds with unfettered voices. In the market we hear "the cry of the baker, the quack, the hawker of miracle drugs," and "curses" mixed in with laughter;[11] elsewhere, Bakhtin recalls the shepherd shouts reported in the prologue introducing *Pantagruel*: "Grrrrr! Grrrr! Kssss!"[12] There are also a range of non-vocal sonorities, including kitchens stuffed with noisy pots and utensils,[13] and men and beasts jangling bells as they go.[14] In such timbres, Bakhtin heard the sonorous component of the carnivalesque—the derisive, yet liberating, opposite to the "official" life of the Middle Ages. While recent scholarship has rightly questioned the historical veracity of Bakhtin's

---

resonated with charivari's concern with the unquiet souls of dead spouses, leading him to observe that "charivari was also related to carnival" (at 267). Later commentators have taken that further, demonstrating that boundaries between charivaric behavior and other established forms of unruly ritual action, such as carnival, were at best blurry. See Jean-Marie Privat, "Sots, sotties, charivari," in *Atti del IV Colloquio della Société internationale pour l'étude du théâtre médiéval*, ed. Maria Chiabò, Frederico Doglio, and Marina Maymone (Viterbo: Centro studi sul teatro medioevale e rinascimentale, 1984), 331–47.

9 The main archival evidence of charivari is in synodal statues, designed to record sources of ecclesiastical discontent and anxiety.

10 The position of Susan Crane in the most recent analysis of charivari. See her *The Performance of Self: Ritual, Clothing, and Identity During the Hundred Years War* (Philadelphia: University of Pennsylvania Press, 2004), 145. See 141–55 for the full discussion. See also Jean-Claude Schmitt, who suggests that charivari was sometimes "for the benefit of a group of youths, the opportunity to finish the night in a tavern." See his *Ghosts in the Middle Ages*, 167.

11 Bakhtin, *Rabelais*, 167.

12 Ibid., 171–73.

13 Ibid., 183–84.

14 Ibid., 214.

social categories,[15] there is nonetheless a value in listening closely to his engagement with Rabelais and his earlier medieval models. For Bakhtin unwittingly opens our ears to registers of social ritual. It is not merely that carnival sound is aggressive or startling: as products of exaggerated verbal intonations, born of a desire to be audible in the rabble of the city, or to enforce the affront of an obscenity, Bakhtin rehears sounds that press not only at the limits of the acceptable in language, but also hover at the fringes of the singing voice. Neither speech nor song, voices taunt the official categories of verbal and musical communication. In turn, the sheer clamor of *Rabelais and his World* articulates a category of derisive sound defined in part by its consistently uneasy relationship to more familiar, and recoverable, forms of spoken and sung communication. It is enriched through work in the disciplines of history and anthropology, which detect a tendency among societies of many epochs and locales to develop noise-making as a strategy for protest, to signal the breaking of social taboos.[16] Such contexts open up new ways to listen to records of charivaric sound.

The medieval soundworlds mediated by Bakhtin also articulate a more fundamental problem, concerning not just the nature of dissenting sounds associated with rituals like charivari, but also their representation. For their sheer evanescence ensure their uneasy relationship to durable, stylized modes of representation. The only certainties of the cries, hoots, and clatterings of the world Bakhtin eavesdrops upon are their resistance to familiar modes of notating and writing, and their slippage between notatable categories of voice. While it may be such sounds' resistance to notation that marked its transgressive power, charivari more than any other sonority we shall encounter in this book raises the question: what, exactly, is there to write about? If the sounds themselves evade recording, where are we to turn for an audible trace?

In this chapter, the status of the charivaric record will be key to reengaging the sonority of the ritual. While a documentary history exists in ecclesiastical records and civic proscription testifying to the social practice of charivari, there is an equally rich body of evidence in which charivaris are part of the fabric of

---

15 For critique of Bakhtin's social categories, questioning his reliance on distinctions between ecclesiastical and lay social groups, see Symes, *A Common Stage*, 208–15. Responding to Bakhtin's interpretation of the charivaric aspects of Adam de la Halle's Artesian play, the *Jeu de la feuillée*, as an embryonic vision of carnival, Symes notes that "in Arras as elsewhere, the institutional boundary lines that produced Bakhtin's carnival were still undrawn during the thirteenth century, and there were not even fixed temporal boundaries within which it could be contained" (p. 209).

16 See Gauvard and Gokalp, "Les Conduites de bruit," 702–4 for discussion of the relationship of noise to the rupture of sexual and metaphysical norms. For a comparative approach to charivaric noise, see Claudie Marcel-Dubois, "La Paramusique dans le charivari français contemporain," in *Le Charivari*, ed. Le Goff and Schmitt, 45–53.

literary, visual, and sometimes musical invention. In these cases, the purpose was less to accurately report on a living practice than to recreate charivari as a narrative event—to translate it via highly deliberate acts of artistic composition. If such records distance us from the social reality, they also offer an unexpected twist to the normally limited story of charivaric sound. For on one famous occasion, charivari found an unlikely amanuensis: song. And in calling upon song to represent its essential opposite, charivari exposes areas of expressive transgression in music, particularly around the boundaries of generic category, words and music, singing and speaking, and sense and sound. In short, it is through the supermusical that charivari finds its musical infinity.

In the rest of this chapter we shall begin with a brief consideration of some rare documentary descriptions of the public ritual from synodal statutes of the fourteenth century, and ways we might "hear" them in the wider spectrum of public performance, and in the theoretical spectrum of *vox*. We shall then turn our attention to the famous scene of charivari in the *Roman de Fauvel*, and explore how charivari became an opportunity to explore transgressions of another kind: to expose the thrilling and subversive edge of the supermusical.

Recording Charivari: The Synodal Statutes

Throughout its history, charivari provoked unease among civil and ecclesiastical authorities. While that unease supports the view that it was a "transgression on transgression," it also ensured it a documentary history, and from the early fourteenth century through to the twentieth, echoes of charivari are enshrined in proscriptive documents such as synodal statutes and letters of remission.[17] Their most consistent and precise references are to sound.[18] Let me summarize the documentary evidence recovered by Vaultier, Le Brun, and Gauvard and Gokalp. While some accounts label sounds in the most general terms, as "din, tumult, scandalous noises" ("vacarme, tumulte, bruits scandaleux"), others offer more concrete information about what must have been an overwhelming and abrasive soundscape. The accounts represent two sorts of sound: instrumental and vocal. Instrumental is perhaps too formal a term,

---

17 Important studies to collect such records are Rogier Vaultier, *Le Folklore pendant la guerre de Cent Ans d'après les Lettres de Rémissions du Trésor des Chartes* (Paris: Librairie Guénégaud, 1965); see esp. 29–44 for discussion of records relating to charivari. Other studies to document and describe accounts are Gauvard and Gokalp, "Les Conduites de bruit," and Lebrun, "Le Charivari à travers les condemnations."

18 The complete list, including modern editions and transcriptions, is given by Lebrun, "Le Charivari à travers les condemnations," 226–28.

for records allude mainly to makeshift instruments: one account describes making sound by "clashing pans, basins, and bells, whistling with the mouth and clicking fingers, by beating rusty instruments and other sonorous things" ("pulsatione patellarum, pelvium et campanarum, eorum oris et manus sibilatione, instrumento aerugiariorum, sive fabricantium, et aliarum rerum sonorosarum"). A characteristic of the instrumental soundworld is thus its percussive, non-pitched, quality. Vocal outrage takes many forms. One account describes a range of defamatory slanders, songs, and accusations directed at the offending couple ("injurias, carmina, libellos diffamatorios contra eosdem sponsos"). The mention of "carmina" here is rare, as voices seem to do everything but sing: accounts describe "clamoring and booing" ("clameurs et huées"), "horrifying and blasphemous shouting and obscene chattering, clamoring harshly and abusively" ("horridis et blasphemis vociferationibus et obscoena loquacitate, injuriosis contumeliosisque clamoribus"). Mention of obscenity here is echoed in other descriptions of words as "ugly and dishonest" ("turpia et inhonesta verba").

Sparse though such sonic remnants may be, the accounts imply an ease with which hullabaloo could be created. Yet it is precisely the simplicity of production that may illuminate charivari's elusive aspect: why such sonority was fitting; what such sound signified. Easy manufacture seems key to defining an ethical register. Most simply, it exaggerates the sense that charivaric performance is *not* music. Indeed, records generate an enormous vocabulary for sound that is profoundly *un*musical, sounds that forgo a privileging of pitch or rhythm, and the register of the singing voice. In their place, we have chatter, clamour, clicking, and hissing, what commentators have termed "paramusic."[19] Situated in the discourses of music, theory, and grammar explored in Elizabeth Leach's work, it qualifies as *vox confusa* in no uncertain terms: it is non-verbal, non-rational, and it is patently unwritable. Yet in another sense, it is laden with signifying potential. In the legal lexicon of the statutes, it is a marker of transgression and has authority not just to expose and coerce an offending couple. The very records that witness to it suggest that it empowered those who performed to unsettle church authority too.

Other kinds of social sounds may help to nuance suggestions of an ethical overtone. Synodal statues were intended to limit behavior, but they were produced in contexts equally adept at endorsing public ritual. A useful point of comparison is the practice of liturgical and civic processions: events designed

---

19 For example in Marcel-Dubois, "La Paramusique." Eugene Vance explores the notion of "paramusic" and "paralanguage" in earlier medieval charivaris in "*Le Jeu de la feuillée* and the Poetics of Charivari," *Modern Language Notes* 100 (1985): 816–17.

to reinforce communal identity.[20] While charivari emphasizes disruption and unregulated movement, processions were intended to coordinate unity. As C. Clifford Flannigan explains, "togetherness or solidarity is the most characteristic feature of processions, a feature that applies to motion itself, the succession of participants in the procession, and even the route which the procession takes, since all participants must go the same way and at the same time."[21] If processing had specific emotional and cognitive goals to create corporate unity,[22] it relied heavily on sound and performance to engineer its effect. Heard comparatively, charivari emerges not as a collection of strange, disturbing noises; we may hear it as *lacking* the sonic ingredients familiar to liturgical processions, and to civic celebrations, pageants, and royal entries. Although distinctions between these two modes of medieval ritual were frequently blurry, they nonetheless employed distinctive instrumental and vocal timbres and forms. It is these sonorities that offer an aural foil to charivaric noise.

While liturgical processions out of the choir, church, and into the streets during the year might vary in scale and geographical scope, they had two distinctive features in common.[23] First, the integration of physical movement with chanting; and second, an emphasis on antiphonal and responsorial chants, or simple, repetitive hymns, during the mobile portions of the procession.

20 For a recent account of the varied forms of medieval processions, see *Moving Subjects: Processional Performance in the Middle Ages and Renaissance*, ed. Kathleen Ashley and Wim Hüsken (Amsterdam: Rodopi, 2001). For two theoretical treatments of medieval processions see essays by Kathleen Ashley, "Introduction: The Moving Subjects of Processional Performance," 7–34, and C. Clifford Flannigan's "The Moving Subject: Medieval Liturgical Processions from a Semiotic and Cultural Perspective," 35–51. See also Noël Coulet, "Processions, éspace urbain, communauté civique," in *Liturgie et musique (IXᵉ–XIVᵉ siècles)*, ed. Marie-Humbert Vicaire, Cahiers de Fanjeaux 17 (Toulouse: Privat, 1982), 381–97.

21 Flannigan, "The Moving Subject," 39.

22 Ashley, "Introduction," 14.

23 There are several studies of individual processions or processional traditions of particular institutions. Studies of French processions contemporary with the early history of charivari include Anne Walters Robertson, *The Service-Books of the Royal Abbey of Saint-Denis: Images of Ritual and Music in the Middle Ages* (Oxford: Clarendon Press, 1991), 251–61. On the music associated with Corpus Christi processions, see Kenneth Kreitner's work on the tradition of fifteenth-century Barcelona, "Music in the Corpus Christi Procession of Fifteenth-Century Barcelona," *Early Music History* 14 (1995): 153–204. For a more comprehensive account of the use of musical instruments and bands in Corpus Christi processions across the Middle Ages, see Edmund Bowles, "Musical Instruments in the Medieval Corpus Christi Procession," *Journal of the American Musicological Society* 17 (1964): 251–60. See also Miri Rubin, *Corpus Christi: The Eucharist in Late Medieval Culture* (Cambridge: Cambridge University Press, 1991), esp. 243–71.

The latter is significant for it meant that liturgical song was not simply the province of a soloist or small group of participants, but involved the many clergy participating in the procession. Those two basic principles are exemplified in Craig Wright's reconstruction of accounts of Palm Sunday in thirteenth-century Chartres.[24] Although the notated missal and ordinals for the procession leave no doubt as to the careful choreography that went into designing the procession, giving participants, or those leading the processional groups, a pre-ordained map of the event, in real time, it was singing that regulated the different groups of clergy in their movement in and out of the cathedral, and to and from the stational stop-offs. A sense of chant as the guiding, directing force of liturgical processing may be seen in instructions for one group of the Chartres processions, the Augustinian canons from Saint-Jean-en-Vallée, who left their abbey to join the crowds of processors in the cathedral. Lined up, two by two, in the chancel, they were given explicit instructions on how to proceed:

> When the time for beginning the procession shall arrive . . . the processions move forward, preceded by banners, a dragon, crosses, and the Gospel books, in which assembly next walk the priests of the parish churches, next the canons of Saint-Cheron, next we canons of Saint-Jean, and finally the canons of the mother church. At the threshold of the chancel, the cantor or succentor of Chartres begins the responsory *In die qua invocavit* with the verse and the repetendum. When that responsory has been sung, however, we canons of Saint-Jean-en-Vallée recommence that responsory with its verse and repetendum, and so with each of the other responsories which the canons of Chartres will sing up to the church of Saint-Barthélemy.[25]

---

24 Craig Wright, "The Palm Sunday Procession in Medieval Chartres," in *The Divine Office in the Latin Middle Ages*, ed. Fassler and Baltzer, 344–71. Wright bases his reconstruction on a series of manuscripts, the oldest, the *Ordo veridicus*, compiled in the first half of the twelfth century, but containing no music. A later notated missal, Chartres, Bibliothèque municipale 520 (copied, according to Wright, as late as 1230), gives an overall sense of liturgical practice at the turn of the thirteenth century, and presumably well into that century. These sources are supplemented with a copy of Bibliothèque municipale 1058, a thirteenth-century expansion of the earlier ordinal. For a full discussion see 345–46.

25 "cum vero tempus progrediendi advenerit, textis et crucibus omnibus in medio chori ordinatis progrediuntur processiones, in quo processu, precedentibus vexillis, dracone, crucibus et textis, progrediuntur deinde presbiteri parrochiales, post canonici Sancti Karauni, deinde nos canonici Sancti Johannis, de hinc canonici matris ecclesie. in ipso autem limine chori cantor carnotensis aut succentor incipit R. *In die qua invocavit* cum versu et regressu. finito responsorio nos vero canonici de Valleia reincipimus eundum

What carried the canons to Saint-Barthélemy was their song. We must imagine how movement to their chant at once signaled and effected their communal identity, in a procession where they were soon to encounter those from other local churches. Chant assured a collectivity, bringing processors together in a harmonious unity. But more practically, communal chanting, often of simple, repetitive hymns, was the vital means of moving large numbers of people through large amounts of space, of keeping participants in line with one another.

If chanting clergy were familiar to the eyes and ears of medieval citizens, they were counterpoint to equally vibrant traditions of secular processions: to celebrate royal or noble entries, weddings, victories, and as part of civic pageants, to name the most common.[26] Notwithstanding that the theatrics of liturgical occasions could press the boundaries of the sacred, secular processions, or secular offshoots of liturgical occasions, were distinct for their use of instruments. While some processions called for huge bands of instrumentalists,[27] the commonplace sound of civic processing was wind instruments and drums. Writing around 1316, the poet and Parisian chancery clerk Jean Maillart

---

responsorium cum versu et regressu, et sic cetera responsoria quod canonici carnotensis cantabunt usque ad ecclesiam beati Bartholomei"; Chartres, Bibliothèque municipale, 529, fol. 58ᵛ, containing the account of the Palm Sunday procession from the perspective of the Abbey of Saint-Jean-en Vallée. The full account in Latin is given by Wright, "Palm Sunday," 359–60, and I quote here from his translation on 351.

26 A useful survey of processional traditions, drawing on evidence from across western Europe, and covering a large temporal span, remains Edmund Bowles, "Musical Instruments in Civic Processions during the Middle Ages," *Acta Musicologica* 33 (1961): 147–61. For two contrasting studies of the public, processional life of individual medieval cities, see Strohm, *Music in Late Medieval Bruges*, and Blake Wilson, *Music and Merchants: The Laudesi Companies of Republican Florence* (Oxford: Clarendon Press, 1992). On the Parisian context of royal processions, see Lawrence Bryant, "The Medieval Entry Ceremony at Paris," in *Coronations: Medieval and Early Modern Monarchic Ritual*, ed. János Bak (Berkeley: University of California Press, 1990), 88–118. For analysis of one of the earliest civic parades which took place at Pentecost, June 7, 1313 in Paris, see Elizabeth A. R. Brown and Nancy Freeman Regalado, " 'Universitas et communitas': The Parade of the Parisians at the Pentecost Feast of 1313," in *Moving Subjects*, ed. Ashley and Hüsken, 117–54; the liturgical and secular intertwined in numerous ways, and so, for example, contemporary chronicles note tableaux of vernacular literary figures such as Renart the fox, quite remote from the primary Pentecostal impetus for the celebrations.

27 For example, one processional tradition in Malines, dating from the mid-fourteenth century, involved many processions spread out over several days. One involved over 100 minstrels playing instruments including viol, guitar, lute, shawm, bombard, crumhorn, cornett, trumpet, and drums. See Bowles, "Musical Instruments in Civic Processions," 160, for further details.

offered a standard ensemble in his fictional account of civic procession in his *Roman du comte d'Anjou*:

Tout la ville est esmüe;
chascun de festoier s'esforce;
partout sonnet cloces a force
tymbres, tabours, trompes, araines
nacaires, cors, musez, doçainnes.[28]

All the city is in uproar;
each of the revelers makes his best effort;
everywhere bells clang
and there are drums, tabours, trumpets, cornets,
nackers, horns, bagpipes, and pipes.

That distinctive brassy sound was repeated in reality time and time again. By the fourteenth century, trumpets and trombones were so central to the public life of a city like Florence, for example, that there was a culture of freelance *pifferi* and *trombadori* who were hired by lay *laudesi* companies for weddings and festive occasions, and also often supported by positions in the Signoria to furnish fanfares for the city's many public processions.[29] And where there were wind instruments, there were invariably drums.[30] Their function: to be piercing and rhythmic enough to be heard and felt across large spaces and thus to coordinate crowds over a large area, to synchronize them in time, and to encourage them to march.

As with charivari, the sounding effect of these collective rituals can be difficult to recover.[31] However, iconographic traces vividly attest to the efficacious meaning of such sound types. Even if the reality might be chaotic, even cacophonous, the ideology of such sounds was bound to ideas of unity: above all, to the synchronizing effects of musical sound. A glimpse of the desired effect can be seen in conventions for representing processions. Artists consistently emphasize order and coordination, with participants shown facing one direction, walking side by side or single file, to suggest group unity. In the *bas-de-page* of fol. 218ᵛ of Paris, Bibliothèque nationale de France, lat. 10484 (the Belleville Breviary), produced in Paris in the early part of the fourteenth century, and decorated by the celebrated artist Jean Pucelle, we see an orderly

28 Jean Maillart, *Le Roman du comte d'Anjou*, ed. Mario Roques (Paris: Honoré Champion, 1931), vv. 6514–18.

29 Wilson, *Music and Merchants*, 152–53.

30 Bowles, "Musical Instruments in Civic Processions," 149.

31 Addressed by Kreitner in "Music in the Corpus Christi Procession," 153, where, he writes, "it is usually impossible to connect the official ceremonial accounts securely to specific, known pieces of music."

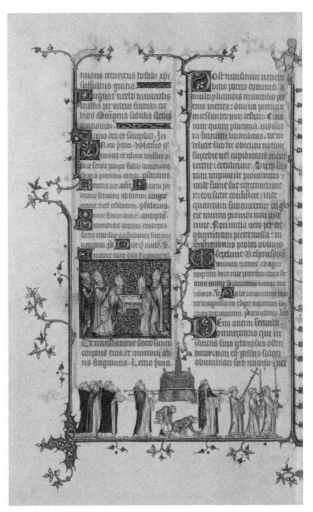

FIGURE 3.1. Paris, Bibliothèque nationale de France, lat. 10484 (the Belleville Breviary), fol. 218ᵛ. By permission of the Bibliothèque nationale de France

procession of Dominicans, typical of the modes for representing processing during this period (see figure 3.1). Undistracted by the lepers who hobble along beneath the relics seeking charitable alms, the group, spread out over significant space, remains in an orderly line. The folds in the copes of the three at the head of the procession reveal them to be leading with the same leg, coordinated by singing monks at the rear. So standard was this kind of processional ordering in the visual domain that it was on occasion a component with which to generate parody. In London, British Library, Add. 49622, a Psalter made for the Use of Sarum dating slightly earlier, we see a procession of hares,

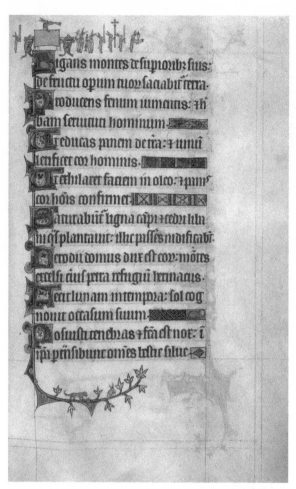

FIGURE 3.2. London, British Library, Add. 49622, fol. 133ʳ. © The British Library Board

leading the burial of a dog (see fol. 133ʳ, in figure 3.2). The cues of sound—hand bells swung by the leader, and the canine trumpeter who sits aloft the funeral bier—conjure the musicality of procession. But it is the orderliness of the hares, their legs neatly aligned to suggest their perfect coordination, that codes the humor here: the stable cue, signaling order, conjures the unthinkable—irrational beasts strutting like humans, in processional harmony.

This brief exploration of sources suggests that while charivaric sound may resist prescription and reproduction, it leaves in its wake a charged sense of social meaning and effects. But what more can be said about the sound? Is it possible to go further, or are we left stranded at the limits of the record? Perhaps it is time for some different questions. For to ask how charivari *sounds* is to follow a trend in charivari studies, to approach it as what Eugene Vance termed "an observable social phenomenon."[32] He was here critiquing the foundational collection of essays on the subject published in 1981 by Jacques Le Goff and Jean-Claude Schmitt under the auspices of the Ecole des Hautes Etudes en Sciences Sociales. With their anthropological approach to the evidence, as remnants of a lived social ritual, and as a trace of that society's cultural values, the essays sought to examine a social reality more than to explore charivari's meaning at moments of its transmission in non-documentary history. It has only been more recently, in the work of literary historians like Vance, Nancy Freeman Regalado, and Susan Crane,[33] that alternative approaches have been suggested. Detecting charivaric references in his reading of a cluster of thirteenth-century French literary texts, Vance suggested that rather than treat these as supplements to evidence of the statutes, we might instead ask how charivaric experience could serve more abstractly poetic preoccupations: thus, he argues, "one cannot properly treat charivari as a 'theme' that one identifies 'in' a given poetic text: rather, an instance of charivari is a convergence of many disparate elements constituting a poetic performance at every level and from beginning to end within the syntax of the work as a whole."[34] It is possible to think of a "mentalité charivarique,"[35] transposable to other social contexts and idioms of representation. As specific case studies illustrate, the rite was often appropriated into highly stylized and refined courtly discourse: restaged still with an intent to challenge, protest, and revel, perhaps, but operating in a different system of authority.[36] How, though, does sound fare in such moments of transposition?

We shall turn now to perhaps the most famous example of charivari's reception, the early fourteenth-century French satire of the *Roman de Fauvel* as preserved in Paris, Bibliothèque nationale de France, f. fr. 146 (hereafter *Fauv*). *Fauv* is so specific and detailed in its representation that it is little wonder some have treated it as an archive of the social practice referred to in the judicial records.[37] It seems to invite such treatment by going out of its way to frame

32 Vance, "*Le Jeu de la feuillée*," 815.

33 See especially Nancy Freeman Regalado, "Masques réels dans le monde de l'imaginaire: Le rite et l'écrit dans le charivari du *Roman de Fauvel*, MS B.N. fr. 146," in *Masques et déguisements dans la littérature médiévale*, ed. Marie-Louise Ollier (Montreal: University of Montreal Press, 1988), 111–26.

34 Vance, "*Le Jeu de la feuillée*," 816.

35 Privat, "Sots, sotties, charivari," 337–38.

36 See especially Regalado, "Masques réels"; Crane, *The Performance of Self*, 140–74; Moll, "Staging Disorder"; and McGavin, "Robert III's 'Rough Music'," for examples of how charivari was appropriated to new and elite social contexts.

37 The tradition of reading *Fauvel* as ethnographic record is the subject of discussion in Schmitt, *Ghosts in the Middle Ages*, 167–69.

itself as an on-the-spot witness to a charivari seen on the streets of Paris. In what follows, I wish to explore the ways *Fauvel* tests the boundaries between an originary ritual event and its translation into the highly contrived medium of literary creation. It is not to deny this charivari its own power of protest: as we shall see, its presence has a highly specific target. My concern is rather with what happens when sounds and acts that pressed the frontiers of lived experience in the social act mutate into the concrete and controlling spaces of writing and song.

The Case of the Roman de Fauvel

Fauv, produced around 1317 in the vicinity of the French royal household in Paris, contains a rich compilation of political poems, chronicles, and songs, all of which allude to unsettling events in the household of Philip IV, le Bel, and his sons.[38] The manuscript is best known for its version of the Old French satire on Capetian politics, the *Roman de Fauvel*, infamous for its wicked horse-hero, Fauvel.[39] The text in *Fauv* is a reworked version of a work by chancery clerk Gervais du Bus, the reworkings attributed in a rubric to one Chaillou de Pesstain. Gervais's original tale, a thinly veiled attack on corruption in the royal realm, recounted the evil horse's ascent, at the will of Dame Fortuna, to rule as king; delighted by his newfound power, the horse sets out to woo the Goddess, and thereby ensure control over her wheels; she is far from amenable, but as consolation she offers him the hand of her henchwoman, Vain Glory. At the hands of Chaillou, the original narrative was massively expanded with illuminations and saturated with the addition of over 169 musical items, from chant to thirteenth-century conductus, to state-of-the art motets. Chaillou also expanded the narrative of Fauvel's nuptials to Vain Glory, and in the account of their wedding night he produced his most spectacular invention: a full-scale charivari.

---

38 For a black-and-white facsimile of the manuscript, see *Le Roman de Fauvel in the Edition of Mesire Chaillou de Pesstain: A Reproduction in Facsimile of the Complete Manuscript, Paris, Bibliothèque Nationale, Fonds Français 146*, ed. Edward Roesner, François Avril, and Nancy Freeman Regalado (New York: Broude Brothers, 1990). The introductory essays offer an in-depth account of the literary, musical, visual, and historical context of the manuscript's production. See also *Fauvel Studies: Allegory, Chronicle, Music, and Image in Paris, Bibliothèque Nationale de France, MS Français 146*, ed. Margaret Bent and Andrew Wathey (Oxford: Clarendon Press, 1998).

39 *Le Roman de Fauvel par Gervais du Bus publié d'après tous les manuscrits connus*, ed. Arthur Långfors, Société des anciens textes français (Paris: Honoré Champion, 1914–19).

As a horse was depicted clambering into bed with a Vice—the ultimate negation of nuptial convention—it is not hard to see why charivari was a witty and apt narrative choice. But it is more than pure entertainment. It probably had a royal target, and was a fitting response to recent nuptial scandals in the royal family.[40] Susan Crane interprets the charivari as an appropriation, as a way for the courtiers who made and read the manuscript to "talk back to the court,"[41] and her reading demonstrates ways the charivari is subtly relocated out of the popular rite of the street and into the highly cultured space, costumes, and music of the court. Charivari depicted is thus a kind of double masquerade: a courtly staging of a rite that was itself a performance of transgression. Such assessments provide a new point of departure for thinking about sound, and for how the essential ingredients of charivaric noise find their equivalence in the courtly idiom.

The key may lie in the larger creative agendas of the manuscript. *Fauv* challenges a number of conventions—poetic, musical, visual, and codicological: the struggle to have the parchment surfaces accommodate so unprecedented an assembly of music, image, and text, and, at the level of the codex, to contain such disparate texts; at the poetic level, Chaillou's expansions both model themselves on, but surpass, with the presence of music, previous models of continuation such as the *Roman de la Rose*.[42] It is within that frame of experimentation that we shall proceed. For in translating charivari, the makers established the ultimate compositional challenge: how to capture on the stillness of parchment a ritual that privileged unwritable sound and unruly action.

It is a challenge that the makers seem keen to emphasize. As charivari commences, the author positions himself as ethnographer, and steps out of the frame of his creation with a promise to record everything exactly as he sees it:

De la maniere et de la guise
de ce chalivali devise

---

40 The scene may resonate with recent marital crises in the Capetian household: in particular, Louis X's speedy marriage to Clémence of Hungary in 1315, three months after the death of his wife Marguerita (who in turn had been one of three royal brides found out for adultery). For further details see *Le Roman de Fauvel*, ed. Roesner, Avril, and Regalado, 11. See also Michelle Bolduc, "Fauvel's Wayward Wives," *Medievalia e humanistica* 32 (2007): 43–62, which further notes the resonances between the charivari and Capetian family politics at the accession of Philip V.

41 Crane, *The Performance of Self*, 154.

42 On the ways *Fauvel* overturns existing models of literary continuation and musical categories see Kevin Brownlee, "Authorial Self-Representation and Literary Models in the *Roman de Fauvel*," in *Fauvel Studies*, ed. Bent and Wathey, 73–103, and Ardis Butterfield, "The Refrain and Transformation of Genre in the *Roman de Fauvel*," ibid., 105–59, and also her *Poetry and Music in Medieval France*, 200–14.

un petitet iceste estoire
Qui ci est faire pour memoire.[43]

On the nature and the look of this charivari I will devise a modest little account, which is made here for memory.

As we consider how he fulfilled that promise, it will be useful to take a brief tour of the scene (see figures 3.3–3.5).[44] It occupies fols. 34^r–36^v, framed at either end by two spectacular three-tier illuminations of the revelers. On fol. 34^r (figure 3.3), we see Fauvel clambering into bed with Vain Glory. The adjacent text tells us that charivari commenced in the streets of Paris, detailing costumes, participants, and sounds, all of which are depicted in the two lower registers of the images. At the bottom of fol. 34^r is a cue for "sotes chançons" sung in the streets, and, turning over, these are recorded in the next column (see figure 3.4). The narrative continues with the arrival of a figure popular in folklore and sometimes conflated with charivari, the hairy demon Hellequin and his troops, fresh from hell, bringing the dead to complain about the transgressions of the living. He is shown at the top of fol. 34^v with his deathly army in rattling wagons. They, too, bring music: a lengthy lay that continues to fol. 36^v, where the charivari concludes with a final three-tier image and more rude songs (see figure 3.5).

At first sight it seems a tour de force of almost pedantic, multimedia documentation. By deploying every possible means of representation—verbal, visual, and musical account—the makers strengthen the effect of the documentary promised in the prefatory cue. However, close analysis shows that the account is far from a straight-forward record, but is rather "a composition, a hybrid ensemble."[45] It quotes and alludes to texts from multiple literary sources and theatrical conventions, and cites elements of folklore, as well, of course, as the actual ritual of charivari. The feat, then, is to have created, under the illusion of realism, an episode of astonishing artifice. This is nowhere truer than in the charivari's soundtrack.

Sound is omnipresent in these folios. The images strain with noisy masked bodies, more than forty crammed and stacked in the tight

43 *Le Roman de Fauvel*, ed. Långfors, Appendix: interpolation du manuscrit *E*, vv. 693–96.

44 As one of the earliest and most thorough accounts of charivari, the *Roman de Fauvel* has received extensive scholarly attention. Key studies of the complete episode (and ones to which I shall primarily refer in developing a new reading of the music) include *Le Roman de Fauvel*, ed. Roesner, Avril, and Regalado, 10–15; Regalado, "Masques réels," 111–26; and Lecco, "Lo *charivari* del *Roman de Fauvel*," 55–85.

45 Regalado, "Masques réels," 123.

FIGURE 3.3. Paris, Bibliothèque nationale de France, f. fr. 146, fol. 34ʳ. By permission of the Bibliothèque nationale de France

architectural registers. Meanwhile, the text groans with detailed sonic information. First, the noises produced by the general mayhem of the action—Hellequin's screeching wagon-wheels:

> Dedens le chariot si ot
> un engin de roes de charetes,
> fors, reddes et moult tres bien faites,
> et au tourner qu'eles fesoient
> sis bastons de fer encontroient
> dedens les moieux bien cloez
> et bien atachiez, or m'oez.[46]

46 *Le Roman de Fauvel*, ed. Långfors, Appendix, vv. 721–27.

FIGURE 3.4. Paris, Bibliothèque nationale de France, f. fr. 146, fol. 34ᵛ. By permission of the Bibliothèque nationale de France

In the chariot there's an engine of wagon-wheels, strong, stiff and so well made that at each turn they make the iron spokes crunch and squeak.

The sound of smashing of windows and doors:

Puis fesoient une crierie,
onques tele ne fu öye:
li un moutret son cul au vent,
li autre rompet un auvent,

FIGURE 3.5. Paris, Bibliothèque nationale de France, f. fr. 146, fol. 36ᵛ. By permission of the Bibliothèque nationale de France

l'un cassoit fenestres et huis,
l'autre getoit le sel ou puis,
l'un getoit le bren aus visages.[47]

Then they make a great cry, such that you have never heard: one reveals his ass to the wind, the other breaks a shed; one smashes windows and doors, another throws salt down a well; one throws bran at onlookers.

47 Ibid., vv. 733–39.

The second category of noise are those made deliberately, by banging make-shift instruments, in unruly parody of the conventional orchestration of civic processions:

> Li uns tenoit une grant poelle,
> l'un le havet, le greïl et le
> pesteil, et l'autre un pot de cuivre,
> et tuit contrefesoient l'ivre,
> l'autre un bacin, et sus feroient
> si fort que trestout estonnoient.[48]

One of them holds a huge pot, another a hook, a griddle, and another a ladle, and another a copper pot. All were feigning drunkenness. Another had a basin, and hit it so hard that he amazed everyone.

The final group of sounds is vocal, covering the entire spectrum from baying, shrieking, to singing the "devil's songs":

> Avec eus portoient deus bieres,
> ou il avoit gent trop avable
> pour chanter la chançon au deable.
> L'un crie corbeilles et venz,
> l'autre de quel part vient li venz.
> Il y ravoit un grant jaiant
> qui aloit trop forment braiant.[49]

With them they carry two funeral biers in which there are people very capable of singing the song of the devil. From one come cries about baskets and wares, from the other come cries from the part the wind comes from. It is led by a giant who goes along braying.

Just once, where the narrator lists the instruments, the lines begin to hiss and clatter:

> Lis uns avoit tantins a vaches
> cousuz sus cuisses et sus naches,
> et au dessus grosses sonnetes,
> au sonner et hochier claretes;
> li autres tabours et cimbales,
> et granz estrumenz orz et sales,
> et cliquetes et macequotes,

48 Ibid., vv. 705–10.
49 Ibid., vv. 742–48.

dont si hauz brais et hautes notes
fesoient que nul ne puet dire.[50]

Some had cowbells sewed to their thighs and buttocks, and overhead
had huge bells that rang and pealed piercingly; others had tabours and
cymbals, and huge, rusty, and dirty instruments, and clackers and
macequotes, which produced such high brayings and high notes as no one
can describe.

While the literary account exploits the phonetic properties of language to
create an audible sound effect, the music goes further. The charivari music is
cued on fol. 34[r] with yet another illusion of documentary:

Ci s'ensiuvent sotes chançons, que cues qui font le chalivali chantent
parmi les rues. Et puise après trouvra on le lay des Hellequines.

Here follow the *sotes chançons* that those who make the charivari sing
throughout the streets. And then afterwards one will find the Lay of the
Hellequins.

The collection (see example 3.1, items 1–9), beginning on the verso, opens
with two refrain-form songs or *fatras* (example 3.1, items 1–2).[51] *Fatras* was a
relatively new poetic genre, in which a pre-existent refrain was split apart, and,
between the opening and closing lines, new, frequently nonsensical or scatological material was placed, borrowing the rhyme scheme of the original
refrain.[52] They are the only two examples in the *roman*, but take their place in
a series of experiments with what Ardis Butterfield has termed semi-lyrics,
that is, genres playing on the opposition of spoken and sung verse. The two
fatras are followed by a clump of refrain-like songs that telescope in length, and
intensify in obscenity (example 3.1, items 3–9). While the songs contain

50 Ibid., vv. 711–19.

51 Patrice Uhl, "Les 'Sotes chançons' du *Roman de Fauvel* (MS E): La symptomatique
indécision du rubricateur," *French Studies* 45 (1991): 385–402, offers the most thorough
literary context for the songs to date.

52 For a commentary on and edition of the *fatras* see Lambert Porter, *La Fatrasie et le
fatras: Essai sur la poésie irrationnelle en France au Moyen Age* (Geneva: Librairie E. Droz,
1960). Other critiques of the *fatras* in the wider context of Old French nonsense poetry
include Patrice Uhl, "Non-sens et parodie dans la fatrasie: Contribution à la localization
du champ interférentiel," *Archiv für das Studium der neueren Sprachen und Literaturen* 144
(1992): 71–97, and Giovanna Angeli, " 'Mundus inversus' et 'perversus' de la fatrasie à la
sottie," *Revue des langues romanes* 86 (1982): 117–32. An excellent summary of the genre
is Bec, *La Lyrique française au Moyen Age*, 1: 171–213.

EXAMPLE 3.1. "Sotes chançons" (items 1–9) (*Fauv*, fol. 34ᵛ)

Item 1

An Diex! on pour - rai ie trou - ver

L'ome qui offri a prouver
que Dieu n'a riens eu firmament?
Ainz dit qu'il le fist estourer
pour ses oës mettre couver,
si le tient Diex mavesement.
Sur ce iure, s'il ne li rent,
q[u]'il le fera tel atourner
a un coq qui a non Climent
que nus ne li pourra donner

con - fort, se - cours n'a - le - ge - ment.

Item 2

En non Dieu, a - gace, a - ga - ce vous n'i fe - rez plus vo

Il n'est nul qui ne vous hace
Pour ce q'uns balais toussi
Quant on li dit: "Sans foace,"
Pour ce qu'il mit en sa nace
La granche [de] Rumegni.
Mes pour ce qu'il s'endormi
A l'issir d'une crevace,
Li dist le fours de Gaigni:
"Se [je] n'ai trios cops de hache,

vous n'i fe - rez plus vo ni."

Item 3

L'au-trier de-hors Pin- qui - gni vi un chat en -

- se - ve - li; dit que es - pou - se - ra lun - di.

Item 4

En Hel - le - quin le quin n'e - le en Hel - [e - quin Hel - le - quin]

EXAMPLE 3.1. (continued)

Item 5

El - les ont peux ou cul, nos da - mes.

Item 6

Tren - te qua - tre pez moy - sis, *etc.*

Item 7

Vos - tre be - le bou-che be - se - ra mon cul.

Item 8

Je vi lex pex de mon cul, en *etc.*

Item 9

Da - me, se vos fours est chaut, *etc.*

textual references that resonate with other contemporary poetic genres,[53] there are no precise literary or musical concordances for the collection. They are followed by a long lay cued to the Hellequin, which concludes with one final filthy refrain. We shall here be concerned with the "sotes chançons" on fol. 34ᵛ.

LISTENING TO THE "SOTES CHANÇONS"

At first glance the songs' lyrics seem filthy enough to be authentic, a view supported by a preliminary assessment of their melodic style—the majority are

53 Butterfield points out that a constellation of ideas from the third item—"chat," "Lundi," and "espousera"—resonate with a similar collection of themes in a collection of *fatrasie* from Arras, dating from the second half of the thirteenth century: "Uns chas emprist a plorer / Si que la mer en alume; / Un Juedi apres souper / La convint il une plume / Quatre truies espouser." See Uhl, "Les 'Sotes chançons' du *Roman de Fauvel* (MS E)," 391, quoting the *fatrasie* from Porter, *La Fatrasie et le fatras*, 123.

short, almost anti-melodic, rhythmically repetitive, and occupy a limited range of little more than a fifth. Small wonder some scholars have interpreted them as documenting contemporary Parisian street songs.[54] It is only when we look at the songs as a collection that a more contrived rationale emerges. The collection is a concentration of new poetic practices of the period that experiment with phonetic sound. In thinking about how genres such as *fatras* stretch poetry's semantic potential in favor of phonetics, Paul Zumthor identifies two categories of poetic nonsense that will be useful to keep in mind here. On the one hand, he illustrates that poetry can exhibit a "non-sense relatif," that is where an individual line may make sense, but where it has little or no connection to its larger context beyond rhyme.[55] On the other, it can also demonstrate "non-sens absolu," where a poetic line has no internal semantic logic, and where the privilege is simply sound. These categories of nonsense extend to the complete collection of "sotes chançons" on fol. 34ᵛ.

Taking their cue from the opening two *fatras*, a genre premised on rhyme sound rather than sense, the refrains experiment with how the phonetic may supplant the semantic. In the first *fatras* the privileging of the "-er," "-ent" rhymes, derived from the endings of the original refrains, is the connective agent of the newly inserted lines; note also the prominence of a secondary vowel sound "i" in the interpolated lines. The semantic effect is typical for a *fatras*: it is a form of "non-sens relatif" in terms of content, having a disjointed semantic effect that is overshadowed by the persisting rhyme sounds binding the whole together:

Item 1

An Diex! on pourrai ie trouver
l'ome qui offri a prouver
que Dieu n'a riens eu firmament?
Ainz dit qu'il le fist estourer
pour ses oës mettre couver,
si le tient Diex mavesement.

---

54 In an exploration of the charivari's connection to folkloric traditions, Margherita Lecco takes for granted the songs' connection to the social ritual, and as having correlations in songs sung in the streets during charivari. See "Lo charivari del *Roman de Fauvel*," 69.

55 Paul Zumthor, "Fatrasie et coq-à-l'âne (de Beaumanoir à Clément Marot)," in *Fin du Moyen Age et Renaissance: Mélanges de philologie française offerts à Robert Guiette* (Antwerp: Nederlandsche Boekhandel, 1961), 5–18. Zumthor explains the distinction between "non-sens relatif" and "non-sens absolu" at p. 12. For further examples of nonsense poetry, see Porter, *La Fatrasie et le fatras*, and *Burlesque et obscénité chez les troubadours: Pour une approche du contre-texte médiéval*, ed. Pierre Bec (Paris: Stock, 1984).

Sur ce iure, s'il ne li rent,
q[u]'il le fera tel atourner
a un coq qui a non Climent
que nus ne li pourra donner
confort, secours n'alegement.

Oh God! Where can I find
the man who offered to prove
that God has nothing in the firmament?
He says instead that he (God) made it
to start his geese hatching,
yet God governed it poorly.
On which he swears that, if he does not apologize,
he will have him treated in such a way
by a rooster named Climent
that no one will be able to give him
comfort, succor, or relief.[56]

The second *fatras* works by the same principle, built around the rhyme sounds
"ace" and "i" derived from its refrains. Note, too, how one of those lines picks up
on the secondary rhyme sound "i" from the first *fatras* as one of its structuring
rhymes. Now the semantic premise is even less secure, and the random assembly
of obscene imagery falls into Zumthor's category of "non-sens absolu":

Item 2

En non Dieu, agace, agace,
il n'est nul qui ne vous hace
pour ce q'uns balais toussi
quant on li dit: "Sans foace,"
pour ce qu'il mit en sa nace
la granche [de] Rumegni.
Mes pour ce qu'il s'endormi
a l'issir d'une crevace,
li dist le fours de Gaigni:
"Se [je] n'ai trios cops de hache,
vous n'i ferez plus vo ni."

In God's name, magpie, magpie,
there is no one who does not hate you

56 Translations for this and following songs in *The Monophonic Songs in the* Roman de
Fauvel, ed. Hans Tischler and Samuel Rosenberg (Lincoln, NE: University of Nebraska
Press, 1991), 125–31, with some minor adjustments.

because a broom coughed
when it was told: "I smell bread,"
because he pulled into his net
the barn of Rumegny.
But because he fell asleep
upon leaving a certain crack,
the oven of Gagny said to him:
"Unless I get three blows with an axe,
you will no longer make your nest here."

As we move from *fatras* to the fully melodic refrains (3–9), the phonetic continues its ascent. The ensuing refrains function like a melodic *fatras* as they are bound through strange leaps of semantic logic, and by the transference of vowel and rhyme sounds across the disparate group. Linguistic sound is the dominant effect in item 3 as the lyrics echo the preceding *fatras* with their obsessive play upon the "i" vowel:

Item 3

L'autrier dehors Pinquigni
vi un chat enseveli;
dit qu'espousera lundi.

The other day outside Pinquigny,
I saw a cat buried;
he said he would marry Monday.

The remaining one-line refrains engage in intense play and movement of sound and sense back and forth between refrains. Item 4 takes the phonetic privilege of language to its limits, in untranslatable rotation of the syllables of Hellequin:

En Hellequin le quin n'ele en Hel[equin Hellequin]

We may hear this revolving pattern more thematically: in the adjacent image, Hellequin's entourage is seen riding in the famous "civiere" associated with the demon—a contraption with no front or back, which thus moves forwards and backwards simultaneously. The topsy-turvy lyrics, verging on the palindromic, take on new meaning as the linguistic equivalent to Hellequin's cart. And the connection operates at a deeper, metaphorical level too: here Hellequin is responsible not merely for the introduction of disturbing, fantastical realms into the real world; in a linguistic sense, now, he is the engineer of semantic confusion, replacing sense with pure, sonorous nonsense. That semantic chaos spills out to the ensuing refrains. The next item (5) begins with "elles," echoing the "elle" heard in the Hellequin refrain. The image of "cul" in that refrain gives rise to the image of "pez" in item 6 that reverts to "cul" in item 7, finally bringing them both together in item 8, "Je ci les peus de mon cul." The final item 9, "<u>Dames</u>, de vos fours," returns us to the opening of the generative sequence, picking up on the last word of item 5 ("Elles ont peux ou cul, nos <u>dames</u>.")

Item 5

Elles ont peux ou cul, nos dames.

Our ladies have lice in the ass.

Item 6

Trente quatre pez moysis, etc.

Thirty-four moldy farts, etc.

Item 7

Vostre bele bouche besera mon cul.

Your beautiful mouth will kiss my ass.

Item 8

Je vi lex pex de mon cul, etc.

I saw the lice in my ass, etc.

Item 9

Dame, se vos fours est chaut, etc.

Lady if your oven is hot, etc.

Poetry here finds the ideal means to stage charivari. In audible ways it recreates "noise" by diminishing language's semantic content in favor of the phonetic. But at a deeper level, by appearing to protest its own semantic premise, it finds another kind of equivalence for charivari's intention. Turning our ear to the melodies, we discover music to be engaged in an audible challenge to its normal regulators. What are these songs exactly? Are they individual refrains, or do they constitute a whole? While the preceding investigation of the poetry suggests connections across the group, does that amount to a "composition"? Viewed from a melodic perspective, the songs pose an ontological question about the very nature of music and of musical composition.

The scribe offers the first clue that each line is regarded as its own individual entity. At the end of several lines, he writes "etc.," suggesting that the melodies are snippets or refrains—that is, extracted from something larger.

The songs are thus a medley of self-sufficient items. Yet like the poetry, they are not without connections. We shall set aside the first *fatras* for a moment (it has a genealogy independent of its companions to which we shall return). From the second *fatras* on down the folio, the songs inhabit the same musical space, which loosely centers around a 5th mode F final, reinforced by consistent emphasis of the attendant and related note C. At the risk of imposing tonal language more modern, the entire collection asserts a powerful sense of an F–A–C triad, as without exception each refrain enters on one of those notes. For the most part, they nearly all remain in the limited melodic spectrum of the fifth. The exception is item 7, which extends c′–f′, thus opening up the upper end of the modal spectrum. In one sense, then, the songs make sense together, and to sing them through is to hear an uncanny sense of relationship between them. Yet from the perspective of the different syllable counts, the absence of fixed rhyme scheme, shifting rhythmic patterns between refrains, and, most fundamental, the absence of coherent melodic conjunctions between endings and beginnings of refrains, the overall effect is of profound musical disjunction. They give the impression of a sonic jigsaw whose pieces have been jumbled up. Put another way, they are a form of musical "non-sens relatif."

Aside from questions of genre and compositional coherence, the collection poses an even more fundamental question about the nature of song. The opening two *fatras*, as examples of "semi-lyric," test the very category of the singing voice. As Butterfield observes of this and related genres in *Fauv*, they pose a basic problem of performance. How is one supposed to "sing" these pieces? Only the first and last lines are notated with music, while the graphic impression of music-less lines reinforces the sense of them as vocally "hybrid." The conclusion is to imagine something half spoken and half sung: neither fully one voice nor another. From the audible perspective, the "sotes chançons" are the ideal embodiment of charivari for their fundamental questioning of familiar categories: speech and song; poetry and music; sense and sound. However, the charivaric dimension does not end in sound alone. Perhaps the most subversive aspect of the songs concerns their challenge to concepts of genre and taxonomy.

THE "SOTES CHANÇONS" AND MISCATEGORIZATION

The collection opens with an illusion of generic specificity, cuing the songs as "sotes chançons."[57] "Sotes chançons" is in one sense an accurate

57 The cue also describes the song sung by the Hellequines as a "lai," a designation repeated in a second cue directly over the song on fol. 34ᵛ. Like the "sotes chançons," the cue "lai" leads to a series of generic contradictions played out with the song's self-designation as a "descort."

description: they are "foolish songs" in terms of their obscene and nonsensical content. However, *sottes chansons* was deployed as a generic tag in at least two other contemporary lyric collections and designated songs quite different in form and content from ours.[58] The implication of mis-cuing is intensified by the fact that the tag is followed by a classifiable genre—*fatras*.[59] This makes the codifying gesture not merely vague, but blatantly incorrect. While it may be the mis-cuing was accidental, it is also possible, indeed likely, that the makers were aware of the contradictory generic implications. For *Fauv* is, more than most manuscripts of this period, obsessively specific in its formal designations, as is evident in the presence at its opening of a detailed table of contents, organized by musical genre. Within the *roman*, the different genres are deployed for narrative ends: so, for instance, the choice to have Fortuna sing Latin conductus—by now a "classic," even antique register amid the Old French lyrics brayed by her suitor, Fauvel—adds a witty twist to her persona— a moralizing voice disguised as a courtly lover. *Fauv* is also actively concerned with transforming and experimenting with genre, and especially with the semi-lyrics.

Fauv is also symptomatic of deep engagement with issues of taxonomy and genre beyond the bindings of the manuscript among composers, poets, and theoreticians.[60] In the thirteenth and fourteenth centuries, the question of the criteria by which one determined the genre was topic of practical debate.[61]

---

58 Oxford, Bodleian Library, Douce 308 and Paris, Bibliothèque nationale de France, f. fr. 24432. Both collections are edited, with an detailed prefatory essay exploring their formal and linguistic features, as well as the usage of the generic tag, in *Deux recueils de sottes chansons: Bodléienne, Douce 308 et Bibliothèque Nationale, fr. 24432*, ed. Arthur Långfors, Annales Academiae Scientiarum Fennicae, BLIII, 4 (Helsinki: [s.n.], 1945). The poems, contrary to the suggestion of their generic label, are void of the scatological or nonsensical content of the songs in *Fauvel*. Långfors argues, though, that the poems are premised on parody, and "pour fonction de faire rire" (at 4), by virtue of their burlesque-like exaggeration of the language and themes of the venerable tradition of *grand chant*. For additional discussion of the *sottes chansons*, and their connection to the poetic genre of *fatrasie*, see Bec, *La Lyrique française*, 167–83, esp. 173–74.

59 As with *sottes chansons*, the term *fatras* appears as a cue to songs that behave as the two opening songs in *Fauvel*. For example, a collection of *fatras* attributed to Wartriquet de Couvin and one "Raimmondin" and dating from the first quarter of the fourteenth century cues them as "li fastras." The manuscript in question is Paris, Bibliothèque nationale de France, f. fr. 14968. For further information see Porter, *La Fatrasie et le fatras*, 145–59.

60 On the lyric context for generic differentiation, in the particular context of the refrain, see Butterfield, *Poetry and Music in Medieval France*, esp. 75–102.

61 For an excellent account of the criteria of genre among theorists of troubadour and trouvère traditions see Elizabeth Aubrey, "Genre as a Determinant of Melody in the Songs

Poetic treatises of the north and south classified songs in terms of their themes or "material," as well as by aspects of their formal organization.[62] On the other hand, we have seen how a treatise like Johannes de Grocheio's *De musica* sought to codify contemporary genres not only by their technical aspects, but also by ethical and social function and meaning.[63]

It is in such contexts that we may wish to think about acts of miscategorization. If genre is determined by "material," then "sotes chançons" is an apt descriptive tag for the songs. But if it cues also formal content and procedure, what ensues fails to follow the expectations of *sottes chansons* and offers instead the formal characteristics of *fatras*, at least in the first two items. Meanwhile, read through a Grocheian lens, the generic contradictions may suggest that the songs evade or overturn a system that seeks to establish not just musical but perhaps also social order. This may also explain the absence of the "sotes chançons" in the index of the manuscript. Their experimental nature, playing with categories of speech and song as well as genre, means they are literally unclassifiable according to existing forms:[64] their very evasion of classification situates them outside the orthodoxy of a formal generic system. What more fitting category, then, than the uncategorizable to make a charivari?

The mis-cue is also part of a complex musical investigation of genre as a compositional convention. The very first song on fol. 34ᵛ, *An Diex*, is the culmination of a narrative of generic transformation and degeneration that plays

---

of the Troubadours and Trouvères," in *Medieval Lyric: Genres in Historical Context*, ed. William Paden (Urbana: University of Illinois Press, 2000), 273–96.

62 The late thirteenth-century Occitan treatise *Doctrina de compondre dictats* describes songs in terms of their topics or themes, and explains how the musical and poetic features reflect the topic. Thus, for example, the "descort" is not simply about discord in love; its melody can also be discordant, "implying that the contour of the melody, like its text, should develop in an unexpected or displeasing way." The treatise reads as follows: "If you wish to make a *descort*, you must speak of love like a man who is distressed by it or a man who cannot have pleasure from his lady and lives in torment. And when this is sung, whenever the tune ought to rise, let it be low; and it does the opposite of all other songs. And it must have three stanzas and one or two tornadas and a refrain. And you can put one or two more words in one stanza than in another, to make it more discordant." See Aubrey, "Genre as a Determinant," 282.

63 On which see Judith Peraino, "Re-Placing Medieval Music," *Journal of the American Musicological Society* 54 (2001): 209–64.

64 The problem is true also for modern editors. As Ardis Butterfield notes, the modern tally of the monophonic songs in *Fauvel* varies considerably, reflecting the generic ambiguity of certain songs. See Butterfield, "The Refrain and the Transformation of Genre," 105.

across the whole manuscript.[65] That *fatras* derives the music and text of its refrains from the motetus of a three-part French motet. The original three-part motet survives in the early fourteenth-century Brussels rotulus (Brussels, Bibliothèque Royale 19606) with a Latin tenor, *Displicebat ei*, an Old French motetus, *An diex*, from which our refrains are borrowed, and a Latin triplum, *Trahunt in precipicia*, part of whose text is based on an older conductus poem.[66] The same motet, in an expanded version, appears earlier in *Fauv* on fol. 6ᵛ (see example 3.2 for the opening measures). There, the original three-part motet was supplemented with a fourth voice, with the Latin text *Quasi non ministerium*; and, to complicate matters, the Old French motetus text, *An diex*, was replaced with a moralizing Latin text, *Ve qui gregi*, a patchwork of two earlier thirteenth-century conductus, one of which is attributable to Philip the Chancellor.[67] In the instantiation as motet, and through its conjunction through texting as conductus, the melody acquires utmost authority by association with the two most highly prized genres of the period. From here, though, a pattern of degeneration commences.

The original French-texted motetus, *An diex*, was not discarded in *Fauv*, and appears in monophonic form (with the same melody, and in the same

65 The complicated contexts and concordances for this song and its hosts were first collated in *L'Hérésie de Fauvel*, ed. Emilie Dahnk, Leipziger Romanistiche Studien 4 (Leipzig: Vogel 1935), li–lxvi.

66 The text only of its motetus voice (including scratched beneath it the Latin tenor designation, indicating therefore that its scribe knew the text from its polyphonic form) survives in the flyleaf of a contemporary monastic manuscript. Ernest Hoepffner first connected these texts, copied in a flyleaf of Paris, Bibliothèque nationale de France, lat. 7682 (although he did not see or note the Latin tenor designation copied beneath it), and connected it to the larger musical context of the motet in *Fauvel*. See his "Chansons françaises du XIIIᵉ siècle (*Ay Dex! ou porrey jen trouver*)," *Romania* 47 (1921): 367–80. The song also contains refrains connecting it to Nevelon d'Amien's *Dit d'Amour*, and also to a monophonic song by Jehan de Lescurel, *Gracieus temps est*, copied in *Fauv*. The *Dit d'Amour* is transcribed in Alfred Jeanroy, "Trois dits d'amour du XIIIᵉ siècle," *Romania* 22 (1893): 45–70, at 54–58. For more on the networks surrounding *An diex*, see Butterfield, "Refrain and the Transformation of Genre," 111–12 and 146–51, and her *Poetry and Music in Medieval France*, 207–9.

67 It quotes with minor adjustments from stanza 4 of *Ve mundo a scandalis* (transmitted in *F*, fol. 426ʳ, as a monophonic conductus) and stanzas 2 and 3 from *Trine vocis tripudio* (transmitted in *F*, fol. 205ʳ and *W1*, fol. 75ᵛ as a three-part conductus), which is also quoted in part of the triplum. Editions may be found in *Notre-Dame and Related Conductus*, ed. Gordon Anderson, 10 vols. (Henryville, PA: Institute of Mediaeval Music, 1979–). A modern edition of the four-part motet appears in *The Roman de Fauvel, The Works of Philippe de Vitry, French Cycles of the Ordinarium missae*, ed. Leo Schrade, Polyphonic Music of the Fourteenth Century 1, with a separate volume of commentary (Monaco: Editions de l'Oiseau-Lyre, 1956; repr. 1984 with a new introduction by Edward H. Roesner).

EXAMPLE 3.2. *Quasi non ministerium/Trahunt in precipicia/Ve qui gregi/Displicebat ei,* mm. 1–7 (*Fauv,* fol. 6ᵛ)

notational language as appears on fol. 6ᵛ) on fol. 26ᵛ (see figure 3.6, and example 3.3 for the opening section).[68] Here it is cued as a "motet enté" and is positioned in the voice of Fauvel, who sings it to woo Fortuna. However, the melody undergoes an important transformation. The original line is fractured, literally "enté." The term *enté* denoted a practice of creating something by either splitting material apart or joining it with new material. As Ardis Butterfield has argued, in literary usage it is connected to the use of refrains, and specifically is "a process of splitting apart refrains and then splicing the fragments to larger sections of text and melody."[69] On fol. 26ᵛ, the original

68 For a complete edition see *The Monophonic Songs,* 97–100.

69 Butterfield, *Poetry and Music in Medieval France,* 227–28; see also her "*Enté*: A Survey and Reassessment of the Term in Thirteenth- and Fourteenth-Century Music and Poetry," *Early Music History* 22 (2003): 67–101. For more on the usage of the term "motet enté" see Mark Everist, *French Motets in the Thirteenth Century: Music, Poetry, and Genre*

FIGURE 3.6. Paris, Bibliothèque nationale de France, f. fr. 146, fol. 26ᵛ. By permission of the Bibliothèque nationale de France

melodic line of the motet is cut into refrain-like sections, with new lines of poetry inserted in between each snippet to create a hybrid or semi-lyric form, similar in concept to the *fatras*. That is, the rhyme endings of the refrains generate the intervening lines of spoken poetry. However, situated in the larger context of refrain songs, the other crucial feature here is that the song overturns the normal procedure of melding musical refrains and lyric poetry

---

(Cambridge: Cambridge University Press, 1994), 81–89, and for an insightful analysis of the term as it relates to the "motet" on fol. 26ᵛ see Judith Peraino, "Monophonic Motets: Sampling and Grafting in the Middle Ages," *Musical Quarterly* 85 (2001): 644–80.

together. As Butterfield explains, whereas single refrains are normally imported into poetry to make larger lyric units, here they turn the process "inside out": "the refrains are not grafted into the work so much as created out of a process of splitting apart another work" (that is, the motet voice from which they derive).[70] The strangeness of this topsy-turvy procedure is reinforced by the vocal effect of rupture conjured by the semi-lyric contrast of speech and song. The narrative context only confirms the sense of generic upset: it is sung by the wicked Fauvel, who here is depicted in his "double" guise—horse-headed and man lower body in one miniature, the order reversed in the other.[71] The hybrid effect of song broken by speech is a fitting voice for such monstrosity.

It is against that backdrop of transformations and generic instability occurring in the motetus voice's movement from fol. 6ᵛ to fol. 26ᵛ that we may hear the final rendition of *An diex* on fol. 34ᵛ. Read chronologically, across the book, the refrain's story is one of downward mobility, through genres and linguistic registers: it begins as part of a motet, the "highest" genre of the group, moves through the hybrid, generically experimental semi-lyric, and ends up now as a *fatras*, spawning poetic nonsense. And what ensues in items 4–9 seems to be a parodic finale to its story. Situating those refrains as conclusion to this narrative of degeneration now offers further insight into their compositional status. For rather as the poetry of the refrains atomized language to uncloak its barest, phonetic essentials, so may the refrain's journey be similarly revelatory. The passage of *An Diex* through the manuscript witnesses the process of a

---

70 Butterfield, *Poetry and Music in Medieval France*, 212.

71 On the changing forms of Fauvel and the implications of his hybridity, see Michael Camille, "Hybridity, Monstrosity, and Bestiality in the *Roman de Fauvel*," in *Fauvel Studies*, ed. Bent and Wathey, 161–74.

whole polyphonic composition reducing to the smallest possible compositional unit: the refrain. By its arrival on fol. 34ᵛ, the little melody has nowhere else to go, musically speaking, and can reduce no further. And yet, this is not the narrative's end. For as we saw, the compositional unit begins to replicate itself in the refrains that spiral into an unruly heap at the bottom of the folio. The sense that each refrain engenders the next is emphasized in the poetry each carries, where, as we have seen, phonic atoms leap from line to line. But in a creative sense, the brood of refrains is profoundly unsettling, for they do not "fit" together in a compositional sense, and even as they sound related, they remain compositionally discrete from one another. Hearing their disjointedness now against the larger framework of generic manipulation, they take on a different meaning. Here they are void of any utility, and lacking the careful attention of compositional grafting—an *enté* whose components fail to "take" to one another—they contravene the usual function of refrain, indeed of genre altogether. As the story of *An diex* illustrates, refrains are normally part of something larger, grafted into, extracted out of, larger pieces of music, and put to work to make new pieces. At the end of fol. 34ᵛ, they cease to behave, and are thus rendered generically sterile as they flout musical sense with their continued production down the folio. The songs may not sound like charivari, but in their generic context, they do not simply reveal the anatomy of musical composition, they also shatter its accepted limits.

CHARIVARI AND THE SUPERMUSICAL

As the preceding discussion has sought to illustrate, the "sotes chançons'" charivaric power lies in audible and inaudible dimensions of meaning, each with connotations of the supermusical. The nature of that effect may be illuminated by ties to the hallmark genre of the supermusical—the motet. For in certain ways, not least through the collection's citational route back to a motet host, the songs exhibit qualities that are distinctly motetish. In their arrangement within the narrative and visual layout of fol. 34ᵛ, they perform the role of a kind of anti-polyphony. In the narrator's fiction of reality, and in the illuminator's crowded depictions of the street, the songs represent as a kind of sonic snapshot—of things heard overlapping and simultaneously in the frenzied ritual. The fact that each song-unit is marked off with the customary decorated capital used in the manuscript to designate a new voice or song adds to the visual impression that these are all part of one monstrous chorus. But aside from those silent cues of the supermusical, it is in their dismemberment of language for its sonic properties—the sheer effect of their nonsensical babble—that the charivaric soundscape encroaches on and overlaps with what is heard amplified in motets. Such a relationship is mutually reinforcing, and it adds to the range of revelatory, ethical, and social meanings encoded in the supermusical effect.

In the next chapter, we shall trace a path of meaningful nonsense heard in the "sotes chançons" back into the field of and around the vernacular motet. Here, the supermusical will find a quite different interlocutor, although one no less concerned with the revelation and protest of social boundaries: the sonority of madness.

4 | Madness and the Eloquence of Nonsense

In this chapter, we examine a sonority that surpasses the creative and social boundaries explored so far. Our starting point is a figure on the fringe of society: the madman. Along with other medieval outcasts, from the wondrous races believed to inhabit spaces at the edge of the world to the poverty-stricken beggars who clattered at the periphery of cities, the madman was traditionally distinguished by a particular kind of sonority, one rooted in nonsense. Yet as we shall hear, he also possessed a unique eloquence, his powers of communication capable of profound revelation. The madman will be revelatory, too, of a particular kind of linguistic effect, and in exploring the sense of madness, we will enter into realms of poetic sound, and specifically those pertaining to poetry's most distinguishing phonetic aspect: rhyme.

Our guide through madness is Adam de la Halle, as famous to musicologists as he is to literary scholars, producing in addition to literary works like the *Jeu de Robin et Marion* and our topic here, the *Jeu de la feuillée*, a substantial corpus of motets, chansons, and rondeaux.[1] As we shall hear, Adam's musical facility manifests also as a sensitivity to the sonority of poetry. In the expressive in-between of words and music he constructed his most monstrous, loquacious, and ultimately eloquent creation. As with the madmen of later literary

---

1 Edition and translation of the literary works and musical lyrics are given in Adam de la Halle, *Œuvres complètes*, ed. and transl. Pierre-Yves Badel (Paris: Livre de Poche, 1995). For editions of the musical works, see *The Lyric Works of Adam de la Hale*, ed. Nigel Wilkins, Corpus mensurabilis musicae 44 (Dallas: American Institute of Musicology, 1967); see too *The Lyrics and Melodies of Adam de la Halle*, ed. and transl. Deborah Hubbard Nelson, melodies ed. Hendrik van der Werf, Garland Library of Medieval Literature 24 (New York: Garland, 1985). For an account of Adam's life and music see Jean Maillard, *Adam de la Halle: Perspective musicale* (Paris: Honoré Champion, 1982).

history, Adam's dervé was endowed with visionary, truth-telling qualities. And when we have heard what he had to say to his community in the *Jeu de la feuillée*, we shall follow him a little further, and listen to how he might also reveal something about the meaning of nonsense in the domain of the supermusical. To begin, though, a walk among the stranger constituencies of the Middle Ages will attune us to the meanings and registers associated with the insane.

Sound at the Edge: Madmen, Monsters, Wildmen, and Marvelous "Others"

The madman and fools of medieval culture take their place in a large cast of marvelous "Others." These range from hybrid shape-shifters, werewolves, the so-called "monstrous races" or "marvelous people" believed to reside in spaces at the edge of the map, to wildmen such as Hellequin, who hailed from realms more metaphysical.[2] They had cousins in the known world, too, among beggars, lepers, prostitutes—those peripheral physically as well as psychologically

2 See especially *The Monstrous Middle Ages*, ed. Bettina Bildhauer and Robert Mills (Toronto: University of Toronto Press, 2003); Jeffrey Cohen, *Of Giants: Sex, Monsters, and the Middle Ages*, Medieval Cultures 17 (Minneapolis: University of Minnesota Press, 1999); John Block Friedman, *The Monstrous Races in Medieval Art and Thought* (Cambridge, MA: Harvard University Press, 1981); *Marvels, Monsters, and Miracles: Studies in the Medieval and Early Modern Imaginations*, ed. Timothy Jones and David Sprunger, Studies in Medieval Culture 42 (Kalamazoo: Medieval Institute Publications, 2002); and David Williams, *Deformed Discourse: The Function of the Monster in Mediaeval Thought and Literature* (Montreal: McGill–Queen's University Press, 1996). On medieval representations of madness see Penelope Doob, *Nebuchadnezzar's Children: Conventions of Madness in Middle English Literature* (New Haven: Yale University Press, 1974); Sylvia Huot, *Madness in Medieval French Literature: Identities Lost and Found* (Oxford: Oxford University Press, 2003); Barbara Swain, *Fools and Folly during the Middle Ages and the Renaissance* (New York: Columbia University Press, 1932); Enid Welsford, *The Fool: His Social and Literary History* (London: Faber, 1968, first published 1935); and *The Fool and the Trickster: Studies in Honour of Enid Welsford*, ed. Paul Williams (Cambridge: D. S. Brewer, 1979). For discussion of medieval maps, see ch. 2, 65, and for the place of the marvelous races in the mapping tradition see Alison Peden, "Medieval Concepts of the Antipodes," *History Today* 45 (1995): 27–33. On werewolves see Asa Simon Mittman, "The Other Close at Hand: Gerald of Wales and the 'Marvels of the West,'" in *The Monstrous Middle Ages*, ed. Bildhauer and Mills, 97–112. See also Bynum, *Metamorphosis and Identity*, which includes examples of werewolves as a lens through which to explore medieval ideas about transformation and identity.

to society.[3] This wondrous collective was bound by a shared challenge to the category of humanness, stretching it either psychologically or physiologically. For example, those shown in world maps and detailed in texts such as Pliny's *Natural History* were located within a hierarchy of humanity: thus they were explicitly related in the genealogy of God and humans, and "alternatively (or even simultaneously) human and sub-human, saved and cursed, rational and savage."[4] The in-betweenness of category, far from denying them agency and meaning, imbued them with revelatory potential, be it to mediate the relationship of humans to the divine, or, as we saw with the hairy revelers and Wildman of the charivari, to shatter social codes. The madman was no less meaning-laden, even as his condition was marked as a loss of reason.

The diagnosis, sources, and genealogy of madness in the Middle Ages illuminate the revelatory power of the insane. In medical traditions exemplified by the likes of Galen, madness was explained as humoral imbalance, leading to a range of psychological outcomes, most commonly mania or melancholy.[5] Common also was a view of madness linked to natural phenomena—the seasonal or lunar cycle—while supernatural causes were another factor, with madness often attributed to demonic possession or moral upset. Madmen cover a broad moral spectrum reflecting the range of provocations, from the biblical "insipiens" of the Psalms[6] to the association of monastics and hermits with the mad and wildmen on account of their austere withdrawal from society,[7] to the melancholic Yvain,[8] to dangerous and violent demoniacs. Yet as with their cohort of the marvelous, the mad were also valued for their efficacious qualities. Although many now question the historical accuracy of Foucault's formulation of the mad as respected and socially accepted for their divine

3 Bronisław Geremek, *The Margins of Medieval Society in Late Medieval Paris*, transl. Jean Birrell (Cambridge: Cambridge University Press, 1987).

4 Paul Freedman, "The Medieval Other: The Middle Ages as Other," in *Marvels, Monsters, and Miracles*, ed. Jones and Sprunger, 1–24, at 3. See also Greta Austin, "Marvelous Peoples or Marvelous Races? Race and the Anglo-Saxon Wonders of the East," ibid., 25–50 .

5 Stanley Jackson, "Unusual Mental States in Medieval Europe I. Medical Syndromes of Mental Disorder: 400–1100 A.D," *Journal of the History of Medicine and Allied Sciences* 27 (1972): 262–97, and Doob, *Nebuchadnezzar's Children*, esp. 11–30.

6 Doob, *Nebuchadnezzar's Children*, 32–33, and for the "insipens," the denier of God commonly depicted in illuminations of Psalms 14 and 53, see Douglas Gifford, "Iconographical Notes towards a Definition of the Medieval Fool," in *The Fool and the Trickster*, ed. Williams, 18–35.

7 John Saward, *Perfect Fools: Folly for Christ's Sake in Catholic and Orthodox Spirituality* (Oxford: Oxford University Press, 1980), esp. 48–79.

8 Anne Hunsaker Hawkins, "Yvain's Madness," *Philological Quarterly* 71 (1992): 377–97.

insights,[9] the revelatory facility of many representations of madness seems indisputable, especially when situated in the broader context of the marvelous. A counter view to Foucault's needs to be considered too: that many representations emphasize the sometimes violent dissociation of the insane from their social environment. If the madman's currency was not always divine, his uneasy relationship to civilized society made him particularly suited to unsettling its foundations, and madness was often depicted as a "shattering . . . [of] social codes as an attempt to get behind them."[10]

What, then, of the symptoms of madness, and especially its sound? Sound is an identifier of the marvelous, and in the case of the madman, it is an essential outward marker of a condition that is otherwise interior or psychological.[11] Greta Austin notes that depictions of monstrous races implied their relationship to human category by virtue of their speech gestures: in other words, they were not irrational beasts, but possessed the capacity for language of their human relatives.[12] Language is also often a facet of the madman's identity, or rather his loss of speech. In its place is either raving clamor, associated with mania, or withdrawn silence, in the case of melancholics. Another sonic identifier is the fool-stick (this would later become the jester's staff)—the characteristic club, to which bells or a rattle might be attached.[13] The sound of the rattle or noisemaker had plenty of audible correlations among other social outcasts, especially associated with beggars and lepers. Like other sounds we have encountered, these were the audible identifiers of a social group. But in the case of the madman, his revelatory function was often explicitly tied to his sound, and especially, as we shall see, to his language. There is, moreover, a musical theme to insanity: namely, the familiar trope of music's curative powers. Sander Gilman traces the thread of thought connecting music's power to temper the

9 Michel Foucault, *Madness and Civilization: A History of Insanity in the Age of Reason*, transl. Richard Howard (London: Routledge, 2001), originally published in French in 1961. For critiques of Foucault on medieval madness see Stephen Harper, " 'So Euyl to Rewlyn': Madness and Authority in *The Book of Margery Kemp*," *Neuphilologische Mitteilungen* 98 (1998): 53–61, at 55, and Huot, *Madness in Medieval French Literature*, 4–5.

10 Hawkins, "Yvain's Madness," 389.

11 David Sprunger, "Depicting the Insane: A Thirteenth-Century Case Study," in *Marvels, Monsters, and Miracles*, ed. Jones and Sprunger, 223–41, at 226.

12 Austin, "Marvelous Peoples or Marvelous Races?," 42–43.

13 William McDonald, "The Fool-Stick: Concerning Tristan's Club in the German Eilhart Tradition," *Euphorion* 82 1988): 127–49; Philippe Menard, "Les Emblèmes de la folie dans la littérature et dans l'art (XIIe–XIIIe siècles)," in *Hommage à Jean-Charles Payen. 'Farai chansoneta novele': Essais sur la liberté créatrice au Moyen Age* (Caen: Centre de publications de l'Université de Caen, 1989), 253–65; and Sprunger, "Depicting the Insane," esp. 233, for a description of fool-sticks appended with a bladder of peas to make a rattle.

body, and to cure mania.[14] In what follows, we shall see another affinity between madness and music: an affinity born at their shared frontier of sound and sense.

The Eloquent Madman in the Jeu de la feuillée

Adam de la Halle's dervé is an unprecedented representation of madness in a play notorious for transgressing formal and generic expectations. To understand his pivotal role, some broader contextualization is necessary, especially so given his intricate connection to the play's subversive social thematics, and to its highly unusual uses of sound. The *Jeu*, dated around 1276 and the earliest extant secular play from this period, may seem a startling subject for a musicologist, for unlike contemporary romances and later secular plays, it is virtually void of song.[15] Yet, as we shall hear, it is highly attuned to the sonorities of its characters and environment.

The play takes its name from a well-known myth concerning the visit of three fairies to Arras, Adam's home town. They appeared in the same spot every year, a small glade in a wood, or *feuillée*. But the fairies are a miraculous interruption in a play primarily concerned with the social politics of Arras, and Adam's poetic identity within that community. It opens with Adam's lengthy address to his friends, Riquier, Hane, and Guillot: he is a wreck, a broken pot, his potential smashed by the corruption of the city. He announces that he will leave for Paris, there to learn the true craft of poetry. His friends and father, Henri, attempt to dissuade him, reminding him not least of his duties to his wife, Maroie. Adam's dilemma forms the essential plot, but the action is constantly interrupted by the comings and goings of gossip-mongering locals: a doctor, the local prostitute, a relic-touting monk, and, most memorably, a young madman, the dervé, trailed by his harried father. On their departure, the fantastical begins to encroach on the local. The clattering Croquesot, emissary of Hellequin and his death army, appears and transmits a courtly missive to one of three fairies on behalf of his master. The fairies, disinterested in the second-hard courtship, settle themselves at a table laid for them by Adam. Two are delighted by their welcome, but the third fairy, Maglore, is furious at a breach of courtly manners: she is missing a knife from her place-setting.

---

14 Sander Gilman, *Disease and Representation: Images of Illness from Madness to AIDS* (Ithaca: Cornell University Press, 1988), esp. 31–32.

15 The play is edited with a French translation in *Œuvres complètes*, 284–375. For an English translation and commentary see Gordon Douglas McGregor, *The Broken Pot Restored: Le Jeu de la feuillée of Adam de la Halle*, The Edward C. Armstrong Monographs on Medieval Literature 6 (Lexington, KY: French Forum, 1991).

She retaliates by putting a curse on Adam, condemning him to life in Arras. In the third and final scene, the action moves seamlessly back into Artesian reality with the fairies' departure. The characters reassemble at the local tavern for drinking, debating, and laughter. Yet at the play's end, Maglore's curse seems eerily fulfilled, for Adam remains in Arras.

If the play feels fantastically strange to a modern audience, the abundant scholarship it has provoked among literary historians can sometimes feel stranger still. This includes psychoanalytical interpretations of father–son relationships in the play, and harebrained archival investigations into the spot where the fairies originally appeared.[16] Some more convincing work relocates the strange work both in terms of the poetics of Adam's corpus and its relationship to the social setting of late thirteenth-century Arras. The play expresses a dilemma familiar in many of Adam's works: creative angst about whether to stay in Arras and endure its corruption, or to leave for Paris, the seat of clerkly learning and wisdom. Entwined with this is the question of Adam's wife, Maroie: if he were to leave her he would also be jeopardizing the source of his lyric inspiration. Adam himself reinforces her status as one-time courtly muse as he runs through a parodic checklist of her now-dissipating attributes.[17] Thus, as Frederick Langley and Sylvia Huot have argued,[18] communal and poetic identity are intertwined in the play: when the community is unsettled, so is the social order that ensures the stability of Adam's essential subject matter of love. Conversely, failure or deceit in love leads to communal disharmony.

From Adam's restlessness to leave his hometown to the tolling of the bells of the local church of St. Nicholas at the end of the play, the city of Arras is a vital—and audible—character in the drama.[19] In her recent book *A Common Stage*, Carol Symes relocates theatrical productions such as the *Jeu* in the context of Arras's highly developed world of civic rituals.[20] Many aspects of the play's action, locales, and characters connect to realities of the city, and especially the fluid boundaries between the church and city people. The "feuillée"

16 The earlier scholarship on the *Jeu* is summarized by Jean Dufournet, "Adam de la Halle et le *Jeu de la feuillée*," *Romania* 86 (1965): 199–245, esp. 199–200.

17 See especially *Jeu*, vv. 51–74 and 81–174.

18 Sylvia Huot, "Transformations of Lyric Voice in the Songs, Motets, and Plays of Adam de la Halle," *Romanic Review* 78 (1987): 148–64, and Frederick Langley, "Community Drama and Community Politics in Thirteenth-Century Arras: Adam de la Halle's *Jeu de la feuillée*," in *Drama and Community: People and Plays in Medieval Europe*, ed. Alan Hindley (Turnhout: Brepols, 1999), 57–75.

19 *Jeu*, vv. 1097–98: "Let's go! The bells of St. Nicholas are starting to toll" ("S'en irons. A saint Nicholai / Commenche a sonner des cloquetes") .

20 Symes, *A Common Stage*. See esp. ch. 4, "Relics and Rites: 'The Play of the Bower' and Other Plays," 183–231.

of the title itself is the clearest symbol of the play's close relationship to its environment. "Feuillées" were literally bowers, makeshift and temporary constructions, decked with foliage, and associated with social gatherings and hospitality.[21] In Arras, there was a specific tradition of "fueillies" in the city's Petit Marché. In this space associated with the city's merchants, the cathedral of Notre Dame commissioned each year from 1221 between Pentecost and Assumption construction of a bower for display of their Marian relics (or "fietre").[22] That bower was at times the site of ferocious altercation between different social groups of Arras, and especially between the monks and canons of the city, and if allusion to the bower in the *Jeu* suggested connection to the site in the Marché, it may thus also have conjured recollection of its associated controversies. There are other echoes of reality more closely connected to Adam's circle. References to a "puy" in the *Jeu* relate not to a singing context among trouvères, as is often reported in musicological accounts.[23] There is in fact no evidence of such practices in Arras. Rather, the term is used interchangeably with the Carité of Arras—a confraternity of jongleurs hosted by the city's cathedral of Notre Dame.

There is one final social resonance to keep in mind. Hinted at by characters such as Hellequin, whom we have seen connected to rituals of charivari, the city of Adam's creation appears to be home to marital intrigues. Although charivari is evidently neither a staged event, nor even referred to by the characters, recurring themes of social unrest invite its performance. As Eugene Vance writes: "Though the *Jeu de la feuillée* may not, itself, give rise to the limited or discrete form of charivari as a modern social scientist would recognize it, the play does posit all the preconditions, both psychic and social, that favor (if not command) the condensation of charivari as an explicit form of social behaviour."[24] While Hellequin is the most explicit cue, Vance detects the charivaric primarily in the sexual undertones that ripple throughout the play. The very opening lines of the play are its essential summons, as Adam threatens to abandon his wife, Maroie, to become a clerk in Paris. But Adam is not the only one guilty of charivari-inducing behavior. Arras abounds with sexual scandal. We learn that Dame Douce the prostitute is pregnant by Adam's married companion, Riquier, while a lengthy diatribe by Maître Henri on bigamy among Artesian clerks plays into the charivaric undertones.[25]

The quasi-autobiographical nature of the play, the references to known locales, to the city's potentially volatile politics, and also to performative

21 Ibid., 193.
22 Ibid., 194–95.
23 Ibid., 216–19.
24 Vance, "*Le Jeu de la feuillée*".
25 *Jeu*, vv. 426–57.

groups, thus situates the *Jeu* at the nexus of fact and fiction,[26] as a product of its environment. It is in the context of the play's thematics of Adam's inner struggle with communal and personal identity and its close relationship to its actual environment that I wish to explore an aspect of the play less frequently discussed. That is, the extraordinarily high level of noise generated by the characters, in contrast to the startling absence of song. The sound of the *Jeu* has been discussed relatively rarely, precisely because it seems to fall neither under the auspices of music nor of literature. At best, it is interpreted as a general, but somewhat ephemeral, soundtrack for the narrative of social unrest. The play thus appears to reflect the real sonic experience of medieval city life, from the scuffles round the cathedral's *feuillée* to social rituals of protest such as charivari. But sound is key both to the plot and also to Adam's ultimate creative dilemma. For if the *Jeu* ultimately agonizes about Adam's creative identity, it is possible that the sound of civic unrest was not just a scene-setter for the play, but also a mimetic challenge. It offered the chance to represent, or find equivalence for, realms of sound that unsettled Adam's familiar creative categories of song and poetry.

How, then, does the *Jeu* sound? From the wordless exclamations of the unruly characters to the volatile syntax of their verbal exchanges that constantly cut across, interrupt, and react to one another, the play, as performed, yoyos up and down the spectrum of vocal intonations. Moreover, these sounds are expressly framed as the displacement of singing. Arras, a city in disarray, is also a city without song. We feel its absence everywhere: characters refer obsessively to Arras's famous singers and to the Puy—the confraternity of jongleurs—but not one puts in an appearance. Elsewhere, characters rant in a pretense of song, and then offer encores. The visitors from hell also bring sound with them, and Croquesot—living up to his croaky-sounding name—enters and departs crooning nonsense rhymes and ringing bells.

In song's absence, the main agent for noise is the language of the characters. At the most basic level of syntax, the *Jeu* bubbles with excessive and volatile sonorities. While the bustling exits and entries of the play's seventeen characters create an unstable sense of movement throughout, so does the verbal interaction between the various groups create a soundtrack of disruption and discontinuity. A performative feature contributing to frantic and unpredictable sound is the frenetic pattern of exclamations and expostulations that occur as characters enter, engage with one another, question, and react to events around them. We must imagine, too, constantly changing vocal inflections and timbres: voice raised, falling, shouting, and tapering off in a succession of reactions from shock, horror, rage, to delight.

26 Symes, *A Common Stage*, 183.

At the more local level, language constantly collapses into wordless, often nonsensical exclamations. For instance, in response to his father's admission that he has no money to give Adam for his studies in Paris, Adam is reduced to a profane and near nonsensical outburst "Quia, kia, kia, kia!"[27] Nor is Adam's linguistic disintegration unique. Elsewhere, the madman's exclamation of "fire!" becomes a chain of meaningless sounds "le fu, le fu, le fu,"[28] while in the tavern, Maître Henri's indignation as he spies the young fool guzzling wine is deliciously onomatopoeic: "le glout! le glout! le glout!"[29] In fact, the Artesians all enjoy the excessive possibilities of their spoken language, exclaiming "Bah!," "Ah!," "Ana!," and "Ooo," in meaningless expostulation. On occasion they come together in vocal unity to taunt the monk in a chorus of moos:

Hane:
Or en faisons tout le vieel
Pour chou c'on dist qu'il se coureche.

The People:
Moie![30]

Hane:
Now let's all be calves, for I'd say that would annoy him!

The People:
Moooooo!

If all the characters are attuned to the boundaries between sense and sound in language, there is one who exists only at that flimsy border. In the young madman, the nameless dervé, Adam created a character who, from a sonic perspective, is the embodiment of civic dissent— a one-man charivari no less. Following in the long tradition of fools and madmen, including Holy Fools and the Feast of Fools, Adam's dervé is, nonetheless, unprecedented.[31] In terms defined in the Galenic tradition, his raving exuberance would be classified as manic. His unruly qualities, with reports of him smashing pots and covering himself with quills, also connect him to literary traditions that conjoin insanity with wildness, such as Yvain and Tristain. But while the dervé exhibits

27 *Jeu*, v. 194.
28 Ibid. v. 1028.
29 Ibid. v. 1053.
30 Ibid. vv. 376–78.
31 On the dervé and his place in the Old French literary tradition see Huot, *Madness in Medieval French Literature*, 59–64; Edelgard DuBruck, "The 'Marvelous' Madman of the *Jeu de la feuillée*," *Neophilologus* 58 (1974): 180–86; and McGregor, *The Broken Pot Restored*, esp. 111–16 and 122–31.

kinship with contemporary representations of madmen, what makes him extraordinary is his experience of language and his sensitivity to verbal sound. In most medieval representations, the insane rarely talk at all, and as we have seen, simply make noise.[32] Our young maniac is exceptional for rarely drawing breath.

The young virtuoso is certainly predictably subversive: he farts, exclaims, bleats, and yells. But his linguistic experience is truly radical. He consistently mishears what is said, and specifically, he experiences words phonetically—grammatically, even—rather than semantically. The misunderstanding occurs with the dervé picking up on the last word each character says and hearing it as a different word that sounds the same. His first appearance offers a spectacular template. As he and his father join the citizens in their cross-examination of the monk and his relics of St. Acaire (associated with the cure of fools), the dervé's father urges him to adore the relics, "venés le saint aourer"; the fool, picking up only on the sound "ourer," rhymes it with "tuer," and flies into a rage of suspicion that those around him plot to kill him:

> Que c'est? Me volés vous tuer?
> Fiex a putain! Leres! Erites!
> Creés vous la ches ypocrites?
> Laissiés m'aler, car je sui rois![33]

> What? You want to kill me?
> Son of a bitch! Thieves! Heretics!
> Do you believe these hypocrites?
> Let me pass, for I am king!

His father, urging him to be quiet, reinforces the sense of noisy disruption his son's skewed acoustic experience of words engenders:

> A! Biaus dous fiex, seés vous cois!
> Ou vous arés des enviaus![34]

> Ah! Dear son, sit down and shut up!
> Or you will take a beating.

But that merely sends the dervé off on another raucous rhyming fantasy. From the rhyme sound "-aus" he conjures the word "crapaus" or "toad," and

---

32 Paulo Valesio, "The Language of Madness in the Renaissance," in *Yearbook of Italian Studies: An Annual Publication of the Italian Cultural Institute* (Florence: Casalini Libri, 1971), 199–234. See esp. 199–200 for discussion of the language of medieval madness.

33 *Jeu*, vv. 392–95.

34 Ibid., vv. 396–97.

continues his bizarre nonsensical leaps by moving with the rhyme sounds, rather than the sense of the language he himself produces: thus in the space of three lines we move from images of toads, to "raines" (frogs), and finally to "araines" (trumpets), the meaning of which he responds to now not with words, but by farting at the assembly, only to ask them if they would like an encore:

> Non ferai! Je sui uns crapaus
> Et si ne mengüe fors raines!
> Escoutés! Je fais les araines.
> Est che bien fait? Ferai je plus?[35]

> No I won't! I am a toad
> And I only eat frogs!
> Listen! I'm making trumpets.
> Did I do well? Shall I do it again?

In the slapstick comedy of the madman's performance, we may detect connections to Arras's public culture of improvisation, the kinds practiced in the Carité.[36] The rhyming frenzy may be nonsensical, but it is in a poetic sense virtuosic, and similar in its "rough" style to genres such as the *jeux-partis*—the improvised dialogue form popular among Artesian trouvères. It is also reminiscent of another genre we saw connected to the representation of charivari in the previous chapter, namely the *fatras*, and its associated genre of *fatrasie*, of which there was a substantial tradition connected with the city.[37] The sense of such a genre as a public performance—a kind of poetry slam—is hinted at in a fourteenth-century compilation of *fatras* by Watriquet de Couvin. In their presentation in Paris, Bibliothèque nationale de France, f. fr. 14968, they are introduced as a contest between Watriquet and one Raimmoudin, for performance before King Philip V: "Here begin the *fatras* that Raimmoudin and Watriquet argued, the day of Easter, before King Philip of France" ("Ci commencent li fastras de quoi Raimmoudin et Watriquet desputerent le jour de Pasques devant le roy Phelippe de France"), a scene visualized in an opening half-folio illumination showing the poets in open-armed declamation.[38]

Set against such contexts, it would be easy to explain the dervé's antics as a comedic sideshow. His function is certainly to entertain, and, Edelgard DuBruck says "we can assume that . . . the audience, if they were awed at first,

---

35 Ibid., vv. 398–401.

36 For discussion of the public life of the Carité see Symes, *A Common Stage*, esp. 222–26.

37 A collection of *fatrasies* in Paris, Bibliothèque de l'Arsenal 3114, fols. 7ᵛ–11ʳ, is rubricated as "Fatrasies d'Arras"; edited in Porter, *La Fatrasie et le fatras*, 109–36.

38 Lambert, *La Fatrasie*, 145–59.

soon fell into roaring laughter."[39] That certainly chimes with his connection to the tradition of *fatras*. Yet when we explore how the Artesians experience the young fool, and also the effects his semantic confusion has on the course of the narrative, it is apparent that his performance is not merely entertainment. In a reading that emphasizes the *Jeu*'s concern with community and social identity, Sylvia Huot interprets the dervé as "the very personification of social disintegration." Language serves both as literal embodiment of the character's identity and as metaphor for social coherence: "characterized by chaotic violence and confusion, incapable of communication or exchange, he is the embodiment of that which must be suppressed and excluded—though never definitively, for he always returns to be sent away again—in order that the social group can achieve coherence and functionality."[40]

A crucial component of the dervé's function as emblem of social disintegration is his sounding, performative aspect. The dervé is carefully staged as "performer" within the play by the ostentatiously aural dimension to his spectacle: although he speaks nonsense, the volatility of his outbursts compels the citizens of Arras to listen. Several features contrive the dervé as a quasi-trouvère, and as a grotesque version of the singers the characters of the *Jeu* seem to spend all the play talking about and waiting to appear. It is evident, for example, in the manner in which the characters engage with him. None of the characters bar the father addresses the madman directly: they direct their reactions and questions about him to his father.[41] In one sense his exclusion signifies his emblematic function, as the dangerous "other" of the community.[42] However, his objectification also generates the impression of the dervé as pure performance, to be observed as an object of contemplation, or as a text to be read. That sense of dervé-as-performance is magnified by is the dervé's constant reference to himself as such, most obviously in his delusional belief that his singing surpasses that of Robert Sommeillon, so-called King of the Puy, and his rivals Gautier de Paux and Thomas de Clari:

Father:
Ha! Biaus dous fiex, seés vous jus!
Si vous metés a genoillons!
Se che non, Robers Soumillons

39 DuBruck, "The 'Marvelous' Madman," 180.

40 Huot, *Madness in Medieval French Literature*, 60.

41 Ibid. 61.

42 As Huot writes: "Clearly he is not considered as a fellow human being or community member. Rather, he is a kind of negative space in the social order, unknowable, ominous, that must be hemmed in and suppressed . . ."; see *Madness in Medieval French Literature*, 61.

Qui est nouviaus prinches du Pui
Vous ferra !

Dervé:
Bien kié lui !
Je sui miex prinches qu'il ne soit.
A sen Pui canchon faire doit,
Par droit, maistre Wautiers As Paus
Et uns autres, leur paringaus,
Qui a non Thoumas de Clari.
L'autr'ier vanter les en oï.
Maistre Wautiers ja s'entremet
De chanter parmi le cornet
Et dist qu'il sera courounés.[43]

Father
Ah! My boy, sit yourself down!
Get on your knees!
Otherwise Robert Someillon
The new "Prince of the Puy"
Will make you!

Dervé
What a load of crap that one is!
I'm a better "prince" than he'll ever be.
At his Puy Master Gautier of Paux
Must perform a song;
And another also, his opponent,
Whose name is Thomas of Clari.
I heard them bragging the other day.
Master Gautier has already concocted something for himself
To sing mingled with trumpets
And says that he will be crowned.

The reactions of characters to his linguistic catastrophes confirm that they listen to him for pure pleasure as much as for sense. Following one outburst, the monk reveals his delight has been truly aural, and asks the father whether the dervé babbles this way when he is on his own:

Aimi! Dieus, qu'il fait bon oïr
Che sot la! Car il dist merveilles.

---

43 *Jeu*, vv. 402–14.

Preudons, dist il tant de brubeilles
Quant il est ensus de le gent?[44]

Friend! Lord, is it good to hear
That fool! For he utters marvels.
Good man, does he speak such babble
When he is away from people?

In describing his son, the father emphasizes not his use of language, but rather sketches a vocality that both includes but also surpasses the single category of singing:

Sire, il n'est onques autrement.
Toudis rede il ou cante ou brait.[45]

Sir, he is never any other way.
He always raves or sings or brays.

These vocalities, reminiscent of the vocabulary used in synodal statues to describe charivaric sound, and of sounds associated with the category of medieval "Others" discussed earlier, explicitly position the boy in a more sonorous, clamorous world than those around him. Like these sonorities, does the dervé's soundworld also have a meaning or effect? If the marvels and monsters have a revelatory function, and charivari a disruptive purpose, does the extravagant display of the boy effect any change?

The father's very next words frame the dervé's sounds as having consequences. For in that world of pure sound, it seems the dervé knows less than he says, but also, perhaps, more:

Et si ne set onques qu'il fait.
Encore set il mains qu'il dist.[46]

He does not know what he does.
But also he knows more than he says.

The father's statement is authenticated when we look more closely at the apparently unintended semantic consequences of the dervé's more sonorous experience of language. Above all, it is his experience of language as rhyme sound that establishes him not just as mad, but ultimately as eloquent. For as well as holding the community in captive awe by his spectacular "performance," the dervé also comes to speak the greatest truth. Moments after his first encounter with Adam, the dervé becomes increasingly verbally volatile, abandoning all

44 Ibid. vv. 520–23.
45 Ibid. vv. 524–25.
46 Ibid. vv. 526–27.

sense, and collapsing into angry exclamations. His father, in an effort to calm him, tells him to quiet himself (the verb "taiser" a reminder again of the orality of the situation): "Taisiés pour les dames!"; from "dames," the dervé alights on the word "bigame":

Dervé:
Qui est chieus clers a cele cape?

Father:
Biaus fiex, c'est uns Parisiens.

Dervé:
Che sanle miex uns pois baiens!
Bau!

Father:
Qu c'est? Taisiés pour les dames!

Dervé:
S'i li sousvenoit des bigames,
Il en seroit mains orgueilleus.

Rikiers:
Enhenc! Maistre Adan, or sont deus!
Bien sai que ceste chi est voie!

Adam:
Que set il qu'il blame ne loe?
Point n'aconte a cose qu'il die.
Ne bigames ne sui je mie,
Et s'en sont il de plus vaillans![47]

Dervé:
Who is that clerk with that gown?

Father:
My boy, he's a Parisian.

Fool:
He has more the air of a bursting peapod!
Bah!

Father:
What's this? Quiet down for the ladies!

47 Ibid. vv. 422–33.

Dervé:
If he remembered the bigamists,
He'd be less full of himself.

Rikiers:
Listen up! Master Adam, he has two!
I know for sure this lady here [Dame Douce] is yours!

Adam:
What does he know that he dishes out blame?
Nothing he says counts for anything.
I am no bigamist, not me,
And there are plenty of them more fancy than I.

Despite Adam's proclamation that the dervé does not know what he is talking about, the seeming non-sequitur of "dames" to "bigames" plants the kernel of the most explosive idea of the entire play: it unleashes from Maître Henri the fact that Arras is rife with bigamists. Bigamy was highly topical in Arras during the period of the *Jeu*, and especially among clerks such as Adam and his cohort in the Carité.[48] It reflects a common practice for clerks to marry: the category of a bigamous clerk covered a broad spectrum of scenarios, from successive marriages, marriage to widows, to adulterous liaisons.[49] What cast such unions into doubt, and what the dervé here alludes to, was ongoing disagreements with the papacy, which forbade marriage under any circumstances among clerks and thus designated them "bigamous." As recently as two years before Adam wrote the *Jeu*, the papacy had handed down another ruling that "bigamous clerks" should be stripped of their ecclesiastical status.[50] With these realities rippling in the background of the *Jeu*, it is not hard to see why the charivaric motif was appropriate. And in such a context, the dervé emerges as the voice of authority—as law-enforcer. Adam's marriage to Maroie, the debates about the paternity of Dame Douce's child, and countless other allusions to marital upset and controversy are all illuminated not just as socially unsettling, but as contravening ecclesiastical law. In other words, just like the fools who would soon start to creep into the literary tradition, the dervé, in his madness, reveals truth.

48 On which see Langley, "Community Drama," 67–72.

49 Ibid. 67. Based on contemporary definitions of "clercs bigames" in the canon lawyer Hostiensis's *Summa aurea* of 1250–53, Langley explains that a bigamous clerk "was a man who had taken minor orders and who had legitimately married successive wives; who had a legitimate spouse, but who had one or more mistresses; who had married a widow; who had married a woman of notorious reputation; who continued to live with a wife whom he knew to be adulterous."

50 Ibid., 69–70.

But we may go further and say that the mechanism for his truth is inextricably linked to language's sound. And there is precise and august method in the dervé's madness. His nonsense is not without eloquence. As he spins rhymes, the dervé is uncannily reminiscent of precepts in contemporary grammar and poetry treatises, and in *ars memorativa*. In such contexts, rhyming was a vital technique for learning and remembering texts, and a starting point for composition. While doggerel rhymes were—and still are—a commonplace mnemonic device, especially for learning languages, they extended into systems using homophonics as an aid to learning and remembering words. John of Garland's *Poetria nova* offers just such an instance.[51] Written in the 1230s, part of the treatise is devoted to techniques of memory designed to aid authors. Drawing on a somewhat hazy understanding of Cicero's *Ad Herennium*, Garland outlines a tripartite spatial system for organizing and storing texts in the chamber of memory.[52] The third of these is in part to aid memorization of "sounds of all types of language" ("omnia genera linguarum sonorum"), and particularly of words that were unfamiliar to readers. On hearing such a word, the reader should place it in the designated memory-space along with a familiar word that sounds the same: a homophonic, or rhyming relationship, then. These could sometimes be words in different languages, and unrelated in any semantic sense to the meaning of the originary word. But through this technique of anchoring like sound with like, the reader could hold onto a word that was semantically unfamiliar.

Such techniques extended to visualization of like-sounding words. In the later fourteenth century, Thomas Bradwardine's *De memoria artificiali adquirenda* (ca. 1335) advocates a similar model, but with a visual component. He explains it thus:

> He should consider and write down for himself the whole possible number of syllables, and should also consider the same number of easily

---

51 John of Garland, *The* Parisiana Poetria *of John of Garland*, ed. and transl. Traugott Lawler (New Haven: Yale University Press, 1974).

52 Ch. 2, subtitled "De arte eligendi," at 36–39 of Traugott's edition. "In the third column let us imagine to be written all kinds of languages, sounds, and voices of the various living creatures, etymologies, explanations of words, distinctions between words, all in alphabetical order; and with a ready mind let each consider what word fits his own language. But since we do not know every language, nor have heard every word, we resort to those which we have heard" ("in tercia columpna intelligamus scribi omnia genera linguarum, sonorum, et vocum diversorum animancium, et ethimologias, interpretationes, differentias, secundum ordinem alphabeti; et leta mente consideret unusquisque que vox conveniat cum lingua sua. sed quia nescimus omnes linguas, nec omnes dictiones audiuimus, recurrimus ad illas quas audiuimus." See Carruthers, *The Book of Memory*, 123–27.

visualizable things known to him, whose name in Latin or his own language or in another language known readily to him may start with or completely coincide with those syllables.[53]

Traces of such practices found their way into literal representation in marginalia and in the visual riddle, or "rebus."[54]

Mary Carruthers underlines how vital such systems were not only to techniques of memory, but also to composition itself. Writing about John of Garland's mnemonics, she argues that "selecting and gathering material one has read is at the heart of successful composition, and . . . this can only occur because one has a trained memory."[55] Situated in such contexts, the madman's apparent "mishearing" of words is also emblematic of a well-schooled memory. He listens homophonically, connecting words heard to those of his memorial system. While the punning nature of his language makes him entertaining, the apparatus of his verbal play also locates him in a venerable tradition of learning and composition. The stakes could not be higher. Consider, for example, the classic dictum of John of Salisbury's description of grammar in his touchstone treatise, *Metalogicon*: "Grammar is the cradle of all philosophy, and in a manner of speaking, the first nurse of the whole study of letters" ("eadem quoque est totius philosophiae cunabulum, et ut ita dixerim totius litteratorii studii altrix prima").[56] Nor, of course, is this an exclusively Latinate tradition. Adam's own aspirations for clerkly (Latinate) learning—the very impetus for his desire in the *Jeu* to go to Paris—are signal of an appropriation of the learned discourse into vernacular poetic production.[57] Yet the dervé seems to surpass all the Artesian clerks for his learned prowess. At the very end of the *Jeu*, the father tells the assembled clerks at the tavern that the night before, he found his crazy boy covered in quills ("Ier le trouvai tout emplumé").[58] Not simply

---

53 Thomas Bradwardine, *De memoria artificiali adquirenda*, quoted from *The Medieval Craft of Memory: An Anthology of Texts and Pictures*, ed. Mary Carruthers and Jan Ziolkowski (Philadelphia: University of Pennsylvania Press, 2002), 211. The translation is from the text transmitted in Cambridge, Fitzwilliam Museum, MS McClean 169 and edited by Carruthers in *Journal of Medieval Latin* 2 (1992): 25–43.

54 Carruthers, *Book of Memory*, 221–57.

55 Ibid., 124.

56 John of Salisbury, *Metalogicon*, Book I, ch. 13, quoting from *Metalogicon*, ed. John Hall and Katharine Keats-Rohan, Corpus Christianorum 98 (Turnhout: Brepols, 1991), 32. The English translation is from *The* Metalogicon *of John of Salisbury: A Twelfth-Century Defense of Verbal and Logical Arts of the* Trivium, transl. David McGarry (Berkeley: University of California Press, 1955), 37.

57 On Adam's appropriation of Latinate writing practices, see Saltzstein, "Relocating the Thirteenth-Century Refrain."

58 *Jeu*, v. 1050.

reinforcing the pathology of his mania, such plenitude of the emblem of writing endows him also with hyperbolic linguistic capability. And in his exhibition of learning, the dervé alone is equipped to unlock himself from verbal meaning, and, in so doing, reveals truth. In a brilliant maneuver, then, the dervé ensures the efficacy of the sonic protest he himself stages. He is both agent of revelation—exposing the bigamy scandal—and agent of resolution, the noisy embodiment of protest. In this linguistic virtuosity, the madman simultaneously resolves Adam's creative dilemma. For he is, after all, Adam's own invention: and as a brilliant experiment with the sound of language, the dervé proves Adam's creative salvation.

*

In the *Jeu*, Adam's madman does more than simply reveal social truth, and more than prove Adam's poetic credentials. His also endows the verbal nonsense with eloquent meaning. More precisely, he endows poetry's defining characteristic—the sound of its rhyme—with a special kind of authority. At the same time, the *Jeu* also makes explicit the connection of such linguistic effect to musical experience. As we have seen, the play depicts a community on high alert for musical performance. We may also compare the *Jeu* to Adam's more famous *Jeu de Robin et Marion*, in which song is the default mode of heightened expression. In the *Jeu de la feuillée*, the constant anticipation of song creates a performative space that is ultimately only filled by the dervé. If he does not sing himself, he creates a sonorous effect that nonetheless has considerable affinity with the missing music. It is a realm of sound-through-language that proves not only entertaining to behold, but is also imbued with moral consequences. And in this hyper-linguistic—or perhaps supermusical—realm, there is not only analogy to musical experience, but also potentially a more explicit and audible correlation: that of pure rhyme sound. In the next part of this chapter, we will listen again to Arras: this time to a landscape portrayed exclusively through song.

Unity, Dissent, and the Meaning of Rhyme in Adam's Motets

The *Jeu* was not the only exploration of poetic identity through metaphors of civic unity and dissent. These themes recur across Adam's corpus. But it is in his motets that they receive their most complex treatment, and it is to the sound of words in two of his motets that we shall attend next: *Aucun se sont* (834)/A Dieu (835)/Super te and Entre Adan (725)/Chief bien seantz (726)/ Aptatur (O 46).

Sylvia Huot first suggested a narrative connection between the motets, and it is not hard to see how they reframe the narrative themes of the *Jeu*.[59] In the texts of *Entre Adan/Chief bien seantz/Aptatur* (see texts below and example 4.1), the poet celebrates communal and personal harmony. The triplum is a classic example of the "bons compaignons" motif explored in chapter 2. In it, Adam is joined by three companions—Hanikel, Hancart, and Gautelot—reminiscent of the Artesian friends of the *Jeu*, Riquier, Hane, and Guillot. Together they dance, sing, drink, play, and entertain, in a joyful performance of communal unity. That concord echoes another sort of contentment in the motetus. It lists the perfections of Adam's beloved—from the "waves and curls" of her hair ("ondés et fremians") to her perfect white teeth ("dens blans"). It is in direct dialogue with the parodic description of his wife Maroie in the *Jeu*, which catalogues not her beauty, but the ravages of time. The lady in the motet at once valorizes the poet's ardor; more importantly, his enchantment (in lines 11–12 of the motetus) is literally that—the lady furnishing him with the matter to turn into his song. Poetry, city, and lovers all stand as metaphors for one another, each the embodiment of harmonious perfection.

Triplum

Entre Adan et Hanikel,
Hancart et Gautelot
a grant esbanoi, qui ot lor revel.
Q[ua]nt il hoquetent, plus tost clapetent que frestel,
5 li damoisel,
mais qu'il aient avant baisié Saint Tortuel.
Et si chantent tout sans livre, viés et nouvel;
Gautelos fait l'ivre
si proprement et si bel, qu'il samble a son musel,
10 qu'il doie traire a sa fin.
Et quant il font le Moulin
ensamble tout quatre
et au plastre batre
en hoquetant,
15 sont si deduisant, si gay, si joiant et si riant
cil quatre enfant
que nule gent tant.

He who hears the revelries of Adam and Hanikel, Hancart and Gautelot has a lot of fun. When they sing hockets they clap louder than a piper can play the pipes, providing they have not already kissed Saint

59 Huot, "Transformations," 153–58.

EXAMPLE 4.1. (continued)

EXAMPLE 4.1. (continued)

25

le Mou - lin   en - sam - ble tout qua - tre   et au

ans,   piz durs et poi - gnans, bou - ti -

III

28

plas - tre batre en ho - que - tant, sont si de - dui -

-ne   sou - le - vant,   ma - niere a - ve -

31

sant,   si gay, si joi - ant et si ri -

nans   et plus li   re - ma - nans

34

- ant cil quatre en - fant   que nu - le gent tant.

ont fait tant d'en - cha[n]t,   que pris est A - dans.

Tortuel [i.e. got drunk]. And they sing totally without books, old or new; Gautelot plays the drunk so exactly and so well, that it seems from his mug that he must be on his last legs. And when the four of them together pretend to be a windmill and beat against the walls, singing hockets, they are so entertaining, the four youths, so gay, so joyous and full of laughter that they surpass all others.

Motetus

1 Chief bien seantz, ondés et fremians,
2 plains frons reluisans et parans,
3 regars atraihans,
4 vairs, humilians, catillans et frians,
5 nés par mesure au viaire afferans,
6 bouchete rians, vermellete, a dens blans,
7 gorge bien naissans, cors reploians,
8 piz durs et poignans, boutine soulevant,
9 maniere avenans
10 et plus li remanans
11 ont fait tant d'encha[n]t,
12 que pris est Adans.

A shapely head, waves and undulations; a wide forehead, gleaming and comely; an alluring glance, blue-gray eyes, cast down, almond-shaped, luscious; a nose made to measure, proportioned to the face; a laughing, little mouth, rosy and red with white teeth; a full neck, a supple neck; breasts hard and pointed; a rounded stomach; a seemly manner and what is more, all the rest spun so much enchantment that Adam was taken.

Tenor

Aptatur: It is fitting.[60]

In the second motet (see texts below and example 4.2), *Aucun se sont*/A Dieu quemant/*Super te*, the creative and narrative premise of *Entre Adan*/*Chief bien seantz*/*Aptatur* is undone. Although Adam is never named as protagonist, his presence is suggested in the motetus, where the "je" first speaks in a refrain borrowed from one of Adam's own rondeaux, "A Dieu quemant amouretes can

---

60 Examples in this chapter are based on editions by Susan Stakel and Joel Relihan in Part IV of *The Montpellier Codex*, ed. Tischler. For an alternative edition of the texts, marked up to indicate competing rhyme schemes, see Robyn Smith, *French Double and Triple Motets in the Montpellier Manuscript: Textual Edition, Translation and Commentary*, Musicological Studies, 68 (Ottawa: Institute of Mediaeval Music, 1997).

EXAMPLE 4.2. *Aucun se sont*/A Dieu quemant/*Super te* (Mo, fols. 288ʳ–290ʳ)

EXAMPLE 4.2. (continued)

-er,   car quant je miex a - mai, plus me con - vint maus en - du -

pour   ce   que   li bour - gois   ont   es - té

- rer;   n'on - ques ce - le   que j'a - moi - e   ne m'i vot mous -

si   fort   me - né, qu'i n'i keurt   drois   ne lois.

- trer   sam - blant   ou   je me de - üs - se con - for - ter ne

Gros   tour - nois   ont   a - vu - glé

II

mer - ci   es - pe - rer.   Tout a - dés me - toit paine   a moi es - chie - ver;

con - tes et rois, jus - ti - ces et pre - las tant de   fois,   que la plus

EXAMPLE 4.2. (continued)

je n'en vois / souspirant en terre estrange" ("I commend love to God, for I am leaving, sighing all the while into foreign lands"), and split, enté style, to frame the opening and close.[61] Here, it is Arras he leaves, sighing as he goes, sick of its vile corruption, while the "bele compagne," echoing the group at the opening of *Entre Adan/Chief bien seantz/Aptatur*, are decamping (line 8). Civic identity is again linked to love. In the triplum, *Aucun se sont*, the protagonist portrays the failure of love as a consequence of betrayal: "Aucun se sont loé d'amours, més je m'en dois plus que nus blasmer / k'onques a nul jour n'i poi loiauté trouver" ("Some have praised love, but I more than any other must blame it, for never was I able to find loyalty in love.")

Triplum

Aucun se sont loé d'amours, més je m'en doi plus que nus blasmer,
k'onques a nul jour n'i poi loiauté trouver.
Je cuidai au premier avoir amie par loiaument ouvrer,
més g'i peüsse longuement baer,
5 car quant je miex amai, plus me convint maus endurer;
n'onques cele que j'amoie ne m'i vot moustrer
samblant ou je me deüsse conforter ne merci esperer.
Tout adés metoit paine a moi eschiever;
trop me douna a penser, ains que je la peüsse oublier.
10 Or sai je bien sanz douter, que loiaus hons est perdus qui veut amer,
ne nus, ce m'est vis, ne s'en doit mesler
fors cil, qui bee a servir de guiler.

Some have praised love, but I more than any other must blame it, for never was I able to find loyalty in love. I thought at first to win a sweetheart by behaving loyally, but I could wait a long time for it, for the better I loved, the more I had to endure pain; the one whom I loved never wanted to show me any sign from which I might take comfort of hope for mercy. She always took great pains to avoid me; I thought of her much before being able to forget her. Now I know well, without a doubt, that a loyal man who wants to love is lost, and no one, in my opinion, should get mixed up in loving, except for him who intends to serve deceptively.

Motetus

A Dieu quemant amouretes, car je n'en vois,
dolens, pour la douçetes, hors du douz païs d'Artois,

---

61 *Lyric Works*, ed. Wilkins, rondeau no. 5.

qui si est mus et destrois
pour ce que li bourgois
5 ont esté si fort mené, qu'i n'i keurt drois ne lois.
Gros tournois
ont avuglé contes et rois, justices et prelas tant de fois,
que la plus bele compagne dont Arras mehaigne,
laissent amis et maisons et hernois
10 et fuient, ça deux, ça trois,
souspirant en terre estrange.

I commend love to God, for I go, sorrowing for the sweet little thing, away from the sweet land of Artois, which is terribly changed and torn apart because the bourgeois have been so mistreated that no rights or laws are upheld. Great tournaments have blinded counts and kings, judges and prelates so many times, that the finest knights which Arras has mistreated are leaving behind friends and houses and equipment and fleeing, here two, here three, sighing all the while, into foreign lands.

Tenor

Super te orta est: Is risen upon thee.

What does music contribute? Most obviously, polyphony permits metaphors of Adam's civic and courtly identities to be displayed in simultaneous juxtaposition. But what of the sound of Adam's two poetic poses? There is a strikingly audible feature of these two pieces whose sound may also contribute to the opposing narratives of the motets. Both, in different ways, exploit the supermusical to downplay the sense of the texts, and to foreground, in its place, the abstract sound of language, or, more precisely, of poetry. As in the *Jeu*, the phonetic takes precedence over the semantic. However, the two motets play with linguistic sound in quite different ways.

Huot first drew attention to the high level of repetition in *Entre Adans/Chief bien seantz/Aptatur*: the motetus text is organized around the single rhyme sound "ans," derived from the sound of Adam's own name that sounds at the beginning and end of the motet.[62] That rhyme sound not only echoes internally, as in line 4, but is also prominent in the triplum, not least when it becomes the rhyming sound of the last section of the poem (lines 14–17). More than metrical patterns, or even regularized syllable counts, what characterizes this poetry is the resonance or repetition of the rhyme sound "-ans" throughout the texts. With the addition of assonance throughout, amplifying that verbal sound, and the creation of competing phonetic emphases through

62 Huot, "Transformations," 155.

secondary rhyme schemes and assonance on the sounds "el" and "-ent," the sound of the poems teeters throughout at the edge of linguistic sense and phonetic sound.[63]

The mesmerizing quality of repetitious rhyme is not lost in performance. In musical context the prominence of the "-ans" rhyme is rather magnified (see example 4.1 above). As well as relentlessly sounding in the individual texts, the polyphonic frame effects many moments of textual counterpoint, as at the opening; elsewhere, as at measures 4 and 13, music brings together the rhyme ending "-ans" of the motetus with phonetically like sounds in the triplum. Finally, from measure 28 to the end, where the triplum text (lines 14–17) asserts the "-ans" rhyme, the composer contrives the different line endings of each voice to coincide, therefore bringing about unison soundings of the "ans" rhyme, culminating with the final sounding of "Adans" in the motetus.

The organization of the motet's tenor adds to this patterning an overwhelming sense of tonal stability and predictability. *Aptatur* is, to begin with, a melody with limited harmonic possibilities, unambiguously revolving around the pole of f; but its rhythmic realization ensures a relentless affirmation of f on almost every single measure: where the tenor sounds c′, the motetus invariably crosses beneath it to f (as at mm. 6 and 7). Onto that pattern of reiteration, Adam constantly contrives to project "-ans" syllables, either in one or both voices. He also exploits elongated, two-perfection cadences to amplify internal rhymes, as at measures 34–35, where the motetus cadences at 35 on f′ via the preceding iteration "tant d'enchant." The constant to-ing and fro-ing between F and C, and the incessant cadencing onto F create the effect of rhyme itself: a constant sense of arrival on the familiar.

There is another strategy by which musical texture helps us to hear the rhyme schemes. Melodic phrases in the motet repertory are commonly determined by the unit of a line of poetry—that is, a line whose ending is marked by a rhyming word. Those endings are usually marked off by a rest following

---

63 This also raises the tricky question of what constitutes "poetry" in this repertory, and indeed in traditions far beyond the medieval. For more on this topic, I direct readers to the fundamental resource for literary taxonomies, Heinrich Lausberg, *Handbook of Literary Rhetoric: A Foundation for Literary Study*, transl. Matthew Bliss et al., and ed. David Orton and R. Dean Anderson (Leiden: Brill, 1998). Here, I work on the generally accepted assumption that the high degree of repetition, assonance, and use of rhyme define the texts as poetry. On rhyme in Old French poetry see Theodor Elwert, *Traité de versification française des origines à nos jours* (Paris: Editions Klincksieck, 1965), esp. 75–111, and Roger Dragonetti, *La Technique poétique des trouvères dans la chanson courtoise: Contribution à l'étude de la rhétorique médiévale* (Bruges: De Tempel, 1960), esp. 404–57 for discussion of rhyme. For discussion of rhyme schemes in Old French motet texts see Smith, *French Double and Triple Motets*, 21–28. I thank Shane Butler for generously sharing his literary expertise with me as I addressed issues of rhyme sound.

the final note; by stasis, the final note falling on a long; with a plica or decorative flourish on the final long; or simply with a cadence.[64] Our motet is no exception. An example of an articulated line ended occurs in measure 3 of the triplum where the long on the final "kel" of "Hanikel" is followed by a rest; the strategy repeats in the motetus, measure 4. While such tactics ensure poetic clarity within the individual voices, there is no assurance that rationale will be audible in performance when heard against the other voices, and the mismatch of phrase lengths (and poetic line-endings) is one of the most powerful parameters to effect the clarity or confusion of words in the genre. *Entre Adans/Chief bien seantz/Aptatur* experiments with different ways of aligning the voices to make phrasing and therefore rhyme endings more audible. That is most evident at the end, where phrase endings of motetus and triplum start lining up. Elsewhere, line endings in one voice overlap with the beginning of a new line in the other voice. That means that we hear a pattern of silence or stasis as one voice ends, coinciding with the beginning of a new line in the other voice. The tenor's movement in longs, punctuated by rests, means that it shadows and supports these patterns. So, for example, at measure 3 silence in the triplum leads into "fremians" in the motetus; as the motetus arrives on its final syllable—the rhyme "ans"—it coincides with the start of the second line "Hancart," the two voices briefly sharing the rhyme sound before the motetus falls silent; at measure 5, the long in the triplum coincides with the opening of the motetus's new line "plains frons," and the assonant echoes on "grant" and "reluisans." These patterns do not help us to understand the texts any better, in a semantic sense—the full verbal context remains aurally elusive. But it does mean that the rhyme sound, and thus the general sense of poetic form, is more transparent in the real time of performance.

If *Entre Adan/Chief bien seantz/Aptatur* projects phonetic clarity, *Aucun se sont/A Dieu quemant/Super te* is designed to generate confusion and concealment (see example 4.2 above). Although rhyme words—line endings—are often followed by silence, the extensive punctuating effects of *Entre Adan/Chief bien seantz/Aptatur* are less consistently used here, and the other tactic of lining up phrases occurs hardly ever. Greater mobility—both tonal and rhythmic—in the tenor means that the piece sounds less predictable than its counterpart. The opening is emblematic of the motet's tendency to confuse verbal sound. The triplum breaks off first at "blasmer" (m. 3), and again at "trouver" (m. 5). That seems to make sense, the phrase ends coinciding with the rhyme sound "-er." However, the opening lines of the motet undermine the potency and authority of that rhyme sound by setting up a competing rhyme through the echo of "d'amours" (at the end of m. 1) and then again after "jour" (at the start of m. 4). The composer might have tackled this by creating two shorter

---

64 Smith, *French Double and Triple Motets*, 21–23.

melodic phrases, thus punctuating the double rhyme scheme. In the event, though, the triplum opens with a single lengthy phrase. Moreover, exactly the same tactic recurs in the opening of the motetus. There the rhyme scheme is even more obscured by the music as between measures 1 and 6 there is no musical punctuation at all. Two sets of rhymes are thus subsumed into a single melodic strand: first, "amouretes" at measure 2, rhyming with "douçetes"; and "en vois" at measure 3 with "Artois" at measure 6.

The clarity of rhyme—or of phrase endings—is further undermined by the tenor melody, "Super te orta." Like "Aptatur," it is grounded in the tonality of F. Yet while the melodic contours of the chant yielded constant affirmation of the F final, "Super te" has markedly fewer cadences on F. Instead, living up to the theme of departure, it hovers in "terre estrange" (to quote from the closing refrain, taken from Adam's rondeau). Phrases end not on strong cadences, but suspended around A or G. To some extent, the motets' shared F final, and consequently the similarity of their melodic range, further encourages such comparative listening: in a purely musical sense, they offer two different renderings of the same world. Heard against *Entre Adans/Chief bien seantz/Aptatur*, then, *Aucun se sont/A Dieu quemant/Super te* seems to conspire to conceal, rather than promote, the clear experience of verbal sound and poetic form, and rather than making opportunities to create phonetic consonance, the piece pits unlike sounds against one another, and against a harmonic background of greater instability.

To be clear: I am not suggesting that *Entre Adan/Chief bien seantz/Aptatur* makes the *meaning* of its texts any clearer than *Aucun se sont/A Dieu quemant/Super te* at the moment of performance. Rather, *both* are mimetic of their texts by virtue of their radically different treatment of verbal sound. Thus one motet expresses civic, personal, and creative harmony by using musical sound and form to reveal clear linguistic consonances; the other expresses the precariousness of Adam's identity as lover and poet by having music pit words against one another, creating sounds impossible to utter in speech alone, and negating the effect of phonetic clarity.

The Supermusical and the Sense of Rhyme

We are in an unusual position with Adams' motets, for their authorial attribution, rare in this repertory, allows us—indeed encourages us—to listen antithetically, while their narrative relationship to the *Jeu* establishes meaning for their contrasting treatment of rhyme sound.[65] Is it simply the prompt of the

65 As well as appearing in the single-author compendium of Adam's works, Paris, Bibliothèque nationale de France, f. fr. 25566 (*Entre Adan/Chief bien seantz/Aptatur* at fol. 36^{r-v}, and *Aucun se sont/A Dieu quemant/Super te* at fols. 34^v–35^r with triplum and

author function that permits us to make these musical connections and to attribute meaning to rhyme sound? Put another way, what evidence is there that Adam's earliest audiences would have heard the distinction as significant, would have even heard the textures differently at all?

Adam's motets were listened to and copied in environments well versed in the wider motet repertory, and it is perhaps against the practice of experimenting with rhyme sound that we should situate Adam's staging verbal sound in these two motets. To think about the motet texture's effect on the *abstract* sound of words, and the possibility of attributing meaning to rhyme sound and its obfuscation, is to run against the grain of many current approaches to the genre as conduit of complex literary meaning, meanings that were often suggested through moments of semantic clarity in the motet's texture (as discussed in chapter 1). My focus on rhyme sound here is not to imply this was the only or most important dimension of the genre. Rather, I want to illuminate the motet's innate potential—by virtue of its texture and its multiple texts—to explore facets of linguistic sound that poetry alone could not. For as Adam's motets suggest, part of the experience of the motet had to do with adjustment of the parameters of the relationship of word to melody to dramatically alter linguistic sound. The supermusical effect of the motet was thus a way not only to experience sheer musical sound; it had potential to make audible the musical properties of words.

A look at the early tradition of motets, but ones also transmitted with Adam's corpus, reveals just how important rhyme sound was in the conception of the genre. In his study of the French motet tradition, Mark Everist emphasizes how crucial the articulation of text through melodic phrasing was as a compositional criterion.[66] That aspect has important consequences for the articulation and audibility of rhyme sound. That is especially true of the earliest representatives of the genre, those connected with the Notre Dame repertory, for the simple reason that the music of a motet often came before the words: earliest motets were often made by texting preexistent clausulae; and later on, the practice of contrafacting was rife, with texts constantly being stripped out and replaced. At a very basic level, then, composers and/or poets often made texts to fit preexistent musical structures. And on occasion, that was seized as an opportunity to play with rhyme sound.

A preexistent clausula could be an opportunity to amplify rhyme. The music of the motet *De jolif cuer* (326)/*Je me quidai* (327)/*Et gaudebit* (M24) (of which there is an extract in example 4.3) is taken from a two-part clausula

---

motetus reversed), they appear in close proximity in *Mo* (*Entre Adan/Chief bien seantz/ Aptatur* at fols. 282^r–283^v, and *Aucun se sont/*A Dieu quemant/*Super te* at fols. 288^v–290^r).

66 Everist, *French Motets in the Thirteenth Century*. Phrasing is a constant theme throughout Everist's study of compositional process. I refer to specific examples below.

in the St. Victor manuscript; its poetic scheme was thus determined by the older structure.[67] The text is as follows:

Triplum (to m. 8)

De jolif cuer doit venir
de faire un treble plesant;

67 It appears as a three-part motet in *W2*, fols. 200ᵛ–201ᵛ and *Mo*, fols. 158ᵛ–160ʳ. The two-part clausula in *St.V*, fol. 289ᵛ, indicates knowledge of its instantiation as at least a two-part motet, as a marginal note gives an incipit of the Old French motetus text "Je me cuidai bien tenir."

por ce voel je maintenir
de signeur Gilon Ferrant.

Motetus (to m. 8)

Je me quidai bien tenir
de chanter dorenevant,
mes Amor, qui son plesir,
fet de moi sans contremant.

Tenor

Et gaudebit

The three-part version here is also transmitted in *Mo* (which also transmits the Adam motets). The two lower voices (the original clausula) move in regular units of four perfections (two measures), marked off either by a rest or decorative fillers. The simple rhythmic pattern of the tenor clicks into the mode 1 rhythm of the motetus voice every other perfection. If that texture alone seemed a poetic invitation—the musical units furnishing ready-made, regular-length poetic units—then a later composer/poet saw in it the possibility for a more ambitious textual scheme. Adding a new triplum, he now created a more elaborate homorhythmic pattern, the matrix for double textual play. The texture of the upper voices is similar in style to a conductus, and it is tempting to imagine that the motet had an earlier instantiation as a conductus-motet: that is, where such a texture would have been texted with a single Latin text.[68] Here, though, the clausula was the chance to play with shared rhyme sound between two *different* texts, and every single melodic unit ends with the same sound: "-ant," and "-ir." Bar occasional aligning of like words, there is no obviously consistent attempt to pit like vowels against like apart from at the ends of poetic lines, and thus the impression of the motet is one of pure rhyme sound.

In some cases, the clear projection of rhyme sound could have symbolic meaning. In *Entre Adan/Chief bien seantz/Aptatur*, we saw how affirmation of the "-ans" rhyme kept the phonetic sound of the name "Adan" in the foreground. Such a technique looks back to the practice of earlier conductus and clausula motets, where the dominance of one particular vowel sound in the new texts may have been intended to amplify through assonance the vowel sound of the original chant melisma on which the upper voices were based.[69] In his exploration of the early repertory, Everist points to a case similar in texture to *De jolif cuer/Je me quidai/Et gaudebit*. In the conductus-motet {*Ad veniam*

---

68 Everist, *French Motets*, 16–38, and see 29–35.

69 Demonstrated in Hans Nathan, "The Function of Text in French 13th-Century Motets," *Musical Quarterly* 28 (1942): 445–62. See also Norman Smith, "The Earliest Motets: Music and Words," *Journal of the Royal Musical Association* 114 (1989): 141–63.

perveniam (635)}/*Ad veniam perveniam* (635)/*Tanquam* (O2), based on a two-part clausula, the newly-composed texts and triplum voice amplify the rhyme "-am," both through copious repetitions of the rhyme sound in the poetry, and through its clear articulation in the conductus-style texture, where upper voice phrase endings coincide precisely. The emphasis on the abstract "-am" rhyme here functions as a form of cue to the liturgical text of the tenor: "Tanqu<u>am</u>."[70]

That same homogeneous texture, however, could produce radically different phonetic effects. Example 4.4 shows the opening of a three-part motet *Quant voi revenir* (126)/*Virgo virginum*/*Hec dies* (M13), extant in *Mo* and *Cl* (again, contemporary with the later repertory).[71] The texts are as follows:

Triplum

Quant voi revenir
d'esté la saison,
que le bois font retenir
tuit cil [jolis] oisillon

Motetus

Virgo virginum,
lumen luminum,
restauratrix hominum,
que portasti Dominum.

Tenor

Hec dies

Its musical texture is almost identical to *De jolif cuer/Je me quidai/Et gaudebit*, the upper voices coordinated with the pattern of the tenor melody that is consistently cut into repeating units of four perfections (two measures). It survives in *Ba* as a Latin double motet, *O mitissima virgo Maria* (128)/*Virgo virginum* (127)/*Hec dies* (M13), using the texture to play with linguistic consonances between the two texts.[72] In the bilingual version, the very texture that amplified rhyme is now an opportunity to create phonetic dissonance, as the music pits unlike sounds together, exaggerating the sheer strangeness, unique to the motet, of sounding French and Latin together.

There are also many examples of the kinds of alternation of staggered and synchronized line-endings we encountered in *Entre Adan/Chief bien seantz/*

70 Everist, *French Motets*, 30–35.

71 *Mo*, fols. 80ᵛ–81ᵛ, where it appears in fascicle 3, part of the old corpus of the manuscript; *Cl*, fols. 388ᵛ–389ʳ.

72 *Ba*, fol. 60ʳ⁻ᵛ.

EXAMPLE 4.4. *Quant voi revenir/Virgo virginum/Hec dies*, mm. 1–6 (*Mo*, fols. 80ᵛ–82ʳ)

Aptatur. Example 4.5 shows *Amours, en qui* (332)/*Art d'amours* (333)/*Et gaudebit* (M24), a unique three-part French motet copied before *De jolif cuer/Je me quidai/ Et gaudebit* in *Mo* at fols. 156ᵛ–158ʳ. The texts are as follows:

Triplum

Amours, en qui j'ai fiance
de merci trover,
par jolie contenance
me fet ce treble acorder.
Car cele au vis cler,
qui samblance
fait tant a loer,
me doune adés remembrance
de joie et baudor mener.

Motetus

Art d'amours ne decevance
ne soloie redouter,
car volenté ne baance
n'avoie d'amer.
Or m'estuet sans reposer

EXAMPLE 4.5. *Amours, en qui j'ai fiance/Art d'amours/Et gaudebit* (Mo, fols. 156ᵛ–158ʳ)

a celi penser,
por qui acointance
puis chanter:
Dieus, j'aim tant, que n'i puis durer.

Tenor

Et gaudebit

A striking aspect of the motet's aural effect is determined by subtle adjust-ment to the length and aligning of melodic phrases—which in this instance is used to create rhyme consonances and echoes. Throughout, the voices march along in strict homorhythmic alignment, while the two upper voices exploit the clarity of such concordant sound to project note-against-syllable declama-tion of their different texts. At the beginning, phrase endings collide precisely at the end of measure 2 to reveal a shared rhyme sound: "-ance." The next line-breaks phase out, but by just a perfection, allowing the ear to catch an echo of another shared rhyme, this time "-er." That same pattern of phrase endings coinciding and phasing out repeats at measure 8 (where the "-er" rhyme now coincides, or "accords," to play on the triplum's "acorder"), and then "cler" in the triplum at measure 9 is echoed a perfection later in the motetus at the beginning of measure 10. The scheme is disrupted by the introduction of a refrain in the motetus in the final section from measure 14, but the voices realign for the final notes of the motet on the "-er" rhyme again.

Given that a polytextual premise will result more often than not in the alignment of unlike sounds—in the manner of Adam's second motet—it is striking just how many motets experiment with texture as a clarifying agent, in the ways illustrated here. To give some more precise sense, consider the motets from the fifth fascicle of *Mo*—perhaps the most comprehensive and abundant representation of the *ars antiqua* motet. Fascicle 5 contains exclu-sively three-part French motets. Given the consonance of language in the dif-ferent voices, it may have invited composers to experiment with emphasizing like sounds or rhymes. A brief look at the texture of the 127 motets in that collection quickly reveals that a large proportion (nearly half) are engaged with manipulating textures that experiment with rhyme alignments. In such cases, the first aural encounter is of a soundworld saturated in clearly articu-lated rhyme sound. What, then, could such a sound signify?

The Power of Rhyme

The ability of texture to make compatible verbal sounds audible may not just be an incidental by-product of putting different texts together in a medium whose concerns often lie in the inaudible, symbolic meanings of the texts it juxtaposes. The experiment in this chapter of situating Adam's play on rhyme in his motets in the wider practice of the tradition opens new ways for hearing the motet's ability to experiment with abstract verbal sound, ways that allow such sound itself to have symbolic meaning. The interaction of Adam's motets with his *Jeu* illuminates the potential for rhyme's consonance in polyphony to signify as positive, perhaps even revelatory. Like the monsters, marvels, and hybrids among whom the dervé took his place, we saw how the sonority associated with his realm of the "Other" is semantically rich. He thus accords with an analysis of the monstrous by Bettina Bildhauer and Robert Mills as "not meaningless, but meaning-laden."[73] As I argued, the madman was "marvelous" in his ability to reveal social truth but, more importantly, for doing so by way of exposing the anatomy and technique of mnemonics and composition itself. Beyond the narrative frame of Adam's works, are there other contexts in which we way hear the unadulterated sound of rhyme in the motet, too, as marvelous?

Earlier in this chapter I suggested how the dervé's rhyming nonsense connected him to a wider tradition of grammar and mnemonics. These contexts also offer ways of interpreting the motet's treatment of text. What the madman and rhyme-enhancing motets have in common is their ability to operate in the phonetic realm, to excavate from words their sound. Poetry naturally exaggerates that sonic aspect of language, precisely because of its dependence on rhyme. It is perhaps no coincidence that one common word for poetry, as distinct from prose, was "rime." Although there are no formal treatises on French versification until the late fourteenth century, the Latin tradition of the *ars poetria* nonetheless sheds light on ways of thinking about rhyme and verbal sound. In the following brief account of the distinction in the third book of Brunetto Latini's *Li livres dou tresor* (ca. 1260), part of which offers a short *ars poetria*, the author explains "prose" and "rime" thus:

> La grant partison de tos parleors est en dui mainieres, une qui est en prose et un autre qui est en rime. Mais li ensengnement de retorique sont comun d'andui, sauve ce que la voie de prose est large et pleniere, si come est ore la comune parleure des jens, mais le sentier de rime est plus estrois et plus fors, si come cellui qui est clos et fermé de murs et de palis, ce est a dire de pois et de nonbre et de mesure certaine, de quoi l'en ne puet ne ne doit trepasser.

> All discourse can be divided into two kinds, one in prose and the other in rhyme. But the teachings of rhetoric are common to both, except that the pathway of prose is broad and full, as is now the common speech of people, but the pathway of rhyme is more narrow and difficult, as is that

73 Bildhauer and Mills, "Introduction," 2.

which is closed in and shut all round by walls and fences, that is to say of weight and of number and of certain measure, which one cannot or should not transgress.[74]

Latini describes rhyme here as a "weight" ("pois"), and although he is referring also to the accent of metrically ordered poetry, there is the sense, too, of the physical, non-semantic effects of rhyme—the pull and leaning towards like sounds. That vernacular authors at least took deliberate pleasure in "pure rhyme" is evident in traditions predating Adam. As Ruth Harvey has argued, the troubadour Marcabru went so far as to invent words—to make up nonsense—for the sake of the rhyme schemes in his songs.[75] Sarah Kay's penetrating study of an Occitan "grammatical" tradition—a collection of vernacular treatises—also illustrates how important rhyme sound was as a principle of composition.[76]

Such contexts also shed light on how contemporaries may have experienced the sound of rhyme in motets: as a facet of linguistic sound identified and sanctioned in a theoretical tradition. There is a more direct connection linking the words of motets to grammatical precepts. Johannes de Grocheio's description of the genre, which gives at least as much emphasis to the text as to the music, has a curious double definition for motet's words. He describes them as having numerous *words* or *texts* ("plura dictamina"), but also as having a structure of multifarious *syllables* ("multimodam discretionem syllabarum").[77] These are not two different kinds of texts, but rather two different conceptions of the same thing: words as poetry, and words as a pattern of syllables and sounds. The origins of such a distinction takes us to the genealogy of language itself. For the steps from syllable to word echo the foundations of grammatical understanding. As discussed in chapter 1, the building blocks of language are rooted in pure sound or "vox." The opening of Donatus's *Ars maior* traces the genealogy of words from "vox" to "littera" and to "syllaba," marking the ascent to words themselves. In grammatical terms, Grocheio's explanation of the

74 Brunetto Latini, *Li Livres dou tresor*, ed. Spurgeon Baldwin (Tempe, AZ: Arizona Center for Medieval and Renaissance Studies, 2003), Book 3, ch. 10; translation from Smith, *French Double and Triple Motets*, 353.

75 Ruth Harvey, "Rhymes and 'Rusty Words' in Marcabru's Songs," *French Studies* 56 (2002): 1–14.

76 Sarah Kay, "Occitan Grammar as a Science of Endings," in *New Medieval Literatures* 11 (2009): 39–61. I am grateful to Professor Kay for sharing this essay with me prior to publication.

77 "The motet is a music assembled from numerous elements, having numerous poetic texts or a multifarious structure of syllables" ("Motetus vero est cantus ex pluribus compositus, habens plura dictamina vel multimodam discretionem syllabum"), quoting from Page, "Johannes de Grocheio on Secular Music," 36.

motet allows for the texts as words—that is semantic units—but also as syllables, the pre-semantic, pre-linguistic building blocks of words. We should read it against a staple definition such as that found in Donatus's *Ars maior*:

> Syllaba est conprehensio litterarum vel unius vocalis enuntio temporum capax.[78]

> A syllable is a grouping of letters or a beat of time for the enunciation of a single vowel.

At the conjunction of poetry, music, and theory, we arrive at the possibility for hearing rhyme not only as a building block for poetry, but as a sound signifying the etymology of language itself. If the proposition to hear in the motet the "origins of language" seems a proto-Romantic gesture, then we should keep in mind the powerful historiographical and genealogical theme among linguists such as Dante.

All the sounds we have listened to up to this point meditate in different ways on the power of language's originary sonority. But of all the literary and musical means of excavating those sounds through language, the motet can perhaps do more to the sound of words than any other medium. If the super-musical seems to disconnect sound from the sense of language, heard another way, it could be said to make the very essence of language accessible to the ears, and nowhere more so than in its play on rhyme. For what is a rhyme, after all, but a kind of sense-less phonetic down-beat within words? In the polytextual setting, it was possible to make audible the pure sound of rhyme unhinged from its semantic context. Rhyme is a phonetic connection between words, not necessarily a semantic one, as Adam's rhyming madman demonstrated. But a motet can go further. Making like rhymes sound together, it could dispense with the semantic context altogether, making audible the sonic source of language.

A Music-less Song

I offer as *envoi* one final witness to music's affinity with the pre-linguistic: a motet that stages an act of singing. A popular occurrence in the vernacular repertory, the voices of this motet nonetheless offer moving ontology of song's non-semantic expressivity. The singing in question occurs in the three-part

---

78 Donatus, *Ars maior*, Part 1. 3, from the edition in Holtz, *Donat et la tradition de l'enseignement grammatical*, 603–7 for the complete definitions of "vox," "littera," and "syllaba."

motet *Par un matinet* (295)/*Lés un bosket* (296)/*Portare* (M34a).[79] The two upper voices rehearse the familiar topic of the *pastourelle*, set over the melisma "Portare" for the Feast of the Assumption. Triplum and motetus present two perspectives of Robin and Marion's relationship, narrated from the external position of an onlooker, and reflect worlds of heightened—non-verbal—sound. In the triplum, Robin spies Marion "sighing" to herself, and then later "lamenting" ("dementer") as she fears Robin's forgetfulness. Sounds of sorrow are then overlaid by Robin's joyful appearance, playing his flute ("flajolant") and laughing ("riant"), and finally, unknowingly perhaps, singing: his final communiqué is a borrowed voice, the refrain *Marote, alons au bois jouer!* (R 1297).

It is the motetus that most eloquently embodies the joyousness of the sounding "letter" of language. The narrator starts with a view of Robin kitted out in his standard Robin-issue of boots, green hat, hood, and so on. Once again he is in a state of hypermusicality, playing his pipe. Marion and her companion Emmelos jump (for joy, perhaps) as they hear him ("l'ot"), and as they do so, the poem tells us of songs heard echoing in the meadows. There is a word for these sounds: "li dorenlos, li dorenlos." They are nonsense vocables, creating words that have no sense, and are often used in this repertory to stand in for "chanson," especially in acts of internal reportage. In this text they are the song in a more literal sense, staged through their own nonsense. Twisting back internally "o" "o," as well as echoing one another, from them rhyme and assonance also emanate, moving across the whole text, assembling resonances with the women "Marot" and "Emmelos," and gathering in words associated with music-making and hearing from "flagelot" to "ot" (meaning both "hearing" and "having"). What echoes—or better, renews—in this poem is rhyme and assonance. In that constant turnover of phonetic likeness, the poem stages something like a motet. I let them "sing" here, music-less:

Triplum

Par un matinet l'autrier
m'aloie esbanoiant;
si comme aloie tous seus pensant,
Marotele vi seant
leis un sentier,
qui son ami atendoit,
Robin, qu'ele amoit tant.
En souspirant disoit:
"Aymi!
Robinet, biaus dous amis,
mise m'avés en oubli!"

---

79 It survives in *Mo*, fols. 282ʳ–283ᵛ and *Ba*, fols. 34ᵛ–35ʳ.

Et quant l'oï si dementer,
pour li reconforter
voil cele part aler,
quant Robins i vint courant
tout flajolant.
Si la prist a acoler
et puis li dist tout en riant:
"Marote, alons au bois jouer!"

The other morning I went out to amuse myself. As I went along, thinking, I spied Marotele sitting beside a path, waiting for her sweetie,
Robin, whom she loved very much. Sighing, she said: "Alas! Robinet,
fair, sweet friend, you have forgotten me!" And when I heard her lament
thus, I wanted to go to her and comfort her, when I saw Robin bound-
ing up, playing his flute. He began to embrace her and then laughing
he said: *"Marote, let's go and play in the woods!"*

Motetus

Lés un bosket vi Robechon,
mout y ot joli vallet:
housiaus ot oins et chapeau vert,
sourcot griset et chaperon.
Il n'estoit pas sans son chienet;
fretel, coutel ot et baston,
sounete avoit,
son flajolot.
Si flagoloit;
Marote saut, quant ele l'ot
et Emmelos, la bele.
Or renouvele
li dorenlos,
li dorenlos
en la praele,
quant chascune pastourele
avoeques li son ami ot.[80]

---

80 *Mo*, fols. 282ʳ–283ᵛ.

Beside a wood I spied Robechon. He was a very handsome chap: oiled boots he had and a green hat, a gray topcoat and hood. He was not without his little dog; he had a pipe, knife, and a stick; he had an instrument, his flute, and he played it; Marote leapt when she heard it and so did the beautiful Emmelos. Now renews [echoes] the "dorenlos, the dorenlos" in the meadow, for each shepherdess has her sweetie with her.

*

Through its unique ability to make rhyme sound transparent, separate from a semantic context, the motet aspired to an eloquence that surpassed even that of the revelatory madman. In the case of Adam's motets, rooted in the vernacular, secular concerns of his city, poetic identity, and relationship to love, the supermusical made audible social and personal unity and dissonance. But the ability to manipulate verbal sound was also a dangerous, at times precarious talent. It had the potential to distort the sound of language in ways that could cause terrible offense. In some quarters the sound of verbal dissonance would have summoned action from the devil himself. While up to now our focus has been largely on the vernacular repertories, it is time to turn our attention to contexts in which the stakes of sense and sound were altogether more fraught. In the remaining chapters I wish to explore the large corpus of devotional motets and "chansons pieuses" in conjunction with a related sphere of sound: the sound of prayer.

5 | Sound in Prayer

The powerful bond between singing and praying in the Middle Ages needs little introduction. In many quarters, the sacred word was synonymous with the sung voice, as the vast repertory of liturgical chant testifies. However, while the official acts of liturgy will play a part in what follows, another practice of prayer will mainly concern us here. To distinguish it from the official, corporate round of liturgical services, historians have often termed this "private devotion," that is, prayer designed for practice by an individual or small group, often alone, or in the presence of a communal liturgical performance. In the mid-thirteenth century, in France and across Europe, such practices exploded, particularly in non-clerical realms, and increasingly in vernacular tongues. The broadening accessibility of the sacred took many forms, from burgeoning cults of Marian devotion to vernacular religious drama and vast civic processions, and is evident, of course, in a larger repertory of devotional song, from vernacular chansons to motets. It expressed itself also as a kind of bibliomania: in the burgeoning market of new forms of prayer books, among them books of hours. These books, the iPads of private devotion, were the means by which many prayed, and are witness to the daily habits of meditation.

At first sight, such books appear remote from concerns of sound, and especially musical sound. They are characterized, rather, by an intense visuality, suggesting their use to be quiet—books for the eyes, more than for the ears. Yet they interlock in numerous ways with a complex practice of sound in prayer. Closer investigation will reveal how they reflected and prompted acts of performance; and how through a sophisticated visual lexicon, they might also provoke interior listening by prompting memory of known sounds, even shocking viewers to configure in the imagination monstrous sounds with no known correlate. I will suggest that prayer books hover at the very boundary of representation and reality. On the one hand, we may see them as encoding and representing the living, often clamorous, habitat of prayer beyond the parchment; on the other, they are themselves a kind of sounding reality—simultaneously a primary site of devotional experience that is imbued, through images of sound, with sonic distraction and reinforcement no less meaningful as that audible in the exterior realm. In both registers—internal and external to the book—they embody a sense of sound in prayer that is efficacious, but also potentially controversial in its power to confuse and disrupt prayer acts. It is in that sonority that we may forge the strongest, perhaps most surprising connection to musical culture.

The other concern in this portion of the book is thus to demonstrate how much the sonority of prayer—material and immaterial—had in common with musical traditions flourishing simultaneously in northern France, above all with the rich corpus of devotional motets and "chansons pieuses." In the first place, prayer offers a fertile new context in which to understand the function and experience of devotional repertories, and encourages us to understand musical experience as prayer-like. It is in the locus of sound, however, that I wish to posit a more revealing relationship. For in attuning to the sonority of prayer books, we discover new contexts for framing the sound of the large corpus of devotional motets. Heard in the wider sonic environment of prayer, the characteristic confusion of the supermusical assumes a very precise meaning; new possibilities emerge for the sense of that sound. Mutually reinforcing, these seemingly disparate materials define a sound that is at once controversial and provocative in its potential for distraction or confusion. Inherent in that sonority is its call for action. In prayer books, as in musical performance, such sound exacts work from its readers and listeners, be it to unravel a didactic message or to transform unfettered sound into devotional sense. Indeed, a final correlation we shall see between these two spheres is not just their shared use of such sonority as impetus for edifying work, but also, on occasion, a sharing of mechanisms by which sonic provocation might be resolved. Each, albeit in very different ways, embodies polyphony as a means of putting sounds and words in relations that cause disturbance to sense, and require action to forge resolution. It will be our task to see how different media—bookish or musical—are both alike and different in their use of polyphony to generate devotional "sound"; and also how the methods of reading, listening, and singing work in free exchange in the process of resolving sound into sense.

The following three chapters are concerned with the sound of prayer as embodied in prayer books, and with how the sense of this sound was informed by, and also facilitated understanding of, contemporary devotional musical practice, especially that of the motet. Before we begin, though, it will be useful to flesh out the environment of prayer and the potential relationship between the two spheres of sound. In the present interlude, I wish to offer a bridge into sound's devotional potential with brief contextualization of two essential aspects: the nature of prayer itself, and the affective bond between praying and singing.

Approaches to Praying

What did it mean to pray? This most complex of questions has most often been approached by defining prayer as a set of ritual practices—of words uttered and actions performed. In turn, the experience has commonly been accessed through the texts by which people prayed. However, there has been shift in emphasis in recent years towards the felt, experiential dimension and to the importance of memory and association on the part of the supplicant. Perhaps the boldest formulation of such an approach occurs in recent essays by Rachel Fulton, and especially in her study of the use and meaning of a twelfth-century manuscript of prayers by St. Anselm.[1] In contrast to thinking of prayer in terms of the texts and rituals of their performance, Fulton privileges experience and effect, as brought about through habits of praying. She writes, "there remains to date a palpable reluctance among academics (as opposed to monastic scholars) to come to terms with the experiential effects such technical practices were likely, or expected, to produce."[2] Her ensuing analysis asks how readers of Anselm's prayers would have used the books in a physical as well as a cognitive sense, and explores how sensations contributed to prayer's meaning and effect: "if we think of it not simply as an activity but a technique—a craft requiring skill—then we will recognize the body, its location in space and time, its movements, its breath, its sensory impressions, as itself as important a tool as the mind for 'making thoughts about God'."[3] One aspect of that more experiential approach is to consider the role of memory and association in the "craft" of prayer. Drawing in particular on Mary Carruthers's study of medieval memorial practices,[4] and engaging with Jean Leclercq's foundational work on meditative reading,[5] Fulton suggests some of the associative and recollected

---

1 Rachel Fulton, "Praying with Anselm at Admont: A Meditation of Practice," *Speculum* 81 (2006): 700–733. This essay also offers a thoughtful and detailed exploration of some of the mainstays in the scholarship on medieval prayer, and I direct readers there for further references to this vast bibliography. See also Fulton's essay " 'Taste and See that the Lord is Sweet' (Ps. 33:9): The Flavor of God in the Monastic West," *Journal of Religion* 86 (2006): 169–204 for further discussion of the sensuality of prayer.

2 Fulton, "Praying with Anselm," 703.

3 Ibid. 720.

4 See especially Carruthers, *The Craft of Thought*.

5 Jean Leclercq, *The Love of Learning and the Desire for God: A Study of Monastic Culture*, transl. Catharine Misrahi (New York: Fordham University Press, 1961, 3rd ed. 1982,

network of texts and images that the words of Anselm may have provoked in his twelfth-century reader. Her hypothetical recreation of a reader's likely process of praying traces a "*ductus*, the flow of ornaments and recollections that would make up her compositional path."[6]

Ideas of prayer's recollective and somatic aspect also feature in work by art historians Beth Williamson and Joan Holladay, who demonstrate that part of the efficacy of a devotional object—a picture, sculpture, or book—was what Williamson terms its devotional "afterglow." In her exploration of altarpieces, Williamson illustrates how an image's association with liturgical ritual might resonate in situations of non-liturgical or devotional use. With regard to an altarpiece by Filippino Lippi, she explains that it

> could adopt a multivalent role: by definition, as an altarpiece it would have been viewed, at least some of the time, in the context of Eucharistic ritual. It might also be expected to retain some kind of Eucharistic or liturgical "afterglow," just by its position on an altar and by its association with the ceremonies performed below it. In addition, it can also function as a cue to various types and levels of devotional thought and activity.[7]

Holladay's essay is especially pertinent to the present project, for the central object of study is a book of hours (the Hours of Jeanne d'Evreux). As Holladay teases out the book's place in Jeanne's library, and its relationship to other texts and objects of the queen's devotional life, she effectively reconstitutes a devotional *ductus*, demonstrating "how certain of her manuscripts—indeed works in other media—may have been related to one another."[8] That the media of association could involve music is demonstrated in Susan Boynton's study of prayers in monastic psalters, which reconstructs an intricate web of liturgical and devotional reference that would be brought to bear in the act of prayer.[9]

---

first published in French in 1957), and his "Ways of Prayer and Contemplation. II: Western," in *Christian Spirituality: Origins to the Twelfth Century*, ed. Bernard McGinn and John Meyendorff, in collaboration with Jean Leclercq, World Spirituality: An Encyclopedic History of the Religious Quest 16 (New York: Crossroad, 1985), 415–26.

6 Fulton, "Praying with Anselm," 730.

7 Beth Williamson, "Altarpieces, Liturgy, and Devotion," *Speculum*, 79 (2004): 341–406, quoting here from 387. For the full discussion of Lippi's "Virgin and Child with Sts. Jerome and Dominic," see 383–87.

8 Joan Holladay, "Fourteenth-Century French Queens as Collectors and Readers of Books: Jeanne d'Evreux and her Contemporaries," *Journal of Medieval History* 32 (2006): 69–100, quoting here from 73.

9 Susan Boynton, "Prayer as Liturgical Performance in Eleventh- and Twelfth-Century Monastic Psalters," *Speculum* 82 (2007): 896–929.

This rich new field of scholarship offers fruitful models for thinking about sound's use in prayer, and also prayer's association with song. The notion of prayerful "ductus" chimes in productive ways with the notion of visual signs of sound as notation—that is, as mnemonic for sound, heard in the inner chambers of the mind. Thus, even in sources that lack conventional notation for music, we may need to attend to other visual cues that prompted aural recollection—a kind of sonic "afterglow." The experience of sound, as somatic memory or as an act of performance, is then an aspect of prayer that needs to be taken as seriously as physical gesture or material and textual association. Conversely, song itself may provoke memorial association with the prayer-act, such that the two modes of performance may be seen to be interchangeable. Thus in reconstructing the dialogue between prayer and sound, there is potential, too, to contribute to the current conversation regarding the medieval experience of prayer. As we reanimate the lost sonority of prayer books and forge associative links between them and musical repertories, there emerges the new possibility that musical listening and performance may themselves be understood as a form of prayer.

Affective Affinities: Song as Prayer

The second context I wish to bring to the exploration of sound in prayer concerns perhaps the most literal connection between prayers and song: their innate affective affinity. While books of hours and Psalters catered to the growing spiritual appetite of lay and clerical supplicants and the desire to create new rituals for praying outside the liturgy, there is also abundant evidence that their music staked out new spiritual territory. One particularly rich example of interaction emerged around the cult of devotion to Mary. In her recent history of the Virgin, Miri Rubin illustrates how the essential humanness and femininity of Mary emphasized in the thirteenth and fourteenth centuries opened up new affective modes of devotion, arguing that Mary "became increasingly an enabling site for reflection on the expression of emotion."[10] This was especially true in non-clerical circles, as the Marian emphasis of books of hours themselves witness. Not surprisingly, song and poetry were another natural consequence, and many vernacular traditions were established in her honor: songs associated with Gautier de Coinci's *Miracles de Nostre Dame*, or the *Cantigas de Santa Maria*, offered fervent counterpoint to devotion to her in words and art.

---

10 Miri Rubin, *Emotion and Devotion: The Meaning of Mary in Medieval Religious Cultures*, The Natalie Zemon Davis Annual Lectures (Budapest: Central European University Press, 2009); see esp. ch. 3, "Emotion and Selves," 79–110. Quoting here from 79. See also her *Mother of God*.

Elsewhere, and not confined to Marian devotion, the Franciscan *laude* were emotional tools suiting the Order's campaign of affective accessibility,[11] while the *laudesi* and *disciplinati* companies of cities like Florence and Siena also recognized the value of having communities sing their devotion together.[12]

In northern France, the trouvère and motet traditions were also host to a large devotional corpus. Although the motet will be our primary focus in subsequent chapters, I shall focus for now on the monophonic repertory, in brief demonstration of song's prayer-like aspect and the deep rootedness of music-making in activities of prayer. In a recent edition and commentary of a core representation, Marcia Epstein estimates that of the roughly 2,000 songs extant produced by trouvères in thirteenth-century France, at least 10 percent had texts on devotional topics.[13] As her analysis illustrates, there were also many ways in which song lyrics echoed popular doctrinal themes and religious symbolism, recast in the idiom of courtly convention.[14] While there is little direct evidence about whom such songs were written for, the absence of erudite clerical doctrine in their texts argues against an exclusively clerical audience. Epstein imagines them as designed for a constituency of lay men and women, from a middle-class or noble social stratum.[15] In other words, their audience was precisely those now also purchasing and praying from prayer books. One obvious social correlation may be seen in the French royal household, where inventories list chansonniers alongside Psalters and books of hours.[16]

---

11 On which see, for example, Alessandro Vettori, "Singing with Angels: Iacopone da Todi's Prayerful Rhetoric," in *Franciscans at Prayer*, ed. Timothy Johnson (Leiden: Brill, 2007), 221–48.

12 See Wilson, *Music and Merchants*, and for an edition of some of the *laude* see *The Florence Laudario: An Edition of Florence, Biblioteca Nazionale centrale, Rari 18*, ed. Blake Wilson, with texts edited and translated by Nello Barbieri, Recent Researches in the Music of the Middle Ages and Early Renaissance 29 (Madison: A-R Editions, 1995).

13 *"Prions en chantant": Devotional Songs of the Trouvères*, ed. and transl. Marcia Epstein (Toronto: University of Toronto Press, 1997), 13.

14 Ibid., 20–53.

15 Ibid., 16.

16 See, for example, the inventory of Clémence of Hungary, widow of Louis X, which contains a chansonnier among an ample stock of devotional books. For a full transcription and commentary, see "Inventaire et vente après décès des biens de la reine Clémence de Hongrie veuve de Louis le Hutin 1328," in Louis Douët-d'Arcq, *Nouveau recueil de comptes de l'argenterie des rois de France* (Paris: Librairie Renouard, 1874), 37–112. The famous inventories relating to the library of Charles V date later than our period of interest, but also reflect the collecting habits of Charles's royal ancestors, and reveal a large body of music books; they list notated books among the collection of liturgical and devotional books. For complete transcriptions see Léopold Delisle, *Recherches sur la librairie de Charles V*, 3 vols. (Paris: Honoré Champion, 1907).

Songbooks, moreover, were produced and decorated by the same artists responsible for the production of prayer books (we shall see this to be the case with the Montpellier Codex), while in cities such as Arras, a renowned center of vernacular song production, there is abundant documentation of the complex interaction of secular and religious ritual.[17] But it is the songs themselves that best illustrate the resonance with prayer texts. Two examples, surviving in manuscripts made in northern France at the end of the thirteenth century, will be considered.[18]

Et cler et lai (R 82) offers explicit indication of the social inclusiveness of vernacular devotional habits, habits that self-evidently now included song.[19] The opening of five-strophe song begins with a call to attention for both "cler et lai":

Et cler et lai
tout sanz delai
or escoutés m'entente:
chançon ferai,
si chanterai de la roïne gente
en qui costéz Dex descendi,
qui de dolor nos desfendi
et de grant tormente.
Chantons en sans atente,
que je me puis mout bien chanter.
De cele devons nos chanter
qui touz nos rendi vie:
Or nos aidiez
et conseillés,
douce virge Marie.

Both cleric and lay,
without delay
listen now to my intention:
I will make a song,
and sing to the noble queen

17 On which see Symes, *A Common Stage.*

18 These are Paris, Bibliothèque nationale de France, f. fr. 24406 (Chansonnier de la Vallière) (*V*); and Paris, Bibliothèque nationale de France, nouv. ac. f. fr. 1050 (Chansonnier de Clairambault) (*X*). They contain thirty and thirty-one devotional songs, respectively. These are the basis of Epstein's edition.

19 The source for the song is *X*, fols. 267ᵛ–268ᵛ. The complete song is edited in *"Prions en chantant"*, 190–93. The translation and transcription quoted here are based on Epstein's with occasional minor adjustments.

into whose sides God descended,
who defended us from pain
and from great torment.
Let us sing of this without delay,
for I can sing well.
We ought to sing of her who gave life to us all:
Now aid and counsel us,
sweet Virgin Mary.

The song also exemplifies a strong bond with the courtly model. It opens with a familiar gesture of intention (to sing about a source of female inspiration) and proclamation of lyric prowess ("je me puis mout bien chanter"). However, the standard motivation of the lady is now displaced to the Virgin. As the song progresses, it lists her moral, physical, and spiritual attributes, as is again common practice. However, the standard courtly tropes merge or are overwritten with imagery imported from a Marian lexicon. In strophe 3, line 1, Mary is the "fountain of pity" ("fons de pitié"); in strophe 4, lines 4–5, she is implored as a source of great mercy, "body without discord, have mercy" ("cors sans descors, / misericors"). Subject position is also an important part of the song's dynamic: notwithstanding the first person of the opening lines, the strophe concludes with a refrain, repeated at the end of all subsequent strophes, that speaks for a collective "nos." Thus the song hovers between personal and communal experience.

Contrast this with a song that enjoys the more passionate possibilities of the first-person subject position. *Je ne vueil plus de sohier* (R 1310) deploys another familiar courtly love topos to establish desolate self-expression.[20] It opens with a declaration that singing must cease. However, whereas in the secular realm such renunciation is often the result of burning desire or failure in love, here it is born of a different kind of passion—love for the Virgin, and the desire to pray rather that sing:

Je ne vueil plus de sohier
chanter, ne faire chançon:
la mere Dieu vueill proier
que me face vrai pardon,
et me face acorde et pes
vers son fil de mes mesfés,
qu'anemis
ne m'ai mort et pris.

20 The source is X, fol. 265ʳ. The complete song is edited in *"Prions en chantant"*, 166–69; my transcription and translation again follow Epstein except for minor adjustments.

Tres douce Marie,
ne m'oubliés mie.

I do not wish to sing of foulness any longer,
nor to make songs:
I want to pray to the mother of God,
that she may grant me true pardon
and set me at peace and accord with her son
regarding my misdeeds,
so that the enemy might not kill and seize me.
Most sweet Mary,
do not forget me.

The song moves on to a more obviously prayer-like laudation of the Virgin, and finally calls on her for intercession, to preserve the protagonist from the devil. As with *Et cler et lai*, the song also makes use of a refrain, here the heart-felt plea that the Virgin *"ne m'oubliés mie."*

There are obvious, audible ties in both songs to the rich Marian prayer tradition. Most noticeably, their vocabulary of Marian representation intersects with the lexicon found in prayers and devotional imagery. Their play on subject position also mirrors some facets of prayer books. *Et cler et lai*'s oscillation between singular and collective expression reminds us of similar changing perspectives found in prayer books, which often mix communal and personal expression. For example, in sections of prayer books devoted to the Hours, which most clearly shadow the form of communal liturgical context, prayers often assume a collective or third-person standpoint, emphasized by the frequent rubric "let us pray" ("oremus"). But books are often host to a range of stand-alone prayers, not just to the Virgin but to many saints and for a variety of causes, both in Latin and the vernacular, and the deeply personal tone of *Je ne vueil plus de sohier* echoes the sentiment of many in a first-person voice. Compare it, for instance, with the opening lines of a first-person vernacular prayer to the Virgin popular in books of hours (and reproduced here from a book of hours in the Walters Art Museum, W 40, produced in Paris in the last quarter of the thirteenth century, typical of the kind we shall see more of presently):

Tres douce dame ie vous cri merci et vous pri que vouz voullez prier vostre chier filz que il ai pitie et merci de moi.

Very sweet lady, I cry to you for mercy, and pray to you that you wish to beg your dear son to have pity and mercy on me.

The similarities rest not only in a common affective vocabulary and personal viewpoint. Songs and prayers also share formal qualities. Both songs conclude each strophe with a brief refrain that appeals directly to Mary for help. In each, the repetition establishes a devotional continuity across the song, the refrain functioning as a kind of spiritual intention. In *Et cler et lai* that repetition is further underscored by a simple aspect of musical design that lends the refrain a mesmerizing memorability. Taking a serpentine form, the song is saturated with repetitions, and the refrain itself is a melodic citation of the song's opening (see example 5.1). The effect is thus one of devotional reinforcement through melodic amplification.

Prayer texts are also by their nature repetitious. The Hours and Psalms were intended for constant reiteration, day after day, week after week. More locally, a feature of the most popular stand-alone prayers is their internal emphasis on counting-out and repetition. Staples such the fifteen *Joys of the Virgin* and the fifteen *Oes* operate around wholesale recitations of familiar prayers such as the *Pater noster* or *Ave Maria* at the conclusion of a verse of prayer. These prayers-within-prayers function as a form of refrain.

EXAMPLE 5.1. *Et cler et lai*, opening strophe (X, fols. 267ᵛ–268ᵛ)

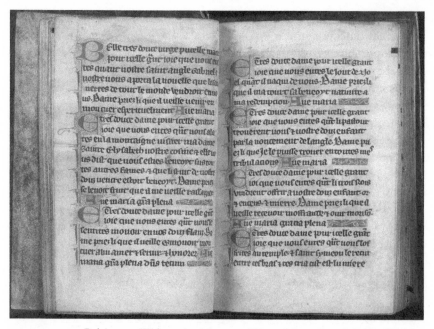

FIGURE 5.1. Baltimore, Walters Art Museum, W 40, fols. 14ᵛ–15ʳ. © The Walters Art Museum

Figure 5.1 [website 5.1] shows fols. 14ᵛ–15ʳ of Walters 40 (measuring 159 × 105 mm), the beginning of the Fifteen Joys of the Virgin. Each of the verses is broken with a recitation of an *Ave Maria*. We see the incipits "Ave maria," marked in red ink, similar in function and look to the refrains in the song.

These intricate associative networks between vernacular art song and texts in prayer books illustrate their profound compatibility at the level of affective purpose. The heightened subjectivity of the trouvère repertory, with its intricate rhetoric of self-representation and expression, was a natural—indeed inevitable—point of reference to develop the ever-personal dimension of prayer. It is against that backdrop that we may explore those other more complex relationships between prayer and sound outlined at the opening of this chapter. For if there is a broad sense in which singing can complement or supplement prayer—a sense in which a song can be like a prayer, and vice versa—in the realm of verbal sound, active performance, and memory, this period witnesses another, much more contentious, compatibility between the two traditions. With our broad contexts in place, it is to evidence of sound's more challenging and controversial place in prayer that we shall turn next.

*

The following three chapters together form a devotional triptych, and attempt to reconstitute the conversation between sound in prayer books and that of the devotional motet. Chapters 6 and 7 reinsert sound into the evidence of prayer books and will show how concerns about the sound heard and produced in prayer informed devotional experience and shaped the act of praying through the book. As this material is new to musicology, I devote the first chapter to a broad contextualization of sound in prayer books. Drawing widely on art historical literature and the history of devotion, this chapter illuminates the range of signs for sound, and explores how the contexts of use and ownership may help explain their function. It is followed in chapter 7 by a close engagement with two books of hours, to show how discourses of sound present in the visual programs may have shaped the experience of prayer. Via case studies, we shall see how the collision of sonorities in prayer book imagery posed a challenge to the eye, but no less to the ear. In resolving the meaning of these visual intrusions of sound, I shall consider the ways the books behave like the polyphonic texture of a motet, not simply as analogy, but as having a musicality akin to the collisions of words familiar in that genre. Chapter 8 brings us back to the motet, and asks how the experience and meaning of sound in prayer might also have influenced musical listening, and the complex negotiation of sense from sound. Devoted to a large corpus of devotional motets in fascicles 1–4 of the Montpellier Codex (*Mo*), it will suggest that the hallmark sonority of confusion in these pieces was related to the concerns of sound in prayer. Not only that, we shall see how prayer books themselves—in their material form and conventions—could offer listeners to the motet the bibliographic mechanism to help them negotiate their way to meaning and sense in the sound of the music. Overarching this portion of *The Sense of Sound* is an attempt to show how the boundaries between activities of prayer and singing were in some instances more fluid than we may imagine, or than is allowed for by the modern categories of "prayer" or "song." A recurring topic in the song repertories eloquently sums up our new trajectory: "prions en chantans."

6 | Sound in Prayer Books

Sometime around the middle of the thirteenth century, the sound of prayer took an unruly turn. As the well-regulated chorus of chant and recitation that filled the chambers of public and private practice was increasingly supplemented by the new media of prayer books, there appeared a startling new dissonance. Bursting out of line endings, clamoring inside illuminated capitals, stalking around the margins, a noisy orchestra of fantastical and outrageous sonorities transformed the soundscape of prayer. Paradoxically, such sound was contingent on the eye as much as the ear; artists' ink and paint rather than the notes and voices of musicians. Yet as we shall see, the visual presence of sound engrained in parchment was a notation of sorts: inscribing audible experience and deeply-felt beliefs relating to sound in prayer.

Before we go further, it is as well to make explicit the intense visuality of prayerful sound.[1] Folios from Cambridge, Trinity College Library, MS B. 11. 22, an early fourteenth-century Flemish book of hours (measuring 168 × 130 mm),

---

1 Lilian Randall, *Images in the Margins of Gothic Manuscripts* (Berkeley: University of California Press, 1966) remains the essential guide to marginalia, offering a comprehensive catalogue of marginalia from devotional manuscripts dating ca. 1250–1400. There are many interpretations of marginalia, to which I shall refer later in the chapter. For now, I direct the reader to the following studies, which offer the most in-depth consideration: Michael Camille, *Image on the Edge: The Margins of Medieval Art* (London: Reaktion Books, 1992); Lucy Freeman Sandler, "Reflections on the Construction of Hybrids in English Gothic Marginal Illustration," in *Art, the Ape of Nature: Studies in Honor of H. W. Janson*, ed. Moshe Barasch and Lucy Freeman Sandler (New York: Harry N. Abrams; Englewood Cliffs: Prentice Hall, 1981), 51–65; ead., "The Word in the Text and the Image in the Margin: The Case of the Luttrell Psalter," *Journal of the Walters Art Gallery* 54 (1996): 87–99, and ead., "In and Around the Text: The Question of Marginality in the Macclesfield

exemplify a commonplace in the cacophony. In figure 6.1 (fols. 19ᵛ–20ʳ), two
tonsured clerics grow out of foliage frames at top and bottom right, bowing or
blowing their instruments, accompanied by a triangle-clanging figure projecting out of a line ending mid-folio. Little wonder the figure above is inspired to
gyrate. They are counterpoint to a vielle-player, sawing at his instrument, and
a trumpeter, who gaze across from the adjacent folio. In figure 6.2 (fol. 36ᵛ),
a dog and man double act stride in from the left with their bagpipes to
create a noisy ensemble with a man swinging bells, and a more modest
trumpet. Such abrasive accompaniments at least had the virtue of being recognizably musical and produced by human agents. They were, however, amplified by gangs of imaginary sound monsters. In figure 6.3, from the margins of
the English-made British Library Add. 42130, fol. 62ᵛ (the Luttrell Psalter,
dating from the 1330s, measuring 350 × 245 mm), a shouting head on legs
runs across the *bas-de-page*;[2] in figure 6.4, from fol. 185ᵛ of the same book,

---

Psalter," in *The Cambridge Illuminations: The Conference Papers*, ed. Stella Panayotova
(London: Harvey Miller, 2007), 105–14.

The bibliography relating to books of hours and Psalters is likewise considerable.
Here I direct readers to some excellent overviews of the tradition. For books of hours see
especially Roger Wieck, *Time Sanctified: The Book of Hours in Medieval Art and Life*, with
essays by Lawrence Poos, Virginia Reinburg, and John Plummer (New York: G. Braziller
in Association with the Walters Art Gallery, 1988). For a recent account of English
prayer books see Eamon Duffy, *Marking the Hours: English People and their Prayers, 1240–
1570* (New Haven: Yale University Press, 2006). On readership and literacy and books of
hours see Paul Saenger, "Books of Hours and the Reading Habits of the Later Middle
Ages," in *The Culture of Print: Power and the Uses of Print in Early Modern Europe*, ed. Roger
Chartier, transl. Lydia Cochrane (Princeton: Princeton University Press, 1989), 141–73.
For an introduction to the forms of the medieval Psalter, see Rosemary Muir Wright,
"Introducing the Medieval Psalter," in *Studies in the Illustration of the Psalter*, ed. Brendan
Cassidy and Rosemary Muir Wright (Stamford: Shaun Tyas, 2000), 1–11. For the early
history of the Psalter see William Noel, *The Harley Psalter*, Cambridge Studies in
Palaeography and Codicology 4 (Cambridge: Cambridge University Press, 1996) and *The
Utrecht Psalter in Medieval Art: Picturing the Psalms of David*, ed. Koert van der Horst,
William Noel, and Wilhelmina Wüstefeld (Tuurdijk: Hes Publishers, 1996). For the
development of Psalters in the thirteenth century see Karen Gould, *The Psalter and Hours
of Yolande of Soissons* (Cambridge, MA: Mediaeval Academy of America, 1978). Michael
Camille's monograph on the fourteenth-century Luttrell Psalter includes additional
information about the later development of the Psalter and the patterns of its decoration
and organization: see *Mirror in Parchment: The Luttrell Psalter and the Making of Medieval
England* (London: Reaktion Books, 1998).

2 For a complete color facsimile see *The Luttrell Psalter: A Facsimile*, with commentary
by Michelle Brown (London: British Library, 2006). See esp. 29–51 for a detailed folio-
by-folio description of the visual programs. The dimensions given are the folio size; with
the cover, the book expands to 370 × 270 mm.

FIGURE 6.1. Cambridge, Trinity College Library, MS B. 11. 22, fols. 19ᵛ–20ʳ. By permission of the Master and Fellows of Trinity College, Cambridge

a strange beast whose nether regions form a trumpet blasts into the margins. Elsewhere, animals have virtuosic musical facility, as in figure 6.5 [website image 6.1], from fol. 82ʳ of Baltimore, Walters Art Museum, W 45, a late thirteenth-century northern French Psalter (measuring 186 × 125 mm), where a rabbit tootles in the margin, "sound lines" from his instrument bell denoting his clamor. Finally, animals themselves are turned into instruments. Consider the scene in figure 6.6, from New York, Metropolitan Museum, Cloisters MS 54.1.2, fols. 34ᵛ–35ʳ (the Hours of Jeanne d'Evreux), a book of hours made in Paris around 1324 (measuring 92 × 60 mm): in the *bas-de-page* of the left-hand verso of the opening two hybrid men emerge from the foliage, blowing on a horn and the tail of a dog (who obliges by yapping).

While such evidence is well known to art historians and others, it remains relatively unfamiliar in musicological accounts. Yet precisely because of their deep implication in the core activity of medieval prayer, such books invite such contemplation. To what extent might we consider the evidence a testimony to sounding experience? How far does it relate to and inform what we more commonly think of as musical matters? What was the effect of the visual representation of so much sound in the experience of prayer? While the scarcity of musical notation explains their absence from musicology, such a lack does not preclude the presence of sound, nor of performance.

As mentioned in the previous chapter, art historians and historians of memory provide one pertinent model for rehearing such evidence. The visualized sounds may function as traces of sounds actually heard or implied, working as a kind of sonic "aftershock," the sounding equivalence to

FIGURE 6.2. Cambridge, Trinity College Library, MS B. 11. 22, fol. 36ᵛ. By permission of the Master and Fellows of Trinity College, Cambridge

Williamson's "afterglow." Furthermore, while noisy marginalia are the obvious indicator of sound, as we shall see, these images are complemented by a diverse array of signs signaling more orthodox performance. Another useful site of art historical investigation that may be helpful is that relating to the utterance and audition of the words in prayer books, and in turn their connection to foundational discourses about medieval language, which understand the letter as the sign for the sounding voice.[3] Indeed, some go so far as to see analogies

3 On which see especially Camille, "Seeing and Reading."

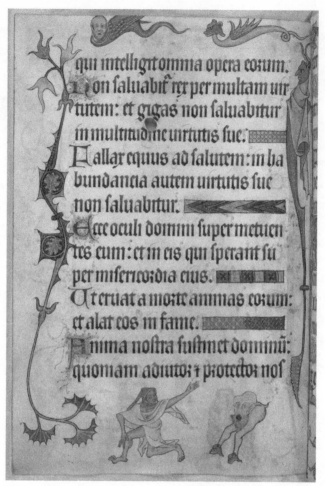

FIGURE 6.3. London British Library, Add. 42130 (the Luttrell Psalter), fol. 62ᵛ. © The British Library Board

with musical notation: images of sound hovering between representations of, and prescriptions for, utterance.[4]

Historians of liturgy and devotion offer some more pragmatic insights into the question of sound, situating prayer books as evidence of wider cultural practices of prayer. By better understanding where and how prayer books were used, and by whom, it is possible to see how signs of sound may be a notation or mnemonic of their environment: contexts vibrating with sound.

4 Ibid., 28–29. Camille makes an analogy with notation as a memory and performance prompt, and argues that decorated capitals "must also have functioned as a mnemonic trigger to regulate the reading performance of the liturgy and the *Opus Dei*."

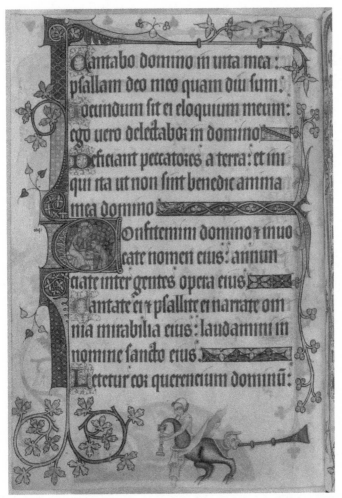

FIGURE 6.4. London, British Library, Add. 42130 (the Luttrell Psalter), fol. 185ᵛ. © The British Library Board

Musicology, too, has some useful theoretical possibilities to contribute. To suggest that visualized sound in prayer books might in some instances be musical involves an ontological adjustment of the very concept of "music." Here it will be helpful to follow a model proposed by Bruce Holsinger, who detects in medieval writing about music ideas quite different from the work-concept dominant in later epochs.[5] Rather, he suggests, the musical traditions of which

5 Holsinger, *Music, Body, and Desire*, 15–17. Holsinger draws here on work by Lydia Goehr, Leo Treitler, and Gary Tomlinson for approaches to music history that unsettle the work-concept.

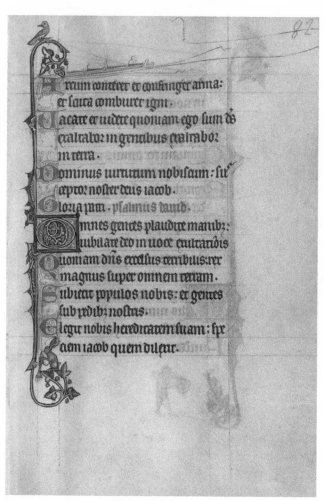

FIGURE 6.5. Baltimore, Walters Art Museum, W 45, fol. 82ʳ. © The Walters Art Museum

theorists write are "components of a thoroughly embodied musicality that integrates theory, manuscript, performer, and listener into a cultural practice invested in the experiencing of sonority."[6] The emphasis on sonority over work means that written and visual testimonies to somatic experience might themselves be considered a form of music.

To illustrate how images in particular may both encode and evoke sonorous experience, we might briefly consider two twelfth-century Cistercians who,

6 Holsinger, *Music, Body, and Desire,* 16.

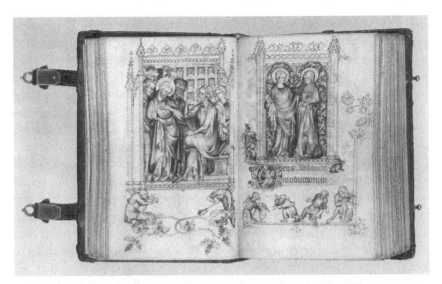

FIGURE 6.6. New York, Metropolitan Museum, Cloisters MS 54.1.2
(the Hours of Jeanne d'Evreux), fols. 34ᵛ–35ʳ. © The Metropolitan Museum
of Art/Art Resource, NY

in expressing their suspicions about the power of the senses, also left traces of
their effects. The first passage, often cited in relation to the later trend for
marginalia seen above,[7] occurs in Bernard of Clairvaux's *Apologia* (dated around
1125). It is a vehement invective against distracting images in monasteries: a
template for Cistercian views on the dangers of liturgical ornament. He
describes how the brethren, devoutly reading their books, would be distracted
by monstrous hybrids: "But in the cloister, under the eyes of the brothers while
they read there, what is that ridiculous monstrosity doing, an amazing kind of
deformed beauty and yet a beautiful deformity?" ("ceterum in claustris, eoram
legentibus fratribus, quid facit illa ridicula monstruositas, mira quaedam
deformis formositas ac formosa deformitas?").[8] When he goes on to describe
an array of fantastical animals and hybrids, the affinity with the later marginal
monsters in prayer books is clear. Similar vivid imagery recurs a few years later

---

7 Randall, *Images in the Margins*, 3–5. Randall begins her catalogue by citing this
passage as precursor to the more widespread tradition of monstrosity in manuscripts that
followed Bernard.

8 From the *Apologia* to William, Abbot of St. Thierry, in the *Tractatus et opuscula*, XII,
28–31, here quoting from 28. Text and translation are from Conrad Rudolph, *The "Things
of Greater Importance": Bernard of Clairvaux's "Apologia" and the Medieval Attitude toward Art*
(Philadelphia: University of Pennsylvania Press, 1990), 282–83.

in the *Speculum caritatis* by Aelred of Rievaulx (touched on in ch. 1), in evocation not of art, but of music. In describing the excesses of polyphony performed in church, Aelred turns to visualization as a means of explaining the problems with sound. Drawing on a classical topic of denunciation—the theater of the Roman satirists—Aelred describes a scene in which male singers become monstrous: like women and horses their gasping and gesturing become a grotesque spectacle.[9] The final shift from sound to sight comes in Aelred's concluding comments, where he damns a situation in which "one would think that they [the common people] had assembled not at an oratory, but at a theatre, not for praying but for watching" ("ut eos non ad oratorium, sed ad theatrum, nec ad orandum, sed ad spectandum").[10] The synesthesic shift here illustrates one mode for thinking of images as musical, and thus serves as a model by which one might "hear" the imagery of prayer books.

The rest of this chapter begins with a look at some evidence for attitudes to sound in prayer and particularly with regard to singing. Following that, we shall devote ourselves to a small corpus of prayer books produced in England, northern France, and areas of French-speaking Flanders between ca. 1270 and 1330, with occasional reference to manuscripts dating later, but frequently cited in the art historical literature, such as the Luttrell Psalter and Vienna, Österreichische Nationalbibliothek, Codex Vindobonensis 1857 (the Hours of Mary of Burgundy, a Flemish book of hours dating ca. 1475). My selected manuscripts involve a cross-section of readers, from monastic users to well-to-do women, and were produced in regions and institutions also known for their cultivation of northern French song repertories. These were the kinds of books that rubbed shoulders with chansonniers and motet compendia, and which were opened up and prayed from by people who in other realms of their lives were accustomed to singing and listening to devotional music. While all images cited here are available in black and white in the pages that follow, the accompanying website to *The Sense of Sound* offers digital color reproductions of examples for which no color facsimile or digital reproduction is otherwise readily accessible, thereby allowing readers a more vivid sense of the visuality of the material.

9 For discussion of the satirical model see Binski, *Becket's Crown*, 262–63.

10 Quoting from Book II, ch. 23 of the *Speculum caritatis*, edited in vol. 1 of *Opera omnia*, ed. Anselm Hoste and Charles Talbot, Corpus Christianorum, continuatio mediaevalis 1–2B, 2D (Turnhout: Brepols, 1971). The Latin is reproduced with an English translation by Randall Rosenfeld in McGee, *The Sound of Medieval Song*, 23–24.

Sound, Prayer, and the Sin of Curiositas

What were the stakes for sound in prayer? What were the associations—positive and negative—of sound, and more practically, what were the expectations of using one's voice? For writers such as Bernard of Clairvaux and Aelred of Rievaulx, there can be little doubt that sound—like images—had the potential to be a deadly distraction. Sights such as the monstrous trumpeter in the Luttrell Psalter would have been doubly damnable, an offense to both senses. How, then, are we to situate the presence of so much outrageous sonic imagery across decades of prayer book production? The scarcity of contemporary accounts relating to the significance and meaning of the visual conventions of our corpus is notorious. Yet in some quarters there were very clear, sometimes dogmatic, ideas about the positive and negative connotations of sound, and the potential for distraction.

One general context is found in evidence relating to liturgical performance. A crucial reference point here is a penetrating study of liturgical practice by Katherine Zieman, which charts among other things the history of what she terms the changing "politics of understanding."[11] Making the important point that for many, learning to read went hand in hand with liturgical instruction, Zieman argues that singing and reading were intricately connected, as dual aspects of educating liturgical practitioners. As the practice of liturgy expanded in the later Middle Ages, and as the expectations of literacy shifted to accommodate a less well-educated congregation of devotees—the sort who might engage in private devotion through their prayer books, or attend Mass and mouth words they did not understand—so did the relationship between sense and sound shift. It was thus possible to perform a text without understanding it, which led to the mangling of pronunciations, and to countless worries about what it could mean to pray without knowing the text. On the other hand, Zieman points to possibilities that the texts uttered, understood or not, had potential to carry powerful meanings—to have a kind of "charisma."[12]

While Zieman's account is largely concerned with the "official" practice of liturgy, her study is a useful point of entry into further exploration of sound and sense in private devotion. Zieman's work is especially important here as it raises the question of how a *singing* voice can complicate notions of sense and inflect experience (an aspect that Zieman deliberately sets aside). Picking up that thread, I wish next to explore some commonplace attitudes to the powers, perils, and sins that musical sound in prayer could bring on. Emanating from centuries of monastic rule and instruction, these discourses were by the thirteenth century so familiar and widely disseminated in sermons, *exempla*,

---

11 Katherine Zieman, *Singing the New Song: Literacy and Liturgy in Late Medieval England* (Philadelphia: University of Pennsylvania Press, 2008).

12 Ibid. 83.

conduct books, and even wall paintings, that they are the natural place to begin to explain the presence of so many sounding signs in prayer books.

We start in the footsteps of prayer's most vigilant monitors. During the Middle Ages, devils and demons made many appearances in contexts of prayer. On many occasions they seemed especially alert to prayer's musical aspect. Three thirteenth-century accounts of devilish intervention will illustrate. The first, most famous of demons, appears among the *exempla* in the *sermones vulgares* of Jacques de Vitry, dating from 1220.[13] Jacques recounts the sighting of the Devil by a certain "holy man" ("sanctus homo"), who saw the Prince of Darkness heaving a big sack out of the choir following Matins. Undaunted, the holy man asked what was in the sack, and was answered thus: "These are the syllables and syncopated words and verses of the psalmody which these clerics in their Matins stole from God" ("hec sunt sillabe et dictione syncopate et versus psalmodie, que isti clerici in hiis matutinis furati sunt Deo.") With these mispronounced ("syncopations") or forgotten words, the Devil had ammunition with which to hold the singers accountable: "These I am reserving diligently for their accusation" ("hec utique ad eorum accusationem diligenter reservo"). This story enjoyed considerable popularity in the Middle Ages, and the Devil, subsequently identified as Tutivillus, appeared in a range of contexts from literary narrative to wall paintings. As well as gathering mispronounced psalmody, he also picked up idle gossip.[14] Zieman notes that by the fifteenth century, the Tutivillus story betrayed anxiety about the disturbance of choral unity, observing that "loyalty to the text was the basis of community."[15] But it was not a matter of words alone. In the public sphere of prayer, singing the right words was important. A later English version makes clear that it is singing, not just reading, that provoked Tutivillus to action: the demonic monitor notes his reliance on failings in "redynge and *in syngynge*" for his work.[16] That there could be so much litter left to scoop up was a reminder

13 *The* Exempla *or Illustrative Stories from the* Sermones vulgares *of Jacques de Vitry*, ed. Thomas Crane (Nendeln: Kraus Reprint, 1967, first published 1890), no. XIX, 6, and a summary and commentary on 140–41.

14 For other citations of the story, see *The* Exempla, 141. On the story see Kathy Cawsey, "Tutivillus and the 'Kyrkchaterars': Strategies of Control in the Middle Ages," *Studies in Philology* 102 (2005), 434–51 and Margaret Jennings, "Tutivillus: The Literary Career of the Recording Demon," *Studies in Philology: Texts and Studies* 74 (1977): 1–93. See also Zieman, *Singing the New Song*, 63–65. The topic of gossip is also taken up in Sandy Bardsley, *Venomous Tongues: Speech and Gender in Late Medieval England*, The Middle Ages Series (Philadelphia: University of Pennsylvania Press, 2006).

15 Zieman, *Singing the New Song*, 64.

16 Quoting from Cawsey, "Tutivillus and the 'Kyrkchaterars'," 434, citing *Myroure of Oure Ladye: A Devotional Treatise on Divine Service*, ed. John Blunt, Early English Text Society 19 (London: Kegan Paul, Trench Kübner and Co., 1873), 54.

of the ways that music could bypass the need for careful diction, and lead to an imbalance in the *vox–verbum* dichotomy.

A second anecdote was written down at roughly the same time, in a didactic text intended for Cistercian novitiates; in it, Caesarius of Heisterbach reveals another problematic aspect of sound in prayer.[17] In chapter 9 of Book IV of his *Dialogus miraculorum*, devoted to the topic of temptation, the devil is once again spotted in church, again with a capacious sack in his left hand ("saccum magnum et longum in sinistra manu tenere").[18] He is listening to the choir of clerics and catching their voices with his right hand to load up his sack. At the end of the service he departs, hauling with him a sack bulging with booty. As the clerics congratulate themselves on having sung so well, the witness observes "you have sung well indeed, but you have sung a sack full" ("bene quidem cantastis, sed saccum plenum cantastis"). In interpreting this scene, Caesarius recalls a Cistercian abbot, who explained that while there was no problem with the sound itself, it was the vainglory with which the clerks pronounced their Psalms that filled up the sack. They sang "voraciously, loudly, and without devotion, raising on high tumultuous voices" ("clamose, non devote, cantantibus, et voces tumultuosas in sublime tollentibus"). And in their self-congratulation at "having praised God well and heartily" ("illis expleto cantu inter se gloriantibus, tamquam qui bene et fortiter Deum laudassent"), the Cistercian noted that "demons rejoice when the voice is upraised in psalmody without humility" ("quantum ex hoc daemones laetentur, si sine humilitate in psalmodia voces exaltentur"). There are obvious echoes here of the old Augustinian trope: the problem of beautiful song surpassing the sense of the words. But by situating his criticism in the specific context of the Office, and seen from the perspective of the supplicant—the singer—Caesarius illustrates more precisely how the thematics of sense and sound take on new meaning in the context of prayer. As an exemplum on temptation, the story suggests that even when mindful of the sins of mispronunciation, a perfect performance could also sway the supplicant to sins of pride and vainglory.

My final example, also from the *Dialogus*, offers insight into a larger anxiety about the prayer experience. In this example, from chapter 5 of Book V, devoted to demons, the choir has begun the antiphonal performance of Psalm 3 from the opening of Matins.[19] It is a pledge of fortitude to God in the face of enemies, beginning "Lord, how are they increased that trouble me," with the

17 Caesarius of Heisterbach *Dialogus miraculorum*, ed. Josef Strange, 2 vols. (Cologne: J. M. Heberle, 1851). For an English translation, see *The Dialogue on Miracles*, transl. Henry von Essen Scott and Charles Swinton Bland, 2 vols., Broadway Medieval Library (New York: Harcourt, Brace and Company, 1929).

18 *Dialogus*, 1:181; translation in *The Dialogue*, 1:204–5.

19 *Dialogus*, 1:281–5; translation in *The Dialogue*, 1:321–25

Psalmist going on to avow in verse 5: "I shall cry out to God with my voice, and God shall answer out of his holy mountain."[20] On cue, the choir fills with a flock of marauding demons, who flit from one side to the other, throwing the choirs off track so that "they no longer knew what they were singing" ("ut prorsus nescirent quid psallerent"). By the end, the two groups are indeed "crying out to the Lord": they are shouting rather than singing ("clamavit chorus contra chorum"), while the intervention of the abbot and prior cannot restore singing or change discord into harmony ("non poterant illos ad viam psalmodiae reducere, neque vocum dissonantias unire"). As well as a dramatic enactment of the theme of the Psalm, the devils offer a larger exemplum: they cause confusion in a most literal sense, resulting in the aural and oral disruption of the prayers. Concern regarding confusion and distraction in prayer—be it literally, verbal confusion, or the interior confusion of a singer bound up in the moment of song rather than prayer—are part of a fundamental preoccupation in prayer: that of *curiositas*.

Curiositas would have been close to Caesarius's heart: drawing on a long tradition of writing from Augustine, John Cassian, and the *Rule of Benedict*, Cistercians such as Bernard of Clairvaux and Aelred of Rievaulx placed special emphasis on the sin, especially in the context of prayer. Defined as a kind of mental or sensual distraction, *curiositas* ultimately led to separation from God, and although its causes were rooted in pride or *luxuria*, practical sources of distraction were often provided by the senses of sight and sound. In his study of *curiositas* among Cistercian writers, Richard Newhauser notes how according to Benedict's rule, monks were to keep their heads bowed and eyes to the ground.[21] In the second part of his *De gradibus humilitatis et superbiae*, Bernard of Clairvaux devotes detailed attention to *curiositas* in his discussion of the range of sins the monk should avoid. There, it is described as a sin of sound, as much as sight, while sound was also a cause and outward sign of *curiositas*: "If you see a monk whom hitherto you have considered a good one, beginning to let his eyes wander wherever he happens to be . . . if you see him with his head held high and his ears straining, you will be able to tell by this external indication that something has changed in the inner man" ("si videris mona-chum, de quo prius bene confidebas, ubicumque stat . . . oculis incipientem vagari, caput erectu, aures portare suspensas, e motibus exterioris hominis

---

20 "Domine, quid multiplicati sunt qui tribulant me?," and "Voce mea ad Dominum clamavi et exaudivit me de monte sancto suo."

21 Richard Newhauser, "The Sin of Curiosity and the Cistercians," in *Erudition at God's Service*, ed. John Sommerfeldt, Studies in Medieval Cistercian History 9 (Kalamazoo: Cistercian Publications, 1987), 71–95.

interiorem immutatum agnoscas").[22] It was these distractions of an exterior, sensual nature that interrupted the interior conversation with God, and ultimately caused a separation from God.[23] Such distraction ultimately manifests in misuse of words, as the monk literally bursts with idle or foolish things to say.[24]

Nor was this a purely theoretical anxiety. During centuries of monastic practice, there was a widespread sensitivity to sonic distraction, especially "strepitus mundi"—noise that might involve loquaciousness on the part of a community, or hubbub from the exterior world. As Scott Bruce notes, abbots of the Carolingian era worried that "the steady drone of human discourse" brought to the monasteries by lay visitors and pilgrims would disturb the monks at prayer, and thus instituted new architectural structures to house guests in quarters out of earshot of the community;[25] in many communities, "roundsmen" ("circatores") patrolled the monastery to check there was no untoward conversing.[26] Such evidence points to the pervasive anxiety about misuse of the voice. There was a fine line between "strepitus" and "tacitus": for a voice singing or murmuring in prayer was entirely permissible—an ideal form of silence. Yet singing too enthusiastically, mispronouncing prayers, or turning to idle gossip made the voice become a danger. As well as underlining the importance of distraction as a concern in prayer, these accounts forge an important link between *curiositas* and the senses, and especially the senses of sight and sound. They also raise the perplexing possibility that the extensive imagery of sound in prayer books was itself a form of distraction, a provocation of *curiositas*.

If these examples illustrate the dangers of sound in prayer, it is also worth considering examples relating to its oral efficacy. In her recent exploration of the rhetorical uses of tropes of sweetness and the sense of taste, Mary Carruthers notes an ancient connection in the biblical tradition that links the sweet taste of melody to knowledge: "the metaphoric *translatio* from gladdening the heart via song to the delight of learning, and from the sweetness of melody to the

---

22 Bernard of Clairvaux, *De gradibus humilitatis et superbiae*, in *S. Bernardi opera* 3: *Tractatus et opuscula*, ed. Jean Leclercq and Henri Roche (Rome: Editiones Cistercienses, 1963), 38–46 for the chapter on *curiositas*, quoting here from 38. The translation is from *In the Steps of Humility*, transl. Geoffrey Webb and Adrian Walker (London: Saint Austin Press, 2001, first printed 1957), 53.

23 Newhauser, "The Sin of Curiosity," 79.

24 See especially the chapter devoted to vainglory, which likens the monk to a bladder swelling to bursting point with the desire to laugh or speak, and therefore breaking silence. See *De gradibus*, 47.

25 Scott Bruce, *Silence and Sign Language in Medieval Monasticism: The Cluniac Tradition c. 900–1200* (Cambridge: Cambridge University Press, 2007), 38–39.

26 Ibid., 48.

sweetness of oratory, is an ancient commonplace."[27] Effective prayer was frequently proven by means of this oral ideal: taste being evidence of perfect utterance. Not all of Caesarius's *exempla* regarding prayer involve devilish warnings. In chapter 49 of Book 7, devoted to Marian miracles, he recalls an anchorite who tasted a "wonderful sweetness" ("mira dulcedinem") every time she uttered the name of Our Lady.[28] The delicious effect was the result of strenuous devotional exercise: "Every day I have been wont to say fifty Ave Marias in her honour, with as many prayers for pardon, and this is why I have gained such sweetness that while I am praying, all the saliva in my mouth seems changed into honey" ("singulis diebus in honore eius quinquaginta Ave Maria, cum totidem veniis dicere consuevi, per quae tantam dulcedinem merui, ut omnis oris mei saliva orationis tempore in mel videatur conversa").

*

Figure 6.7 shows the opening of Lauds for the Hours of the Virgin, from fol. 29[r] of a book of hours produced around 1300 in the northeastern region of France (Cambrai, Médiathèque municipale, MS 87, measuring 165 × 113 mm). It was probably made for a lay woman and, as with many such books, the owner would here, as elsewhere in the manuscript, have seen herself painted into the scene. Imagine her for a moment at her early morning prayer: book open, her eyes may be drawn to the central meditative image—filling out the round spaces of the capital "D" of the Office's opening "Deus in adiutorium," the letter a mirror to her own devotional pursuits. But she has alarming company. Tugging at the dress of a lady is none other than the Devil himself: an exemplum of the perils of temptation and *curiositas*.[29] In this case, it is specifically the distraction of sonic pleasure that threatens to lure our fervent lady off course. Across the folio, but clearly within her sightline, we see a curly-haired man, heel kicked out, engaging in musical delight. He strums his gittern, the very embodiment of the sin of *luxuria* and what Adelaide Bennett calls "the allurement to erotic adventures."[30] Together, the Devil, woman, and

27 Mary Carruthers, "Sweetness," *Speculum* 81 (2006), 999–1113, at 1005.

28 *Dialogus*, 2:69–70; translation in *The Dialogue*, 1:533–34.

29 Adelaide Bennett, "A Woman's Power of Prayer Versus the Devil in a Book of Hours of ca. 1300," in *Image and Belief: Studies in Celebration of the Eightieth Anniversary of the Index of Christian Art*, ed. Colum Hourihane (Princeton: Princeton University Press, 1999), 89–108. For more on the didactic program of this manuscript see Bennett's "Christ's Five Wounds in the Aves of the Vita Christi in a Book of Hours about 1300," in *Tributes in Honor of James Marrow: Studies in Painting and Manuscript Illumination of the Late Middle Ages and Northern Renaissance*, ed. Jeffrey Hamburger and Anne Korteweg (London: Harvey Miller, 2006), 75–84.

30 Bennett, "A Woman's Power of Prayer," 92–93. See n. 10 for the identification of the figure as *luxuria*.

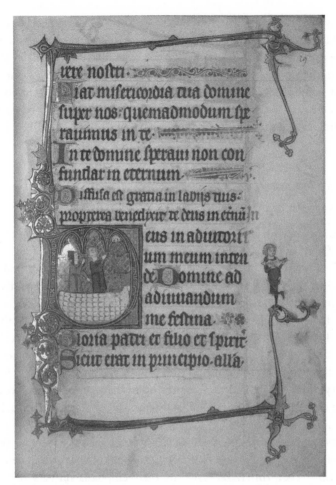

FIGURE 6.7. Cambrai, Médiathèque municipale, MS 87, fol. 29ʳ. By permission of the Médiathèque municipale of Cambrai

musician offer a lesson in the perils and precautions of sound in prayer: beware the distractions of pleasure as embodied in music. What is more, Lauds was by no means the only didactic site in this book: other aspects of the book's imagery and texts designed it simultaneously as prayer book and conduct manual, schooling its owner in the dangers of temptations and virtues such as penitence and obedience.[31]

This example indicates not only how prayer books might echo more codified and orthodox concerns about prayer. It also illustrates how such books could also be *about* prayer, building into the prayer-act a kind of active pedagogy.

31 Ibid., 102.

For the woman who once used this book, to pray may have been to reflect on the worldly perils that might distract her from unfettered connection with the sacred personalities of her manuscript. It is time now to take the evidence on its own terms, and to explore what such books may have to say about the efficacy and perils of their sounding embodiment. If the Hours themselves often took on a didactic form, then it will be fitting for us to explore the evidence in eight parts: each a small lesson in sound in prayer.

An Office for Sound in Prayer Books
MATINS: BEGINNINGS

A brief word to begin about the development of prayer books in the thirteenth century. Of all the spin-offs of the official books of the liturgy, the Psalter and the book of hours were the most popular, and became famous for making the Latin rite of the clergy accessible to a wide lay audience. The Psalms, as the basic core of the eight daily offices, were the best known of all sacred texts, familiar to lay and clerical audiences alike, and it is little wonder that they were the first to break away, materially speaking, from official liturgical books, such as the Breviary.[32] Growing in popularity as an independent book from the middle of the eleventh century, they also served a secondary function: the simplicity of the Latin, and their centrality to daily prayer, meant that these were the texts learned by heart, and subsequently the Psalter was the book by which many learned to read.[33]

Psalters nearly always contained ancillary texts, such as Hours for the Dead and prayers for the Virgin; and in many ways books of hours were their natural outgrowth.[34] They differ, however, in their emphasis on sets of Offices.[35] Alongside the standard Hours of the Virgin and the Office of the Dead, many other devotional offices for a variety of saints and commemorations were

32 On the books of the medieval liturgy see in particular Andrew Hughes, *Medieval Manuscripts for the Mass and Offices: A Guide to their Use and Terminology* (Toronto: University of Toronto Press, 1982).

33 See above, n. 1, for general histories of the Psalter. For an excellent analysis of a thirteenth-century Psalter designed for a lay female reader, see Gould, *The Psalter and Hours of Yolande of Soissons*. Michael Camille's monograph *Mirror in Parchment*, on the fourteenth-century Luttrell Psalter, includes additional information about the later development of the Psalter and the patterns of its decoration and organization.

34 See above, n. 1, for general bibliography relating to books of hours. For a succinct introduction to their emergence and use, see Wieck's "Introduction" in his *Time Sanctified*, 27–32.

35 For further context for the medieval Offices see *The Divine Office*, ed. Fassler and Baltzer.

collated to suit the devotional tastes of individual readers. Such Hours followed the pattern of the eight offices, and often either abbreviated existing
liturgical Hours or constructed new Hours in a kind of pick-and-mix from a
range of existing liturgies. They were frequently copied with a standardized
pictorial program, and together, text and images provided a blueprint for daily
devotion. These core texts interacted with supplemental materials, which
included calendars, depicting the zodiac and labors of the months, and inter-
lacing the official feasts of the church with obituaries of family or community
members or local saints; litanies for saints; and a vast corpus of personal prayers
and devotions, free-standing from the main hours of the day.[36] In both secular
and religious environments, such books were not only prized treasures and
daily talismans, tucked into pockets or hung from girdles: they were also reliquaries of sorts, personalized by their particularization to different saints and
feasts, and also carried the memory of a lifetime's use, memories which surely
intensified as books were often passed down to children and grandchildren.[37]
While many of the books we shall explore were of value for the beauty of their
artistry, it is important to remember that their owners cherished them for their
intimate connection to the sacred congregations they saw in them daily; and
also for their more personal stories, told in the shaky handwriting and multiple
shades of ink used to inscribe the deceased into their calendars. They were also
books demanding strenuous attention and active use, and were often filled
with signs and instructions intended to direct the reader's path in prayer. It is
to the more orthodox signs of sound that we shall turn first.

LAUDS: SIGNS OF LISTENING, SIGNS OF PERFORMANCE

Fundamentally letters are shapes indicated by voices. Hence they represent things which they bring to mind through the windows of the eyes.
Frequently they speak voiceless the utterances of the absent.[38]

This famous dictum by John of Salisbury on the intractably oral nature of the
written word has frequently served as entry into a topos in book decoration of

---

36 Wieck's *Time Sanctified* provides useful accounts of all the main sections common
in books of hours.

37 On the personalized aspect of prayer books see Duffy, *Marking the Hours*.

38 From ch. 13, Book 1 of John of Salisbury, *Metalogicon*, ed. Hall and Keats-Rohan,
32: "Littere autem id est figurae primo uocem indices sunt, deinde rerum quas animae
per oculorum fenestras opponunt, et frequenter absentium dicta sine uoce loquunter."
Translation here from Michael Clanchy, *From Memory to Written Record: England 1066–
1307*, 2nd ed. (Oxford: Blackwell, 1993). For a complete translation of the treatise, see
The Metalogicon *of John of Salisbury*, transl. McGarry.

the Middle Ages.[39] We have seen how the relationship of sound to language was central for many medieval grammarians, musicians, and theologians: it was no less a source of fascination for image-makers. If the letter is in a literal sense inaudible, artists of the Middle Ages nonetheless developed a sophisticated visual lexicon to represent its performance, audibility, and sometimes to encourage its readers to supply its voice—to utter the absent. While iconography relating to verbal sound is not limited to prayer books, and is visible also in a range of media from stained-glass windows to frescos, its abundance in the context of prayer is indicative of the significance of sound.

An important antecedent is in the corpus of illuminated Psalters of the eleventh and twelfth centuries.[40] In his account of their iconography, William Noel explains how artists represented the experience of Psalm texts by a range of means: from figures pointing and staring at the text on the page; to the development of speech scrolls, indicating utterance; to the writing rolls and codices to signify the word as written authority.[41] By the thirteenth century such signs were so well used as to be instantly decipherable. Among the most prevalent signals are figures in and around the text, pointing at it, or engaging it with a beady-eyed stare: what Michael Camille characterizes as the "oral witness within the written text."[42] Consider, for example, Walters Art Museum W 104, a book of hours produced in Arras in the early fourteenth century. A slim, hand-sized book (measuring 170 × 123 mm), its margins are among the most highly populated of its genre, filled with a range of holy folk paying avid attention to the text. Figure 6.8 [website figure 6.2] (fol. 71ʳ, from its Litany) shows saintly figures at the edges of the folio, looking across the text frame, staring intently at the prayers (here, their own litanies, performed by the open-mouthed clerics in the main illumination at left).[43]

39 The most thorough exploration of the relationship of art to discourses of the orality of language is Camille, "Seeing and Reading." Camille draws also on Clanchy's *From Memory*, of which see esp. 253–93.

40 On which see esp. Noel, *The Harley Psalter*.

41 See William Noel, "The Utrecht Psalter in England: Continuity and Experiment," in *The Utrecht Psalter*, 121–65, and esp. 159–64 for discussion of the signs for uttered and written word.

42 Camille, "Seeing and Reading," 28, and *passim* for further information on signals of oral performance in manuscript decoration.

43 For this and other manuscripts cited from the Walters collection, I direct readers to the following excellent catalogue and exhibition entries: Lilian Randall assisted by Judith Oliver, *Medieval and Renaissance Manuscripts in the Walters Art Gallery*, 1: *France, 875–1420* (Baltimore: Johns Hopkins University Press, 1989) and Lilian Randall with the assistance of Judith Oliver, Christopher Clarkson, and Claudia Mark, *Medieval and Renaissance Manuscripts in the Walters Art Gallery*, 3: *Belgium, 1250–1530*, part 1 (Baltimore: Johns Hopkins University Press, 1997). In addition, several of the books of hours in the

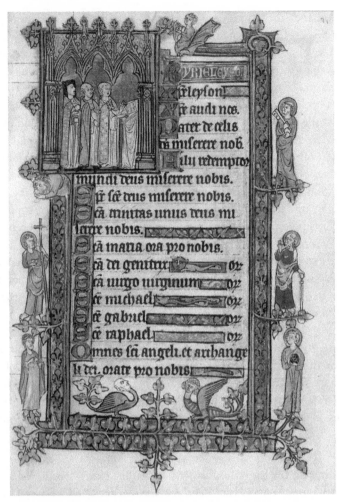

FIGURE 6.8. Baltimore, Walters Art Museum, W 104, fol. 71ʳ. © The Walters Art Museum

The iconography of scrolls offers even more nuance, suggesting in wispy mobility something akin to the motion of the voice. In the Paris Psalter Paris, Bibliothèque nationale de France lat. 8846, produced in Paris around 1200, William Noel detects meaning in the inflection and direction of scrolls. The psalmist is shown with scrolls that alternately droop downwards and roll energetically up, as graphic illustration of Psalm 29: "In the evening weeping shall

collection are the evidential basis for Wieck's *Time Sanctified*, and he also includes a short description as well as several plates. For W 104 see Wieck, *Time Sanctified*, catalogue no. 8, pp. 173–74; Randall, catalogue no. 55, pp. 143–45.

have place; and in the morning gladness."[44] Scrolls are also commonplace in the later corpus. In books of hours they are a fixture by virtue of their standard usage in two scenes in the Infancy cycle that commonly punctuated the Hours of the Virgin.[45] Opening images for Matins (Annunciation) and Terce (Annunciation of the Shepherds) make use of scrolls as a signal of vocal communication: the angel Gabriel to Mary and the heavenly host to the shepherds. Speech scrolls might also appear at the head of prayer sections, and especially in those directed to the Virgin. She was often shown in her popular role as intercessor: one standard image type showed her in intimate communication with her supplicant, the two bound in dialogue by the presence of connective scrolls.[46] Some representations show extravagantly curly scrolls, meditatively meandering upwards; sometimes scrolls spring unruffled from supplicant to intercessor, suggesting the directed urgency of the plea. A vivid sense of the "tone" of a scroll as uttered communiqué can be seen in Cambridge, Trinity B. 11. 22, where several times in sections devoted to prayers for the dead, and for the intercession of saints, a supplicant is seen tossing a scroll that unfurls upwards to the outstretched hand of an angel, inscribed with the words "Memento mei domine," as in figure 6.9 (fol. 147ʳ).

The Macclesfield Psalter (Cambridge, Fitzwilliam Museum, MS 1-2005, measuring 170 × 108 mm), produced in East Anglia in the second or third decade of the fourteenth century, offers examples of another use of scrolls. Figure 6.10 (fol. 161ᵛ) shows the opening verse of Psalm 109, which begins with an ostentatious speech act: "Dixit Dominus domino."[47] As the Lord addresses David, the folio is caught up in acts of utterance and audition.

44 Noel, "The Utrecht Psalter," 159–60 for his discussion of speech scrolls. The passage in question comes from Psalm 29:6: "Ad vesperum demorabitur fletus, et ad matutinum laetitia."

45 Description and illustration of the standard cycle is given in Wieck, *Time Sanctified*, 60–66. The common images, starting with Matins, were Annunciation, Visitation, Nativity, Annunciation of the Shepherds, Adoration of the Magi, Presentation in the Temple, Flight into Egypt (or Massacre of the Innocents), Coronation of the Virgin (or Flight into Egypt, Massacre of the Innocents, Assumption, or Death of the Virgin).

46 For an account of Mary's role as intercessor and the associated iconography, see Catherine Oakes, Ora pro nobis: *The Virgin as Intercessor in Medieval Art and Devotion* (Turnhout, Harvey Miller, 2008). As Oakes points out, there were two main branches of Mary's intercessory role. First, where she listens to the prayers of individual supplicants; second, where she intercedes to God directly. The former is most commonly depicted in books of hours. For discussion of that type and for further illustrations, see esp. 37–64.

47 "The Lord said unto my Lord: Sit thou at my right hand: Until I make thy enemies thy footstool" ("Dixit Dominus Domino meo sede a dextris meis donec ponam inimicos tuos scabillum pedum tuorum"). For a facsimile see *The Macclesfield Psalter: A Complete Facsimile*, ed. Stella Panayotova (London, Thames and Hudson Ltd., 2008).

FIGURE 6.9. Cambridge, Trinity College Library, B. 11. 22, fol. 147^r. By permission of the Master and Fellows of Trinity College, Cambridge

The communication is signaled in the central initial with elaborate hand gestures, while disembodied heads tilt this way and that the better to "hear" the Psalm. In the *bas-de-page*, the scroll is put to use again as the figures beneath mirror the action in the initial. One throws an empty scroll across to his interlocutor, the visual sign of the active voice.

PRIME: RESPONSIVE LISTENING

That the invocations to sound and listening were successful, that the text was understood as resonant, is suggested by another category of sign: the

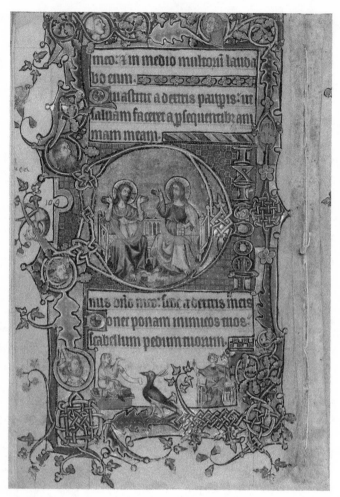

FIGURE 6.10. Cambridge, Fitzwilliam Museum, MS 1-2005 (the Macclesfield Psalter), fol. 161ᵛ. By permission of the Syndics of the Fitzwilliam Museum, Cambridge

responsive listener. There are numerous instances in which marginal figures appear to "hear" one another. Sometimes the simple gesture of a cupped ear and a head swiveled signals rapt listening. But on other occasions listening is depicted as an embodied activity. In figure 6.11, British Library Stowe 17 (fol. 112ʳ), a book of hours from Maastricht produced around 1300 (measuring 95 × 64 mm), a woman plays a vielle, making music for two dancers: a leaping man and cape-clad dog, prancing at the center. In figure 6.12 [see website, figure 6.3], from a French book of hours contemporary with this, Walters Art Museum W 90 (measuring 130 × 100 mm), there are two signals of responsive listening (from fol. 22ʳ). In the main illumination of Annunciation, the Virgin's

FIGURE 6.11. London, British Library, Stowe 17, fol. 112ʳ (detail). © The British Library Board

hand gestures suggest her startled recoil, taken by surprise by the arrival of the angel. In the margins, a figure dances to the music of a trumpet pointed into the text. These examples also illustrate the frequently contrapuntal nature of sound constructed by signs. In both cases, dance music is independent of and concurrent with other sounds implied by the text. As we shall see, the possibility for disruption brought about by these sonic simultaneities is nowhere more common than in the margins, where multiple musics compete for attention.

TERCE: CUE THE VOICE, CUE THE MEMORY

What would the viewer of a book make of such signs? In the case of scrolls, they might represent the sentiment and even inflection of an audible voice, or trigger a memory of its performance; but could they do more? Approached from a more musical perspective, scrolls invite comparison with notation: they describe the shape or direction of the voice. Like notation, they might also cue sound. Michael Camille first suggested the analogy, proposing a connection between the function of decorating capital letters and neumatic notation.[48]

48 Camille, "Seeing and Reading," 29.

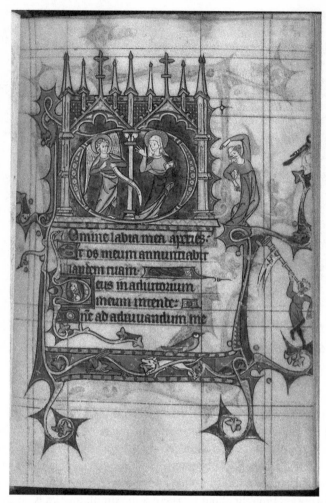

FIGURE 6.12. Baltimore, Walters Art Museum, W 90, fol. 22ʳ. © The Walters Art Museum

Building on the widely accepted notion of notation's partial and mnemonic function, Camille suggested that visual embellishment of letters could likewise be a "mnemonic trigger." We can pursue this further: could a sign such as a scroll also encourage engagement of the living voice itself?

One category of scroll seems especially well suited to prescribing sound: that associated with the two Annunciation scenes in the Hours of the Virgin. Both have roots in famous acts of utterance. The Annunciation of the Virgin, seen at Matins, cites the angel's greeting to Mary from Luke, 1:24, a vocal act that itself spawned one of the most frequently uttered prayers in the Middle Ages: "Ave Maria, gratia plena, dominus tecum." In images of the Annunciation of the Shepherds at Terce, scrolls recall the scriptural words verbatim of the heavenly host reported in Luke 2:14: "Gloria in excelsis deo." Incipits of both texts were frequently inscribed on the scrolls, and these abbreviations are easy to understand as prompts, inviting performance of the full texts. The practice of "realizing" scrolls may have been informed by other media. Beth Williamson's study of iconography of the Madonna of Humility in the fourteenth century includes discussion of a diptych by Benedetto di Bindo, dating from ca. 1400–1405, depicting the Madonna of Humility and St. Jerome. Surrounded by accoutrements of domestic life—bobbins and spools of thread—the Madonna sits nursing the Christ Child, while a book lies open beside her, its text visible to the viewer.[49] It is Psalm 69:2, "Deus in adiutorium meum intende" on the left leaf and "Domine ad iuvandum me" on the other, the opening versicle and response common in all but one of the canonical Hours. The book is perhaps to be understood as the Madonna's own book of hours, and here it may perform the function of vocal and spiritual cue to viewers, themselves perhaps familiar with the practice of praying from such a book. As Williamson speculates: "The text of such inscription on the open book in Benedetto di Bindo's painting would have provided cues to correct prayerful behaviour and focused devotion for an individual using the diptych to direct his or her private spiritual activities."[50]

Let us now consider some scrolls *in situ*. Walters Art Museum W 90, scene of the marginal dancer, places considerable emphasis on its visual programs. In addition to the familiar Infancy cycle in its Hours of the Virgin, the manuscript opens with a series of full-folio, wordless illuminations of Creation.[51] Visual meditation was thus a prominent feature of the owner's experience. Directly following the Creation sequence, on fol. 22[r], the Hours of the Virgin opens with the standard Matins image of Annunciation (see above, figure 6.12, and website figure 6.3). The Virgin and Angel adopt traditional stances and attributes: the Virgin is seated before an open book, Gabriel brandishes a scroll. Here, though, the scroll is void of words. Looking forward to fol. 67[v], the opening of Terce, shown in figure 6.13 [website figure 6.4], the Annunciation of the Shepherds reveals another mute proffering—an empty message. In these cases, particularly given the book's emphasis on visual meditation, the blank scroll may be understood not so much as vocal absence as an imperative: to supply the voice, to ventriloquize the scene.

49 The picture in question is now housed in the Philadelphia Museum of Art.

50 Beth Williamson, *The Madonna of Humility: Development, Dissemination and Reception, c. 1340–1400*, Bristol Studies in Medieval Culture (Woodbridge: Boydell & Brewer, 2009), 158–59, at 159.

51 See fols. 15[v]–21[r]. For contents and description of the manuscript see Wieck, *Time Sanctified*, catalogue no. 7, pp. 173–74; Randall, *Medieval and Renaissance Manuscripts*, I, catalogue no. 54, pp. 138–42.

FIGURE 6.13. Baltimore, Walters Art Museum, W 90, fol. 67ᵛ. © The Walters Art Museum

In the case of the Annunciation of the Shepherds, the question of what words—and indeed what voice—would have been complicated by a competing textual convention. The scene of Terce as represented in figure 6.14 [website figure 6.5] from fol. 72ᵛ of an early fourteenth-century book of hours from the region of Amiens, Walters Art Museum W 38 (measuring 118 × 81 mm), ascribes some alternative words to the angel: "Puer natus est nobis."[52]

52 For contents and description of the manuscript see Wieck, *Time Sanctified*, catalogue no. 10, pp. 175–76; Randall, *Medieval and Renaissance Manuscripts*, vol. 1, catalogue no. 58, pp. 153–55.

FIGURE 6.14. Baltimore, Walters Art Museum, W 38, fol. 72ᵛ. © The Walters
Art Museum

These are scripturally fitting for the Nativity, referring to the famous Isaian
prophecy 9:6,[53] which is given typological realization in the Gospel of
Matthew. However, the words would also have had resounding liturgical

53 "For a child is born to us, and a son is given to us, and the government is upon his
shoulder: and his name shall be called Wonderful, Counsellor, God the Mighty, the Father
of the world to come, the Prince of Peace" ("Parvulus enim natus est nobis et filius datus
est nobis, et factus est principatus super umerum eius, et vocabitur nomen eius
Admirabilis, consiliarius, Deus fortis, Pater futuri saeculi, Princeps pacis.")

association: they are the opening of the Introit for the Mass on Nativity.[54] If the scroll citation was thus scripturally incorrect, it was in another sense profoundly provocative, encouraging typological and musical associations.

Later books of hours are even more explicit about potential musical association: in Annunciation of the Shepherd scenes, angels are often shown singing from notated rolls. Music also creeps into scenes of Marian intercession. Over the course of the Middle Ages many of the standard Marian prayers such as *O intemerata* were set to music, a trend also reflected in the iconography of these scenes. In figure 6.15, the female supplicant of London, British Library, Harley MS 2900, fol. 200[r], a French-made book of hours of ca. 1430–40 of the Sarum Use (measuring 240 × 157 mm), kneels above the text of her prayer *O intemerata*, while her scroll wafts upwards to the Virgin, the prayer's incipit echoed as inscription. In the background, two angels huddle over a musical-ized version of the prayer. In all these cases, we see examples of how the sonic sign of the scroll invites not only active, vocal participation. The scroll also unfurls into an associative chain of melodic, performative, scriptural connections and memories, powerfully mnemonic of manifold incarnations of the words.

SEXT: MUSICAL TRACES - FORM AND CONTENT OF BOOKS OF HOURS

While imagery in prayer books is highly attuned to sound, a closer look at the form and content of their texts reveals numerous traces of prior musicality. At first sight, the general absence of notation in books of hours and Psalters simply suggests that these were not books from which one was intended to sing. Such a lacuna is not surprising. Most books were not created to fulfill a strictly liturgical and communal function. However, many prayers had intricate connections to the official liturgy. Some Hours common in books of hours and Psalters did double service and were fully viable for communal—and sung— performance. One important example was the Office of the Dead, which followed the precise liturgical prescription found in the Breviary.[55] While one could recite the office daily in private remembrance of one's departed family or community members, the presence of complete or partially complete prayers could permit the owner to take her book into public performance of rituals for

---

54 "Unto us a child is born and a son is given, and the government is upon his shoulder: and his name shall be called Angel of mighty counsel" ("Puer natus est nobis et filius datus est nobis: cuius imperium super humerum eius et vocabitur nomen eius magni consilii Angelus.")

55 For a transcription of the incipits of the Hours of Matins, Lauds, Vespers, and Compline, see Wieck, *Time Sanctified*, 166–67.

FIGURE 6.15. London, British Library, Harley 2900, fol. 200ʳ. © The British Library Board

the dead. Prayer books sometimes reflect that versatility. The standard iconographical opening of the Hours typically depict prayers in the public setting—the readers in a kind of semi-private state as they huddle over their individual manuscripts. Walters Art Museum W 104, fol. 74ʳ, shown in figure 6.16 [website figure 6.5], exaggerates that tension of public and private use. The folio is from the opening of the Vigil for the Dead. The central scene depicts the public rite, as clergy gather round the coffin, the celebrant performing from a book. They are joined in the margins by a gathering of solitary readers of all kinds, each holding a book in hand. They represent the position of the reader herself, who, following their gaze, may likewise be witness to the public scene,

FIGURE 6.16. Baltimore, Walters Art Museum, W 104, fol. 74ʳ. © The Walters Art Museum

either in person or in memory. Rarer, but indicative of the potential for singing in these portions of the manuscript, are instances of notation. Figure 6.17 is from Philadelphia, University of Pennsylvania Rare Book and Manuscript Department, MS Codex 1063 (measuring 95 × 60 mm), fols. 53ᵛ–54ʳ. It shows part of the Office of the Dead from a book of hours following Sarum Use and dated around 1450, which contains fully singable notation throughout. Quite possibly this book was for the private use of a cleric, but transportable into the communal setting for performance of the rites of the dead.

The Hours of the Virgin is also resonant with unsung voices. Its history long predates its life in books of hours, and evidence of the so-called "Little Office of the Virgin" dates back to the Carolingian era and persisted

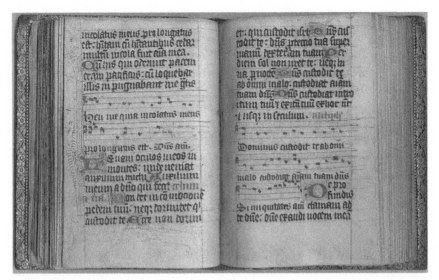

FIGURE 6.17. Philadelphia, University of Pennsylvania Rare Book and Manuscript Department, Codex 1063, fols. 53ᵛ–54ʳ. By permission of the University of Pennsylvania Rare Book and Manuscript Department

well into the later Middle Ages.[56] These Hours had many instantiations in largely communal, liturgical settings: there are copious records of their sung performance by religious communities in tandem with the daily liturgical requirements of the Sanctorale and Temporale. Rebecca Baltzer has documented how in the cathedral of Notre Dame in Paris the Little Office was performed in the choir, and most days "shadowed" the performance of the regular Offices.[57]

The prayers of these Hours would have been doubly resonant for a reader of a book of hours, as the original program of prayers was drawn from a host of pre-existent chants from a range of liturgical contexts. Indeed, part of the power of the devotion to Mary seems to have been the prayers' web of association with other feasts in her honor. Thus even to those least attuned to liturgical practice, the Hours of the Virgin were texts that would have instilled the mnemonic tug of musical association. They included some of the best-loved and most mobile of Marian hymns and antiphons. Favorites such as the *Ave maris stella* (the hymn for Vespers) and the *Salve regina* (often sung at the end

56 On which see Rebecca Baltzer, "The Little Office of the Virgin and Mary's Role at Paris," in *The Divine Office*, ed. Fassler and Baltzer, 463–84. For an introduction to the Hours of the Virgin in books of hours, see also Wieck, *Time Sanctified*, 60–72.

57 Baltzer, "The Little Office," 465.

of Compline) were highly disseminated in a melodic form beyond the liturgical setting, and it would be hard to imagine sight of the words of such texts
without memory of the melody. A closer look at the contents of the individual
Hours reveals the entire Office to be a patchwork of texts drawn from liturgical—and therefore chanted—contexts,[58] meaning that every portion of the
Hours—whether the ubiquitous Psalms or the highly specific antiphon texts—
had potential for musical association. The Hours of Jeanne d'Evreux (about
which we will hear more in the following chapter) will serve as a brief case
study in the inherent musicality of the prayers.[59] Matins follows a modified
version of the liturgical form of the Office, with an abbreviation of the standard
three nocturnes to one. Throughout, every hymn, antiphon, versicle, and

58 For a full transcription of the Hours according to thirteenth-century Parisian Use,
see Baltzer, "The Little Office," 474–81; see also Wieck, *Time Sanctified*, 159–61 for a
transcription of the incipits of the main prayers for the Hours. For another useful source
relating to the Hours appearance in books of hours, including incipits and information
relating to regional variants, see the "tutorial" section of the online resource *CHD Center
for Håndskriftstudier i Danmark*, http://www.chd.dk/index.html. This is a more developed
version of the classic "Madan" text for determining localization, on which see Falconer
Madan, "Hours of the Virgin (Tests for Localization)," *Bodleian Quarterly Record* 3 (1920),
40–44, and his "The Localization of Manuscripts," in *Essays in History Presented to Reginald
Lane Poole*, ed. Henry Davis (Oxford: Clarendon Press, 1927), 5–29. For those less familiar with the Hours, a good introduction to the prayers is the English translation of Vespers
and Compline from an early fifteenth-century English manuscript, the Hours of Isabel
Ruddock, housed in Bristol City Library, Bristol Public Library MS 14, in *Women's Books
of Hours in Medieval England: Selected Texts Translated from Latin, Anglo-Norman French and
Middle English*, transl. Charity Scott-Stokes (Cambridge: D. S. Brewer, 2006), 39–46.
An effective way to trace liturgical contexts for texts of any of the Hours commonly found
in books of hours is via *Cantus: A Database for Latin Ecclesiastical Chant*, http://
cantusdatabase.org.

59 The Hours in this manuscript differ in several respects to the form outlined in
Wieck, and follow a Dominican Use. A complete transcription of all the Hours and
prayers is given by Barbara Drake Boehm in the commentary to the complete color facsimile: *Die Stundenbuch der Jeanne d'Evreux/The Hours of Jeanne d'Evreux*. With Commentary
by Barbara Drake Boehm, Abigail Quandt, and Willian Wixom (Lucerne: Faksimile
Verlag; New York: Metropolitan Museum of Art, 1998). All references here cite the
English-language publication of the facsimile. See commentary volume 421–34 for a
transcription of the incipits of the Hours of the Virgin by Catherine Gros. For a partial
color facsimile of the manuscript, more widely available than the 1998 volume, see *The
Hours of Jeanne d'Evreux, Queen of France, at the Cloisters, the Metropolitan Museum of Art*.
With an introduction by James Rorimer (New York: Metropolitan Museum of Art,
1957). See too the CD-Rom of the manuscript: *The Hours of Jeanne d'Evreux: A Prayer
Book for a Queen*. CD-Rom. With commentary by Barbara Drake Boehm (New York:
Metropolitan Museum of Art, 1998).

Table 6.1. Summary of liturgical references in Matins, Hours of the Virgin

Genre	Incipit	Liturgical source
Invitatory	*Regem virginis filium*	Matins, Feast of Vigil of the Assumption (Invitatory Antiphon)
Hymn	*Quem terra pontus*	Matins, Assumption (Hymn)
Antiphon	*Benedicta tu*	Matins, Annunciation (Responsory verse)
Versicle	*Diffusa est*	Terce, Nativity (Responsory verse)
Responsory	*Sancta et immaculata*	Matins, Nativity of the Virgin (Responsory)
Responsory	*Beata es Maria*	Various Marian feasts (Antiphon for the Magnificat)
Responsory	*Felix namque es*	Nativity of the Virgin (Responsory)

responsory has a melodic correlate, drawn from a range of feasts, most commonly those associated with the Virgin. Table 6.1 offers a summary.

Given the latent musicality of their texts, it is little wonder that we encounter evidence that those engaged in private devotion may have felt bound to raise their voices in song. Michael Clanchy points to Matthew Paris's account of the attempted murder of Henry III of England in 1238, when one of the perpetrators was overheard by a lady of the household: "She was still awake because she was reciting (literally 'chanting', 'psaltabat') her Psalter by candlelight."[60] It may be that such readers saw in their books a form of notation that even encouraged them to vary their vocalization. For although cases of musical notation are rare, that is not the end to the potentially musical texture of the prayer texts, and especially to the recall of prior musical association of so many of their texts. It was not just textual association that imported musical memory. A broad survey of books reveals that format and layout remain sensitive to the change of texts and vocal registers (from the intonation

60 Michael Clanchy, "Images of Ladies with Prayer Books: What Do They Signify?," in *The Church and the Book: Papers Read at the 2000 Summer Meeting and the 2001 Winter Meeting of the Ecclesiastical History Society*, ed. Robert Swanson (Woodbridge: Boydell & Brewer, 2004), 106–22, at 111. The account is from *Matthaei Parisiensis monachi Sancti Albani Chronica Majora*, ed. Henry Luard, 7 vols., Rerum Britannicarum medii aevi scriptores 57 (London: Longman and Co., 1872–83), 2:497 and 4:200.

of Psalms to strophic hymns to the neumatic melodification of responsories and antiphons). This is notation of sorts, too.

Consider again the Hours of Jeanne d'Evreux. It encodes through rubric and layout the musicality of the texts. It is ruled throughout with identical line spacings. However, the scribe makes use of two different script sizes—one occupying the entire line space, the other much smaller, using roughly half the space. The scale of the text is commissioned to reflect changes of melodic type implied by the texts. Taking a sample of folios of Matins, figures 6.18–6.20 (fols. 20^v, 21^r, and 22^r), we see that the most melodic texts—the antiphons, responsories, verses, and versicles—are written in a smaller size than those of the Psalms. The former are associated with a more melodically varied vocal style, while the Psalms demand a simpler, recitational voice. Meanwhile, the latter are beautifully set up to reflect the distinction of verses, with the start of each punctuated by a colored capital letter. Finally, the scribe is assiduous in the use of red rubrics, sometimes abbreviated, to signal the shift of text genre. The book thus creates something like a visual map of the musical memory. It may also have had a practical use. For those learning their prayers, perhaps not yet literate in Latin, it offered clear cues for the movement from one section of prayer to the next. Such a set-up was ideal for the intended owner, a young queen, Jeanne d'Evreux. One could imagine her listening to her confessor recite or chant the Offices, perhaps joining in with the texts she knew by heart, until she eventually came to know her prayers well enough to assume an independent voice.

If books invite their individual users to attune to the communal context, what more evidence is there of where books were used? For to be engaged in an individual act of prayer one did not necessarily have to be alone. It is time now to think outside the books, to their contexts of use: as we shall see, the voices within the books are joined by an often clamorous chorus of voices in their immediate exterior.

NONE: SONIC DISTRACTIONS AND THE LOCATIONS FOR PRAYER

A classic and much reproduced example of the fact that prayer books were used for private meditation is an image from a much later book, the Hours of Mary of Burgundy, shown in figure 6.21.[61] A lady—presumed to be Mary—is alone with her book.[62] The shutters of her chamber open onto a chapel, where she is

61 For a facsimile see *The Hours of Mary of Burgundy: Codex Vindobonensis 1857, Vienna, Osterreichische Nationalbibliothek*, ed. with commentary by Erik Inglis (London: Harvey Miller, 1995).

62 Most agree on the identity of Mary here. For an alternative reading, arguing that the lady represents Mary's stepmother, Margaret of York, and that Margaret may have

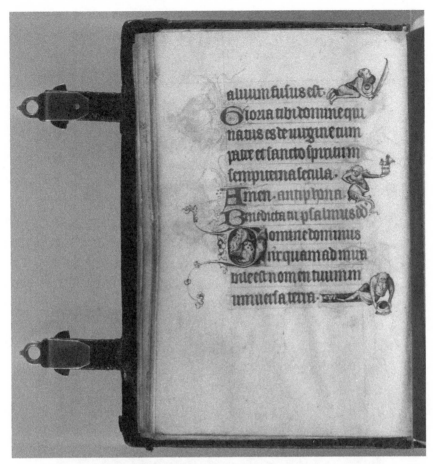

FIGURE 6.18. New York, Metropolitan Museum, Cloisters MS 54.1.2 (the Hours of Jeanne d'Evreux), fol. 20ᵛ. © The Metropolitan Museum of Art/Art Resource, NY

projected into an audience with the Virgin. It is what Diana Webb describes as a "visionary image": the space beyond the shutters is a representation of her interior meditation.[63] The many images of solitary devotion in a domestic

---

commissioned the book for Mary, see Anne Hagopian Van Buren, Review of Otto Pächt and Dagmar Thoss, *Die illuminierten Handschriften und Inkunabeln der flämische Schule II*," *Speculum* 68 (1993): 1187–90. My thanks to Beth Williamson for pointing this out to me.

63 Diana Webb, "Domestic Space and Devotion in the Middle Ages," in *Defining the Holy: Sacred Space in Medieval and Early Modern Europe*, ed. Andrew Spicer and Sarah Hamilton (Aldershot: Ashgate, 2005), 44.

FIGURE 6.19. New York, Metropolitan Museum, Cloisters MS 54.1.2 (the Hours of Jeanne d'Evreux), fol. 21ʳ. © The Metropolitan Museum of Art/Art Resource, NY

setting have often fueled a notion of prayer as a quiet, contemplative pursuit. The reality could not be more different. Books opened up spaces rife with sonorous effects, and also with aural distraction, be it in the clamor of the memory or the literal space of prayer's pursuit. And in startling ways, books themselves, in encoding sights of such sound, were themselves a form of sonic distraction.

To relocate prayer books in their full sonic environment involves a shift of perspective, and especially a revision of the category of "private." As we saw in the previous section, some books were customized for use in communal liturgical settings, and recalled prior public contexts. But even books without those

FIGURE 6.20. New York, Metropolitan Museum, Cloisters MS 54.1.2 (the Hours of Jeanne d'Evreux), fol. 22^r. © The Metropolitan Museum of Art/Art Resource, NY

attributes found their way into public venues. So, while the sight of Mary of Burgundy alone may be designed as a contemplative prompt, a cue for her to imagine a one-to-one relationship with the Virgin, such a projection could easily have taken place in a context where Mary herself was far from alone.[64] In this case, the image of liturgical space viewed from the domestic interior

64 On which see Wieck, *Books of Hours*, 44, and Clanchy, "Images of Ladies with Prayer Books," 120.

FIGURE 6.21. Vienna, Osterreichische Nationalbibliothek, Codex Vindobonensis 1857 (the Hours of Mary of Burgundy), fol. 14ᵛ. Foto Marburg/Art Resource, NY

had some correlations in reality. For some elite members of society, there were indeed windows opening out onto ecclesiastical space. As Webb points out, Mary's tomb monument, in the choir of the church of Our Lady in Bruges, was adjacent to a small chapel with a window-seat, constructed by Louis de Gruuthuse in 1472 so that he might have access to the church from his house.[65]

65 Webb, "Domestic Space," 44. For more on the relationship between such "visionary" images and real locales, see also Paul Crossley, "The Man from Inner Space: Architecture and Meditation in the Choir of St Laurence in Nuremberg," in *Medieval Art—Recent Perspectives: A Memorial Tribute to C. R. Dodwell*, ed. Gale Owen Crocker and Timothy Graham (Manchester: St. Martin's Press, 1998), 165–82.

It was just one case of what Eamon Duffy describes as the "privatization of religion" in the corporate setting in the later Middle Ages, including provision for a family pew in church, or a domestic chapel at home. In these ways, he argues, the "boundaries between private and public, individual and corporate, are . . . permeable."[66]

Some examples will illustrate the variety of devotional contexts. A fascinating source is Guillaume de St. Pathus's *Vie de saint Louis*, the life of the great Capetian King Louis IX, canonized in 1297.[67] Dating from 1303, the *Vie*, although undoubtedly biased to emphasize the saintly aspects of his life, offers valuable insights. Intended in part as a moral exemplum for his royal progeny, the *Vie* contains a detailed account of Louis's devotional habits. Chapter 6 concerns his "devocion fervent" and charts his adherence to the official structure of the Divine Office. The main locale is his chapel and the *Vie* recounts Louis's hectic to-ing and fro-ing between this venue and various royal sites, where he joins the assembly of clerks and chaplains. However, the assembled clergy perform the Mass and Offices "in raised voices with notes" ("a voix haut et a note")—that is, fully sung—while Louis is described in the company of his chaplain, praying "with lowered voice" ("a voix basse").[68]

Louis also found time in this Olympian timetable for more solitary, chamber-bound reflection. Chapter 8 describes him as "devoted to God in prayer" ("qui est en devotement Dieu prier"). This reflects a less structured pattern of devotion centered around free-standing prayers, performed both in his private chamber and in the chapel, and occurring in between the canonical Hours: a dual activity that mirrors the format of many books of hours, which contain Offices but are frequently supplemented with private prayers and devotions. And the prayers described in this chapter echo the kinds common in prayer books. The *Vie* describes an aerobic-style round of fifty *Ave Marias*, each one

66 Duffy, *Marking the Hours*, 54–55.

67 *Vie de saint Louis par Guillaume de Saint-Pathus*, ed. Henri-François Delaborde (Paris: Alphonse Picard et fils, 1899).

68 See, for example, the celebration of Matins: "And the custom that the blessed king observed with regard to the Divine Office was thus: the blessed king got up in the middle of the night and had his clerks and chaplains called, and then they entered the chapel in the presence of the king each night; and then they sang in raised voices with notes the Matins of the day and then of Our Lady, and for this the blessed king never left without saying one or other of the Matins in this same chapel, in a low voice with one of his chaplains" ("Et la costume que li benoiez rois gardoit en[vers] le service Dieu estoit tele: li benoiez rois se levoit a mie nuit et fesoit apeler clers et chapelains, et lors il entroient en la chapele en la presence du rois chascune nuit; et lors chantoient a haute voiz et a note matines du jour et puis de Nostre Dame, et pour ce ne lessoit pas li benoiez rois que il ne deist les unes et les autres matines en cele meesme chapele a basse voiz avec un de ses chapelains"). French text from *Vie de saint Louis*, 33.

uttered on standing up from a genuflection.[69] The form here bears comparison with a prayer in Cambridge, Trinity B. 11. 22 (fol. 118ʳ), which offers provision in a French rubric for kneeling and praying an *Adoremus te Christe* in between recitations of Psalms: "Se vous aues aucunes tribulations de adversites. Se dites ces psaumes et le fin de chascun psaume dires vous as genous ce verset [followed by *Adoremus te Christe*]."

There is ample evidence of people of less lofty social echelons situating personal prayer in a range of settings, from the bedchamber to the church. The early thirteenth-century English *Ancrene Wisse*, a handbook for anchoresses, instructs readers to recite prayers and the well-known hymn *Veni creator spiritus* on waking up, at the side of the bed and in the privacy of the bedchamber, and to continue to recite prayers as they dress, telling them: "Make much use of these words and keep them in your mouth often on every occasion that you can, whether you are sitting and standing."[70] Here the bedchamber does double service as oratory. On the other hand, as Duffy points out, the *Ancrene Wisse* also takes for granted that young women readers of the manual would attend and listen to the public liturgy of the church, while their own prayers revolved around the abbreviated Hours of the Virgin and portions of the Office of the Dead.[71] There is a sense that these simultaneities had the potential to create dissonance, the one utterance interfering with the other. The author warns his readers to keep their voices down when praying in the presence of a priest in active celebration of the Mass: "Listen to the priest's hours as far as you can; but you must not recite verses or sing so he can hear it."[72]

Set against such contexts, one category of image common in the margins of prayer books takes on new significance: as visual trace of the experience of the sonic environment. Consider the marginal surround of figure 6.22, from

---

69 "The saintly king genuflected each day in the evening fifty times, and each time stood upright, and then genuflected again, and each time that he genuflected he said an *Ave Maria* as quietly as possible" ("li sainz rois s'agenoilloit chascun jour au soir cinquante foiz et a chascune foiz se levoit tout droit, et donc se ragenoilloit, et a chascune foiz que il s'agenoilloit, il disoit mout a loisir un *Ave Maria*"). French text from *Vie de saint Louis*, 54.

70 As noted in Webb, "Domestic Space," 29. Quoting here from *Ancrene Wisse: Guide for Anchoresses*, transl. Hugh White (London: Penguin Books, 1993), 9. The preamble to this instruction reads thus: "When you first rise, bless yourself and say *In nomine Patris et Filii et Spiritui Sancti, Amen*, and begin at once *Veni, Creator Spiritus* with your eyes and hands raised up to the heaven, bending forward on your knees upon the bed; and say the whole hymn through like this, with the versicle *Emitte Spiritum tuum* and the prayer *Deus, qui corda fidelium*. After this, putting on your shoes and dressing, say *Pater noster* and *Credo*."

71 Duffy, *Marking the Hours*, 7.

72 *Ancrene Wisse*, 24.

FIGURE 6.22. London, British Library, Add. 36684, fol. 125ʳ. © The British Library Board

London, British Library Add. 36684, and English book of hours made for a female reader, dating from ca. 1320 (measuring 152 × 112 mm). In the scheme of images for the Office of the Dead and Commendation of the Soul—the portions of the book containing the most strictly liturgical texts—the illuminator follows the convention of other manuscripts by representing a scene of corporate congregation around the coffin. However, the edges of the central scene, filled with a strange fantasy of book-bearing witnesses, including the disembodied head of a female onlooker, transform the frame into something like a choir-screen. The exterior figures listen in, and strain to see, the action of the liturgical rite, just as in reality any lay female supplicant would have done.

An even stranger, more distracting sense of contexts is suggested in Walters Art Museum W 88, a French Psalter dating from 1300 (measuring 110 × 70 mm).[73] A personal feature of this manuscript is the exhaustive fantasia of the *bas-de-page*: the entire lower register of the manuscript hosts a parade of drolleries. While at first sight appearing to be a random assortment of hybrids and scatological distractions, a closer look reveals this layer to be systematic in its hallucinatory snapshot of situated uses. Flying and running across the folios are an eclectic congregation of readers. In the mix are a number of hybrid figures: human heads on animal legs; bodies with winged heads. Among them are a number of tonsured clerics and women, holding their own books or reading from legged lecterns. In figure 6.23 [website figure 6.6] we see a fantastical conjunction of these groups: on the right, fol. 141ʳ, a female reader, book in hand (deploying the sign of performance), is led astray by the beaky strutting creature before her, and held aloft by her winged bottom, from which protrudes the tonsured cleric, gazing across the opening at the scene on fol. 140ᵛ of a man and a boar. As in London, British Library Add. 36684, the mixture of human constituencies in this motley crew of the imaginary echoes the sense of community in which a book such as this would have been used. Amid the copious signs of performance, there is another recurring theme: that of sound. Trumpets blare and vielles scrape, sometimes right in the thick of those signs of use. In figure 6.24 [website figure 6.7], fol. 38r, a three-piece hybrid with devoted reader to the right, listener to the left, is interrupted in its midriff by a trumpet player. An even more arresting sense of competing sounds may be found in the *bas-de-page* of an unusual musical appendage to this manuscript. In figure 6.25 [website figure 6.8], fol. 181ʳ, a man and bagpiper are in musical colloquy in competition with the voice of the interlocutor's loquacious nether regions. This grotesque ensemble is in the shadow of the lyrics of a conductus by Philip the Chancellor, its musical association apparent for all to see in the bright red rubric that introduces it as "suauissima viellatura beate uirginis edita a magistro philippo Cancellario parisiensi".[74] All such disturbing sound

---

73 Wieck, *Time Sanctified*, catalogue no. 80, p. 208; Randall, *Medieval and Renaissance Manuscripts*, 3, catalogue no. 222, pp. 67–72.

74 The sequence is *Que est ista que ascendit transiens deserta*. It survives in two other sources and was transcribed in *Analecta hymnica medii aevi*, 9: *Sequentiae ineditae: Liturgische Prosen des Mittelalters*, pt. 2, ed. Guido Maria Dreves (Leipzig: O. R. Resiland, 1890), 58–60. The version in Walters 88 is transcribed with critical apparatus in Thomas Payne, "Poetry, Politics, and Polyphony: Philip the Chancellor's Contribution to the Music of the Notre Dame School," 3 vols. (Ph.D. diss., University of Chicago, 1991), 3: 614–16. Payne's dissertation remains the authoritative work on Philip the Chancellor.

FIGURE 6.23. Baltimore, Walters Art Museum, W 88, fols. 140ᵛ–141ʳ. © The Walters Art Museum

may be no figment of the artistic imagination. Situating the book for a moment in the physical environments of prayer, or into memories of its use, such a sighting may be understood as a translation of sorts—the book's twisted visions of sound may have mimicked the distracting, action-packed nature of reality.

Before we turn closer attention to the breakdown of sense in marginalia, I want to address ways in which prayer books were themselves caught up in a reality of prayer characterized by linguistic confusion. For many of those devotedly reciting, and trying to ignore the noise of prayers around them, the world made no verbal sense at all. For some, the images in their books would have been the only aspect that was coherent. By contrast, the sound of Latin prayer— in their surroundings, perhaps even coming from their own mouths—was nothing less than incomprehensible babble.

Full identifications of this and other song lyrics in this portion of the manuscript, including transcriptions of their rubrics, are provided in Lilian Randall's description of W 88. See *Medieval and Renaissance Manuscripts*, 3:68–69 for the account of this portion of the manuscript.

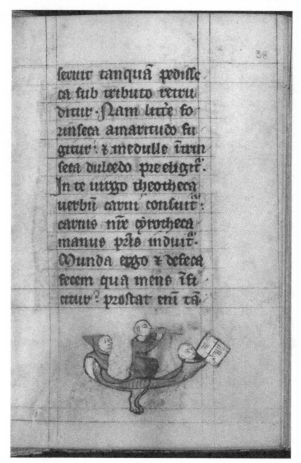

FIGURE 6.24. Baltimore, Walters Art Museum, W 88, fol. 38ʳ. © The Walters Art Mueusm

VESPERS: OWNERS AND THEIR SENSE OF SOUND

The history of sound in prayer is also a history of medieval literacy. Some owners of prayer books might not have been able to read their contents. For others, the folios turned open to a range of languages (Latin, French, English) in which they were entirely fluent. For others still, prayer books became comprehensible over time: they were also the means by which they learned their letters, and perhaps eventually the sense those combinations of letters signified. Questions of sense and sound were thus at the foreground of the prayer book.

In his study of literacy and reading habits in medieval books of hours, Paul Saenger draws a useful distinction between "phonetic literacy" and "comprehension literacy." In the former, a reader might be able to "decode texts syllable

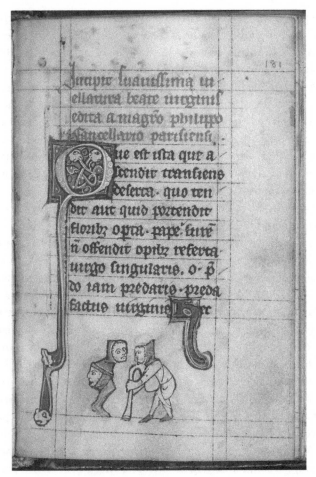

FIGURE 6.25. Baltimore, Walters Art Museum, W 88, fol. 181ʳ. © The Walters Art Museum

by syllable and to pronounce them orally."[75] Saenger describes here the essential program for learning to read in the Middle Ages, which in its early stages did not necessarily involve comprehension. By contrast, those with comprehension literacy had the ability "to decode a written text silently, word by word, and to understand fully in the very act of gazing upon it."[76] Nor were these two modes discrete. Many clerics might have comprehension literacy in Latin, while many more, and many lay people, might have comprehension literacy only in the vernacular, and phonetic literacy in Latin.

75 Saenger, "Books of Hours," 142–43.
76 Ibid., 142.

Where phonetic literacy applied at least in the early stages of experiencing the prayer book, sounding out the text was an essential part of its experience, as was—especially in the case of Psalters—chanting it out. As dictated by the discipline of grammar, the starting place for learning letters and language was through sound: sounding out letters and then learning by rote as stepping stones to eventual comprehension. As Michael Clanchy notes, "'reading' (legere) and 'understanding' (intellegere) were recognized as distinct and progressive stages of attainment." Not only that, he argues, "the essential element in reading was correct pronunciation." Clanchy cites examples of monastic regimes in which "legere" preceded "intellegere," "as a form of reading without understanding."[77]

Taking up the theme in the context of liturgy, Katherine Zieman's work explores the many connections between singing and reading. Liturgical instruction was synonymous with learning to read and, given the pervasive musicality of the liturgy, was therefore connected to singing. With the rise of more popular modes of devotion, the potential to learn liturgy without knowing the meaning increased. Treatises on the Mass, and writers such as Chaucer and Langland, are witness to a culture in which lay people might hear, and choristers perform, words they did not understand—evidence of what Zieman terms an "extragrammatical literacy."[78] In the public arena of liturgy, then, understanding was not necessarily as critical as the utterance itself.[79]

Books of hours and Psalters were caught in the flux of these competing literacies, and catered to all types. Many bear traces of customization. A number of manuscripts contain prayers in the vernacular, as counterpart to the Latin Offices and Psalms.[80] Among the manuscripts discussed in this chapter, Cambrai, Médiathèque municipale 87 offers perhaps the best example of a bilingual prayer book, containing an extensive selection of French prayers. The book was designed with careful attention to the spiritual edification of its

77 Clanchy, "Images of Ladies with Prayer Books," 110. For a more extensive account of medieval literacy and memory, see also Clanchy, *From Memory*.

78 See especially Zieman, *Singing the New Song*, 114–27.

79 Ibid., 125.

80 The essential sourcebook for the tradition of French prayers is Jean Sonet, *Répertoire d'incipit de prières en ancien français* (Geneva: Droz, 1956). See also the following two publications, which update and correct Sonet's original catalogue: Keith Val Sinclair, *Prières en ancien français: Nouvelles références, renseignements complémentaires, indications bibliographiques, corrections et tables des articles du Répertoire de Sonet* (Hamden: Archon Books, 1978) and Pierre Rézeau, *Répertoire d'incipits des prières françaises à la fin du Moyen Age: Addenda et corrigenda aux répertoires de Sonet et Sinclair* (Geneva: Droz, 1986). For a selection of prayers in books of hours produced in England see *Women's Books of Hours*, transl. Scott-Stokes, which includes texts translated from Latin, Anglo-Norman French, and Middle English.

female user, and the presence of prayers that would have been semantically accessible indicates how much phonetic and semantic concerns were bound into prayerful experience.[81] Indeed, the history of female literacy is deeply entwined with the history of books of hours and Psalters.[82] The strong presence of the vernacular in prayer books persisted until the Offices themselves were translated: the exquisite little Hours in Baltimore, Walters Art Museum W 89 (the Hours of Isabelle de Coucy), dating from ca. 1380 and of Parisian provenance, is one of the earliest such examples.[83] Elsewhere, there are cases not just of independent Latin and vernacular sections, but of hybridized units with extensive vernacular rubrics and glosses on Latin texts, thus offering a form of translation that was semantically elusive. An elaborate instance of the hybridizing of Latin Hours occurs in Walters Art Museum W 102, made in England ca. 1300, probably for a monastic user.[84] We shall be looking closely at this book in the next chapter. For now, though, we can note its extensive use of Old French rubrics and commentaries as gloss to Latin prayers. Cambridge, Trinity B. 11. 22 likewise includes practical instructions in French relating to prayer sequences. These alternations of languages play on the registers of the respective languages, but they may also imply readers operating at two levels of literacy: understanding fully the French, but able perhaps only to sound out the letters of the Latin.

It is this context of polylingualism, of varied and changeable literacies, and the book's role in teaching language and letters, that we may situate discourses of pronunciation and distraction. Not only was the potential to mis-sound words high. In contexts of extragrammatical literacy, the unhinging of sound from sense meant sound's sensual pull, unfettered by meaning, had potential to stir the body to distraction. As we have seen, there is one site in prayer books where artists seemed especially attuned to sound's relationship to sense: the marginalia. It is there we shall now turn, to see playing out all the many frequencies—and also perils—of sounding prayer.

81 On which see Bennett, "A Woman's Power of Prayer," and on the French prayers see too her "Christ's Five Wounds."

82 A point made by Bennett, "A Thirteenth-Century French Book of Hours," 29. For further discussion of women's readership of prayer books see also Clanchy, "Images of Ladies with Prayer Books"; Gould, *The Psalter and Hours of Yolande of Soissons*; and Susan Groag Bell, "Medieval Women Book Owners: Arbiters of Lay Piety and Ambassadors of Culture," *Signs* 7 (1982): 742–68.

83 Wieck, *Time Sanctified*, catalogue no. 14, p. 179; Randall, *Medieval and Renaissance Manuscripts*, 1, catalogue no. 73, pp. 194–95.

84 Wieck, *Time Sanctified*, catalogue no. 111, pp. 221–22. For a detailed description of the manuscript, its contents, and a partial transcription of the French rubrics, see Florence McCulloch, "The Funeral of Renart the Fox in a Walters Book of Hours," *Journal of the Walters Art Gallery* 25–6 (1962–63): 8–27.

For nineteenth-century collectors who snipped them out for private delectation or prudishly covered them over, to modern tourists who purchase postcard close-ups from museum gift shops, medieval marginalia were and are a source of fascination and controversy. Subject to exhaustive investigation by art historians, perhaps the only consensus regarding their meaning for medieval readers is their resistance to systematic decoding. Pioneering work to catalogue and analyze marginal imagery demonstrated a degree of consistency: in the forms of particular image types, and in their appearance across a broad spectrum of manuscripts.[85] However, such images seem to resist certain resolution. One thing is clear: that while the strangeness of the monsters and hybrids populating margins led some early commentators to feel suspicion, categorizing them as "hideous creatures . . . [that] can hardly have been normal,"[86] marginal art was not void of significance, nor incidental to the texts it elaborated. Rather, the margins were semantically excessive, purveyors of multiple meanings, often erudite in their allusive nature, drawing widely on classic, biblical, and romance sources, citing proverbs and fables. Through close attention, case by case, the margins inject meaning into the prayers they appear to defy.

Throughout this chapter we have had glimpses of the noisy nature of marginalia. To understand what and how such sound signifies, we need to consider some general principles by which they operate on prayer texts. For that, we shall summon Lucy Freeman Sandler as *cicerone*, and specifically her recent essay on the margins of the Macclesfield Psalter.[87] Drawing together work from the preceding two decades, notably Camille's famous *Image on the Edge* as well as her own extensive publications on the subject, Sandler sets out three common scholarly viewpoints, and suggests a new one. The first, influenced by Bakhtinian concepts, categorizes marginalia as "liminal." Monstrosities or obscenities invert the stable, authorized world that produces the texts they frame. They shock the viewer, but in offering a foil to the familiar they also have a potentially pedagogical function: to illuminate the orthodox; to challenge but ultimately uphold its authority. A second approach concerns the

85 Randall's *Images in the Margins* remains an essential reference. Based on a survey of hundreds of manuscripts containing marginalia, Randall's catalogue indexed marginalia according to thousands of types, including human and animal, mythological, biblical, and literary allusion, and gestural category, to name but a few. Among her categories are several pertaining to music and instruments. Another classic reference text for the systematic and analytical approach to marginalia is Sandler's "Reflections on the Construction of Hybrids," 51–65.

86 Sandler, "In and Around the Text," 106, n. 20, here quoting Eric Millar, *The Luttrell Psalter* (London: British Museum, 1931), 16, on the Luttrell Psalter.

87 Sandler, "In and Around the Text," 105–14.

word–image relationship—the "imagines verborum." Sometimes marginal imagery radically decontextualizes, with no obvious correlation to the word it may adorn. At other times, though, closer investigation of seeming disjunctions reveals images as complex etymologies of sense and sound. Finally, Sandler draws attention to the "societal meaning" of the margins. That approach identifies in marginalia elements that derive from the social world of a book's production, and which thus offer earthly counterpoint to the spiritual source of the prayer texts. The Luttrell Psalter is such an example, renowned for its detailed depictions of daily life in the world of its owner.[88] Sandler's essay also emphasizes marginalia as an assertion of artistic individuality. Like no other category of image, marginalia invite invention on the part of the artist: to define the margins as a site of personal creativity reinforces the fact that images had semantic intention.

If these categories offer ways to understand how margins relate to their texts, the purpose of such operations has also been widely debated. For Mary Carruthers, the images had an ancillary function: to serve as mnemonics for the texts they decorate.[89] Relating marginalia to a rare account of the utility of extraordinary images in Thomas Bradwardine's *De memoria artificiali adquirenda*, Carruthers suggests that the more outrageously scatological or sexualized the image, the greater its mnemonic potential.[90] On the other hand, Michael Clanchy argues that grotesque marginalia are an indicator of "equivocation,"[91] and that "by drawing the eye away from the body of the text to that surrounding pictorial forms of penmanship, grotesques remind the reader that the letters themselves are not the truth."[92] Clanchy also points to the realism inherent in much hybrid or grotesque imagery as a source of their ambiguous ethical standing vis-à-vis the words they accompany: something recognizably human or otherwise known transformed into a form utterly unfamiliar poses problems. He goes on: "letters metamorphosize into mythical creatures, animals change size and act like human beings, sacred words become the playthings of equivocators and blasphemers."[93] If images represent equivocation, and incite distraction, they also—by nature of their precarious semantic status—demand a kind of devotional labor on the part of the reader.

88 See especially Michelle Brown, *The World of the Luttrell Psalter* (London: British Library, 2006).

89 Carruthers, *Book of Memory*, esp. 226–29 and 245–48.

90 For a translation of key portions see *The Medieval Craft of Memory*, ed. Carruthers and Ziolkowski, 205–14.

91 Clanchy, *From Memory*, 291; for discussion of grotesques see 290–93.

92 Ibid., 291.

93 Ibid., 292.

Images were thus "visual injunctions for action," and called on supplicants to resolve their meaning in relation to the text.[94]

All these accounts open up ways to think about sound's role. We shall pursue two. The first relates to the function of free-floating sound images—those not explicitly tied to specific words but in general opposition to their spiritual host; another concerns sounding aspects of "imagines verborum." Let us consider the large number of free-floating, seemingly non-referential, sound images that frequent the margins. By contrast to certain other sonic conventions such as scrolls, gesturing figures, and so on, these images are strange, often hybrid in nature, and less readily decipherable. We saw some at the opening of this chapter, among them chatty hybrids, trumpet-blaring creatures, and so on. They appear with varying degrees of deliberateness. Some are "fillers"—images that repeat at line endings or *bas-de-page* across entire manuscripts. Others seem to be placed with more intent. For example, the bagpiping wolf in the foliage margin in figure 6.26 [website figure 6.9] from Walters Art Museum W 45, fol. 116ᵛ, is typical of the kinds of imaginative instrumentalists who pop up throughout that book (compare, for example, with figure 6.5, website figure 6.1, from the same manuscript). Walters Art Museum W 88, which we have already seen to have a highly developed vocabulary of reader-supplicant hybrids, also offers a highly imaginative musical theme. In figure 6.27 [website figure 6.10] (fol. 185ᵛ) a two-tier monster with a triple-sided face blows trumpets either side; in figure 6.28 [website figure 6.11] (fol. 48ʳ) one half of a hybrid bows a vielle while the other turns to listen.

In these cases, it is impossible to attribute specific meaning to any single image since they resist correlation with the verbal context. However, to read them within a currency of artistic economy—as meaningless fillers—is to ignore their powerful effect. Seen from the viewpoint of margins representing the "other" to the center, and within the broader context of concern with sound, they stage a constant reminder of the threat of *curiositas*: be it the distractions of environment, of the voice's shaky grasp of verbal sound, or the memory of musical pleasure. With the turn of each folio, and the eye craving the minutia of detail, such images ultimately have a regulatory potential: the viewer is entrapped again and again by the sight of sounds she is enjoined to guard against.

The second category of sounding images is the "imagines verborum"—images related explicitly, and often physically, to specific words. Many conventions of the word-image look back to an older tradition of Psalm illustration, and also tie in with the double function of prayer books as primers.[95] In many instances, they reveal deep sensitivity to and reliance on the oral/aural

94 Sandler, "In and Around the Text," 109.
95 A point made by Michael Camille in *Mirror in Parchment*, 162.

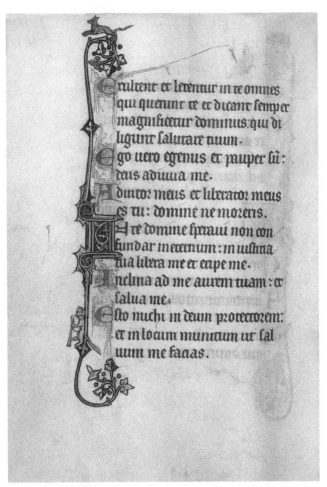

FIGURE 6.26. Baltimore, Walters Art Museum, W 45, fol. 116ᵛ. © The Walters Art Museum.

properties of language: as letter and utterance; as sense and sound. Some decorated letters and line endings offer a general prompt for the oral, embodied nature of words. There are cases of figures nested within capital letters who then shout out or play instruments. Elsewhere, figures chomp on decorative foliage fronds and borders, to suggest the literal ways in which words are savored in the mouth, and with obvious reference to the medieval discourses of *meditatio* and *ruminatio*. Images of vomiting and defecation likewise invite association with the gastric notion of the embodied text. A further category of "imagines verborum" establishes mimetic relationships. Few artists seem able to resist the opportunity to visualize the exclamatory or jubilatory sentiments of words. Jean Pucelle, artist of the Hours of Jeanne d'Evreux, was especially

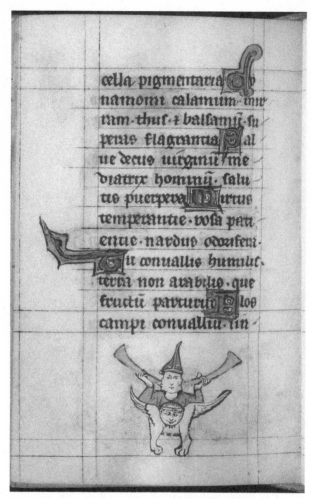

FIGURE 6.27. Baltimore, Walters Art Museum, W 88, fol. 185ᵛ. © The Walters Art Museum

responsive to words relating to sound, and his Hours are full of images that listen. One example will suffice, from the opening of Psalm 99, beginning with the word "Iubilate" at the opening of Lauds for the Hours of the Virgin.[96] In figure 6.29 (fol. 37ʳ), the "I" is extended into a small turret-like structure, from which a man leans out to blow a trumpet. This captures the injunction of "Iubilate," while the architectural setting also refers the Psalm's fourth

96 Psalm 99:2: "Sing joyfully to God, all the earth; serve ye the Lord with gladness. Come in before his presence with exceeding great joy" ("Iubilate Domino, omnis terra, servite Domino in laetitia, introite in conspectu eius in exsultatione").

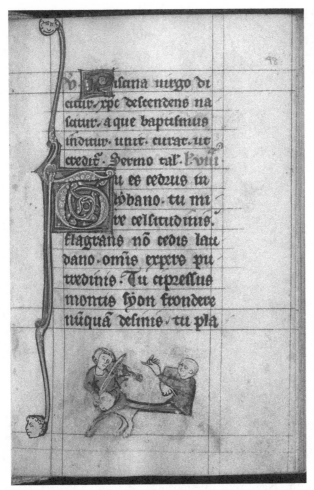

FIGURE 6.28. Baltimore, Walters Art Museum, W 88, fol. 48ʳ. © The Walters Art Museum

verse: "Go ye into his gates with praise, into his courts with hymns: and give glory to him. Praise ye his name" ("Introite portas eius in confessione, atria eius in hymnis, confitemini illi: laudate nomen eius.")

A final category concerns images' relationship to the sound of words. These are not necessarily images of sound; they rather visualize concepts derived from a phonetic encounter. Analysis by Sandler and Camille helps explain how seemingly nonsensical images "hear" the multiple meanings in the text, establishing a relationship to verbal sense and sound that mimics the varied literacy of many medieval supplicants. If prayer inhabits a fluid semantic field, these images seem to push language to a new limit by representing words within words, by listening bi- sometimes trilingually to the texts.

FIGURE 6.29. New York, Metropolitan Museum, Cloisters MS 54.1.2 (the Hours of Jeanne d'Evreux), fol. 37ʳ. © The Metropolitan Museum of Art/Art Resource, NY

The process of "hearing" through "seeing" often involves a kind of atomization of words, breaking them down syllable by syllable—Sandler terms it "visual syllabification"—as would have been the case in the schoolroom or primer.[97] Exaggerating the extragrammatical experience of Latin, artists are likely to pick up the most shocking words within words. As Camille recounts, "a popular joke of the age asked which was the 'dirtiest' word in the Psalter—the answer was conculcavit, which combines the word for cunt (con); ass (cul)

97 Sandler, "The Word in the Text," 92.

and prick (vit),"[98] all of which body parts were frequent visual topics in margins. Perhaps the most eloquent example is the Luttrell Psalter, where the images listen to the Psalms as three languages: Latin, French, and English. Thus, Camille writes, "even though only one language—Latin—is actually written down on the pages of the psalter, two others are voiced around it, floating between its lines and articulating some of its most powerful pictures."[99] Not only do images play with the sound of words within words, on occasion they make more tenuous semantic associations. Sandler cites an instance where a figure holds an arrow over the syllable "spec" from the word "conspecto," playing out the phonetic echo with "conspicere" and "spiculum."[100]

It is not hard to see why random imagery seems removed from prayer. However, understood in the wider context of meditation, and in the larger discourses relating to sound, they assume a different meaning. For both Sandler and Camille, the "imagines verborum" ultimately have an efficacious effect, pushing readers to make associations—semantic and phonetic—and thereby enriching the experience of reading. As we have seen, part of those riches were borne of verbal sound: as Camille reminds us: "word and image are equal on the pages . . . both would have been thought of as conventional and secondary representations, external to, but always referring back to, the spontaneous springs of speech."[101]

It is also in that intersection of sight and sound that prayer's musical aspect reveals itself. Throughout this chapter, we have seen the multiple ways in which images can control, prompt, judge, and notate the sounding performance of prayer. Sonic imagery can also distract, mimicking through sight its audible effect. The silent page thus enshrines records of sound—that sonic "afterglow"—that are more than simple prescriptions. They trace paths of memory, sensation, feeling, and thought about, and provoked by, sound. These all invite contemplation of the sound of prayer not just as an audible event, but also as personal experience: sometimes striving to listen to the word; sometimes driven by the noise of the surrounding oratory or visual hubbub of the manuscript, or by shaky literacy, to slip into an experience of prayer as meaningless clamor. More important than the possibility for audible affinity between wordy prayers and verbose music is the potential for the sonority of each to carry meaning and provoke action. Above all, it is during the tussle for meaning that the "imagines verborum" reveal their most striking affinity with music. These record not just the semantic superabundance of words; they are reminders of how such potency is a matter of sound, a product of word's

98 Camille, *Image on the Edge*, 38–9.
99 Camille, *Mirror in Parchment*, 170.
100 Sandler, "The Word in the Text," 92.
101 Camille, *Mirror in Parchment*, 174.

phonetic aspect. As images make audible the polyphony of language, they also invite meditation that implies another bond with music. For to uncloak a resolution of word and image, of sense and sound, is to engage in a mode of reading that allows multiple voices to co-exist, and multiple media to work—and in different ways to sound—simultaneously. It is in this polyphonic rigor of praying that we will find perhaps the most startling intersection with musical experience.

I wish next to "listen" to acts of prayer, to invite the reader to experience prayer books as innately musical. It is time now to assemble the lessons of sound, and see how they are put to work in individual acts of prayer. The next chapter offers two close readings of prayer books that not only set the signs of sound to active work. The work they demand of their devotees to decipher lessons and meanings from their sonic signs will also illuminate my closing suggestion—that praying with sound was infused with a kind of musicality, was itself a kind of music-making.

7 | Praying with Sound: The Hours of Jeanne d'Evreux and Walters Art Museum W 102

Voice Lessons: The Hours of Jeanne d'Evreux

If books were audible, an encounter with the sonorities of our first manuscript, New York, Metropolitan Museum, Cloisters MS 54.1.2 (the Hours of Jeanne d'Evreux), would prompt deafened recoil (see fols. 15ᵛ–16ʳ, shown in figure 7.1). So tiny a manuscript—a mere 89 × 62 mm—has a surprisingly large and controversial voice.[1] While we have glimpsed some of its sounds in the preceding chapter, a closer look reveals that the artist of the Hours, Jean Pucelle, was virtuosic in his use of the lexicon. From his brilliant deployment of the familiar to his invention of new categories of musical monstrosity, Pucelle created nothing short of a master class in sounding prayer.

If the book is a remarkable record of artistic agency, it is no less precious for its wealth of cultural memory. Few artifacts of its kind offer so much evidence regarding owner and purpose.[2] In thinking about how visual sonorities shape prayer, we are thus in the unusual position of knowing a good deal about the

---

1 For references to facsimiles of the manuscript, see chapter 6, n. 62, 220–21.

2 For the bibliographical context, see the commentary volume of the 1998 color facsimile *Die Stundenbuch/The Hours*. The following essays are pertinent to issues of context and use: Madeline Caviness, "Patron or Matron? A Capetian Bride and a *Vade mecum* for her Marriage Bed," *Speculum* 68 (1993): 333–62; Joan Holladay, "The Education of Jeanne d'Evreux: Personal Piety and Dynastic Salvation in her Book of Hours at the Cloisters," *Art History* 17 (1994): 585–611; her "Fourteenth-Century French Queens"; and Gerald Guest, "A Discourse on the Poor: The Hours of Jeanne d'Evreux," *Viator* 26 (1995): 153–80.

FIGURE 7.1. New York, Metropolitan Museum, Cloisters MS 54.1.2 (the Hours of Jeanne d'Evreux), fols. 15ᵛ–16ʳ. © The Metropolitan Museum of Art/Art Resource, NY

intended reader, her social context, and the range of devotional and didactic materials that would have informed her experience and determined her meditative "ductus."[3]

Although a good deal has been written about the historical context of the Hours, it will be helpful to recall the turbulent events surrounding its creation. It is widely accepted that the book was made for the young Capetian bride Jeanne d'Evreux for her wedding (1324), at the age of fourteen, to Charles IV. (A small book for small hands, then.) The pressures on the child-bride are well known. As Charles's third wife, she inherited a royal legacy saturated not only in the reproductive angst to bear sons, but also with an unusually fraught and violent outlook on marriage. In the years preceding, both Charles and his older brothers had been involved in adultery scandals that concluded in divorce, and in castration for certain of the offending parties—these were the same events that inspired the charivari explored in chapter 3.[4] If the humiliations of adultery had haunted Charles's early married years, then the death of his second wife, Marie of Luxembourg, as she gave birth to a son who lived a mere week, left the king contemplating the worst crisis any monarch could face. By late 1324, Charles looked to a future that saw the extinction of the Capetian line: as he embarked, sonless, on marriage with his young cousin, the stakes were high indeed. Prayer might easily be imagined to be the final and ultimate recourse for all concerned parties.

Everything about the contents of Jeanne's book implies careful customization for the tense moment of her accession. Along with a standard calendar (fols. 1^v–13^r), Hours of the Virgin (fols. 15^v–101^r), and Penitential Psalms and Litany (fols. 183^r–209^r), the book contains Hours of St. Louis (fols. 102^v–180^r)—an Office confected especially for private use from two recently composed liturgical (and communal) Offices for the saint.[5] Louis IX was of course the

---

3 Holladay, "Fourteenth-Century French Queens".

4 For the political aspect see Caviness, "Patron or Matron?," 32–36.

5 M. Cecilia Gaposchkin, "Philip the Fair, the Dominicans, and the Liturgical Office for Louis IX: New Perspectives on *Ludovicus decus regnantium*," *Plainsong and Medieval Music* 13 (2004): 33–61. There were several offices in circulation following Louis's canonization in 1297, the most famous among them *Ludovicus decus regnantium*, and the one which was in use in the Sainte-Chapelle. The Hours of Jeanne d'Evreux, however, contains a much-abridged version beginning with the incipit *Sanctus voluntatem*. This is based on two other full versions of the Office suitable for sung liturgical use. The first was the *Nunc laudare*, which was written very soon after the canonization and for use at the Dominican convent of Saint-Louis de Poissy, founded by Philip the Fair in 1297. The second was the *Exultemus omnes*, composed to celebrate the translation of the head of St. Louis to the Sainte-Chapelle from Saint-Denis in 1306. The privatized version of these Offices in the Hours of Jeanne d'Evreux draws largely on antiphons and hymns. It also appeared in other books made for Capetian women, including books of hours made

ideal inspiration: in addition to his legendary devotional skills (which we saw in the previous chapter), genealogy constructed him as spiritual exemplum. He was great-grandfather not only to Jeanne, but also to her husband Charles.[6] Family and religious duty were thus entwined to create in these prayers the ultimate personal daily routine. Meanwhile, the original artistry of Pucelle, from the unusual washed-out effect of *grisaille* to a brilliant double cycle of Passion and Infancy for the Hours of the Virgin, to the creation of a visual exemplum of Louis's *vita* to accompany his Hours, and above all to the scandalous and unexpected marginal decorations, tailored the book precisely to the queen's prayerful hands.

This exquisite book's currency beyond its material value is further suggested by its fate at the end of Jeanne's life. Widowed at the age of eighteen, Jeanne never remarried, living out the ensuing decades close to the royal court, where it seems she grew to become a sophisticated reader and collector. In a will drawn up in 1371, her book of hours is revealed not only as a continuous presence in her extensive library but also as something she held precious.[7] It is one of three items she singled out in a codicil to leave as bequest, in this case to the current king, Charles V, who himself seems to have treasured it as he might a relic: his inventories reveal he kept it in his private study at his palace in Vincennes, as opposed to the famous library he had had built at the palace of the Louvre in 1367–68, and where most of his collection resided.[8]

Even this brief outline suggests how highly charged any act of prayer from this book must have been. Nor was it simply meaningful for the moment of its creation. It would have changed over time, in response to Jeanne's life

---

for Jeanne de Navarre, Blanche of Burgundy, and Marie de Navarre. For full details of these books see Gaposchkin, 37–38, n. 26. For a complete transcription of the *Sanctus voluntatem* as it appears in the Hours of Jeanne d'Evreux, see *Die Stundenbuch/The Hours*, 435–57.

6 Jeanne, born in 1310, was the daughter of Louis d'Evreux (son of Philip III le Hardi and half-brother of Philip IV, le Bel), and Marguerite d'Artois. Her husband, Charles, was the son of Philip IV and Jeanne de Champagne and the last of the Capetian kings.

7 Details in Holladay, "Fourteenth-Century French Queens." The will and extracts from the codicil are in Constant Leber, *Collection des meilleurs dissertations, notices et traités particuliers relatifs à l'histoire de France*, 20 vols. (Paris: G.-A. Dentu, 1838), 19: 120–69. The original note reads: "A very small book of prayers that King Charles, God keep his soul, had made for Madame, which Pucelle illuminated." ("Un bien petit livret d'oroisons que le roy Charles, dont Diex ait l'âme, avoit faict faire por Madame, que Pucelle enlumina.")

8 On the book's relic-like status, see Holladay, 'Fourteenth-Century French Queens," 70; in n. 2 she notes that the 1380 inventory lists the manuscript. The inventory is transcribed in Delisle, *Recherches sur la librairie de Charles V*; see vol. 2, no. 244 for the entry pertaining to Jeanne's book.

experiences from marriage, pregnancy, motherhood, to widowhood. Imagine her in old age, drawing up the codicil, when her book would have been her life's memory; and imagine that memory—the relic now reliquary for Jeanne's own exemplary life—as the book passed on to Charles. For now, though, it is with that originary moment of creation and teaching that we shall be concerned. Part relic, part *vita* of the venerable ancestor, Jeanne's book, like so many other books of hours, was also a conduct book, designed to school the young queen in her devotional and queenly duties.

First some preliminary soundings. Today, most glimpse the book through the glass of the display-case at the Cloisters Museum of the Metropolitan Museum in New York. Others, keener to see more, may hunt down a copy of the limited-edition color facsimile, which comes to the reader in a box lined with blue velvet and furnished with its own magnifying glass. That ancillary aid is emblem of the fundamental visceral effect: the sheer effort required to see, and the book's miniature stature designed to engross and ensnare. The reproduction in figure 7.1 is to scale, and gives some sense of the challenge. Squinting into the folios, the eyes adjust to visual excess on a Lilliputian scale. As we saw in the previous chapter, the layout of the text of the Hours is eloquently particular. Yet the words are a still presence on parchment that swarms with activity, the eye drawn here and there, tracing erratic lines that may run counter to the flow of words. It is not chaos, even if the first impression is of such. Art historian Madeline Caviness distinguishes between four main areas of activity: first, luxurious, framed depictions of hagiographical or biblical scenes, enhanced with color; second, figures just on the periphery of the main frame, perhaps within a decorated capital, and occupying what Caviness calls "another (time-)frame," by being separate from the scriptural narrative of the main image; third, *bas-de-page* and margins; and finally the monstrous line-fillers, line-endings, and figures around decorated capitals.[9] The effect of vigorous and often competing visual activity is to swamp the words, producing a kind of "struggle against the ordered lines of the written word (which constitute the prayers), *and powerful distractions to be resisted by the reader intent on her devotions*" (my emphasis).[10] That struggle to see, and the tussle to stay focused on words, is thus the very embodiment of the dangers of *curiositas*, a danger exaggerated by the effort the book demands to scrutinize its distractions. It requires eye-strain in a most literal sense, as the reader peers in to decipher things that had better not be revealed. That physical effect is the hallmark of the sin itself. Recall Bernard of Clairvaux's famous evocation of the curious monk as one with roaming eyes and straining ears. Here the eyes perform the work of the straining ear. And to see—and hear—what, exactly?

9 Caviness, "Patron or Matron?," 32.
10 Ibid., 46.

Folio after folio, line after line, word after word, the eye tunes into a medley of sounds as noisy as they are here tiny: from the familiar sight of orthodox curly scrolls, to shouting, trumpeting, and gnashing line-endings; to figures screaming inside capitals; to music-obsessed monsters roaming the *bas-de-page*. Few books are so consistently imaginative, so systematic, in their creation of sonority. And the sensual mismatching—the distraction of straining to see unruly sound—is a template for one of the book's most powerful lessons. While the young Queen Jeanne was to learn much from her book about queenship and the virtues of her ancestor, her Hours was also a primer in some more essential instruction. Her wedding present was also a voice lesson.

DIDACTIC CONTEXTS

To establish a background for reading the sonority of the Hours, we might first consider the book's more obvious didactic programs. In the past fifteen years, several studies have illuminated Pucelle's carefully wrought discourses on queenship and their relationship to the politics of Jeanne's marriage. In its pedagogical impulse, the book resonates with the tradition of the Mirror of Princes, of which there was also a healthy subgenre concerned with queenship.[11] The late Capetians were particularly assiduous in their cultivation of such literature, the most famous witness being the treatise *De regimine principum*, written by the celebrated theologian Giles of Rome and dedicated to the then future Philip IV in the 1270s.[12] They also commissioned works widely read by women: Vincent of Beauvais's *De eruditione filiorum nobilium* dating from around 1265 and commissioned by Margeurite, wife of Louis IX, and the early fourteenth-century *Speculum dominarum* of Durand de Champagne,

---

11 *Medieval Queenship*, ed. John Carmi Parsons (New York: St. Martin's Press, 1993); *Queens and Queenship in Medieval Europe: Proceedings of a Conference Held at King's College London, April 1995*, ed. Anne Duggan (Woodbridge: Boydell & Brewer, 1997); and Janet Nelson, "Medieval Queenship," in *Women in Medieval Western European Culture*, ed. Linda Mitchell (New York: Garland, 1999), 179–207. On women's conduct literature see Diane Bornstein, *The Lady in the Tower: Medieval Courtesy Literature for Women* (Hamden, CT: Archon Books, 1983) and Alice Hentsch, *De la littérature didactique du Moyen Age s'adressant spécialement aux femmes* (Cahors: Conselant, 1903).

12 There is no complete edition of the text. For a recent edition of an early Middle English translation of the rule, see *The Governance of Kings and Princes: John Trevisa's Middle English Translation of the "De regimine principum" of Aegidius Romanus*, ed. David Fowler, Charles Briggs, and Paul Remley, Garland Medieval Texts 19 (New York: Garland, 1997), on which see Charles Briggs, *Giles of Rome's* De regimine principum: *Reading and Writing Politics at Court and University, c. 1275–c. 1525*, Cambridge Studies in Palaeography and Codicology 5 (Cambridge: Cambridge University Press, 1999).

confessor of Philip IV's wife, Jeanne de Navarre, and dedicated to her.[13] If the young Jeanne d'Evreux may not have known such works first-hand, she became familiar with them later in life, acquiring several such texts for her library.[14] Another influential body of literature entwined with the genre of the Mirror of Princes was that documenting the life and miracles of St. Louis, following his canonization in 1297.[15] Louis was the ultimate royal exemplum, as the meeting ground for the ideal confection of kingship and sanctity. Seen against such contexts, the iconography of the Hours begins to make sense.

Louis was central to Pucelle's pedagogical regime. His importance is testified not just in the prayers of the Hours themselves, but also through the highly original image cycle Pucelle devised, drawing on the earliest codified lives and miracles.[16] Unconstrained by visual convention, Pucelle was at liberty to determine the emphasis. The cycle fashions Louis as moral and spiritual model, and by highlighting his good deeds and charity—feeding a leprous monk (Lauds, fols. 123ᵛ–124ʳ, shown in figure 7.2), tending the sick (Prime, fols. 142ᵛ–143ʳ), washing the feet of the poor (Terce, fols. 148ᵛ–149ʳ)—created a curriculum of civic duty for Jeanne.

Drawing out a more combative didactic theme, Madeline Caviness's account reveals lessons in the manuscript relating to gender.[17] While the exemplum of St. Louis reinforces themes of duty, education, and charity, other images foreground blatant sexuality and bawdy and lascivious activities to impress on Jeanne the need for chastity and fidelity—values her predecessors so obviously

13 Vincent of Beauvais, *De eruditione filiorum nobilium*, ed. Arpad Steiner (Cambridge, MA: The Mediaeval Academy of America, 1938). There is no complete edition of the *Speculum dominarum*, which also circulated in a French translation as *Miroir des dames*. For extracts see Léopold Delisle, "Durand de Champagne," *Histoire littéraire de la France*, vol. 30 (Paris: Imprimerie nationale, 1888). See too Holladay, "The Education of Jeanne d'Evreux," 601–603.

14 Jeanne owned a copy of the *Miroir aux dames* of Watriquet de Couvin, which was an allegorical tale about the nature of women. She also acquired a French translation of the *De regimine principum* from the library of Clémence of Hungary. For reconstruction of Jeanne's library see Holladay, "Fourteenth-Century French Queens," 82–91.

15 The earliest is the 1303 *Vie et miracles de saint Louis*, by Guillaume de Saint-Pathus. The *Vie*, discussed in chapter 6, is edited in *Vie de saint Louis par Guillaume de Saint-Pathus*, ed. Delaborde. The *Miracles* are edited in *Les Miracles de saint Louis*, ed. Percival Fay (Paris: Honoré Champion, 1931). Another important source was Joinville's life, dating from 1309, for which see *Histoire de saint Louis*, ed. Natalis de Wailly, Société de l'histoire de France 144 (Paris: Renouart, 1868).

16 Holladay, "The Education of Jeanne d'Evreux," 586–99. For interpretation of images in the cycle relating to Louis's charity and their relationship to literary accounts of Louis's *vita*, see Guest, "Discourses on the Poor," 166–79.

17 Caviness, "Patron or Matron?"

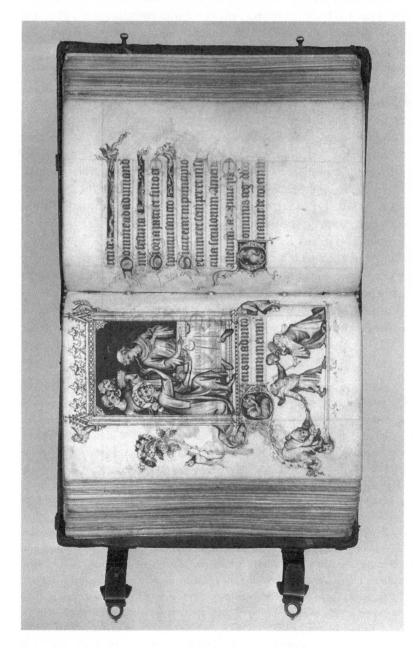

FIGURE 7.2. New York, Metropolitan Museum, Cloisters MS 54.1.2 (the Hours of Jeanne d'Evreux), fols. 123ᵛ–124ᶠ. © The Metropolitan Museum of Art/Art Resource, NY

lacked. In reference to the scene of Betrayal at the opening of Matins for the Hours of the Virgin (see above, figure 7.1), Caviness points to the "concentration of male aggression": a male-only scene (exaggerated by the presence across the opening of the feminized space of the Annunciation), alive with the phallic contours of the bristling collection of spears and crossbows.[18] Meanwhile, the sight of men riding rams and tilting the barrel at center exploits a range of colloquial and anatomical associations to suggest lasciviousness.[19] These are just a few of the ways that the folios host the lessons of gender, their purpose to exploit the habitual nature of prayer to keep ideas of marriage and sex at the front of Jeanne's mind.[20]

It is within this pedagogical framework that we may situate concerns with sound in prayer. It may also be that Pucelle derived inspiration from the same literary corpus from which he determined themes relating to royal duty and female moderation. We have seen already in the previous chapter that Guillaume de Saint-Pathus's *Vie de saint Louis* devoted considerable space to the saint's devotional practices. That alone underscored the importance of prayer as exemplary activity. But Guillaume went further still and, with his royal audience in mind, included details relating to Louis's own ambitions for the devotional life of his offspring—both male and female. Louis, it seems, had precise ideas not just about the importance of prayer in the life of his progeny, but also about priorities of the respective genders. For women, it seems, the voice and its potential for distraction was of paramount importance.

In two places, Guillaume cites Louis directly, claiming the source to be letters the king wrote to his children, Philip (later Philip III, 1245–85) and Isabelle (1241–71). For subsequent generations, these must have been akin to a verbal relic—as authoritative and personal as the actual relics of the saint/ancestor that also circulated. While Philip is instructed to treat his people with care, and to show special generosity towards the religious, the messages for Louis's daughter pertain exclusively to how she should pray. Here, Louis's instructions reveal anxiety about distraction, and insist on careful attention to verbal performance:

Chiere fille, oiez volentiers le service de sainte Eglise; et quant vos serez au service, gardez que vos ne musez ne ne dites paroles vaines. Dites voz oroisons en pes ou de bouche ou de pensee, et especiaument quant li cors Nostre Seigneur Jhesu Christ sera present a la messe. . . . Et oez

18 Ibid., 39–41, at 39.
19 Ibid. 40.
20 Ibid. 43.

volentiers parler de Nostre Seigneur [en sermons et en] parlemenz privez ensement.[21]

Dear daughter, go gladly to hear the service of the Holy Church; and when you are in the service, take care that you do not daydream or utter vain words. Say your prayers in a measured fashion, either by mouth or in thought, and especially when the body of Our Lord Jesus Christ is present at the Mass. . . . And listen gladly to words spoken about Our Lord [in sermons and] spread in private conversations.

The theme of sensual moderation is also common in contemporary conduct literature for women. Durand de Champagne's *Speculum dominarum* of 1305 is especially relevant, as it was written with queenly duty in mind.[22] The treatise is organized in three parts: on the condition of women; on their education; and on their spiritual life. Resonating throughout is the topic of appropriate female virtues and dangerous vices, and especially those connected with the senses. In Part I, §3, devoted to the acquisition of spiritual grace, Durand stresses the importance of modest deportment—particularly in "speech, facial expression and gestures."[23] Among his list of vices leading to spiritual fall from grace are some familiar favorites: loquaciousness and *curiositas*.[24] It is little wonder that Durand, who as confessor was daily involved in instruction of his regal subject, should emphasize devotional reading as having an important role to play in maintaining spiritual grace.[25] However, with echoes of the old Bernadine invective about decorative distraction, he offers a startling warning to forms of reading that can inspire *curiositas*, singling out beautiful books favored by

---

21 Chapter 6; *Vie de saint Louis*, 52. See also *The Teachings of Saint Louis: A Critical Text*, ed. David O'Connell (Chapel Hill: University of North Carolina Press, 1972) and *The Instructions of Saint Louis: A Critical Text*, ed. David O'Connell (Chapel Hill: University of North Carolina Press, 1979).

22 There is no modern edition. Partial transcriptions and translations are given in Delisle, "Durand de Champagne" and Bornstein, *The Lady in the Tower*, 79–82. The original survives in Paris, Bibliothèque nationale de France, f. fr. 610.

23 Quoting from Bornstein, *The Lady in the Tower*, 81.

24 Ibid., 81. Similar emphasis on the importance of modesty in physical comportment occurs in *La clef d'amors*, a free translation of Ovid's *Art of Love* dating from the late thirteenth century. See "La Clef d'amors," ed. Auguste Doutrepont, *Bibliotheca normannica* 5 (Halle: Max Niemeyer, 1890): 1–152. For more on this see Bornstein, *The Lady in the Tower*, 40–41.

25 Delisle, "Durant de Champagne," 313: "For a woman, there is no more honest and salutary occupation for her edification than to read about or listen to precepts and exempla for her consolation and instruction." ("Pour une dame, c'est une honnête et salutaire occupation que de lire ou d'écouter des préceptes et des exemples propre à l'édifier, à la consoler et à l'instruire.")

clerics for particular criticism.[26] This aside sheds some fascinating light on a contemporary perception of Jeanne's Hours, and reinforces the fact that, while the prayer book was a source of spiritual edification, its visual decorations were by Durand's reckoning a perilous distraction—or perhaps a devotional challenge.

These texts may have one final lesson. While we know very little of the manner of Jeanne's schooling, the circumstances of the creation of much Capetian conduct literature offer their own model. Many of their authors shared a profession: as tutors and confessors to royal children, girls among them. That they dedicated their texts to their pupils implies a fixing of lessons that must have been an on-going part of the daily discourse. In the case of confessors, who frequently accompanied their charges in their daily prayers, their texts may be understood as a codification of their lessons. Although we have no record of Jeanne's confessor, like her cousins, aunts, and uncles, it is likely she would have had similar company. These texts, then, offer us the unseen voices that may have accompanied her as she first turned the folios of her new book of hours. As we now turn to its vocal instruction, we shall see how the flow of instructive voices across the preceding decades, right back to Louis himself, would have taken shape on the folios themselves.

LESSON I: RAISING THE VOICE

We begin with a familiar scene of vocal direction: an Annunciation. Figure 7.3, fols. 61^v–62^r, comes from the opening of Terce for the Hours of the Virgin. To the right, at the start of the prayers, we see the expected scene of the Annunciation of the Shepherds from the Infancy cycle; to the left, a scene from the Passion cycle that runs concurrently. We should focus on the Nativity hillside, which at first sight appears to reiterate standard iconography. In the framed image a group of shepherds, surrounded by their flock, gaze up to the angel on the right-hand side, who appears, scroll in hand, to impart the good news. There are several interesting amplifications to this basic picture. First, looking outside the frame, we see a bagpiper, who is more usually associated with the internal, rustic scenery of the hillside, now transposed to the initial D of the versicle "Deus in adiutorium." He hunches over, his back to the scriptural scene, and engages in a duet with a trumpeter who grows out of the base frame and the bell of whose instrument is delicately connected to the letter, so that the round curves of the "D" look like a kind of bubble of sound

26 Part I; §3, warning against those who have books which are beautiful and distracting rather than truthful and useful ("plus quaerunt habere libros pulchros et curiosos quam veraces et utiles minus pulchros"), as transcribed in Delisle, "Durand de Champagne," 314.

FIGURE 7.3. New York, Metropolitan Museum, Cloisters MS 54.1.2 (the Hours of Jeanne d'Evreux), fols. 61ᵛ–62ʳ. © The Metropolitan Museum of Art/Art Resource, NY

emanating from his trumpet. The transference of figures from the central, biblical scene to the margins, a space Caviness has argued is closer to the "real time" of Jeanne's reading, is suggested first by the miniature pastoral scene at the bottom left of the *bas-de-page*, where a pair of sheep doze under a tree; and at the right, where two rustic figures carrying herding cudgels look up, witness to the miracle. The dog that accompanies them acts as a further link between the two worlds—echoing the dog at the bottom right of the framed image. Finally, angels hanging from the frame at the top left and right, hurling scrolls, appear to have flown directly out of the scene, the heavenly host breaking into the real world beyond the historical, biblical representation.

The fluidity of the boundaries between real and biblical time is further articulated by two figures at either side of the frame, looking into the Annunciation, rapt in concentration. Their gaze compels the reader to follow, letting the imagination penetrate the frame, projecting themselves into the scene. But they are being asked to do more than simply contemplate biblical truth. The intense gaze is also standard in the lexicon of sound signs as a signal of attentive listening. Via a medley of symbols, these figures invite the reader to *hear* the scene. The clearest invocation is suggested by the man at the middle of the *bas-de-page*, whose body is poised in the classic gesture of listening: he looks up at the scene, cupping his ear with his hand the better to hear, and also the better to focus his ear away from the noisy duet to the left.

Pucelle's realization of conventions thus stages in the margins of the Annunciation an urgent call to listening. But there is something more. As is usual, the angel holds a scroll, one that would normally contain the words of the exclamation "Gloria in excelsis deo." While the scroll is turned upwards, implying jubilation, some curious features seem to focus attention on sound and performance. In the earlier Annunciation of the Virgin at the opening of Matins (see above, figure 7.1, fols. 15^v–16^r)—indeed, on other occasions in the manuscript where there are writing surfaces depicted within images—the artist supplied words, or marks to symbolize them. Thus, in the workings of this manuscript, the empty scroll seems self-conscious. Following our earlier discussion of scrolls, the absence of words here makes the instruction to attend to the missing sound even more intense. Simply put, it calls on the reader to raise her voice, to supply what is not there, what the folio so actively encourages her to hear. If the intensity of the other sound signs on the folio is not enough to urge the supplicant to insert her voice into the scene, there is another important cue. Scrolls also feature in the space of real time, courtesy of the two daredevil angels at the top left and right. We have seen scroll exchanges between angels and mortals in other manuscripts, but in reverse configuration, with angels stretching earthwards to pluck the praying voices upward. This was the case in Cambridge, Trinity B 11. 22 (see above, figure 6.9). Here, the reversal is something like a reproach. Tracing the configuration of signs, their empty scrolls, aimed at the two dreamy listener/observers, sail down like a couple of pregnant pauses: spaces inviting—indeed, demanding—vocal completion.

Why such urgency? The imperative tone may be in proportion to some threats to prayer. Down in the *bas-de-page*, the roaming shepherds seem have wandered over from a scene a couple of Hours earlier. At the bottom of the opening of Lauds (see figure 7.4, fols. 34ᵛ–35ʳ), we see another rustic scene, where men stomp to the music of the bagpiper (here down from his capital, furnishing live music). Just overhead is the scene of the Visitation, a celebration of fertility that would have been especially pertinent to Jeanne. What of the barn-dance beneath, though? According to Caviness's reading, the constant sighting of bagpipes has particularly phallic association.[27] In this scene, it may be emblem of a kind of "base appetite," while the act of dance summons connotations of lascivious pleasure.[28] They are in other words a warning against carnality: when read against the didactic literature for queens, they perform a morality tale to reinforce the upholding of ideals of virtue and modesty. The figures at the bottom of Terce carry with them lingering association with the scene of Lauds, and may thus explain the ferocity of the call to envoice the sacred word: at stake here is nothing less than Jeanne's womanly virtue.

While the scene of Terce illustrates how Pucelle manipulates conventions for representing sound, it also reveals something about why Jeanne's correct elocution might be bound into other moral themes of the book. Nor is this an isolated or incidental lesson, but one carefully wrought throughout the manuscript. In another key moment in the manuscript, Pucelle set out something like a syllabus for sound in prayer. And where better to establish such a curriculum than at the threshold of prayers for an ancestor renowned for his devotional prowess?

LESSON 2: LOUIS EDUCATES JEANNE

There is no better way to offer instruction on prayer than to depict the act itself. The opening of the Hours of St. Louis, shown in figure 7.5 (fols. 102ᵛ–103ʳ), does just that: not once but twice. To the left, we see the crowned figure of a woman at her prie-dieu. This is the young queen Jeanne in the second of two scenes to depict her (the other occurs at Matins for the Hours of the Virgin). She is at prayer, before a book, and looks out to a small chapel tomb, on top of which St. Louis himself appears. Views about the site the image refers to differ: some interpret this as Louis's own tomb in Saint-Denis, others as a chapel at the abbey, built in 1299, soon after his canonization,

27 Caviness, "Patron or Matron?," 49.

28 Jonathan Alexander, "Dancing in the Streets," *Journal of the Walters Art Gallery* 54 (1996): 147–62.

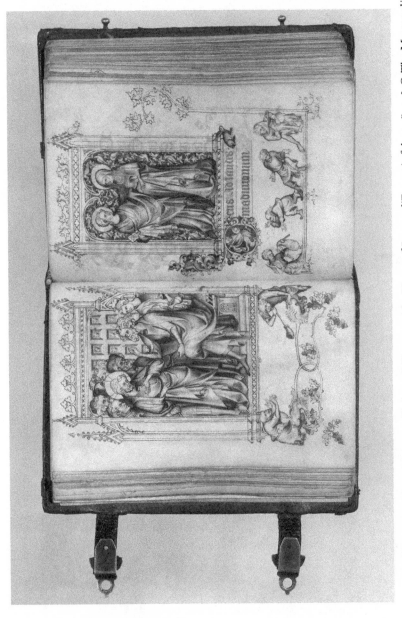

FIGURE 7.4. New York, Metropolitan Museum, Cloisters MS 54.1.2 (the Hours of Jeanne d'Evreux), fols. 34^v–35^r. © The Metropolitan Museum of Art/Art Resource, NY

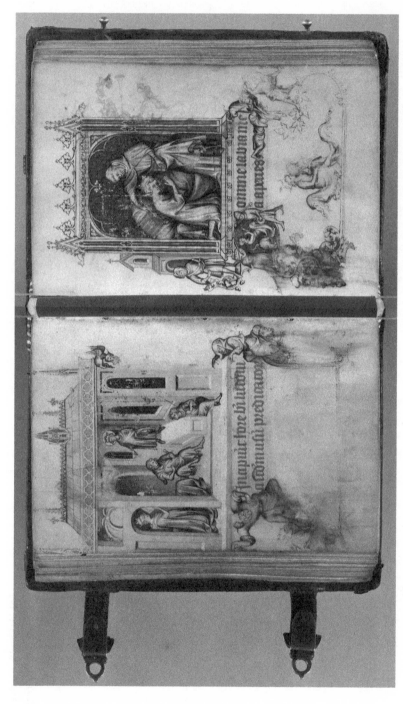

FIGURE 7.5 New York, Metropolitan Museum, Cloisters MS 54.1.2 (the Hours of Jeanne d'Evreux), fols. 102ᵛ–103ʳ. © The Metropolitan Museum of Art/Art Resource, NY

in which a small statue was placed.[29] Either way, the scene refers Jeanne to known locales associated with devotion to her ancestor, and also transforms him into a visual topic of meditation. Across the opening, ahead of the opening versicle for Matins, a second scene of prayer is under way, rather more ferocious than Jeanne's quiet contemplation. This time it is Louis himself, likewise kneeling on a prie-dieu located in a more private space: the cushion and fabric slabs situate him in his chamber—a common scene of prayer. He is being lashed, rather daintily, by a tonsured monk. Holladay identifies the scene as that described in Guillaume de Saint-Pathus's *Vie*, detailing how once a week and three times during Lent, as part of his routine of prayer and devotion, he retired alone to his chamber with one Brother Geoffrey, where he confessed his sins and received discipline with three knotted cords.[30]

While much of the focus has been on how the ensuing images instruct Jeanne in matters of charity and royal duty through Louis's visible example, another aspect of the Matins opening bears further scrutiny. The instruction here is not simply that Jeanne attend to the lessons of the *vita*. It is more literal. Mimicking Louis's kneeling stance, with the echo even of the bed of his chamber in which he said his prayers, Jeanne is here to attend to the importance of prayer itself. Visible in both scenes is a small prayer book. These books within the book affirm the Hours themselves as key aids in the act of prayer.

As we attend to the other details of this opening, a clear lesson unfolds to explain why discipline—and especially the discipline of sound—may be a crucial component of prayer. While the framed illuminations establish the central lesson, the margins and line-endings contribute additional subversive voices. Jeanne mimics Louis's stance across the opening, but she is also echoed in the facing *bas-de-page*. Tracing the line diagonally down the opening from the praying Jeanne—indeed within a sight line reinforced by figures in right of the chapel, right of the red rubric, and at left of decorated capitals—the eye arrives at another crowned figure. Riding on the back of a bearded monster, she sits entranced, bowing a vielle. While the praying Jeanne is fixing her eyes on her prayer book, and at the scene of Louis just beyond, the sight lines defined here may draw her eyes to an alternative route, or represent the possibility of another enraptured experience of prayer. Indeed, the "other" Jeanne has eyes likewise fixed in attentive listening, and gazes up, musicking all the while, to the kerfuffle of figures coming out of the line-ending of the versicle for Matins. These figures, the very definition of "imagines verborum," are the embodiment of

29 See Holladay, "The Education of Jeanne d'Evreux," 597, drawing on Elizabeth A. R. Brown, "The Chapels and Cult of Saint Louis at Saint-Denis," *Mediaevalia* 10 (1988): 279–331, and esp. 292–95 for discussion of the tomb monument.

30 Holladay, "The Education of Jeanne d'Evreux," 598. The passage occurs in chapter 14 of the *Vie*. See *Vie de saint Louis*, 122–23.

verbal distraction, and in turn interpret the versicle as a suspenseful hiatus: the line of prayer reads "O Lord, open up my lips" ("Domine labia mea aperies"). It will take the folio turn to supply the resolution "and my mouth will bring forth thy praise" ("et os meum annuntiabit laudem tuam"). Poised on that turn, the line-ending is the very depiction of an open mouth, a visualized gawp no less.

The open mouth, the no-man's-land of prayer, is simultaneously a site of *curiositas*. The musical Jeanne just below is not merely riveted by the sight of the line-ending. She has turned her back on the other, more devout visual opportunities of the folio: the images of St. Louis and the letters of the prayer. And she rides on the back of a monster who is likewise caught up in distraction, his eyes turned to the swollen foliage hanging from the letter "D" of "Domine." In the language of the margins, distraction is thus tied explicitly to musical sound. The marginal Jeanne bows a vielle as if she is making music to the line-ending. Allowing the signs and interaction of senses to play out, the scene seems to caution against sensual pleasures of sound as a source of distraction in prayer, the sort that can lead that open mouth to all kinds of verbal confusion and vocal pleasure. Music here is also a powerful metaphor, serving as a short-hand for distractions of sight as well.

That the marginal exchanges are more than incidental and all part of the "lesson" is suggested by a final echo between center and periphery. Discipline is also afoot in the margins. While Louis receives his lashes from Brother Geoffrey, a burly figure in the right margin swings a cudgel at the offending line-ending, as if to beat it back into the pure letter. It is counterpointed by a soldier figure who takes aim at a distraction in the letter "D"—another figure riding the back of a hybrid. These attempts to tame the voice to rightful utterance only add to the distraction.

The lesson of Matins is sustained through the ensuing Hours by a process of reinforcement. While the single-folio illuminations of the remaining Hours expound the themes of charity and alms-giving, the margins, line-endings, and capitals of their recto counterparts continue the theme of music-making as distraction, and the orality of the text. With the exception of Lauds, sound and text production (and consumption) feature prominently. Prime, Terce, and Sext each fill their capital "D"s of the versicle "Deus in adiutorium" with music and open-mouthed reading; Nones has a figure chomping into the versicle's foliage; Vespers features a huge twirling open-mouthed figure grooving to harping margins and strumming line-endings; and Compline once again squashes music into the versicle, while a fluting hybrid fills the margins (see figure 7.6, fol. 174^r).

There is a final aspect of these figures to note. Here, as elsewhere, Pucelle creates some of the most imaginative and original music-making monsters of the repertory of prayer books. Sometimes, instruments are evoked for their sexual connotations, as with the bagpipes. But another feature is sound's

FIGURE 7.6. New York, Metropolitan Museum, Cloisters MS 54.1.2 (the Hours of Jeanne d'Evreux), fol. 174ʳ. © The Metropolitan Museum of Art/Art Resource, NY

embodied nature. As Bruce Holsinger has observed, the constant likening of bodies to instruments in the Middle Ages—the body likened to the strummed harp, or the beaten drum—serves many metaphors for musical experience, as well as its ability to inspire pleasure and pain, and its pedagogical power.[31] In the medium of images, and especially in the freedom of marginalia, Pucelle transformed the correlation between musical experience and bodily sensation into a recurring visual theme. It is striking how many marginal musicians hug

31 Holsinger, *Music, Body, and Desire*.

strings close to their bodies, almost as if they are strumming themselves; and there are many cases where it is hard to know where the body ends and instrument begins, as pipes shoot out of torsos. The harper in the final "D" of Compline (see above, figure 7.6) is perhaps the best illustration of this graphic and metaphorical entanglement of body and music: he is cross-legged, but plays his harp with an almost yogic contortion, with his strumming right arm tucked under and around his right knee. The image stresses the sheer sensuality of sound, as if to remind the supplicant of the greatest potential of all regarding sound in prayer: the pleasure of one's own body as instrument of the word. Here, in the prayer-act, they are not simply metaphor. As "afterglow" of musical experience, and simultaneously also as visual pleasure, perhaps also distraction, the images are imbued with their own unique kind of musicality—heard and felt internally, in the body of the supplicant.

Polyphonic Prayer: Hours of the Passion in Walters 102

Our second round of prayer comes from the Walters Art Museum in Baltimore, W 102, an English book of hours dating from the early fourteenth century— see figure 7.7, showing the manuscript open to fols. 28ᵛ–29ʳ [website figure 7.1]. It contains unusual sets of prayers and Hours. Despite the reshuffling of its contents when it was rebound in the nineteenth century, it is possible to determine that the original order was as follows: Hours of the Virgin; Abbreviated Hours; Hours of the Holy Spirit; Seven Penitential Psalms, Litany, and Collects; Fifteen Gradual or Penitential Psalms; Office of the Dead; Hours of the Passion; and assorted prayers, readings, and canonical hours in honor of St. Catherine.[32]

By contrast to the Hours of Jeanne d'Evreux, there is little evidence about provenance and ownership, or about how the book was used. Based on the presence of a prayer to St. Julian in the final section of the manuscript, and on the identification of Augustinian Use in the Abbreviated Hours, Dorothy Miner proposed an Augustinian provenance, suggesting the foundation of St. Julian near Saint Albans Abbey as a possible candidate. Florence McCulloch, however, reasoned that given the larger amount of devotional material for St. Catherine, another plausible provenance might be an institution dedicated

---

32 Listed in full with folio numbers in McCulloch, "The Funeral of Renart the Fox," 13; her article includes the most detailed codicological description to date. See, too, *Illuminated Books of the Middle Ages and Renaissance, Walters Art Gallery Exhibition Catalogue*, ed. Dorothy Miner (Baltimore: Johns Hopkins University Press, 1949), 56.

FIGURE 7.7. Baltimore, Walters Art Museum, W 102, fols. 28ᵛ–29ʳ. © The Walters Art Museum

to her, rather than to St. Julian, and suggested the Hospital of St. Catherine in London.[33]

The book itself offers some clues. It measures 267 × 184 mm, larger than many others we have explored, but still of a scale (and a weight) suitable for personal use. The prayers are extensively rubricated in Old French, and appear sometimes to situate use in a religious, institutional context. This is especially true of the Office of the Dead, which concludes with lengthy rubrics explaining how to integrate and regulate recitation of the Offices within the framework of the liturgical year. That strongly suggests monastic or convent use, and someone who followed the corporate round of liturgical services, who indeed may have brought this book into public liturgical observance in the Office of the Dead, but for whom the other contents were for personal use. About who that person might have been W 102 is tantalizingly contradictory. Like other prayer books, it contains many images of readers, but their gender varies. In the Office of the Dead, for example, the classic image of the Requiem shows tonsured monks reading from books at the side of a coffin, as at fol. 55^r, shown in figure 7.8 [website figure 7.2]. Yet the Hours of the Virgin strongly suggest female use. The openings of each Hour do not follow the Infancy cycle, but rather fill each of the "D"s with the figure of a kneeling woman, as in fol. 88^v, from the opening of Prime, figure 7.9 [website figure 7.3]. Finally, there is also the matter of the extensive use of Old French rubrics and commentary. Old French might normally point to a strong literacy in that language, and perhaps only phonetic literacy in Latin. However, the bilingualism here may rather point to a user not only comfortable and literate in both languages, but also able to capitalize on the different registers of the two languages for productive spiritual ends. As we move more deeply to engage its prayers, images, and instructions, it will be clear that its makers designed a demanding devotional program. Someone versed in monastic modes of exegesis and also familiar with vernacular culture would have been ideally equipped to realize its potential.

I have left the book's most unusual feature until last. From the painted capitals and fuller folio illuminations to the delicate pen-work flourishes that fill the margins, the artistic conception of the book is of the highest quality and rarely conventional (as evident in figure 7.7). Although we know nothing of its artist (or artists), the sheer originality of its decorative style is striking. As with Pucelle's Hours, there is a powerful sense throughout of the artist's agency, and of his images as a creative directive to the reader. Perhaps his most original—even anomalous—conception is a visual intrusion into prayer unprecedented in its scope and material proportions. It is also one of the most musical.

33 McCulloch, "The Funeral of Renart," 25–26.

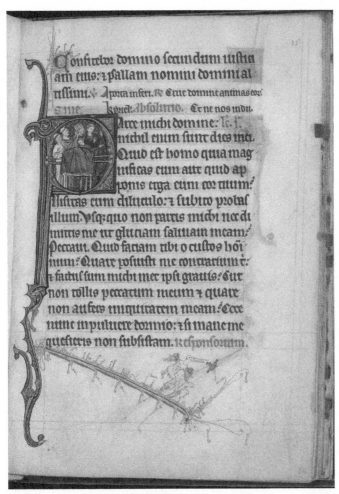

FIGURE 7.8. Baltimore, Walters Art Museum, W 102, fol. 55ʳ. © The Walters Art Museum

The moment falls deep in the manuscript: beginning on fol. 73ʳ, the close of Office of the Dead, just prior to, and extending into, the Hours of the Passion— the complete sequence is given in figures 7.10–7.18 [website figures 7.4–7.12]. The reader is confronted with a startling image: a white ram, walking jauntily along on its hind legs and, hooves notwithstanding, swinging two hand bells (figure 7.10, website figure 7.4). Turning over, we see that the ram is a straggler in a procession, and follows an elephant, trunk aloft, trumpeting into the text, who in turn shadows a horned bull playing a horn (figure 7.11; website figure 7.5). On the next opening a bright blue horse playing the drum and tabor struts behind an ass, juggling bell and recorder between hooves (figure 7.12; website figure 7.6). Turning over again, a grinning dog wraps his fangs around

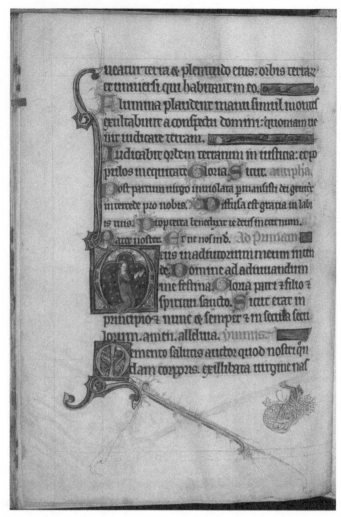

FIGURE 7.9. Baltimore, Walters Art Museum, W 102, fol. 88ᵛ. © The Walters Art Museum

bagpipes, while on the facing folio a family of apes looks in horror at the grotesque face gawping at them from the margins (figure 7.13; website figure 7.7). This innovative use of parchment reaches its apotheosis as we turn over one last time: stretched across the opening, a large antlered stag shares the burden of a funeral bier with a cat (figure 7.14; website figure 7.8). (We shall return to the identity of the wooly-faced corpse poking out from under the bier in a moment.) On the verso, a cockerel swinging a censer with his beak follows a wolf, done up like a bishop, leaning on a crozier (figure 7.15; website figure 7.9); and next a cat, beating a drum, marches behind a venerable-looking goat, carrying a cross (figure 7.16; website figure 7.10). Padding across the penultimate

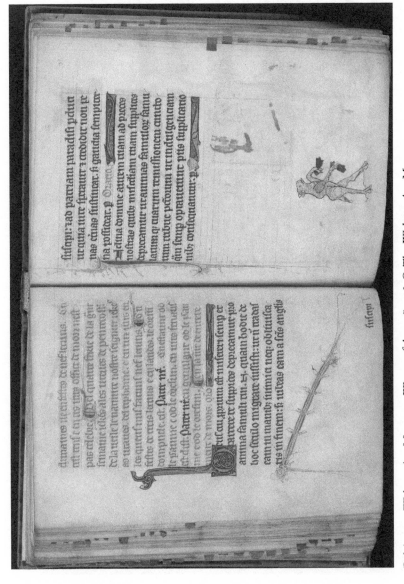

FIGURE 7.10. Baltimore, Walters Art Museum, W 102, fols. 72ᵛ–73ʳ. © The Walters Art Museum

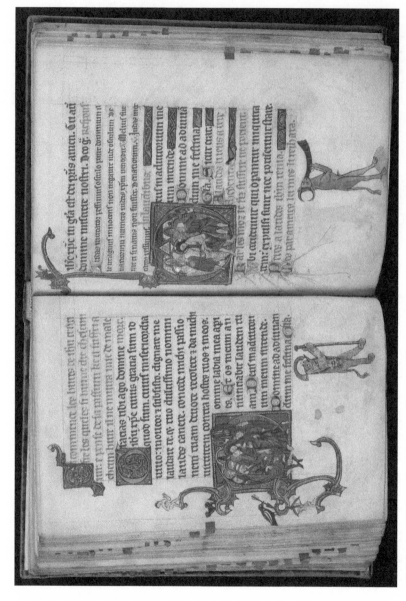

FIGURE 7.11. Baltimore, Walters Art Museum, W 102, fols. 73ᵛ–74ᶠ. © The Walters Art Museum

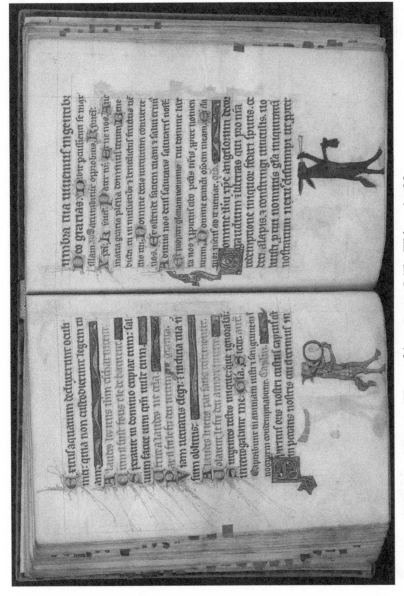

FIGURE 7.12. Baltimore, Walters Art Museum, W 102, fols. 74ᵛ–75ʳ. © The Walters Art Museum

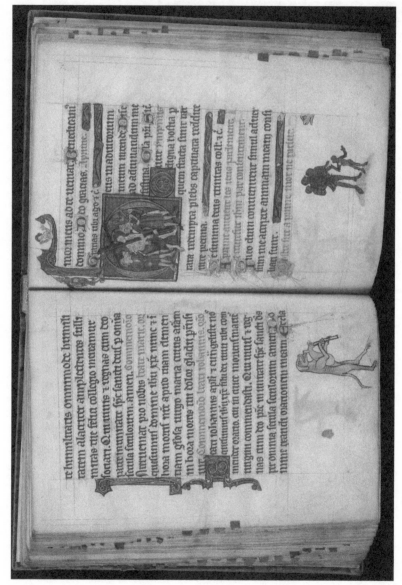

FIGURE 7.13. Baltimore, Walters Art Museum, W 102, fols. 75ᵛ–76ᶠ. © The Walters Art Museum

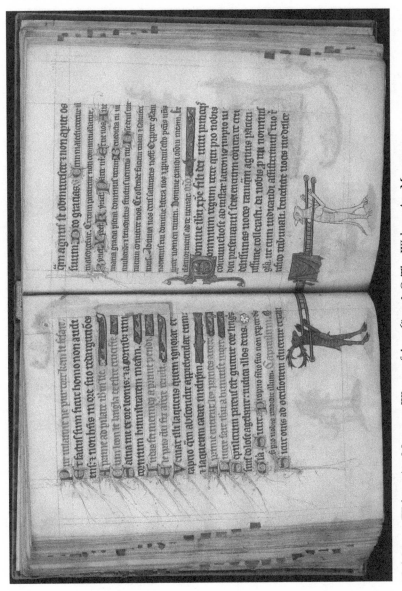

FIGURE 7.14. Baltimore, Walters Art Museum, W 102, fols. 76ᵛ–77ᶠ. © The Walters Art Museum

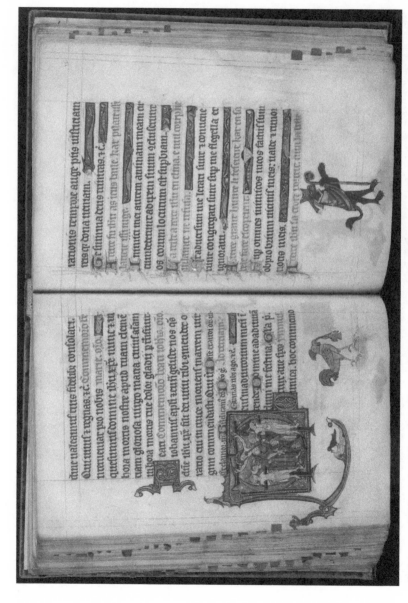

FIGURE 7.15. Baltimore, Walters Art Museum, W 102, fols. 77ᵛ–78ʳ. © The Walters Art Museum

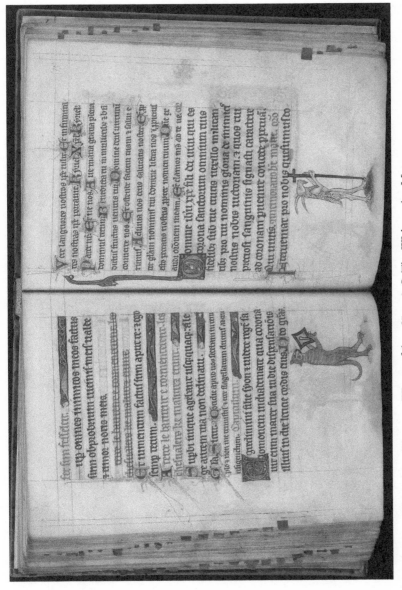

FIGURE 7.16. Baltimore, Walters Art Museum, W 102, fols. 78ᵛ–79ʳ. © The Walters Art Museum

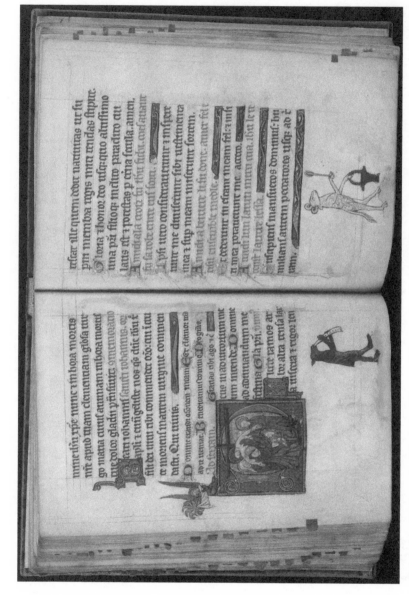

FIGURE 7.17. Baltimore, Walters Art Museum, W 102, fols. 79ᵛ–80ʳ. © The Walters Art Museum

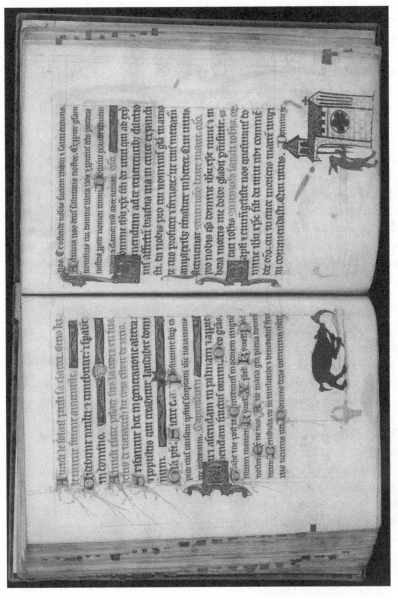

FIGURE 7.18. Baltimore, Walters Art Museum, W 102, fols. 80ᵛ–81ʳ. © The Walters Art Museum

opening, a bear blows on a shawm, following the lead of a splendid curly-horned ram, who *asperges* the route with holy water (figure 7.17; website figure 7.11). The procession reaches its end as the only animal to make use of its four paws to walk, the wild boar, carries a tool, perhaps to dig a grave, and leads us up to a church door, where a giant rabbit sounds the bells (figure 7.18; website figure 7.12).

In whose honor is this lavish, deathly procession to the grave? Florence McCulloch connected the sequence to a scene from the popular thirteenth-century Old French *Roman de Renart*. Constantly read, and often rewritten, with anonymous writers adding additional episodes or branches to the core story of the evil fox, the scene shown here, branch XVII, was among the best known of the tales: the story of his fake death. Renart swoons after losing a game of chess and the other animals, taking him for dead, waste no time in preparing his funeral. This includes a full-blown twittered, hooted, and squeaked Vespers service; a wake; a Requiem Mass, with obscene sermons; and, as our scene depicts, a procession to the burial ground. As Renart is placed in the ground and doused with holy water, he comes to and, rejuvenated, leaps out to seize the rooster Chantecler by the throat before fleeing the scene. Here is the earliest version of the passage from Branch XVII on which the scene is based, with King Noble, the lion, assembling the animal kingdom to designate their roles in the procession:

"Chanteclers, prenez l'encensier
Dont vous le cors escenseroiz.
Brichemer et vous porteroiz
La biere au baron de franc lin,
Et vous le mouton dant Delin.
Ysengrin se deportera
En la croiz que il portera.
Chascun fera de son labour:
La chievre prandra un tabour
De quoi ele ira tabourant,
Et le roncin sire Ferrant
Harpera, tiex est mon plesir,
Un sien galois, tout a loisir,
Ne viel pas que se voist tardant.
Les cierges porteront ardant
Couart li lievres et Tibert
Li chaz et l'escoufle Hubert.
Quant le cors enterer iront,
Les souriz les sains sonneront,
Ainssi con mon conseil le loe,
Et li singes fera la moe.

Bernart metra le cors en terre:
Meilleur de li n'i convient querre."
Ainssi con li rois le conmande
Le font, nus respot n'i demande.
Le cors aporterent a grant feste,
Qui descouverte avoit la teste.
Brun l'ours, qui la poe avoit grosse,
Ot appareilliee la fosse,
Qui moult bien i ot entendu.[34]

"Chantecler, take the censer to honor his corpse. Brichemer and you, Sire Belin the sheep, carry the coffin of this baron of noble lineage. Ysengrin will occupy himself carrying the cross. Everyone has his job: the goat will carry and play the tabor; Ferrant the cart horse will interpret on the harp, such is my pleasure, one of those Galois melodies, for the delight of all, but I want him to begin immediately. Couart the hare and Tibert the cat and Hubert the kite will carry lighted candles. When the cortège departs, the mice will ring the bells as is pleasing to me. The monkey will make faces. It's Bernard who will put the body in the ground: futile to look for anyone better than him." Without delay, they carried out the king's orders. With great pomp, they carried the body, whose face they left uncovered. Brun the bear had carefully prepared the ditch beforehand, with his powerful paws.

While the procession is a witness to the popularity of the Renart fable and its transmission to painted media, its function at the local level of the manuscript remains unclear. McCulloch reads it as juxtaposition of the sacred and profane, arguing that, along with the numerous marginal drawings and line-endings, the sequence "must not only have delighted the eye, but also tempted . . . the mind to flee pious thoughts and pursue more lively matters."[35] Elsewhere she suggests the animals' presence "appealed to the eternal comic sense of the reader and spectator."[36] It seems plausible to understand the scene as entertaining distraction. However, as we consider precisely how this

---

34 The Renart manuscript tradition is complex, reflecting the story's transformation across generations of readers and writers. I quote from *Le Roman de Renart*, ed. Armand Strubel with the collaboration of Robert Bellon, Dominique Boutet, and Sylvie Lefèvre (Paris: Gallimard, 1998), which includes a French translation. See Strubel's introductory essay for a useful account of the manuscript tradition, and the manuscripts and editions on which his present edition is based: lxxiii–lxxx. Quoting here from Branch XVIII, vv. 1027–49, p. 716. Translations here are my own.

35 McCulloch, "Funeral of Renart," 26.

36 Ibid., 12.

interruption of "pious thoughts" occurs, and what such distraction signified in relation to the meaning of the prayers, humor gives way to something more serious. In what follows, we shall look more closely at the interaction of the prayers and the procession, and in particular consider the effect of music on the experience: the trail of animals suggests both noisy, processional sound and movement through time and space. In this regard, the rarity in this period of the Hours of the Passion may suggest that these folios were deemed worthy of special treatment by the makers of the book. We should also explore the contents of the prayers themselves, to see what in narrative and scriptural terms the eye tempts the mind away from.

The choice of animals, and Renart in particular, as marginal counterpoint to the main texts would have implied moral coding to certain medieval readers. Coming from a long tradition of beast fables, the *Roman de Renart* was one among a series of Old French *romans* to feature animals as central characters, their purpose often to offer a biting, if humorous, critique of human social and political order by transposing it into the animal kingdom.[37] That Renart functioned as moral exemplum is further supported by evidence of the fox outside the literary text, in England as well as France. Work by Kenneth Varty and Clive Rouse shows that Renart had an extensive visual life, particularly in wall paintings, both in churches and secular settings, including this very scene in stained glass at York Minster, and in painted panels in Gloucester Cathedral with traces of musical notation; and there are many other marginal representations of Renart's *cortège* in another contemporary devotional manuscripts.[38] If readers knew the story from walls, carvings, and manuscripts, they may also have known it from urban theater. As Nancy Freeman Regalado has shown, scenes from the *roman* were performed as tableaux during massive urban

---

37 On the older tradition see Jan Ziolkowski, *Talking Animals: Medieval Latin Beast Poetry, 750–1150* (Philadelphia: University of Pennsylvania Press, 1993). The fox story continued to be retold. See, for example, *Renart le nouvel*, attributed to Jacquemart Gielée (ca. 1288) and *Renart le contrefait* (dating between 1319 and 1342).

38 See Kenneth Varty, "The Death and Resurrection of Reynard in Mediaeval Literature and Art," *Nottingham Mediaeval Studies* 10 (1966): 70–93, and "The Pursuit of Reynard in Mediaeval English Literature and Art," *Nottingham Mediaeval Studies* 8 (1964): 62–81; Kenneth Varty and Clive Rouse, "Medieval Paintings of Reynard the Fox in Gloucester Cathedral and Some Other Related Examples," *Archaeological Journal* 133 (1976): 104–17. On iconography of the fox's death and resurrection, see Kenneth Varty, *Reynard, Renart, Reinaert and Other Foxes in Medieval England: The Iconographic Evidence. A Study of the Illustrating of Fox Lore and Reynard the Fox Stories in England during the Middle Ages* (Amsterdam: Amsterdam University Press, 1999), 131–62. Varty includes a brief description of W 102 at 139–48.

festivities in Paris, in Pentecost 1313, when Edward II visited the city.[39] Particularly relevant here is the way in which performance (in paint and on stage) served a didactic function: the trickster fox, and the corrupt animal kingdom in which he operated, served time and again as a brilliant, memorable challenge to religious and civic orders in the venues. Thus, in accounting for the foxy tales amid the religious tableaux in Paris, Regalado traces Renart back to a Latin tradition of beast fables, cultivated in monastic and court circles: there, she argues, their exemplary function was overt, the stories intended to have a moral function. By the fourteenth century, as well as evoking Renart simply for "fun," she suggests the fox was also invested with "pointed moral and political commentary."[40] It may have been the potency of Renart as an exemplum that motivated its inclusion in the margins of W 102. A glimpse of his bushy tail may have cued monastic readers to a certain mode of reading, one in which they understood that Renart was present to challenge, but ultimately teach them something.

What lessons do the animals bear? While in popular culture Renart had a pointed political meaning—as a challenge to secular authority—it is striking how many instances of his representation outside literature occur in liturgical or devotional contexts: carved into misericords, painted on church pillars, in the compound of the cathedral. But in W 102, while clearly situated in a monastic and prayerful setting, it would be hard to suggest that the fox challenges any particular secular or religious institutional authority. Rather, the layout and form of the book itself press Renart to signify against a much more startling "baron": namely, Christ himself, whose Passion is told in the prayers in the space directly above Renart's funeral.

A closer look reveals a choreography of images against text contrived to create an intricate tapestry of liturgical, scriptural, and romance narrative. The most accessible meaning is through the alignment of Renart's death with that of the crucified Christ. Each of the eight Hours of the Passion begins with an illuminated capital, which, read as a sequence, illustrates the main chronology of the Passion. Matins begins with the Betrayal of Christ, then follow the Flagellation (Lauds), Carrying of the Cross (Prime), Crucifixion (Terce), Descent from the Cross (Sext), Entombment (None), Resurrection (Vespers), and the Tree of Jesse (Compline). As the animals take Renart to his grave, they counterpoint the events leading to Christ's death and entombment. In animal time, however, the cycle ends on fol. 81: just prior to the commencement of None, commemorating the entombment, and ends at the point in the narrative where

39 Nancy Freeman Regalado, "Staging the 'Roman de Renart': Medieval Theater and the Diffusion of Political Concerns into Popular Culture," *Mediaevalia* 18 (1995): 111–42.

40 Ibid., 128.

Renart is lowered into the ground. The alignment with Christ's life continues, by implication, in the empty *bas-de-page* that follows. As Vespers remembers Christ's resurrection, the reader might be prompted to think of another miraculous resurrection, as Renart awakens, and leaps out of the grave.

The first obvious effect of the animal procession seems to be simple parody. However, this is only the beginning. To understand better the sonorous implications of the animals, we must now look to the texts of the prayers themselves. The Hours of the Passion are unlike any other in the contemporary prayer book corpus, and offer an unusual transparency with regard to the kind of devotional experience their maker intended them to effect. While a great deal of work remains to be done on these prayers, we shall here touch on the main feature of devotional organization, and illuminate an essential compatibility with the animal narrative threaded through.

The Hours open with a French rubric which indicates their devotional purpose: "Here begin the hours of Jesus crucified, which if one says them each day and thinks of the passion that he suffered at each hour he will not die a bad death" ("Ci commence les hures de Jesus crucifié les queles si hume die chescun iur e pense de la passiun ke il suffri a cheun heur il ne murra mie de male mor").[41] The intention to create a mode by which one can "pense de la passiun" is realized in what follows: a meditative reconstruction of the Passion. Time—and an intricate web of competing temporalities—is at the heart of the program, as organizing principle and affective engine. The Hours of course mark the passage of a single day in the life of the supplicant, from nighttime Matins to evening Compline. Each of the eight hours is organized around an event from Holy Week, as noted above. There is also some alignment of the present-liturgical and historical-biblical, as the creator seems to coordinate the precise time of day at which certain events of the Passion occurred with the clock of the daily Office. Thus, the nighttime betrayal of Jesus falls at Matins, in the hours of darkness.

If the illuminations thus prompt the supplicant to contemplation of historical-biblical time, the prayers themselves present another unprecedented temporal meditation. Each Hour follows an identical ground plan, and thus departs from most other Hours, which adopt the order of regular, communal liturgical offices. In the Hours of the Passion, however, the format of each Hour falls into three main sections. The opening versicle "Deus in adiutorium" is followed by a section of a well-known hymn. The second section, the core of each Hour, comprises alternation of short biblical passages in Latin, often Psalms, with Old French rhyming couplets. The final section comprises an antiphon, *capitulum*, and prayers to the Virgin and St. John. Much of the material is drawn from liturgies associated with the Passion, or is of a somber, penitential nature.

41 McCulloch, "The Funeral of 'Renart'," 23.

Striking also is the abundance of material with musical association. The citation of hymns in particular at the start of each Hour establishes a lyrical tone. Nowhere is this more fervent than in the second main section of each Hour.

These portions create a highly emotional—and lyrical—expression of the overarching program of the Passion. Old French rhyming couplets elaborate narrative and temporal cues to dramatize events of the Passion, offering miniature meditations for the reader. Thinking back to the rubrical instructions of the opening, they provide the reader with the essential materials through which to think of Christ's passion, and more importantly to think themselves into the scene. A brief sample of three couplets from Lauds will illustrate:

> Peres a laudes Iesum denia,
> Mes par ameres lermes li rechata.

> At Lauds Peter denied Jesus,
> But by bitter tears he redeemed it to him.

> A laudes les ieus Iesum escharnirent,
> Cum il fust fous e le debatirent.

> At Lauds the Jews mocked Jesus,
> As if he were mad, and they struck him.

> Verité a laudes ne cela
> Par li fu le fiz deu verement granta.

> At Lauds he did not hide the truth,
> For he was God's son, he truthfully admitted.[42]

Time, again, is the prompt. The couplets each share opening formulae that ground the historical event of the Passion in a time of day shared by the present-liturgical of the prayer's performance. For Lauds, each meditation begins "A laudes," at Prime it is 'A Prime" and so on. Thus far, the reader uses her real-time of prayer as an affective portal to imagine the exact moment—in the historical past—at which Christ's suffering unfolded.

The Latin verses interwoven through the Old French couplets provide a final temporal provocation, one reliant in part on the innately lyrical register of its texts. The alternation of languages is signaled by different ink colors, red (Old French) alternating with black (Latin). The effect is also to highlight another kind of alternation: of time itself. As mentioned previously, the overwhelming source for the Latin interpolations is the Psalms. So while the Old French couplets reflect New Testament time, the Latin speaks from the Old Testament. That juxtaposition, in a context already hypersensitive to time, invites typological investigation—a common form of allegorical investigation

---

42 Transcribed in McCulloch, "The Funeral of 'Renart'," 27.

of Old and New Testament relationships in the medieval tradition of biblical exegesis.[43] Closer reading reveals a brilliantly wrought program, such that every event described in the time of Passion is reiterated—and uttered—from the Old Testament perspective of the Psalmist. Let us now reconnect the couplets with their Psalms:

The first Old French couplet, recalling Peter's denial of Christ, is followed by an extract from Psalm 118:136:

Peres a laudes Iesum denia,
Mes par ameres lermes li rechata.

At Lauds Peter denied Jesus.
But by bitter tears he redeemed it to him.

Exitus aquarum deduxerunt oculi mei, quia non custodierunt legem tuam.

My eyes have sent forth springs of water, because they have not kept thy law.

Here, the Old French cue transforms the Psalm into the voice of Peter, and third-person Old French is reconfigured in the first-person position of the Psalm.

In the next scene, the scourging of Christ is recalled and amplified retroactively with reference to Psalm 21:9:

A laudes les ieus Iesum escharnirent,
Cum il fust fous e le debatirent.

At Lauds the Jews mocked Jesus
As if they were mad, and they struck him.

Speravit in domino, eripiat eum, salvum faciet eum quoniam vult eum.

He trusted in the Lord, let him rescue him, let him deliver him, seeing he delighteth in him.

The Psalm here speaks from the position of Jesus, awaiting God's intervention. The connections to the Passion are also intensified by this Psalm's use in the liturgy for the Stripping of the Altar on Maundy Thursday.

---

43 Northrop Frye, *The Great Code: The Bible and Literature* (New York: Harcourt Brace Jovanovich, 1982). In thinking about W 102 from a typological perspective, I learned a great deal from Cordula Grewe's reading of some much later artistic uses of the medieval model. See her *Painting the Sacred in the Age of Romanticism* (Farnham: Ashgate, 2009), esp. 39–43.

Finally, in recalling Jesus's declaration to Pilate, Psalm 118:30 is now re-envoiced as the voice of Christ himself:

Verité a laudes ne cela
Par li fu le fiz deu verement granta.

At Lauds He did not hide the truth,
For he was God's Son, he truthfully admitted.

Viam veritatis elegi, et iudicia tua non sum oblitus.

I have chosen the way of truth, and thy judgments have I laid before me.

The multiple temporalities in the Hours of the Passion, especially in the typological design of the Old French and Psalms, create a meditative pathway into the Passion whereby the supplicant herself is brought into the historical past of the Passion as if in her own real time. It is not simply the temporal relationships that establish the gateways to make present the past. The vocal registers of the texts themselves contribute to the temporal alchemy, making multiple musical resonances besides those images strutting beneath the margins. Much of the affective power of the exegesis rests in remembering the words were intended to be uttered. The alternation of Old French and Latin recalls models such as lyric-interpolated romance, where there is a shift from narrative to lyric mode. Like the prayers, contemporary manuscripts of lyric-interpolated romances often set their lyrics apart by means of colored ink. The choice of Psalms as the Old Testament source calls on a very specific lyricism: they are, after all, songs. The notion of singing out typological relations adds to the intensity of the meditative experience: to sing is to embody the "I" of the text, to become in the moment of performance both the voice of the Psalmist and the New Testament character the Psalm is staged to prefigure. Finally, the rooting of these temporalities in the real present of the liturgical hour, the moment at which the supplicant is praying, also commissions the singing self to experience the present as a moment of culmination and consolidation of sacred history.

If this discussion illustrates the complexity of the temporal and lyrical program of the prayers, it also suggests how high the devotional stakes are and encourages alternative interpretations of the *cortège* beneath. Entertainment or humor do not seem satisfactory explanations for its presence; and the obvious resolution of Renard as Christ's parody seems simplistic set against the other narratives. Marching in to the beat of their vernacular and romance temporality, what other alternatives are there to realize the animals within the typological time frame?

There is no easy solution. But perhaps that is part of their purpose: to demand interpretive attention, to clamor for hermeneutic resolution, and to extract contemplative work from their readers. We can take up the challenge, and offer two suggestions for how the animals' music may play into the texture of time running overhead. Most simply, of course, they are a signal of irrationality, in the technical sense of *musica*. And that shocking appearance of animals—not humans—adhering to musical order, and bringing with them elaborate narrative contexts, cannot help but draw the supplicant's attentions away from prayer. Here, the visual lure of brightly colored images implying a cacophony of instruments and animal voices mimics the effects of the sounds represented. And if we cannot actually "hear" their music, there is another way that the intrusion of musical mimesis interrupts the flow of prayer. The performative space translates into material presence, and processional time is marked by units of folios. The parchment itself assumes processional meaning, and dramatically destabilizes prayer, or rather exploits its limits as a medium for representing musical experience. Perhaps the most unusual aspect of W 102 is that its procession is spread over several folios rather than a single folio or opening: it is one of only a few manuscripts to use the margins in that way, to generate simultaneous narratives.[44] Faced with the first (or perhaps last?) animal in the sequence, the impulse is, of course, to follow the trail through to its conclusion, and thus to experience the form of the book much faster in the sequential movement of its prayer texts than their liturgical time frame permits. It encourages the reader to flip through the prayers, rather than pausing to reflect on them in the correct order of the Hours; more fundamentally, it also creates a conflicting sense of time—experienced as the turn of the folios—that overrides the sacred time of the main texts. In a context of prayer that is insistent on staying "in the moment" of the specific Hour, the temptation to turn folios ensnares the reader into an act of *curiositas*.

If the space of the procession thus represents a threat to prayer's efficacy, then another temporal dimension of its sound ultimately creates a profoundly productive turn. While the movement of the procession through parchment invites a forward-moving progression by speeding through the Hours, a closer look reveals a second temporality in play. While movement through parchment implies motion, or a movement through musical time, what is represented here is in fact stillness. As the band stretches out over space, the creatures are bound together in a single moment in time, time marked by the notes sounding on the instruments they play, instruments they hear across the parchment spaces. At that junction of real subject (movement, temporal

---

44 The Luttrell Psalter develops narrative sequences across the space of several folios. For example, fols. 86^r–96^v unfurl the Life of Christ, while fols. 170^r–173^v depict scenes of farming. However, in these cases the individual folios or openings alone represent a single narrative event, one in a longer narrative sequence. In W 102, the folios are akin to a single shot, and depict one event over several folios.

progression, the passage of musical time) and material (parchment, paint), time is suspended: the animals are completely synchronized, marching to the same tempo, poised, their left paws, claws, and hooves in mid-air, on an eternal upbeat. That unsettling tension between parchment space, pushing us forward, and musical time, frozen, in turn generates a cross-rhythm that now finally harmonizes with—perhaps even resolves—the temporal aspect of the prayers themselves. The rowdy, noisy, visually tantalizing procession beneath does not merely distract. Renart's narrative creates the impossible: a single moment at which all temporalities of the prayers co-exist. The clanging musicality of the processional moment works something like a tenor in a typological motet: holding its voices together in the parchment eternity of a single moment.

The Musicality of Prayer

From the formal model of St. Louis down to the unpredictable flurry of marginalia, Jeanne's Hours not only sought to set out doctrines relating to utterance, distraction, and the dangers of her sensual experience. The book itself may also be read as a notation for the experience of prayer, not simply a conduit of messages. Similarly, the daring design of the musical procession in W 102 invites a distraction embodied in the forbidden turn of folios. In their ingenious designs, both artists were in essence at prayer, and made for their readers meditative experiences rife with unresolved meaning, inviting contemplation of images, utterance of words, and associations with a range of other pedagogical texts and sonic experiences. Although we can illuminate the individual components by which supplicants of these manuscripts may have constructed their devotional sense, and suggest some interpretations, it is much harder to know what the experience itself may have felt like, and especially how the silent sonority of prayer had its effect. Throughout this chapter, though, a recurring theme in the suggested readings invites analogy with altogether different media. Although the currency is the ephemeral and spontaneous medium of sound, polyphony, like prayer, offers a framework for experiencing semantic multiplicity simultaneously.

In both manuscripts, sound is not simply a didactic topic: it may also offer supplicants an affective and meditative reference point for the act of prayer. In W 102, the typological design of the Hours of the Passion and the unusual material challenge of the marching animals rely on the reader's ability to conceive temporally disparate events simultaneously. In creating a lesson in prayer, artist Jean Pucelle relied on a mode of meaning-making that likewise engaged all manner of narratives at once. In analysis of the theme of charity in the Hours of St. Louis, for example, Gerald Guest observes how meanings are created through a negotiation of visual registers: "In Jeanne's *Hours* neither miniature nor margin can be read in isolation—the two play off one another to create meaning."[45] Although the psychological and physiological experiences of medieval prayer are beyond the limits of the evidence, analogies with contemporary musical practice may ultimately offer insights into aspects of history that are normally elusive. Prayer's investment in discourses relating to sound and music, and its use of visual juxtaposition and narrative simultaneities to create devotional challenges, implies an experience akin to musical listening, especially listening to the motet. While polyphony is often appropriated by literary scholars and art historians as analogy for semantic simultaneity in art and texts, I wish in my usage to keep the sounding, musical dimension in play. For in the case of sound in prayer books, I hope to have shown that the signs of sound had the potential to prompt recollection of real sonorities, and also in their unsettling juxtapositions to create disturbance and distractions to the eyes that provoked the mind's ear to respond and ultimately to seek out sense. That said, the musicality of these books operates in a realm different from that of audible performance, and it will fall to our concluding chapter to examine not just the correlations between the medium of prayer books and motets, but also the differences.

The final chapter of this devotional trio will thus explore the possibility of a reciprocity between prayerful experience and musical experience, at the level of a shared concern with sound's efficacies and dangers in the realm of meditative practice. As well as giving musical sound a new sonorous context, the polyphonic aspect to the construction of meaning in prayer books also offers new ways to situate meaning in devotional motets. Not only that, we shall see how the very forms and visual schemes that shaped the experience of prayer books on occasion seeped into the physical design of motet compendia. In a material sense, as well as a sonorous sense, singing was an opportunity for prayer.

45 Guest, "A Discourse on the Poor," 165.

8 | Devotional Listening and the Montpellier Codex

Motets as Prayers

We begin with two motets that from a textual perspective are indistinguishable from prayers. Examples 8.1 and 8.2 forge instant association with the Marian emphasis of books of hours, by appropriating verbatim texts commonly uttered or chanted in prayer. The first example, *Salve, mater misericordie* (694)/*Salve, regina* (695)/*Flos filius* [*eius*] (O16),[1] is built on a tenor melisma from the Marian responsory for the feasts of the Assumption and Nativity of the Virgin, *Stirps Jesse*.[2] Its motetus and triplum are likewise on Marian themes, and offer ingenious play on one of the best-known Marian antiphons, the *Salve regina*. The motetus text is a wholesale citation of the text, and opens with the familiar hail to Mary as "regina misericordie." The triplum, glossing the text, replaces "regina" with "mater," opening "Salve, mater misericordie," foreshadowing an adjustment to the antiphon in the early fourteenth century in which the opening line read "Salve, regina, mater misericordie." The triplum goes on to emphasize the motherly and protective aspect of the Virgin, while its

1 The motet is unique to *Mo*, fols. 109ᵛ–110ᵛ, and the motetus melody is incomplete. It is edited in *The Montpellier Codex*, ed. Tischler, no. 72.

2 "The stalk of Jesse produced a branch: and the branch a flower. And upon this flower the bountiful spirit came to rest. V: The Virgin mother of God is the branch, *the flower her son*." ("Stirps Jesse produxit virgam: virgaque florem. Et super hanc florem requiescit spiritus almus. V: Virgo dei genetrix virga est, *flos filius eius*.")

EXAMPLE 8.1. *Salve, mater misericordie/Salve, regina misericordie/Flos filius [eius]*, mm. 1–16 (*Mo*, fols. 109ᵛ–110ᵛ)

reference to her as "flower of modesty" ("flos pudicie") chimes with the floral symbolism of the original chant "root" beneath.

Triplum

Salve, mater misericordie,
summi patris mater et filia,
porta celi, domus mundicie,
via vite, mundi leticia,
celestium civium gloria,
lux hominum, origo venie,
spes salutis, flos pudicie,
debilium convalescentia!
Virgo pia,

huius fletus audi familie,
propicia
in flebili valle miserie!
Fons gratie,
per te nobis post hec exilia
detur frui sanctorum requie
feliciter in celi curia,
ubi sedes in throno glorie,
O suavis, O dulcis Maria.

Hail, mother of compassion, mother and daughter of the highest Father, gate of heaven, abode of purity, path of life, happiness of the world, glory of the heavenly host, light of mankind, source of pardon, hope of salvation, flower of modesty, convalescence of the sick! Pious Virgin, hear the weeping of this family, be kind in this mournful valley of misery! Font of grace, may it be granted us that through you, after this exile, we enjoy the rest of the saints happily in the heavenly court, where you sit on the throne of glory, O gentle and sweet Mary.

Motetus

Salve, regina misericordie,
vita, dulcedo et spes nostra, salve!
Ad te clamamus,
exules filii Eve;
ad te suspiramus
gementes et flentes in hac lacrimarum valle.
Eya! Ergo, advocata nostra,
illos tuos misericordes . . .

Hail, queen of compassion, life, sweetness, and our hope, hail! To you we cry, the exiled children of Eve; to you we sigh, moaning and weeping in this valley of tears. Hail! Therefore, O our patron, those your compassionate . . .

Tenor

Flos filius [eius]

The motet *in toto* is thus a passionate amplification of one of the best-known Marian prayers. The *Salve regina* was not only commonly sung at the conclusion of Compline, it was frequently found as a stand-alone in prayer books, as is shown in figure 8.1 from fol. 32ᵛ of Walters Art Museum, W 40, the Parisian book of hours we encountered in chapter 5. There, the *Salve regina* follows a sequence of prayers to the Virgin. To encounter the motet either as singer, listener, or reader is thus to be drawn instantly into the habit, and habitat, of prayer.

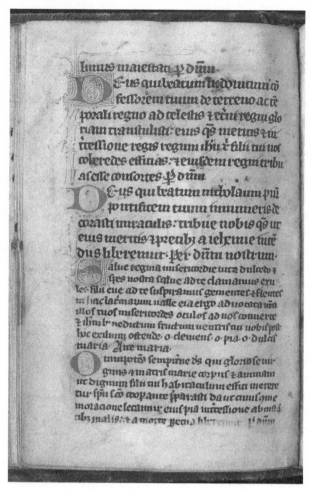

FIGURE 8.1. Baltimore, Walters Art Museum, W 40, fol. 32ᵛ. © The Walters Art Museum

Our second example, the motet *Ave beatissima civitas* (394)/*Ave, Maria* (395)/*Ave maris stella* (M85a) (example 8.2),[3] offers another model for transforming prayers into motets. Its tenor comprises two statements of the melody of the Marian hymn *Ave maris stella*, popular again from the book of hours, where it was sung or recited at Vespers in the Hours of the Virgin. Notwithstanding the propensity of motet tenors to draw on the repertory of liturgical chants, it

3 The motet appears in *Mo*, fols. 93ᵛ–94ʳ, and *Cl*, fol. 384ʳ. The incipits appear in an index of a musical collection, now lost, in London, British Library, Harley 978. There are also various other musical settings of the *Ave beatissima* text. It is edited in *The Montpellier Codex*, ed. Tischler, no. 55.

EXAMPLE 8.2. *Ave beatissima civitas/Ave, Maria, gratia plena/Ave maris stella* (*Mo*, fols. 93ᵛ–94ʳ)

EXAMPLE 8.2. (continued)

is an unusual—and unusually melodious—choice. The wholesale citation of prayers continues in the motetus, which comprises a near-complete statement of the *Ave Maria*. The triplum, newly composed for the motet, taking up the theme of Marian laudation and supplication, is an A, B, C of Marian devotion, with each word beginning with a different letter of the alphabet.

Triplum

Ave beatissima civitas, divinitas, eterno felix gaudio habitaculum iusti-tie, karissimum lilium, mater nobilis! Obsecra plasmatorem, quatenus redemptos sanguine tueatur, ut viventes Xristo ymnizemus; zima.

Hail, most blessed city, divinity, happy in eternal joy, dwelling of jus-tice, most dear lily, noble mother! Beg the Creator to watch over those who are redeemed by His blood, that we may, while living, sing a hymn to Christ; zima.

Motetus

Ave, Maria, gratia plena! Dominus tecum; benedicta tu in mulieribus et benedictus fructus ventris tui, amen. Natum dulcissimum pro nobis peccatoribus exora, beata Maria!

Hail, Mary, full of grace! The Lord is with thee; blessed art thou amongst women, and blessed is the fruit of thy womb, amen. Entreat your most sweet son on behalf of us sinners, O blessed Mary!

Tenor

Ave maris stella

Both examples demonstrate how prayers were sometimes recycled for use as texts for *ars antiqua* motets. They are extreme instances of what scholars have long recognized to be a devotional priority in the genre. Be it in the texting of liturgical clausulae, the explicitly sacred trajectory of newly composed Latin motets of this kind, or in the allegorical model of bilingual or vernacular motets that align secular commonplaces with a sacred counterpart, a powerful hermeneutic of the genre is its incessant construction and reconstruction of devotional topics. Their presence has fuelled many thoughtful analyses and interpretations whose aim is to unpack from motets—through textual and musical analysis—a range of sacred meanings.[4] Resonant with such work, my starting point here of prayers within motets is intended to stir some even more basic considerations. With such a direct correlation to acts of prayer, these pieces provoke us to consider now how the sonic environment of prayer explored in the preceding two chapters may help us attune to the transformative impact of musical sound on devotional texts. Heard against the discourses of sound in prayer, and positioned with a practice of devotional listening informed by the experiences of praying through the medium of prayer books, the supermusical hubbub of the genre assumes a specific meaning. The sense of its sound is shaped, I suggest, by the sonorities known and thought about in prayer. Thus while previous chapters have shown how the supermusical could connote urban magnificence, civic dissent, madness, and so forth, cast now in the context of devotion, the motet's unknowable verbosity manifest in its surface effect has potentially edifying and dangerous possibilities. In what follows, I wish now to rehear the devotional motet in light of prayer's sonic environment, and ask afresh—what is the sense of its sound?

Let us first permit our examples their voices. One might hear the polytextual effect as pure hyperbole, the supermusical here akin to the sacred charisma of nonsense to which Katherine Zieman has referred. In both these

4 On which see Sylvia Huot, *Allegorical Play in the Old French Motet: The Sacred and the Profane in Thirteenth-Century Polyphony* (Stanford: Stanford University Press, 1997). Other important studies connecting motets to traditions of trope and gloss include Dolores Pesce, "Beyond Glossing: The Old Made New in *Mout me fu grief/Robin m'aime/Portare*," in *Hearing the Motet: Essays on the Motet of the Middle Ages and Renaissance*, ed. Dolores Pesce (New York: Oxford University Press, 1997), 28–51; Gerald Hoekstra, "The French Motet as Trope: Multiple Levels of Meaning in *Quant florist la violete/El mois de mai/Et gaudebit*," *Speculum* 73 (1998): 32–57; Lisa Colton, "The Articulation of Virginity in the Medieval *Chanson de nonne*," *Journal of the Royal Musical Association* 133 (2008): 159–88; and Susan Kidwell, "Elaboration through Exhortation: Troping Motets for the Common of Martyrs," *Plainsong and Medieval Music* 5 (1996): 153–73.

motets, it is fitting to allow for such meanings, given their enactment of two familiar Marian stances: laudation and a plea for intercession. They are both soundings of prayer texts driven by the desire to be heard by the Virgin. Their multi-voicedness permits them a superlative aural effect a mono-textual prayer alone could not.

Ave beatissima civitas/Ave, Maria/Ave maris stella is even more complex in its construction of hyperbole, as in its alphabet of praise it harnesses all letters as language fitting for the Virgin. Elsewhere, its texts establish a connection between praise and singing. In calling the Virgin to pray for the gathered, it characterizes their pleas as songs. Thus the triplum prayer concludes with the collective "ymnizemus"—meaning "we sing hymns"—to describe the act of supplication. The entire motet is a musicalization of the trope of intercession. It deploys two moments of strategic phonetic alignment between the upper voices to direct the ecstatic hubbub to its Marian audience. Triplum and motetus begin with the unanimous declamation "Ave," while in measure 2 they again congregate on shared syllables "i" and "a," which boost the motetus's statement of the name "Maria." The same tactic repeats in the closing measures, again to amplify the statement of "Maria" in the motetus. These striking verbal events thus frame the motet with brief yet effective devotional cues—"Ave!"—and cast the motet's intervening hyperbolic clamor as directed to divine ears. In this way, the motet embodies the impulse of *magnificat.*

While such readings allow the motet's primary sonic effect a positive meaning, the wider lessons of sound in prayer must also urge caution. As we saw, verbal confusion—not to say evidence of unmediated musical pleasure—in some quarters generated work for the devil. Like the unresolved marginal obscenities and monstrosities of the "imagines verborum," sound may be understood as an invocation to action. If prayer provides us with fresh contexts for understanding the ambiguous potential of the motet's sound, it may also provide tools to effect and explain its semantic resolution. Above all, it creates an environment for what we may term devotional listening: listening that is itself a form of prayer. I deliberately adopt the term "listening" here, even though much of what follows involves exploration of the genre's material instantiation, and hypotheses of multifaceted meditative relations to the sounding object. Indeed, by listening, I mean to include many of the experiences of motets that Sylvia Huot termed "reading" in her own study (that is, to include singing, hearing, reading, remembering, and also composing).[5]

---

5 Huot, *Allegorical Play*, 1–2. She writes: "the word *reading* refers to the understanding or interpretation of any text, including one destined for performance. . . . *reading* in its modern usage carries implications of critical analysis that are lacking from *hearing*, *listening*, or *singing*. The reading in question might be that of a composer or that of a musician who participated in the performance of the motet, or that of an audience

However, my default to "listening" is an encouragement to keep primary the sensory impression of sound. While I suggested that the simultaneities of sonic representation in prayer books functioned as polyphony, including their having an aural/oral dimension, the motet's polyphony must now account for the vibrating, sounding reality of its performance. And it is the motet's sound, I suggest, that is simultaneously the object of devotion, and equally its greatest adversary.

In the rest of this chapter I take up the negotiation of sound and sense as it pertains to devotional motets, and suggest that sometimes the means by which medieval listeners resolved the problem of sonic temptation was by recourse to the familiar routines of prayer. Devotional motets were similar to prayer books—rife with temptation and sonic provocation, and full of the potential for devotional illumination. On one occasion, the question of how to make sense of sound was answered in part by means of a material solution, and in what follows, I will explore how manuscript context could shape a devotional "ductus" that mimicked and interacted with the meaning of motets as heard. The manuscript in question is one of the most famous and comprehensive sources for the thirteenth-century motet (and also source for the two motets with which we began): the Montpellier Codex (*Mo*).[6] This book lends itself extremely well to exploration as prayer-through-song. Although, as we shall see, debates about the book's provenance, dating, and function remain unresolved, we know a little of the artists of its splendid program of illuminations. Among their other commissions, including some books made for a cardinal undoubtedly skilled in the practices of prayer, were liturgical manuscripts, including books for private prayer such as Psalters.[7] Furthermore, a tantalizing hypothesis suggested by Catherine Parsoneault about the owner of the book likewise locates it in a culture of prayer, one directly related to the Hours of Jeanne d'Evreux discussed previously. Based on manuscript inventories of the Capetian household, references to motet performance in literary sources, and

---

member who heard it. . . . the term includes visual and aural reception as well as meditation on the piece." Questions of listening and reading are also taken up in Clark, " 'S'en dirai chançonete'."

6 For a fascimile and edition see *Polyphonies du XIIIe siècle: Le manuscrit H 196 de la Faculté de Médecine de Montpellier*, ed. Yvonne Rokseth, 4 vols. (Paris: Editions de l'Oiseau-Lyre, 1935–39); for a more recent edition, along with complete transcriptions and translations of the motet texts, see *The Montpellier Codex*, ed. Tischler.

7 See Robert Branner's *Manuscript Painting in Paris during the Reign of Saint Louis: A Study of Styles* (Berkeley: University of California Press, 1977), 130–37, and especially his list of manuscripts designated the "Cholet Group" and "Royal Psalter Group," 237–39. These include manuscripts whose illuminations were executed by artists working on portions of *Mo*. Although some of Branner's designations and datings have now been revised, his lists nonetheless offer useful context for *Mo*'s imagery.

drawing on a reading of the book's illuminations, Parsoneault made a provocative suggestion. Namely, that *Mo* was made for a Capetian queen, one well versed in reading and known for her cultivation of the arts.[8] The queen in question was Marie of Brabant, wife of Philip III: none other than the grandmother of Jeanne d'Evreux herself.

In what follows, I offer a model for devotional listening in *Mo*. In exploring the interaction of manuscript design, illumination, liturgical allusion, texts, and musical sound, I offer a hypothesis for how medieval listeners made sense of devotional motets, showing how dimensions of sound, memory, and material object could serve as something like an experience of prayer. To begin, though, I need to introduce the manuscript. For as well as being the most comprehensive of contemporary motet compendia, it is also the most notoriously complex.

Introducing Montpellier
PRESTIGE OR PERFORMANCE?

Mo is justly famous as a witness to medieval musical culture. Dating from the end of the thirteenth century, and containing over 350 motets organized into eight fascicles according to voice numbers and languages, the *Mo* repertory derives from all stages of the genre's developments:

> Fascicle 1: conductus, organum
> Fascicle 2: four-part French motets
> Fascicle 3: four-part bilingual motets
> Fascicle 4: three-part Latin double motets
> Fascicle 5: three-part French motets
> Fascicle 6: two-part French motets
> Fascicle 7: variety of three-part motets
> Fascicle 8: variety of three-part motets

Within the rationale ordering motets by voice types, the book is also loosely chronological, beginning with the oldest representatives of the genre, and ending with the most recent. In part because of that design, the earlier portions are dominated by overtly sacred items (common in the earliest stages of the genre), with motets less bound by devotional themes falling in later portions of the book. If the manuscript is a treasure for its comprehensive scope, it is equally prized for its material value. Partly because of its lavish program

---

8 Catherine Parsoneault, "The Montpellier Codex: Royal Influence and Musical Taste in Late Thirteenth-Century France" (Ph.D. diss., University of Texas at Austin, 2001). See especially chapter 4.

of illuminations, particularly the spectacular marginal illuminations and historiated capitals with which each of the book's eight fascicles opens, the book's function is little understood: on the one hand, its material quality suggests an object of prestige and display more than a repository for performance, or indeed for any practical "use"; on the other, its encyclopedic scope, its often meticulous notation implies an active possibility for performance.

The problem of determining *Mo*'s function—as (passive) object of display or (active) text for performance—reflects common criteria for categorizing compendia of this period. For example, in characterizing the trend to anthologize motets at the end of the thirteenth century, Patricia Norwood makes the following distinction:

> Were they merely anthologies of an important and popular art form? Were they, then, merely compiled for purposes of display? Or were these manuscripts intended to be vehicles for performance? Indeed, were any of these collections prepared in such a way that performance from them was possible?[9]

There is no reason why *Mo* could not have served multiple functions. Certainly, it is clear that the book is neither simply just a score for performance, notwithstanding its decipherable notation and clear underlay, nor just a prestige object. The comprehensive scope of its contents, resonant with contemporary encyclopedic theoretical approaches to musical genre, also suggests that the compilation was not merely a practical act of containment, but could also be a structure for thinking about the materials inscribed. In engaging the book with the larger context of thirteenth-century book production and reading habits, it will be fruitful to explore the ways the physicality of the object interacted with and informed the experience or memory of the sounding life of its motets; that its luxuriousness, which may encourage us to regard it as a prestige book, engages in precise and productive ways with the sense of the music it transmits.

THE MAKING OF MONTPELLIER

It is not hard to see why there may be resistance to the suggestion that the pictorial and compilatory forms were intended to do more than embellish. According to many accounts, the book came into its current form over decades, with numerous scribes and artists working on it in. This implies that what we now see was a piecemeal production where, at best, design strategy evolved in the act of creation. It is little surprise, given the book's complexity, that its

9 Patricia Norwood, "Performance Manuscripts from the Thirteenth Century?," *College Music Symposium* 26 (1986): 92–96.

codicological life has dominated accounts by art historians and musicologists alike. While my purpose is not to resolve the thorny debates regarding dating and chronology, I need to outline some recent thinking concerning the book's mysterious genesis, not least because a central preoccupation is whether or not it was conceived of, and read, as an integrated whole.

Until recently, the consensus was that *Mo* was put together somewhat arbitrarily, produced in distinct stages over a considerable span of time rather than conceived according to a single compilatory plan from the outset.[10] The established view was that the book was produced in three basic units.[11] Yvonne Rokseth's assessment of scribal hands led her to argue that fascicles 1–6 were a single unit, and the earliest portion of the book, dating ca. 1280, with fascicle 7 copied at the turn of the century, and fascicle 8 still later.[12] That view was modified by Robert Branner's analysis of the decorative components of the book. His grouping differed in one important matter: he demonstrated that the artists who produced fascicle 1 also worked on fascicle 7. He also modified the dating, situating fascicles 2–6 as the oldest part of the book, datable by virtue of their connection to another family of datable manuscripts

---

10 The manuscript has been subject to intensive analysis over the years by art historians and musicologists. Key studies that also include synthesis and critique of previous scholarship are Mary Wolinski, "The Montpellier Codex: Its Compilation, Notation, and Implications for the Chronology of the Thirteenth-Century Motet" (Ph.D. diss., Brandeis University, 1988), and her "The Compilation of the Montpellier Codex," *Early Music History* 11 (1992): 263–301. See too Parsoneault, "The Montpellier Codex." Parsoneault includes a critique of Wolinski's most radical arguments at 135–49. Both authors build on Mark Everist's assessment of the manuscript and the earlier scholarship in *Polyphonic Music in Thirteenth-Century France: Aspects of Sources and Distribution* (New York: Garland, 1989), esp. 110–34. More recently, Alison Stones has added further evidence relating to the dating of certain fascicles: see "Les Manuscrits du Cardinal Jean Cholet et l'enluminure Beauvaisienne vers le fin du XIIIème siècle," in *L'Art gothique dans l'Oise et ses environs (XIIème–XIVème siècle): Architecture civile et religieuse, peinture murale, sculpture et arts précieux. Colloque international organisé à Beauvais les 10 et 11 octobre 1998 par le Groupe d'Étude des Monuments et Oeuvres d'Art de l'Oise et du Beauvais* (Beauvais: GEMOB, 2001), 230–68, esp. 251–57. All these works rely on older scholarship, in particular the essay in volume 4 of *Polyphonies du XIIIème siècle*, ed. Rokseth, which offered the first thorough analysis of scribal hands, drawing on the older, less reliable account of Gustav Jacobsthal, "Die Texte der Liederhandschrift von Montpellier H. 196," *Zeitschrift für romanische Philologie* 3 (1879): 526–56, and 4 (1880): 278–317. For a recent description of the manuscript, including discussion of dating, see also Alison Stones, *Manuscripts Illuminated in France: Gothic Manuscripts, 1260–1320* (Turnhout: Brepols, forthcoming). See catalogue entry I: 24. I am very grateful to Professor Stones for generously sharing this work with me prior to publication.

11 Wolinksi, "The Compilation," 264–65.

12 *Polyphonies*, ed. Rokseth, 4:28–30.

to ca. 1260–90 (therefore opening the possibility these fascicles were produced earlier than Rokseth originally proposed); fascicles 1 and 7 in the last years of the thirteenth century; and fascicle 8 a little later, around 1300.[13]

That framework for understanding *Mo*'s physical composition has persisted ever since, with various minor modifications to dating and to scribal and artistic involvement across the manuscript. However, Mary Wolinski's painstaking codicological assessment uncovered new evidence showing that some scribes and artists worked across fascicles previously thought to be codicologically discrete. Crucially, she posits connections between scribes of fascicles 1 and 7 and 2–6, and suggests that artists involved in fascicle 7 also had a hand in fascicle 8. Thus, she argues, there is "substantial evidence that scribes and painters of *Mo* worked simultaneously."[14] Although scholars have argued against Wolinski's position, both in print and public discussion, new evidence uncovered by Alison Stones postdating those studies mentioned may strengthen Wolinski's position, or at least encourage a view of *Mo* as codicologically more integrated.[15]

Stones's essay is a detailed reassessment of manuscripts owned by Cardinal Cholet (d. 1292), and others produced by the circle from which Cholet's books came. Branner had earlier connected the *Mo* illuminations in fascicles 2–6 to a network of books known as the "Cholet," "Henry VIII," and "Royal Psalter" groups, their colophons or marks linking them explicitly to other books by the same artists in each group. Stones's return to some of these books, especially those connected with Cholet, and the discovery of other manuscripts (some datable) allowed her to make some new suggestions for dating the artwork not only of fascicles 2–6, but also 1 and 7. Although Stones, as Branner himself, often builds families of manuscripts based on stylistic identifications alone, she nonetheless arrives at conclusions that chime in interesting ways with Wolinski's vision of *Mo*.

Two elements are pertinent. First, based on her comparison between the artists of fascicles 1 and 7 and those of the Beauvais Psalter (now housed in New York, Pierpont Morgan Library, M 98), the St. Denis Missal (Paris, Bibliothèque nationale de France, lat. 1107), the London Evangeliary (London, British Library, Add. 17341), and a collection of medical treatises in Kraków, Biblioteka Jagiellońska 816, Stones argues that "stylistic echoes invite us to push the dating of fascicles I and VII of *Mo* several years later than M 98

13 Branner, *Manuscript Painting*, 130–37.

14 Wolinski, "The Compilation," 274.

15 Parsoneault summarizes the unpublished commentary on Wolinski's views in "The Montpellier Codex," 136.

[New York, Morgan Library 98], closer to 1280–86 than to 1276–80."[16] Second, on the basis of an intricate network of connections to the Murthly Hours (National Library of Edinburgh, MS 21000), some of whose decorations are posited to be from the 1280s or 1290s, and which was decorated by artists also connected to the decorative schemes of *Mo*'s so-called Old Corpus (fascicles 2–6), Stones suggests a dating for that portion of *Mo* that is not only much later, but also closer to the time of the decoration of fascicles 1 and 7: "on the early side of the decade 1280–90, about the same moment as the execution of fascicles 1 and 7."[17] These redatings do not necessarily prove all work within these fascicles happened at the same time. Mark Everist makes the important point that the historiated capitals were among the last portions of the book to be executed, and could have been added relatively late after the copying of the notation.[18] However, even if the sections of the manuscript were produced by different ateliers and at a later stage, Stones's hypothesis about datings opens the possibility, in accordance with Wolinksi's thesis, that some aspects of the book's design could have been conceived and undertaken at roughly the same time.

We will never know the full story of *Mo*'s genesis: as analysis brings its physical creation ever more into focus, it reveals a codicological picture that is only more complicated and open-ended. As Parsoneault and Wolinski show, some scribes moved across the fascicles, but their movement is not necessarily mirrored by the illuminators. On the other hand, the revised dating of the artwork suggests the book's fascicles were produced much closer together than was originally thought. In the face of such evidence, the traditional desire—to understand *Mo* as a series of disparate elements—is no less likely than the possibility that its component parts were made with some view to their eventual place in a larger whole. What is lost in relinquishing that framework of *Mo* as product of codicological chance? Or, to put it another way, why might we resist seeing the book as more integrated? One answer may lie in a long-standing musicological reading of the style of the motets across the manuscript. Dating back to the earliest stylistic critiques of the *ars antiqua* motet by Ludwig, the *Mo* repertory has been broken into old- and new-style motets. The oldest layer was identified as fascicle 1 (containing organal settings) and fascicles 2–6 (two, three, and four-part motets); fascicles 7 and 8, by contrast, were thought progressively more modern, with fascicle 8's repertory being the closest extant

16 "échoes stylistiques . . . invitent à pousser la datation des fascicules 1 et VII de *Mo* quelques années plus tard que M 98 – plutôt vers 1280–86 que vers 1276–80." Stones, "Les Manuscrits du Cardinal Jean Cholet," 253.

17 "un peu plus tôt dans la décennie de 1280–90, à peu près ou même moment que l'exécution des fascicules I et VII." Ibid., 257.

18 Everist, *Polyphonic Music*, 118–27, esp. 125–26.

precursors of the *ars nova* motet.[19] The pairing of musical/stylistic and codico-logical evidence has nurtured an instinct to argue that the book's chronological representation of the motet is reflected by, and reflects, the narrative of its physical genesis.

Let us look again at the manuscript, and consider some aspects that create coherence—even a meaning—in its physical organization. It is worth remind-ing ourselves of some more basic visual congruence between the different fas-cicles. Namely, the stunning program with which each fascicle begins, and its consistency in designing each to have an "opening." Even if the illuminations were entered at a later stage, the layout of each fascicle was set up with a view to their inclusion. Their effect: a vivid, visual punctuation across the manu-script, rather like a series of bookmarks. Not merely decorative, they serve the function of *accessus*, allowing for speedy location of particular genres of motets, which, as we saw, define the contents of the individual fascicles. Simply put, the illuminations and marginalia not only communicate artistic value: they reinforce a strategy of musical organization.

Then there is the compilatory strategy itself. As well as the obvious generic distinctions of the fascicles, *Mo* simultaneously operates a chronological scheme. The traditional understanding of *Mo* is, as we saw, as compiling representatives of the tradition from the earliest examples (long predating the book's creation) to motets whose composition was probably contemporary with the copying of the latest sections of the book. Both genre and chronology may themselves be expressive strategies. In one respect, *Mo* is retrospective, a *summa* of the motet that began with Notre Dame polyphony. The presence of the first fascicle, which contains organa and conductus, music that predates the genre of the motet, is especially powerful in casting the book as a "history" of the tradition. That almost historiographical rationale resonates with other musical and liter-ary manuscripts, not least the Notre Dame repertory and contemporary trou-badour and trouvère chansonniers, many of which were compiled decades after their contents were first in use. They often had a retrospective rationale. Edward Roesner notes that the repertory in *F*, for example, marks "an overall progres-sion from old to new, with the more recent genre of the motet appearing late in the manuscript . . . and the presumably relatively modern refrain songs coming at the end."[20] The organization within subgenres of the motet likewise

---

19   This may be traced back to Friedrich Ludwig's "Studien über die Geschichte der mehrstimmigen Musik in Mittelalter II: Die 50 Beispiele Coussemakers aus der Handschrift von Montpellier," *Sammelbände der Internationalen Musikgesellschaft*, 5 (1903–1904), 200–203.

20   *Antiphonarium, seu, Magnus liber organi de gradali et antiphonario: Color Microfiche Edition of the Manuscript Firenze, Biblioteca medicea laurenziana, Pluteus 29.1*, with introduc-tion by Edward Roesner (Munich: Helga Lengenfelder, 1996), 25.

echoes compilatory gestures in contemporary music books. This is true in the Notre Dame manuscripts, and in vernacular collections (such as Oxford, Bodleian Library, Douce 308, a poetry collection organized by genre). A little later than *Mo*, there is the *Roman de Fauvel*, which as we saw in chapter 3 opens with a table of contents organizing the interpolated items via genre. In its distribution of generic categories *within* the motet tradition, and projected onto the chronological trajectory, *Mo* may thus be read not just as a historiographical record of a musical past, but also quasi-theoretically, as an account of the evolution of a genre: from its sacred origins, through the largely devotional motets up to fascicle 5, and then beyond, moving towards topical and musical multiplicity that reaches its apotheosis in fascicles 7 and 8, where the stricter generic principle gives way to variety.

Portions of the book that from physical analysis seem to have been added late reveal sensitivity to the schema of the earlier compendium. This is true of fascicle 8, which in one sense works as a stand-alone *libellus* compiling exempla of the most recent representatives of the genre. However, its opening mirrors almost exactly that of fascicle 1 (both open with *Deus in adiutorium* settings and standard imagery of singers in their historiated initial "D"s). While it was not uncommon to open musical collections with *Deus in adiutorium* settings—borrowing the opening versicle of seven of the eight Hours to create a bibliographic gesture of a "beginning"—the similarity of layout in *Mo* creates a bookend to mirror the opening of the manuscript.

Other features (often characterized as codicological anomaly) assume new coherence when reading *Mo*'s organization as more deliberate. If historical and generic order draws attention to the overwhelming devotional bent of the early motet up to the end of fascicle 4, an unusual decorative feature at the end of that fascicle marks off these early fascicles as separate from the increasingly secular trajectory thereafter. Figure 8.2 shows fol. 111^r, the recto facing the close of fascicle 4, which culminates on fols. 109^v–110^v with the incomplete copy of *Salve, mater misericordie/Salve, regina misericordie/Flos filius [eius]* (the motet with which we began). While physically part of fascicle 5, its textless polyphonic *In seculum* settings are musically outside that fascicle's contents, which contains three-part French double motets. Turning to fols. 111^v–112^r, the first main opening of fascicle 5 (figure 8.3) has its own elaborate decorative scheme with historiated capitals and *bas-de-page* decoration, typical in layout to the openings of other fascicles in the manuscript. In other words, it is on fol. 111^v, not 111^r, that the new fascicle begins, according to the schema of the other fascicles. Parsoneault reads the curious appearance of the *In seculum* folio as "somewhat anomalous," and accounts for it as a filler, the folio originally left blank "because of the need to use an entire opening for the layout of the first motet in each fascicle"; as she points out, this is the case earlier, in fascicles 2, 3, and 4, where the recto of the new gathering was left blank to allow the

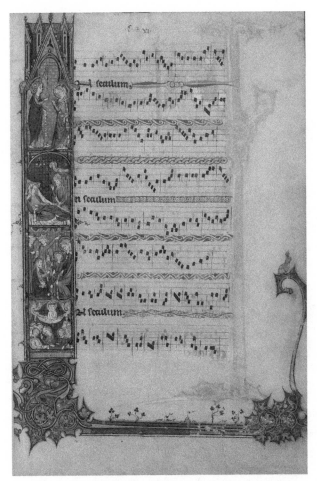

FIGURE 8.2. Montpellier, Bibliothèque Interuniversitaire, Section Médecine, H 196, fol. 111ʳ. By permission of the BIU, Montpellier

opening to mark the beginning of the new fascicle.[21] The missing ending of the motet, moreover, is confusing here, as the blank space of fol. 111ʳ could have been used to contain the missing few lines of music.

If from a codicological perspective this transition is understood as "anomalous," we should nevertheless consider the thematic implications of its effect. As suggested above, the transition between fascicles 4 and 5 marks a natural boundary in the subject matter of the motets: from devotional, largely Marian themes into motets whose texts have more overtly secular themes. Folio 111ʳ thus emphatically flags an important junction in the book as a whole, the boundaries between sacred and secular. Not only that, music's presence here

21 Parsoneault, "The Montpellier Codex," 103.

FIGURE 8.3. Montpellier, Bibliothèque Interuniversitaire, Section Médecine, H 196, fols. 111^v–112^r. By permission of the BIU, Montpellier.

reinforces that sense of the shape of the codex as a whole. For the *In seculum* settings sound earlier in the book, right after the *Deus in adiutorium* settings of fascicle 1 (there will be more to say about these settings presently). There, the upper voices are texted with Old French lyrical texts; here those texts vanish to leave just the bare voices. For now, we shall leave aside questions of the meaning of that lost lyric on fol. 111ʳ, and the possible motivation for the Marian imagery in the historiated border that decorates the folio. However, the pattern of musical echoes and use of the junction of the two fascicles here stages a material interjection, or a hiatus, marking a rite of passage. Leaving the unambiguously devotional landscape of fascicles 1–4, the book now progresses into a new lyric space of the vernacular motet.

Listening with Devotion: Fascicles 1–4

The next section explores three related aspects of the devotional design of the first part of *Mo*, three ways in which the book's shapes, decorations, and order of its contents prompt the reader to a meditative engagement with its music, attempting to extrapolate sense from musical substance whose sounding incarnation defies easy understanding. We will adopt a prayerful attitude to the book, opening its folios with memory of the prayer books recently worked through in chapters 6 and 7. We begin with fascicle 1—the threshold of the collection—and consider how it sets the reader on a devotional pilgrimage that reaches its apotheosis at the junction of fascicles 4 and 5.

DEUS IN ADIUTORIUM

Made up of conductus, clausulae, and organal settings, several with concordances in the Notre Dame manuscripts, and attributable in some cases to Perotin (see table 8.1), fascicle 1 is blatantly old-fashioned and seemingly discrete from the rest of the book. Even though the physical evidence now allows us to tie the fascicle's creation to the larger scheme of the manuscript, few studies dwell on the polyphony's presence in the book. Why was material both stylistically and functionally distinct from the main body deemed a fitting opening? Read in context, it has at the very least a symbolic function, positioned as venerable precursor of the motet. That feature is made more explicit by the fact that no fewer than seven of the seventeen four-part motets in fascicle 2, the oldest motet corpus in the manuscript, are based on clausulae extant in the main core of Notre Dame manuscripts;[22] furthermore, two motets in fascicle 4

22 Motets 19, 21, 22, 26, 29, 31, and 35, according to Tischler's numbering.

Table 8.1. The contents of fascicle 1 of *Mo*

Item	Folio	Incipit and attribution	Genre	Concordances
1 (1)	1ʳ	*Deus in adiutorium* (troped)	3-part conductus	*Ba*, folio 62ᵛ; *Tu*, folio Eʳ; *Da*, folio 1aʳ; *MuC*, folio 31ᵛ
2 (2)	1ᵛ–3ʳ	*Je n'aimerai autre* (211)/*In seculum* (M13)	4-part hocket-motet (*In seculum longum*)	Without quadruplum in *Ba*, folio 63ᵛ; *Ma*, folio 122ᵛ; *Mo*, folio 111ᵛ. Without triplum, but with motetus text and quadruplum in *Cl*, folios 387ʳ–187ᵛ (765) and *Mo*, folios 187ᵛ–189ʳ
3 (3)	2ᵛ–4ʳ	*Je n'aimerai autre* (211)/*In seculum* (M13)	4-part hocket-motet (*In seculum breve*)	Without quadruplum in *Ba*, 64ʳ
4 (4)	4ᵛ	*Benedicamus Domino*	3-part clausula	Unicum
5 (5)	5ʳ	*Portare* (M22)	3-part clausula	Unicum
6 (6–8)	5ᵛ–8ʳ	R: *Virgo.* V: *Sponsus amat* (O40)	3-part organum	*F*, folios 33ᵛ–34ᵛ; *W2*, folios 12ᵛ–14ʳ
7 (9–10)	9ʳ–12ᵛ	*Alleluia.* V: *Nativitas* (M 38) Perotin	3-part organum	*F*, folios 31ʳ–32ᵛ; *W1*, folios 6ʳ–7ᵛ; *W2*, 16ʳ–17ᵛ
8 (11–13)	13ʳ–16ʳ	R: *Sancte Germane.* V: *O Sanctei Germane* (O27)	3-part organum	*F*, folios 34ᵛ–36ʳ; *W1*, folios 5ʳ–6ʳ; *W2*, folios 10ʳ–12ᵛ
9 (14–15)	16ᵛ–20ʳ	*Alleluia.* V: *Posui adiutorium* (M51) Perotin	3-part organum	*F*, 36ʳ–37ᵛ
10 (16–18)	20ʳ–22ʳ	R: *Abiecto.* V: *Rigat lacrimis* (O41)	3-part organum	Unicum

(the collection of Latin double motets) are also based on clausulae, one of them on a section first heard in its unadulterated liturgical form in fascicle 1.[23]

Fascicle 1, then, establishes a sonorous historical context in which to hear the collection. But by virtue of the unambiguously liturgical function of almost all of its music, it also initiates a devotional context. Several other aspects of contents and presentation position the reader in a prayerful frame of

23 Motet 62, *Ex semine/Ex semine/Ex semine*, based on a clausula from the famous three-part organal setting *Alleluya: Nativitas*, for the Feast of the Assumption.

FIGURE 8.4. Montpellier, Bibliothèque Interuniversitaire, Section Médecine, H 196, fol. 1ʳ. By permission of the BIU, Montpellier

mind on entering the manuscript. The most obvious cue is the first item on fol. 1ʳ: the conductus setting of the *Deus in adiutorium* trope (see figure 8.4).[24] As noted above, it serves a bibliographic function, signaling a "beginning." Given the largely liturgical bent of the collection, it would be as well to allow devotional meanings to resonate. In prayer books, the "D"s of the opening versicle of each of the Hours were frequently the frame for programs of devotional images, most commonly, the Infancy or Passion Cycles in the Hours of

24 *The Montpellier Codex*, ed. Tischler, vol. 1, no. 1.

the Virgin. The purpose of the images was to offer an emotionally immediate meditative focal point, a portal into prayer.

Associated with such contexts, the *Deus in adiutorium* has meditative potential—as a ruminative space. In *Mo*, the devotional prompt is recommissioned to evoke the act of singing as the medium of prayer. The initial "D" is illuminated with a small choir of tonsured men gathered around a choirbook, mouths open, their bodies falling into the gestures of song. The image is not unique to *Mo*, and was a familiar part of the iconography of the polyphonic *Deus in adiutorium* convention.[25] However, the image plays out in provocative ways with the text of the trope (of which *Mo* is the earliest source). The textual expansions of the versicle exaggerate with performerly and musical reference the imperative of the original, which reads: ("Deus in adiutorium meum intende. Domine ad adiuvandum me festina" ("Lord, make speed to save me. Lord, make haste to help me"). Like the texts of *Ave beatissima/Ave, Maria/Ave Maris stella*, the first verse trope redirects the original versicle not just as a prayer for intercession, but also as a song. The text of the second verse, collapsing into the incantatory repetitions of "Amen" and "Alleluia," exaggerates the sense of itself as jubilant song, while in the manuscript, the clamor of the supermusical realization of sacred words is conveyed through the abbreviations as well, which render the words as a chain of nonsense vocibles: "Am am alla. Am am alla. Am am alla. Am am alla" (see figure 8.4).

Deus, in adiutorium
intende laborantium,
ad doloris remedium
festina in auxilium,
ut chorus noster psallere
possit et laudes dicere
tibi, Christe, rex glorie:
Gloria tibi, Domine!

Lord, make haste to help the suffering, come to their aid to relieve their sorrow, that our choir may sing and give you praise, Christ, King of Glory; glory to you, O Lord!

In te, Christe, credentium
miserearis omnium,
qui es Deus in secula,
seculorum, in gloria!

25 For more on this convention, see Wolinski, "The Compilation," 290, and Ursula Günther, "Les Versions polyphoniques du *Deus in adiutorium*," *Cahiers de civilization médiévale* 31 (1988): 111–22.

Amen, amen, alleluya;
amen, amen, alleluya;
amen, amen, alleluya;
amen, amen, alleluya!

O Christ, have mercy on all who believe in you, for you are God forever and ever, in glory! Amen, amen, alleluia; amen, amen, alleluia; amen, amen, alleluia; amen, amen, alleluia![26]

In its conjunction of memory of other devotional contexts of the prayer, of sight, sound, and voice, the opening folio of *Mo* is thus a miniature devotional exercise, readying the reader to embark on prayer.

It is somewhat startling, then, that the next item is the apparent anomaly of the fascicle. The two three-part textless *In seculum* discant settings (items 2 and 3) that follow are surprising in their addition of a quadruplum, in whose Old French text the protagonist is in a state not of spiritual sorrow (recall the "ad doloris remedium" of the *Deus in adiutorium* setting), but of courtly love-sickness. We shall return to them presently. For now, let us move on, through the clausulae and revered organal settings—a trip down memory lane of the motet tradition—to the close of the fascicle, where the meditative theme seems to resolve. While most of the fascicle's music has concordances among the Notre Dame manuscripts, the last item (item 10) is unique to *Mo*. It is a three-part setting of a chant identified by Edward Roesner as from the sixth responsory of Matins for the Office of St. William of Bourges, celebrated on 10 January.[27] William, a convert to the Cistercian Order, reluctantly agreed to be archbishop of Bourges in 1200, a post he held until his death in 1208.[28] It is an unusual conclusion for a fascicle that contains some of the great Perotinian organa, for feasts more mainstream than William's. On the other hand, a setting of the liturgy of an archbishop follows as natural conclusion to the two preceding items (items 8 and 9), *Sancte Germane. V: O Sancte Germane* and *Alleluia. V: Posui adiutorium*, which are based on chants from the Common of a Bishop Confessor. That unusual directing of the fascicle towards the celebration of bishops may point to the interests, or even roles, of potential dedicatees of the manuscript. For now, though, I am interested in how the *vita* of the saint, and the text of the chant itself, direct the reader's devotion.

It would be hard to find a better exemplum of the virtues of meditation and prayer. William's reluctance to accept the bishopric was due to his preference for an ascetic life over institutional politics. Clothed in the ultimate accessory of asceticism—the hair shirt—his prayer skills were renowned, and his

26 Texts from *The Montpellier Codex*, ed. Tischler, 4:1.
27 The identification is reported in Wolinski, "The Compilation," 291.
28 *The Montpellier Codex*, ed. Tischler, nos. 16–18.

fondness for intensive meditation was highlighted in his *vita* as evidence of his sanctity.[29] That piety was emphasized in the texts of the Offices of the saint, no more so than in the text of the chant setting in *Mo*:

R: Abiecto

V: Rigat ora lacrimis uberrimis orans in cubiculo pro populo. Gloria patri et filio et spiritui sancto.

R: Abject.

V: My face is wet from copious tears when I pray in my chamber for my people. Glory be to the Father and to the Son and to the Holy Spirit.[30]

Abjection is closely associated with the doctrine of compunction, popular in monastic and devotional writing throughout the period. It was a deeply aspirational state, an intense desire for heaven attainable through rigorous spiritual concentration, which promised release from despair. Tears have a specific currency. As Jean Leclercq writes: "the desire for Heaven inspires many texts on tears. The tears of desire, born of the compunction of love, are a gift from Our Lord; . . . these 'suave tears' engendered by the perception of God's sweetness, by the desire to enjoy it eternally, are accompanied by sighs, which are not sighs of sadness, but of hopeful desire."[31] The locus of William's solitary abjection in the Office text—the chamber—also has a genealogy. As Mary Carruthers argues: "in classical as in monastic rhetoric, withdrawal to one's chamber indicates a state of mind, the entry to the 'place' of meditative silence which was thought essential for invention."[32] Finally, it is hard to read this chant text without thinking of more venerable abjects: Augustine, tearfully alone at the moment of conversion; Boethius, weeping in his bed prior to Philosophy's arrival. Tears, within a doctrine of compunction, are "the exterior expression of the greater activity, prayer between the individual and God."[33] Within the established textual authorities for abjection in the later Middle

---

29 *Acta sanctorum quotquot toto orbe coluntur, vel a catholicis scriptoribus celebrantur quæ ex latinis et græcis, aliarumque gentium antiquis monumentis collegit*, ed. Johannes Bollandus, vol. 1 (Paris : V. Palmé, 1863), 627–39. See especially 629–30 for an account of his ascetic attributes, including abstinence from meat, eschewing of luxurious clothes, and his ability to bring peace to situations of noise, tumult, and controversy ("inter mundanos strepitus et aulae tumultus, inter litigantium rixas et controversias, pacem pectoris ita coluit . . .").

30 Texts from *The Montpellier Codex*, ed. Tischler, 4:2.

31 Leclercq, *The Love of Learning*, 58–59; drawing on the writings of Jean Fécamp.

32 Carruthers, *The Craft of Thought*, 174.

33 Sandra McEntire, *The Doctrine of Compunction in Medieval England: Holy Tears*, Studies in Mediaeval Literature 8 (Lewiston, NY: The Edwin Mellen Press, 1990), 55.

Ages was at least one connecting the compunctive experience directly with a sounding, even musical, one—Augustine's *Confessions*:

Quantum flevi in hymnis et canticis tuis, suave sonantis ecclesiae tuae vocibus commotus acriter! Voces illae influebant auribus meis, et eliquabatur veritas in cor meum, et exaestuabat inde affectus pietatis, et currebant lacrimae, et bene mihi erat cum eis.

How I wept during your hymns and songs! I was deeply moved by the music of the sweet chants of your Church. The sounds flowed into my ears and the truth was distilled in my heart. This caused the feelings of devotion to overflow. Tears ran, and it was good for me to have that experience.[34]

From the meditative chorus at the start of the fascicle to William's tearful abjection at the end, the polyphony framed within may not simply be a liturgical miscellany: it sets a devotional tone, leading the reader into a state of spiritual readiness for what is to ensue.

If the onslaught of motets with vernacular, lyric texts in fascicles 2 and 3 seems jarring, fascicle 1's other crucial directive may concern precisely that juxtaposition—sacred with secular—that is a central dynamic of the genre. For William's tears are not the first we encounter in fascicle 1. The saint has a lyric counterpart. Returning now to the *In seculum* settings (items 2 and 3), we find the courtly protagonist, the lover, immersed in a form of *courtly* abjection, brought on by longing not for God but for his lady:

Je n'amerai
autre que cele, que j'ai
de fin cuer amee.
Je li ai m'amour dounee.
ne ja ne m'en quier partir
De li pour noif ne pour gelee.
Dieus, que li dirae,
la bele qui a mon cuer et m'amour?
Pour li sui en grant dolour
n'i ai repos ne nuit ne jour,
quant je remir sa bouchete,
sa tres frechete coulour.
Ses atour
n'est pas villains
mes plans est de douçour,

34 Augustine, *Confessions*, Book 9, ch. 6, ed. O'Donnell, 1:109. English translation from *St. Augustine: Confessions*, transl. Chadwick, 164.

de courtoisie et d'ounour.
Hé, douce amie!
Trop main dure vie,
en plour
tous jours
pour vous sui:
Alegiés moi mes grans dolours!

Never will I love anyone but her whom I have loved with a true heart.
To her, I have given my love and neither ice nor snow will ever make me
want to part from her. God, what will I say to her, to the fair one who
has my heart and my love? On her account do I suffer greatly—I can
rest neither night nor day when I remember her little mouth and her
color so fresh. Her character is not churlish, rather it is full of gentle-
ness, courtesy, and honor. Oh, sweet beloved! I live such a hard life:
I am always crying on account of you. Lighten my great sorrow![35]

While in one sense out of place in its liturgical surround, nearly all the lovelorn protagonist's utterances find a sacred counterpoint. His suffering in love is
as tearfully compunctive as William's, the two of them "en plour." In
such close material proximity to the *Deus in adiutorium* setting, both his declaration of sorrow and his imploring for divine intervention reiterate, in lyric
translation, the sentiments of that prayer. Thus the choir of the *Deus in adiutorium* pleads with the Lord to hasten to ease their sorrow "ad doloris remedium";
the lover, meanwhile, sleeplessly "en dolour," likewise begs for mercy: "Alegiés
moi mes grans dolours!"

Experienced in the real time of the manuscript, the lover's complaint insti-
gates a conversion across the fascicle, as lyric desire transforms into spiritual
longing, as courtliness dissolves into religiosity. We may read the courtly lover
allegorically, mimicking in the trappings of lyric yearning the desire for God
expressed in the first-person perspective of the chant text. Read in this way,
the compilatory order mimics other media where such elisions and tensions
reside: that seen in prayer books, where multiple registers of sound run concurrently; and of course the genre of the motet itself, where the juxtaposition of
secular and sacred in allegorical relationships is commonplace.

We need look only to fascicle 2 to see how easily a motet can stage such
congruence. Indeed, the teary lover and his longed-for addressee appear to
linger on, to be uncloaked, through the juxtaposition of voices, as the pose of
supplicant and Virgin. The first motet in fascicle 2, and the first item
immediately following the organum for William of Bourges, contains a torrent
of tears, split between three texts that span the sacred and the secular.

35 Texts from *The Montpellier Codex*, ed. Tischler, 4:1.

The quadruplum of *Qui la vaudroit* (220)/*Qui d'amors* (218)/*Qui longuement pour-roit* (219)/*Nostrum*[36] advocates constancy, patience, and loyalty to the lady, "the most wonderful perfumed flower among ladies" ("la dame des flours de toutes odours"), common imagery for the Virgin; the triplum resides in a more erotic sphere, where love is synonymous with pleasure, speaking of "he who desires to take pleasure in love" ("qui d'amors velt bien joir"); the motetus, ambiguously poised between sacred and secular, enacting the juxtaposition of the upper voices, reveals that pain and tears are the authentication of true love, so that "one often finds tears and weeping [in love]" ("l'en i a sovent lermes et plors"). As even this simple example suggests, embedded in the series of visual prompts, liturgical allusions, and compilatory order of fascicle 1 is not only a lesson in devotion, but also an exemplum for devotional listening to the motet itself: the fascicle is a linear, material representation of the simultaneity of the motet in performance.

The lesson does not end here, however. We shall next trace the path of the *In seculum* settings from fascicle 1 to their reappearance as closure to fascicle 4. In a recent study of Marian symbolism of spring in repertories of the late Middle Ages, David Rothenberg reveals fascinating new dimensions of the relationship of Eastertide liturgy and its vernal associations with imagery relating to the Virgin.[37] As he writes: "when either Mary or an earthly maiden was aligned with the wonders of the spring season, she absorbed the salvic potential of the Resurrection."[38] One rich environment for those alignments was in motets, and particularly those on Easter chants. Among the most popular settings to align the topos of spring with the Virgin are those on the *In seculum* melisma, derived from the gradual *Hec dies* for Easter Sunday.

The two *In seculum* settings in *Mo*, Rothenberg argues, had possible use as springtime dances. While the *In seculum* melisma was one of the most popular sources for discant clausulae, these two are part of an unusual group of five pieces, probably dating from the mid-thirteenth century, characterized by their use of hocket and rhythmic experimentation (the second *Mo* setting is a rhythmically shortened version of the first).[39] One setting in *Ba* contains the incipit "In seculum viellatoris," which points to instrumental use. That hypothesis makes sense, too, of another frequent association of the chant with Marianized *pastourelle* texts, which abound with references to dance. It is in

36 Fols. 23ᵛ–25ʳ in *Mo*. Texts from *The Montpellier Codex*, ed. Tischler, no. 19.

37 David Rothenberg, "The Marian Symbolism of Spring, ca. 1200–ca. 1500: Two Case Studies," *Journal of the American Musicological Society* 59 (2006): 319–98. See too his book, *Marian Devotion and Secular Song in Medieval and Renaissance Music* (New York: Oxford University Press, 2011).

38 Rothenberg, "The Marian Symbolism," 320.

39 For discussion of these pieces, see ibid., 337–41.

light of the common conjunction of Mary with the Easter theme that Rothenberg interprets the second appearance of the *In seculum* settings in *Mo*, textless, at the end of fascicle 4. There, they are beamed by the large historiated letter "I" in which four key scenes in the life of the Virgin are depicted: Annunciation, Nativity, Adoration of the Magi, and the Assumption (see above, figure 8.2). The reappearance, in fascicle 5, of a three-part setting (the original texted quadruplum as triplum and a new text for the motetus) completes the Marian-springtime-Easter fusion, adding a love song, directed to a lady shrouded in springtime beauty, to the lovelorn complaint of the older quadruplum voice.

Read in their fuller codicological setting, though, the appearance marks the culmination of a larger conversion across the four fascicles, which is the natural turning point in the manuscript from overtly devotional motets to those with a more secular and allegorical bent. This juncture also marks the consolidation of a Marian conversion. If the Old French texts of the original *In seculum* settings vanish on fol. 111^r, they are translated and transformed into the visual column that runs down the folio. While the addressee of the lover's desire in fascicle 1 has an implied lyric persona, she is now transfigured as none other than the Virgin. The conversion from the secular to the sacred beloved, articulated by the musical repetition, is developed also in the images adorning the opening of the intervening fascicles 2 (fols. 23^v–24^r) and 3 (fols. 63^v–64^r) (see figures 8.5 and 8.6). Narrating the transformation, they show us, in fascicle 2, a courtly (untonsured) lover kneeling before his lady; distance is narrowed in fascicle 3, and the lady's two faces—secular and sacred—are vividly juxtaposed across the space of the opening. By fascicle 4, the transformation to the sacred realm is complete (fols. 87^v–88^r, see figure 8.7). Echoing across these spaces, the *In seculum* settings articulate a musical arc, mapping a space of profound devotional intent. The object of devotion: Mary—*mater dolorosa, mediatrix*, and *redemptrix*.

THE FACES OF MARY

The elision of Marian and Eastertide topics in *Mo* taps into complex and heartfelt symbolism related to the Virgin. Above all, it emphasizes Mary's close relationship to the redemptive meaning of the crucifixion, a relationship forged through her shared physical and emotional suffering. Through a range of material and musical means, the makers of *Mo* drew attention to three related aspects of Marian devotion popular at the time of the book's creation. As *mater dolorosa*, Mary's pain at the loss of her son was understood as a form of sacrifice, establishing the mother's co-redemptive potential. In turn, the very human, relatable nature of her pain made her the ideal mediator between God and man. Let us look briefly at these key formulations of the faces of Mary.

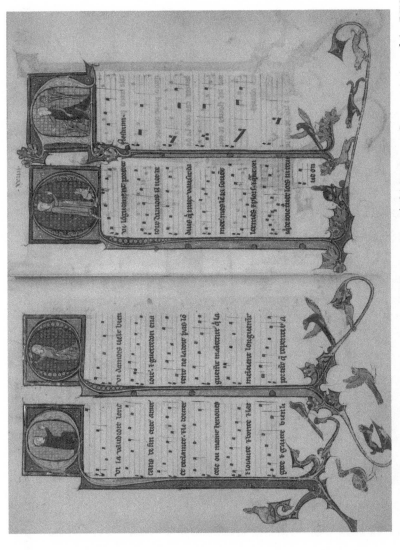

FIGURE 8.5 Montpellier, Bibliothèque Interuniversitaire, Section Médecine, H 196, fols. 23ᵛ–24ʳ. By permission of the BIU, Montpellier

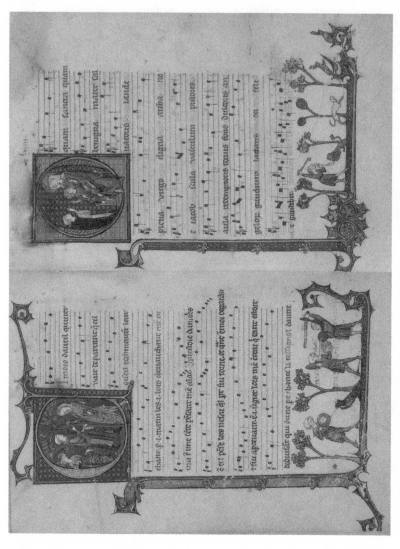

FIGURE 8.6 Montpellier, Bibliothèque Interuniversitaire, Section Médecine, H 196, fols. 63ᵛ–64ʳ. By permission of the BIU, Montpellier

Mary's salvific potency is the topic of recent work by Rachel Fulton and Miri Rubin, particularly with regard to medieval attitudes towards Mary's role in the Passion.[40] Looking to the previous century, Rachel Fulton identifies ways that writers such as Anselm of Canterbury and Bernard of Clairvaux, writing as the cult of Marian devotion began to take flight, emphasized the experience of the Virgin in the Passion. The correspondences—between mother and Savior—were especially apparent in accounts of Mary's dramatic trauma at the Cross. Consider, for instance, the writings of Arnold of Bonneval (biographer of Bernard), who examines Mary's physical pain at her son's crucifixion:

> Jesus, about to breathe his last . . . honors his mother with such great affection that he turns to her from the cross and speaks with her, intimating how great her merits and grace were with him, she whom alone he looked to at that moment, when his head wounded, his hands and feet pierced, he was about to die. For his mother's affection so moved him that at that moment there was for Christ and Mary but one will, and both offered one holocaust equally to God: she in the blood of her heart, he in the blood of his body . . . she was wounded in spirit and co-crucified in affection (*concrucifigebatur affectu*); for just as the nails and lance drove into the flesh of Christ, so she suffered in her mind with the natural compassion and anguish of maternal affection . . . For without a doubt in this sanctuary could be seen two altars, the one in the breast of Mary, the other in the body of Christ. Christ immolated his flesh, Mary her spirit.[41]

By the later thirteenth century, such theology had found its way into more immediate and widespread forms, as a familiar symbol in new affective devotional materials, none more vivid than the hymn *Stabat mater dolorosa*.[42] The theme also played out in books of hours: recall the Hours of Jeanne d'Evreux, where the double campaign of illuminations through the Hours of the Virgin unfurls the narratives of the Passion and the Virgin simultaneously. At Prime, the connections between Mary's suffering and that of her son are made graphically apparent as the scene of the Nativity is adjacent to the scourging of

40 Fulton, *From Judgment to Passion* and Rubin, *Mother of God*.

41 Arnold of Bonneval, *Libellus de laudibus b. Mariae virginis*, in *Patrologia cursus completus: series Latina*, ed. Jacques-Paul Migne, vol. 189 (Paris: Migne, 1841–64), cols. 1721, 1731, and his *Tractatus de septem verbis Domini in cruce*, ibid., col. 1694; quoting here from Rachel Fulton's translation, *From Judgment to Passion*, 425. For more on Arnold's treatment of the Virgin, see Luigi Gambero, *Mary in the Middle Ages: The Blessed Virgin Mary in the Thought of Late Latin Theologians*, transl. Thomas Buffer (San Francisco: Ignatius Press, 2000), 148–54.

42 See Rubin, *Mother of God*, 243–49.

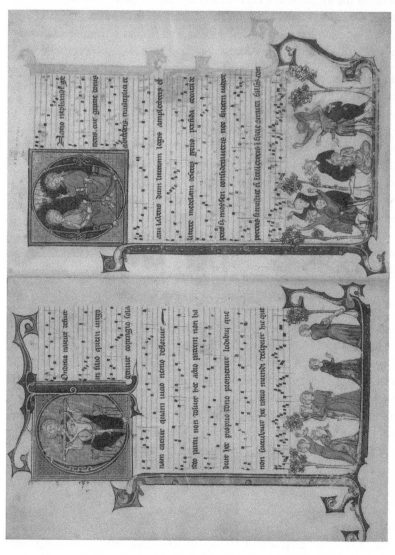

FIGURE 8.7 Montpellier, Bibliothèque Interuniversitaire, Section Médecine, H 196, fols. 87ᵛ–88ʳ. By permission of the BIU, Montpellier

Christ: the mother's agony here ironically makes up for the pangs that were remarkably absent at her son's birth. Such juxtapositions construct the Virgin as mother, but also metaphorically as the Cross bearing Christ. She was co-Redeemer of mankind, but also because of her deeply human sense of loss, the ideal mediatrix between man and God.

Mo draws upon precisely these aspects, reaching its apotheosis in the Marian/Easter finale of fascicle 4. Let us consider briefly how these themes assemble at the fascicle's end. It is fitting that the musical consummation of the first four fascicles is the motet *Salve, regina misericordie/Salve, mater misericordie/Flos filius eius* (no. 22) (with which we opened this chapter), an eloquent materialization of Mary's multiple identities. The motet is also a perfect musicalization of the Marian pageant depicted down the left-hand side of fol. 111ʳ. The motet's unusual split of the "regina" and "mater" between triplum and motetus (see above, example 8.1) forces their co-existence by sounding them simultaneously. It is a miniature theology of the Virgin, whose maternal suffering elevated her salvific status to that of Queen of Heaven. Not only that, these are the same facets emphasized in the pictorial scheme on the facing folio, which celebrate her motherhood (in the Nativity), and her royalty (in the image of the Assumption). And there is another, perhaps more consoling, message in the fascicle's conclusion. Like the *Salve regina* antiphon, the assembling of motet, *In seculum* settings, and images here constructs a message of mercy, and of hope in the face of suffering. For the Marian invocations "Salve, mater misericordie" and "Salve, regina misericordie" are answered in the Easter gradual source of the *In seculum* chant, whose full text is:

Hec dies quam fecit Dominus: exsultemus et letemur in ea.

V: Confitemini Domino, quoniam bonus: quoniam *in seculum misericordia eius.*

This day that the Lord hath made: let us exult and rejoice in it.

V: Praise the Lord, for he is good: *for his mercy endureth forever.* (My emphasis)

Mother and Son are thus co-mingled in the act of devotional listening that spans visual, aural, oral, and memorial processes. Together they offer a message of mercy and redemption to their supplicants.

If these *material* gestures of juxtaposition mirror the motet's own texture, the two working in relation to deepen devotional meaning in the music and manuscript, how do these thematics shape the listener's relationship to the main material of the first four fascicles—music's *sounding* instantiation? How, specifically, does *sound* articulate these messages? As we reach the close of this chapter, and indeed of the whole enterprise of *The Sense of Sound*, let me open *Mo* one last time, to engage in an act of listening, to a motet drawn from the devotional heart of the manuscript.

Au doz mois de mai/Crux, forma penitentie/Sustinere (example 8.3) is the sixth of eleven three-part bilingual motets that form fascicle 3.[43] Work by Dolores Pesce and Sylvia Huot on this motet and related versions has revealed intricate networks of Marian allusion.[44] The motet is built over the tenor "Sustinere" ("to bear"), a lengthy melisma from the Alleluia from the Feast of the Finding, Reception, and Exaltation of the Holy Cross; the same melody, with textual alterations, did double service for the Feast of the Assumption, where the verb "sustinere" is changed to "portare."[45] The tenor choice is apt, as it is mimetic of the texts it sings—its musical function is literally to "carry" or "sustain" the upper voices, one of which is a literary representation of the Cross. It is apt in another sense, too, for the double liturgical reference of the chant already entwines Marian and redemptive themes: the mother, like the Cross, is symbol of salvation; like the Cross, she bears Christ. As the text of the Assumption Alleluia has it: "Sweet virgin, sweet mother, bearing the sweet weight" ("Dulcis virgo, dulcis mater, dulcia ferens pondera.")

Those overlapping symbols are played out in the juxtaposition of the motetus and triplum: the motetus, a catalogue of the virtues of the Cross, calling on supplicants to carry the cross themselves in their daily lives in order to assuage their sin; the triplum, by contrast, a *pastourelle*, recording a lyric lament of Robin's Marion (who is frequently cast as the secular counterpart to the Virgin). She, too, is weighed down by the grief of her loss, indeed, her grief is reminiscent of the plea of the lover at the end of the fascicle 1 *In seculum* settings, where he implores his addressee to "lighten" his "great sorrow" ("Alegiés

---

43 *The Montpellier Codex*, ed. Tischler, no. 40. Fascicle 3 was supplemented by four additional motets in a later hand. The motet has a complex genealogy. It survives in *Mo* at fols. 74ᵛ–76ʳ; the same version is extant also in *Cl*, fol. 375ʳ⁻ᵛ. A contrafacted version appears in the *Ba*, fol. 11ʳ: there, the triplum melody appears with the Latin text, *Cruci Domini* (277). For an edition of the *Ba* version, see *Compositions of the Bamberg Manuscript: Bamberg, Staatsbibliothek, Lit. 115 (olim Ed.IV.6)*, ed. Gordon Anderson with translations of French texts by Robyn Smith, Corpus mensurabilis musicae 75 (Rome: American Institute of Musicology, 1977), no. 19. A third version appears in *MuB*, fol. Vʳ⁻ᵛ, where the triplum appears with another Latin text, *Arbor nobilis* (276), thematically similar to *Cruci Domini*.

44 For a discussion of the *Mo* version, see Huot, *Allegorical Play*, 133–37. For a discussion of the Latin version, including detailed discussion of the Christological symbolism of the texts, and of the relationship between words and music, see Pesce, "The Significance of Text," esp. 96–7 and 100. Pesce also discusses the imagery and liturgical context of the motet's tenor in "Beyond Glossing."

45 For an account of these two liturgies, and the symbolism of their connection, see Pesce, "Beyond Glossing," 39–42. See also Huot, *Allegorical Play*, 136.

EXAMPLE 8.3. (continued)

moi mes grans dolours!"). Cross and lady are once again bound together, this time, though, through the simultaneity of performance:

Triplum

Au doz mois de mai
en un vergier flori m'en entrai,
trovei pastorele desoz un glai;
ses agneaus gardoit
et si se dementoit,
si com je voz dirai :
"Robin, doz amis,
perdu voz ai;
a grant dolor de vos me departirai!"
Lés li m'assis,
si l'acolai;
esbahie la trovai
pour l'amour Robin,
qui de li s'est partis:
s'en estoit en grant esmai.

In the sweet month of May I went into a flowering orchard. I came upon a shepherdess under a bush; she was guarding her sheep and grieving, as I will tell you: "Robin, sweet lover, I have lost you; I will depart from you in great sorrow!" I sat beside her and embraced her. I found her overwhelmed by her love for Robin, who had left her: she had great sorrow.

Motetus

Crux, forma penitentie,
gratie
clavis, clava peccati, venie
vena, radix ligni iusticie,
via vite, vexillum glorie,
sponsi le[c]tus in meridie,
lux plenarie
nubem luens tristicie,
serenum conscientie:
hanc homo portet,
ha[n]c se confortet,
crucem oportet,
si vis {lucis} vere
gaudia sustinere.

Cross, form of penitence, key of grace, staff of sin, source of mercy; root of the tree of justice, path of life, banner of glory, bridegroom's nuptial couch at noon, full light, chasing away the cloud of sorrow, clearing up the conscience: let humankind carry this, let them take comfort in it. One must bear the cross if one wants the joys of true light.

Tenor

Sustinere: to bear.[46]

It is not hard to see how the devotional elisions and transfigurations performed elsewhere by the codex help to reframe meaning in the motet. The polyphonic structure enables the lady of the courtly triplum to slip easily out of her lyric mantle, and into that of the Virgin, reiterating the series of conversions witnessed in the music and images of fascicles 1 and 4. The lyric/sacred parallels, moreover, are worked out in minute detail: at the monophonic level of the triplum text imagery; and also vertically, in the alignments between motetus and triplum text that comes about through performance. Thus, embedded in the simple, *pastourelle* narrative, Marion's lovelorn story echoes key elements of the Virgin's sorrow: Marion weeps for Robin just as Mary wept for the loss of her son; Marion is found alone at the foot of a bush, in a leafy glade, the lyricized locus of Mary at the foot of the Cross.[47] Within the polyphonic matrix, the meanings are deepened still further and, as Huot argues, "invite allegorical reading."[48] Marian's sorrow in measure 23 of the triplum is pitted against the image of the Cross as comforter—"nubem luens tristicie" ("washing away the cloud of sorrow"), the juxtaposition offering, Huot suggests, comfort to grief.[49]

If the reading thus far uncovers meanings accessible through a meditative, perhaps visual, contemplation of the motet, what of meaning in *sound*? The Marian prompts within the codex may certainly provoke semantic engagement. Some of the juxtapositions and allegorical parallels are made audible through the techniques of silence and verbal counterpointing in the piece, as emphasized by Pesce in her study of the Latin double version of the motet. Silences in one or the other upper voice allow fragments of the text to be heard: thus the texture foregrounds words such as "penitentie" (m. 3) and "peccati" (m. 7), suitable themes in a meditation on the symbolism of the Cross.[50] Extending Pesce's approach, another technique for generating audible

46 Translation from Huot, *Allegorical Play*, 135, with minor adjustments.
47 For more on the Marian imagery, see Huot, *Allegorical Play*, 129–131.
48 Ibid., 133.
49 Ibid., 136.
50 Pesce, "Significance of Text," 96.

emphasis is that of textual counterpoint—where compatible words from different voices are sounded in close proximity. If these verbal moments may not be so clearly audible as words proclaimed where other voices are silent, they are, perhaps, moments of semantic congruence picked up by performers. In the bilingual version, the different texts frequently appear to brush against one another's meanings: for example, at measure 11 the French word "glai" in the triplum is followed by the beginning of "ligni" in the next beat—bringing together the locus of the orchard with the tree of the Cross; later, at measure 23, "dolor" in the triplum is followed by its Latinized counterpart "tristicie."

There is another means by which the motet generates meaningful textual simultaneity, however, one that relies on the inner voice, as it were, one produced when the outer voice engages the interior musical memory. As noted above, the Old French triplum exists in *Ba* as a Latin text, *Cruci domini*:

Cruci domini
sit cunctis horis laus parata,
per quam homini
salus est data,
que sustinuit
illum qui rapuit
omnium peccata
carne sua mortificata,
que in cruce fuit sacrificata.
Quam est ergo venerandum
ac laudandum
hoc lignum,
quod solum dignum
vite fuit vere
precium sustinere!

To the Cross of Christ may praise be given at all hours, through which salvation was given to man; which held him who snatched away the sins of all by his body given over to death, when it was sacrificed on the Cross. Therefore, how worthy of veneration and praiseworthy is this tree, which alone was worthy to sustain the price of the true life![51]

It is difficult to be certain which version came first. Gordon Anderson argued that the *Ba* Latin version was a contrafactum of the bilingual version.[52]

---

51 Text and translation from *Compositions of the Bamberg Manuscript*, lxxxiv.

52 Gordon Anderson, "Notre Dame Bilingual Motets: A Study in the History of Music c. 1215–1245," *Miscellanea musicologica Australia* 3 (1968): 50–144, at 87.

However, based on internal musical evidence, Dolores Pesce argued that the Latin triplum text fit its music perhaps better than the Old French. She pointed to the startling melodic disjunction at measures 19–22 of the triplum, where the melody arcs an entire octave, concluding at measure 21 with the strong downward articulation of a G triad. For Pesce, this was tantamount to "word-painting," as it coincided in the Latin text with the most intense textual reference, "carne sua mortificata." As she noted, though, the triplum's transmission of Marion's words "Robin, doz ami, perdu voz ai" "may offer less dramatic impact . . . but certainly they could be appropriate for the startlingly disjunct musical line found in those measures."[53] If we cannot prove chronology, by the time *Mo* came into being, it is possible, indeed likely, given the bilingual motet's transmission in the so-called "old" layer of music—that both versions had been in existence for some time, and that some or all of the makers or readers of *Mo* may have known the music in both guises. That it survives in two manuscripts that are roughly contemporaneous indicates that both versions were at some stage in circulation simultaneously.

More pertinent here than chronology is the possibility that one version prompts recollection of the other. For that musical disjunction at measures 19–22 does not merely flag significant words within the individual versions, but also summons what is absent. In rehearing the Latin text, the performer of or listener to *Mo* may have better understood the allegorical possibilities of Marion's tearful speech, her "grant dolor" at his departure. The reason for her lament is hidden in the memory—of the physical and psychic meaning of Crucifixion recalled in the words "carne sua mortificata que in cruce fuit sacrificata." It summons the most dramatic, dynamic moment of its revelation—the fraught exchange between Christ and the Virgin at the site of the Cross, where, recalling Arnold, the intensity of the Virgin's loss was equivalent to her son's bodily sacrifice—the Virgin at that moment "co-crucified," her suffering as salvific a gesture as her son's. As Rubin writes, "Mary came to encompass all the pain associated with the Crucifixion as a drama of loss and bereavement."[54]

It is also at this moment in the Passion narrative where Mary swooned, the moment where she lost the power of language, uttering just a wordless sob that was paradoxically akin to the cry of birth.[55] It is here, finally, that the motet's sounds—actual and remembered—converge and contribute to its meaning. For it, too, is rendered speechless—in the supermusical excess of language, and counterpoint of the singer's inner and outer voices. *In toto*, it is a sonorous

53 Pesce, "The Significance of Text," 100.

54 Rubin, *Mother of God*, 246.

55 See Amy Neff, "The Pain of *Compassio*: Mary's Labor at the Foot of the Cross," *Art Bulletin* 80 (1998): 254–73.

equivalent of the wordless sob, and at the same time a provocation for interpretations that are only partially decipherable in the hubbub of the musical reality, indeed which exist to be teased out in the meditative contemplation of things heard and remembered.

*

It is with this startling intersection of sonorities—a mother's swoon; the audible and inaudible voices of song; the precarious phonetics of prayer—that I now draw to a close. If the possibility that such entanglement of sound was a meaningful part of sonic experience in the Middle Ages seemed an unusual proposition at the outset of this book, I hope I have illuminated how such relationships could be productive and instructive. In tracing connections between musical sound and soundscapes as diverse as city hubbub and a madman's nonsensical ravings, I have sought to reunite sonorities that medieval writers, musicians, artists, book-makers, and listeners were evidently keen to align. In mapping the contours of these listening environments, I have hoped to create a fresh emphasis on the *sound* of the past, and to suggest ways in which its sensual impression enshrined a range of meanings—from dissent to laudation, from sublime devotion to earthly complaint.

In my story, musical sound has often featured center stage, and the motet in a lead role. The emphasis on the motet has been inevitable, given that genre's special status in the repertories of the thirteenth and early fourteenth centuries as a conduit and melting pot for so many other musical traditions. If the motet is spokesperson for its time, it is also the most distinctive audible marker of the turn to the supermusical, the most exaggerated example of a kind of music in which sound asserts itself though and beyond words. While I have chosen to trace the story of the supermusical primarily through the motet, in part to offer an alternative to the analysis-led approaches that have tended to dominate motet scholarship, I hope my book will inspire investigation of the supermusical sonority in other genres. Forms such as the *fatras, fatrasies*, and semi-lyric genres in *Fauvel* would be one place to turn, and we may trace the influence as far ahead as the polyphonic ballade and rondeau, to name just a few. Beyond the concerns of medieval musicology, consideration of this sonority may also yield interesting connections to the long-standing theme in music history of all the semantic complications music's presence brings to language, and such sound's connections to realms sublime and metaphysical.

Here, though, my context for listening into the supermusical has been tightly circumscribed by evidence connecting music to a broader investigation of sound ca. 1260–1330. And if music, by virtue of my musicological affiliation, inevitably began with star billing in the enterprise, then the other sonorities examined have together emerged as a co-star of no less expressive stature. In seeking out the audible interlocutor to the supermusical, and how other sounds could help illuminate its meanings, evidence for the profound ways in which the acoustic environment once shaped the experience of medieval communities has become ever more apparent. Here, too, I hope my book will invite future investigation, and encourage others to turn an ear to the acoustic past. For the most part, the attempt to listen back for those most capricious and accidental soundworlds is an effort that will be met only with silence. But the acoustic trace, and its configuring from sounding reality to cultural meaning, is, I have argued, accessible among the rich evidence of the arts. Here, translation of sounds regarded as ineffable or unruly (realms resistant to prescriptive notation) often resulted in representations that are audible and performable, as well as prompting of the inner ear and imagination. Through them, we may hear a range of social imperatives, and perhaps, here and there, a faint echo of something more literal. These are sonorities, I believe, worth more attention for those interested in bringing sound back into the normally quiet space of history.

We hear in them, too, a congruence with the supermusical—the evasion of sense in the madman; the cacophonous confusion of the urban *magnificat*; the poly-linguistic babble of prayer. In allowing those sonorities to brush up against one another again, I hope to have shown how music that resisted easy semantic decoding could be meaningful, resonating in sonic counterpoint with soundscapes imbued with all manner of values and warnings. But by the same token, music may perform its own benevolent act. Listening reciprocally to the evidence, the unlikely alignments between these sonorities gives to the soundscape its own new currency. It allows a new possibility: that the experience of the sounding world, in all its instantiations, real and reconfigured, could be felt to be musical.

At the opening of his book *The Audible Past*, Jonathan Sterne reminds us of the scientific fact of sound's essential bond to its listeners.[1] He writes: "human beings reside at the center of any meaningful definition of sound . . . As part of a larger physical phenomenon of vibration, sound is a product of the human senses and not a thing in the world apart from humans. Sound is a little piece of the vibrating world."[2] Sterne's point is as true for the Middle Ages as it is for our own time. Provoked by evidence of genres such as the motet, by the increasingly visible traces of musical voices with the emergence of new notational styles and compendia, and by the relentless staging of singing in the vernacular lyric, my book has drawn on the humanizing potential of theories such as Sterne's to reframe the meaning of musical sound in medieval France. In doing so, I have attended to traces of song's once vibrant presence, and, allowing for its innate connection to people and their environment, have pursued its trajectories into its "vibrating world"—the locale in which associations and meanings were forged. In this formulation, listeners are the mediators of song's sense, and, I have suggested, did not experience music in a hermeneutic vacuum, but rather in constant and productive dialogue with other forms of sonic experience.

If I have been inspired in my efforts by musicology's turn to issues of liveness, listening, and performance, then I have also been attentive to some recent reminders of our bounded relationship to certain modes of writing history. With the 2005 publication of Richard Taruskin's *New Oxford History of Music* comes the reminder that we cannot do without the story, and that the small

1 Sterne, *The Audible Past.*
2 Ibid., 11.

pockets of history turned over by the various fields within the discipline are also determined by and understood within the context of a larger historical narrative.[3] While Taruskin's multi-volume work is testimony to the necessity of the historical framework, a refreshing and provocative aspect of the *History* is the candor with which the author accounts for the historical threads he has chosen to pursue, and those he has not. History, we are reminded, is contingent, too, on the choices of the tellers. Indeed, a productive theme in reviews of this work has been the opportunity to reflect not simply of the nature of Taruskin's authorial choices, but more generally on how the discipline has come to privilege certain trajectories over others.[4]

Particularly pertinent to the broad perception of medieval music has been Taruskin's decision to trace a narrative path shaped through the dichotomies of oral and literate practices of music, forging a path for which there is material evidence (musical texts and objects), or as one review represents it, a history of music that has a history.[5] Medieval repertories figure large in that story, and in volume 1 Taruskin's "curtain goes up" on the originary moment of musical writing, with the notations of early chant repertories. This gesture also illustrates the unusual position in which medievalists find themselves in the larger scheme of the discipline with regard to the responsibilities and priorities surrounding the narrative of the Western tradition. For by default, more than by design, medieval music often serves as the discipline's scene-setter. Taruskin's history is unusual in devoting as much space as it does to a period that often figures as a brief preliminary to the "main" tradition (normally devoted to music post ca. 1700). Notwithstanding the lively and imaginative work afoot within the subfield of medieval musicology, and Taruskin's skillful representation of the period, perhaps more than any epoch of music history it suffers from a certain kind of typecasting, fulfilling a role of mysterious, half-seen premonition of the big stories to come.

That familiar caricature may in turn reflect later investments and priorities regarding the definition of music more than authentically medieval ones: often privileged, then, are the originary moments of harmony and counterpoint; notation; melody and rhythm, and so forth—attributes of a musical text, of the thing we can still see, touch, and reconstruct, and which resemble, too, things

3 Richard Taruskin, *The Oxford History of Western Music*, 6 vols. (New York and Oxford: Oxford University Press, 2005).

4 Taruskin's *History* has been widely reviewed. Two review-articles that most clearly engage with the larger issues of history-writing are Charles Rosen, "From the Troubadours to Frank Sinatra," *New York Review of Books*, Part I in 53/3 (2006), 41–45 and Part II in 53/4 (2006), 44–49, and Gary Tomlinson, "Monumental Musicology," *Journal of the Royal Musical Association* 132 (2007): 349–74.

5 Rosen, "From the Troubadours," Part I, 41.

to come. Texts all figure prominently, and necessarily, in the story, and reflect also the philological origins of the study of medieval music and the continued priority of its study, then and now deeply involved with the material trace of sound. The material text of medieval song has been foundational and essential to my own relationship to the repertories I study, and the physical stuff of music has evidently played its part in this book. However, the current climate of historiographical self-reflection invites some reconsideration, and the fruitful opportunity to wonder why we tell the stories we tell. Reflecting on medieval music in the context of the larger portrait of a Western musical tradition, it seems newly evident what aspects of the sonic past slip into the wings, making way for the more accessible and visible evidence. Lost in the muddle of material history are the things we cannot see, the things we cannot hear, and, also, things that do seem unfamiliar and disconnected from the things we have come to define as music. Evidence of emotional responses, of conceptions of musicality defined in relation to medieval linguistics and theology, of a polyphony that is driven more by improvisational prowess than fascination with counterpoint... the list could go on. Lost also in the history of song is the history of its *sound*, its audible presence often muted by the very scholarly acts that attempt to ascribe meaning to it. These are not unlike the "invisible topics" of which Barbara Rosenwein speaks in making her case for a study of the emotional Middle Ages. Perhaps the most exciting, if paradoxical, outcome of musicology's current reevaluation of both musical liveness and deadness, its presentness and its pastness, is the opportunity it affords those of us engaging medieval materials to wonder about the living, vibrant, human experience of song right back at the most distantly past frontiers of the tradition.

I bring one final voice into the fray. For beyond the bounds of musicology, many of these issues have had more widespread treatment in Edward Said's lectures and essays on ethics and democracy within the humanities as a whole. Said's call for "democratic criticism" seems especially resonant with the issues Taruskin and others raise on the nature of music history, for it likewise addresses the complex responsibilities before humanists in representing a fully democratic picture of their subjects. On the question of history, Said, too, recognizes the desire to trace traditions to be a natural scholarly impulse, and has a good deal to say about the way scholarly narrative desire can overshadow a reality more diverse and complex than history-telling allows for. Indeed, he has some hard words for those representing the earlier end of the temporal spectrum:

> It is little short of scandalous, for instance, that nearly every medieval studies program in our universities routinely overlooks one of the high points of medieval culture, namely, Muslim Andalusia before 1492, and that, as Martin Bernal has shown for ancient Greece, the complex intermingling of European, African, and Semitic cultures has been

laundered clean of that heterogeneity so troublesome to current humanism.[6]

He goes on:

> When will we stop allowing ourselves to think of humanism as a form of smugness and not as an unsettling adventure in difference, in alternative traditions, in texts that need new deciphering within a much wider context than has hitherto been given them?[7]

To be sure, decades-worth of the growth of the discipline of ethnomusicology, and in medieval studies the flourishing and well-established fields devoted to the Greek musical tradition and the influence of Arabic philosophy on Latinate music theory, are clear encouragement of a future of a more equal cultural and historical representation, while the current political and institutional tendency to foster and support interdisciplinary initiatives implies a hopeful future for a more "intermingled" vision of history. But another vital place for change can fruitfully be sought within the most familiar stories. For with every retelling, the groove of history is etched still deeper, made smoother, so the gap of history is little more than a slip of time. In the collective endeavor of "democratic criticism," it is perhaps the job of those working with the most familiar stories to take a step back, to look again, to seek the new and unfamiliar, the more innately human, in what we believe we know well. *The Sense of Sound* has endeavored to offer an alternative account, rather than a corrective, of a period of imaginative creativity in late thirteenth- and early fourteenth-century France. My account has tried to position sound, listening, and creative community at the center of the picture normally driven by analytic, textual, and philological imperatives. I have tried through those traditional practices of close engagement with the records of history, albeit records that are not normally brought into dialogue, to find a trace of sound's presence, and to scrutinize its effects. Yet, notwithstanding the serious nature of Said's manifesto, my book has also attempted to shift the perspective on the familiar in a mode that keeps central the nature of the material. For as we gather around the matter of song, it is important to keep in mind its principle of community, and song's (sound's) eternal capacity—in medieval Paris, or on Exeter High Street—to form connections between people, and to shape their (our) sense of self and other. And so at the same time that it has experimented in unsettling the familiar narratives of music history, *The Sense of Sound* has aspired, also, to the spirit of adventure.

---

6 Edward Said, *Humanism and Democratic Criticism* (New York: Columbia University Press, 2004), 54.

7 Ibid., 55.

Manuscripts

Baltimore, Walters Art Museum, W 38.
Baltimore, Walters Art Museum, W 40.
Baltimore, Walters Art Museum, W 41.
Baltimore, Walters Art Museum, W 45.
Baltimore, Walters Art Museum, W 85.
Baltimore, Walters Art Museum, W 88.
Baltimore, Walters Art Museum, W 90.
Baltimore, Walters Art Museum, W 102.
Baltimore, Walters Art Museum, W 104.
Baltimore, Walters Art Museum, W 115.
Bamberg, Staatsbibliothek, Lit. 115 (*olim* Ed.IV.6).
Cambrai, Médiathèque municipale, MS 87.
Cambridge, Fitzwilliam Museum, MS 1-2005 (the Macclesfield Psalter).
Cambridge, Trinity College Library, MS B 11. 22.
Darmstadt, Hessische Landes- und Hochschulbibliothek, 3471.
Florence, Biblioteca Medicea Laurenziana, Pluteus 29.1.
Leuven, Universiteitsbibliotheek, frag. Herenthals.
London, British Library, Add. 42130 (the Luttrell Psalter).
London, British Library, Add. 49622.
London, British Library, Harley 2900.
London, British Library, Stowe 17.
Madrid, Biblioteca Nacional, 20486.
Montpellier, Bibliothèque Interuniversitaire, Section Médecine, H 196 (Montpellier Codex).
Munich, Bayerische Staatsbibliothek, lat. 16444.
Munich, Bayerische Staatsbibliothek, lat. 5539.
New York, Metropolitan Museum, Cloisters MS 54.1.2 (the Hours of Jeanne d'Evreux).

Oxford, Bodleian Library, Douce 308.

Paris, Bibliothèque nationale de France, f. fr. 146.

Paris, Bibliothèque nationale de France, f. fr. 610.

Paris, Bibliothèque nationale de France, f. fr. 837.

Paris, Bibliothèque nationale de France, f. fr. 2090–2092.

Paris, Bibliothèque nationale de France, f. fr. 12615 (Chansonnier de Noailles).

Paris, Bibliothèque nationale de France, f. fr. 14968.

Paris, Bibliothèque nationale de France, f. fr. 24406 (Chansonnier de la Vallière).

Paris, Bibliothèque nationale de France, f. fr. 24432.

Paris, Bibliothèque nationale de France, lat. 803.

Paris, Bibliothèque nationale de France, lat. 8846.

Paris, Bibliothèque nationale de France, lat. 10484 (the Belleville Breviary).

Paris, Bibliothèque nationale de France, lat. 15139 (the St. Victor manuscript).

Paris, Bibliothèque nationale de France, nouv. ac. f. fr. 1050 (Chansonnier de Clairambault).

Paris, Bibliothèque nationale de France, nouv. ac. f. fr.13521 (La Clayette)

Philadelphia, University of Pennsylvania Rare Book and Manuscript Library, MS Codex 1063.

Turin, Biblioteca Nazionale (*olim* Reale), MS varia 42.

Vienna, Österreichische Nationalbibliothek, Codex Vindobonensis 1857 (the Hours of Mary of Burgundy).

Wolfenbüttel, Herzog August Bibliothek, 628

Wolfenbüttel, Herzog August Bibliothek, 1099 (*olim* Helmst. 1206)

Primary Texts, Musical Editions, and Facsimiles

Abbot Suger on the Abbey Church of St. Denis and its Art Treasures. Ed. and transl. Erwin Panofsky. 2nd ed. Princeton: Princeton University Press, 1979.

Acta sanctorum quotquot toto orbe coluntur, vel a catholicis scriptoribus celebrantur quæ ex latinis et græcis, aliarumque gentium antiquis monumentis collegit. Ed. Johannes Bollandus. Vol. 1. Paris: V. Palmé, 1863.

Adam de la Halle. *The Lyric Works of Adam de la Hale.* Ed. Nigel Wilkins. Corpus mensurabilis musicae 44. Dallas: American Institute of Musicology, 1967.

———. *The Lyrics and Melodies of Adam de la Halle.* Ed. and transl. Deborah Hubbard Nelson, melodies ed. Hendrik van der Werf. Garland Library of Medieval Literature 24. New York: Garland, 1985.

———. *Œuvres complètes.* Ed. and transl. Pierre-Yves Badel. Paris: Livre de Poche, 1995.

Aelred of Rievaulx. *The Mirror of Charity.* Transl. Elizabeth Connor. Cistercian Fathers Series 17. Kalamazoo: Cistercian Publications, 1990.

———. *Opera omnia.* Ed. Anselm Hoste and Charles Talbot. Corpus Christianorum, continuatio mediaevalis 1–2B, 2D. Turnhout: Brepols, 1971.

Ein altfranzösischer Motettenkodex: Faksimile-Ausgabe der HS La Clayette, Paris, Bibl. Nat. nouv. acq. fr. 13521. Ed. Friedrich Gennrich. Summa musicae medii aevi 6. Darmstadt: n.publ., 1958.

Analecta hymnica medii aevi. Ed. Clemens Blume and Guido Maria Dreves. 55 vols. Leipzig: O. R. Resiland, 1886; repr. 1961.

Ancrene Wisse: Guide for Anchoresses. Transl. Hugh White. London: Penguin, 1993.

Antiphonarium, seu, magnus liber organi de gradali et antiphonario: Color Microfiche Edition of the Manuscript Firenze, Biblioteca medicea laurenziana, Pluteus 29.1. With introduction by Edward Roesner. Munich: Helga Lengenfelder, 1996.

Arnold of Bonneval. *Libellus de laudibus b. Mariae virginis.* In *Patrologia cursus completus: series Latina.* Ed. Jacques-Paul Migne. Vol. 189, cols. 1721–34. Paris: Migne, 1841–64.

———. *Tractatus de septem verbis Domini in cruce.* In *Patrologia cursus completus: series Latina.* Ed. Jacques-Paul Migne. Vol. 189, cols. 1677–1726. Paris: Migne, 1841–64.

Augustine of Hippo. *Confessions.* Ed. with an English commentary by James O'Donnell. 3 vols. Oxford: Clarendon Press, 1992.

———. *Enarrationes in Psalmos.* Ed. Eligius Dekkers and Johannes Fraipon. Corpus Christianorum series Latina 38–40. Turnhout: Brepols, 1990.

———. *St. Augustine: Confessions.* Transl. Henry Chadwick. Oxford: Oxford University Press, 1991, repr. 1998.

———. *De doctrina Christiana.* Ed. Roger Green. Oxford Early Christian Texts. Oxford: Clarendon Press, 1995.

Bernard of Clairvaux. "De gradibus humilitatis et superbiae." In *S. Bernardi opera 3: Tractatus et opuscula.* Ed. Jean Leclercq and Henri Rochais. Rome: Editiones Cistercienses, 1963.

———. *In the Steps of Humility.* Transl. Geoffrey Webb and Adrian Walker. London: Saint Austin, 2001, originally published 1957.

Bradwardine, Thomas. "Thomas Bradwardine's *De memoria artificiali adquirenda.*" Ed. Mary Carruthers. *Journal of Medieval Latin* 2 (1992): 25–43.

Brunetto Latini. *Li Livres dou tresor.* Ed. Spurgeon Baldwin. Tempe, AZ: Arizona Center for Medieval and Renaissance Studies, 2003.

Burlesque et obscénité chez les troubadours: Pour une approche du contre-texte médiéval, ed. Pierre Bec. Paris: Stock, 1984.

Caesarius of Heisterbach. *The Dialogue on Miracles.* Transl. Henry von Essen Scott and Charles Swinton Bland. 2 vols. Broadway Medieval Library. New York: Harcourt, Brace and Company, 1929.

———. *Dialogus miraculorum.* Ed. Josef Strange. 2 vols. Cologne: J. M. Heberle, 1851.

Cantus: A Database for Latin Ecclesiastical Chant: http://cantusdatabase.org/.

Cent motets du XIIIᵉ siècle, publiés après le manuscrit Ed. IV. 6 de Bamberg. Ed. Pierre Aubry. 3 vols. Paris : Rouart, Lerolle and Geuthner, 1908; repr. New York: Broude Brothers, 1964.

CHD Center for Håndskriftstudier i Danmark: http://www.chd.dk/index.html.

Chrétien de Troyes. *Yvain: The Knight of the Lion.* Transl. Burton Raffel. New Haven: Yale University Press, 1987.

Cicero. *Ad C. Herennium de ratione dicendi (Rhetorica ad Herennium).* Ed. and transl. Harry Kaplan. London: Heinemann, 1954.

"La Clef d'amors." Ed. Auguste Doutrepont. *Bibliotheca normannica* 5: 1–152. Halle: Max Niemeyer, 1890.

Compositions of the Bamberg Manuscript: Bamberg, Staatsbibliothek, Lit. 115 (olim Ed.IV.6). Ed. Gordon Anderson with transl. of French texts by Robyn Smith. Corpus mensurabilis musicae 75. Rome: American Institute of Musicology, 1977.

Corpus antiphonalium officii. Ed. René-Jean Hesbert. 6 vols. Rerum ecclesiasticarum documenta, series maior, fontes 7–12. Rome: Herder, 1963–79.

Dante. *De vulgari eloquentia.* Ed. and transl. Steven Botterill. Cambridge Medieval Classics 5. Cambridge: Cambridge University Press, 1996.

Deux recueils de sottes chansons: Bodléienne, Douce 308 et Bibliothèque Nationale, fr. 24432. Ed. Arthur Långfors, Annales Academiae Scientiarum Fennicae, BLIII, 4. Helsinki: [s.n.], 1945.

The Earliest Motets (to circa 1270): A Complete Comparative Edition. Ed. Hans Tischler. 3 vols. New Haven: Yale University Press, 1982.

Facsimile Reproduction of the Manuscript Wolfenbüttel, 1099 (1206). Ed. Luther Dittmer. Publications of Mediaeval Music Manuscripts 2. Brooklyn: Institute of Mediaeval Music, 1960.

Festive Troped Masses from the Eleventh Century: Christmas and Easter in the Aquitaine. Ed. Charlotte Roederer. Madison: A-R Editions, 1989.

The Florence Laudario: An Edition of Florence, Biblioteca Nazionale Centrale, Rari 18. Ed. Blake Wilson, with texts ed. and transl. by Nello Barbieri. Recent Researches in the Music of the Middle Ages and Early Renaissance 29. Madison: A-R Editions, 1995.

Geoffrey of Vinsauf. *The* Poetria Nova *and its Sources in Early Rhetorical Doctrine.* Ed. and transl. Ernest Gallo. The Hague: Mouton, 1971.

Guillaume de Machaut. *Le Jugement du roy de Behaigne and Remede de Fortune.* Ed. James Wimsatt and William Kibler, music ed. Rebecca Baltzer. Athens, GA: University of Georgia Press, 1988.

Guillaume de Saint-Pathus. *Les Miracles de saint Louis.* Ed. Percival Fay. Paris: Honoré Champion, 1931.

———. *Vie de saint Louis par Guillaume de Saint-Pathus.* Ed. Henri-François Delaborde. Paris: Alphonse Picard et fils, 1899.

Guillaume de Villeneuve. "Les Crieries de Paris." In *Proverbes et dictons populaires avec les dits du mercier et des marchands, et les crieries de Paris aux xiiiᵉ et xivᵉ siècles.* Ed. Charles Crapelet, 137–46. Paris: Imprimerie de Crapelet, 1831.

Guillot de Paris. *Le Dit des rues de Paris par Guillot: Manuscrit du quatorzième siècle, vers l'an 1300.* Compiled in a collection of essays by Louis Lazare. Paris: n.d.

———. *Le Dit des rues de Paris (1300) par Guillot (de Paris) avec preface, notes et glossaire par Edgar Mareuse, suivi d'un plan de Paris sous Philippe-le-Bel.* Paris: Librairie générale, 1875.

———. *Les Rues de Paris mises en vers à la fin du 13ᵉ siècle par Guillot publiées d'après un manuscrit du 14ᵉ siècle.* Paris: Baillieu, 1866.

L'Hérésie de Fauvel. Ed. Emilie Dahnk. Leipziger Romanistiche Studien 4. Leipzig: Vogel, 1935.

The Holy Bible: The Catholic Bible, Douay–Rheims Version. New York: Benziger Brothers, 1941, first published 1750.

The Hours of Jeanne d'Evreux: A Prayer Book for a Queen. CD-Rom. With commentary by Barbara Drake Boehm. New York: Metropolitan Museum of Art, 1998.

The Hours of Jeanne d'Evreux, Queen of France, at the Cloisters, the Metropolitan Museum of Art. With an introduction by James Rorimer. New York: Metropolitan Museum of Art, 1957.

The Hours of Mary of Burgundy: Codex Vindobonensis 1857, Vienna Osterreichische Nationalbibliothek. Ed. with commentary by Erik Inglis. London: Harvey Miller, 1995.

Hugh of St. Victor. *Didascalicon, De studio legendi: A Critical Text.* Ed. Charles Buttimer. The Catholic University of America, Studies in Medieval and Renaissance Latin 10. Washington, DC: The Catholic University Press, 1939.

———. *The Didascalicon of Hugh of St. Victor: A Medieval Guide to the Arts.* Transl. Jerome Taylor. New York: Columbia University Press, 1961, repr. 1991.

In Old Paris: An Anthology of Source Descriptions, 1323–1790. Ed. and transl. Robert Berger. New York: Italica Press, 2002.

The Instructions of Saint Louis: A Critical Text. Ed. David O'Connell. Chapel Hill: University of North Carolina Press, 1979.

Introitus-Tropen I: Das Repertoire der südfranzösischen Tropare des 10. und 11. Jahrhunderts. Ed. Günther Weiß. Kassel: Bärenreiter, 1970.

Jacques de Liège. *Jacobi Leodiensis Speculum musicae.* Ed. Roger Bragard. 7 vols. Corpus scriptorum de musica 3. Rome: American Institute of Musicology, 1955–73.

Jacques de Vitry, *The* Exempla *or Illustrative Stories from the* Sermones vulgares *of Jacques de Vitry.* Ed. Thomas Crane. Nendeln: Kraus Reprint, 1967, first published 1890.

Jean de Jandun. "Tractatus de laudibus Parisius." In *Paris et ses historiens aux XIVe et XVe siècles.* Ed. Le Roux de Lincy and Lazare Maurice Tisserand, 3–79. Paris: Imprimerie Impériale, 1867.

Johannes de Grocheio. In *Die Quellenhandschriften zum Musiktraktat des Johannes de Grocheio.* Ed. Ernest Rohloff. Leipzig: Deutscher Verlag für Musik, 1972.

———. In Christopher Page. "Johannes de Grocheio on Secular Music: A Corrected Text and a New Translation." *Plainsong and Medieval Music* 2 (1993): 17–41.

John of Garland. *The Dictionarius of John de Garlande.* Transl. Barbara Blatt Rubin. Lawrence, KS: Coronado Press, 1981.

———. *The* Parisiana Poetria *of John of Garland.* Ed. and transl. Traugott Lawler. New Haven: Yale University Press, 1974.

John of Salisbury. *Metalogicon.* Ed. John Hall and Katharine Keats-Rohan. Corpus Christianorum 98. Turnhout: Brepols, 1991.

———. *The* Metalogicon *of John of Salisbury: A Twelfth-Century Defense of Verbal and Logical Arts of the* Trivium. Transl. David McGarry. Berkeley: University of California Press, 1955.

———. *Policraticus.* Ed. Katharine Keats-Rohan. Corpus Christianorum 118. Turnhout: Brepols, 1993.

John Trevisa. *The Governance of Kings and Princes: John Trevisa's Middle English Translation of the "De regimine principum" of Aegidius Romanus.* Ed. David Fowler, Charles Briggs, and Paul Remley. Garland Medieval Texts 19. New York: Garland, 1997.

Joinville. *Histoire de saint Louis,* ed. Natalis de Wailly. Société de l'histoire de France 144. Paris: Renouart, 1868.

Kempe, Margery. *The Book of Margery Kempe.* Transl. Barry Windeatt. Harmondsworth: Penguin, 1985.

Légende de Saint Denis: Reproduction des miniatures du manuscrit original présenté en 1317 au Roi Philippe le Long. Ed. Henry Martin. Paris: Honoré Champion, 1908.

The Luttrell Psalter: A Facsimile. With commentary by Michelle Brown. London: British Library, 2006.

The Macclesfield Psalter: A Complete Facsimile. Ed. Stella Panayotova. London, Thames and Hudson Ltd., 2008.

Le Magnus liber organi de Notre-Dame de Paris. Ed. under the direction of Edward Roesner. 6 vols. Monaco: Editions de l'Oiseau-Lyre, 1993–.

Maillart, Jean. *Le Roman du comte d'Anjou.* Ed. Mario Roques. Paris: Honoré Champion, 1931.

Matthew Paris. *Matthaei Parisiensis monachi Sancti Albani Chronica Majora.* Ed. Henry Luard. 7 vols. Rerum Britannicarum medii aevi scriptores 57. London: Longman and Co., 1872–83.

Die mittelalterliche Musikhandschrift, W1: Vollständige Reproduktion des "Notre Dame" Manuskripts der Herzog August Bibliothek Wolfenbüttel Cod. Guelf. 628 Helmst. Ed. Martin Staehelin. Wiesbaden: Harrassowitz, 1995.

The Monophonic Songs in the Roman de Fauvel. Ed. Hans Tischler and Samuel Rosenberg. Lincoln, NE: University of Nebraska Press, 1991.

The Montpellier Codex. Ed. Hans Tischler, with translations by Susan Stakel and Joel Relihan. 4 vols. Recent Researches in the Music of the Middle Ages and Early Renaissance, 5–8. Madison: A-R Editions, 1978–85.

Motets of the Manuscript La Clayette: Paris, Bibliothèque Nationale, nouv. acq. f. fr. 13521. Ed. Gordon Anderson with translation of French texts by Elizabeth Close. Corpus mensurabilis musicae 68. Rome: American Institute of Musicology, 1975.

Les "Motets wallons" du manuscrit de Turin: vari 42. Ed. Antoine Auda. 2 vols. Brussels: the author, 1953.

Myroure of Oure Ladye: A Devotional Treatise on Divine Service. Ed. John Blunt. Early English Text Society 19. London: Kegan Paul, Trench Kübner and Co. 1873.

Notre-Dame and Related Conductus. Ed. Gordon Anderson. 10 vols. Henryville, PA: Institute of Mediaeval Music, 1979–.

Nouveau recueil de contes, dits, fabliaux et autres pièces inédites des XIIIᵉ, XIVᵉ et XVᵉ siècles. Ed. Achille Jubinal. Geneva: Slatkin Reprints, 1975; first published 1842.

Pliny the Elder. *Natural History.* Transl. Harris Rackham, 10 vols. Loeb Classical Library. Cambridge, MA: Harvard University Press, 1939.

Polyphonies du XIIIᵉ siècle: Le manuscrit H 196 de la Faculté de Médecine de Montpellier. Ed. Yvonne Rokseth. 4 vols. Paris: Editions de l'Oiseau-Lyre, 1935–1939.

"Prions en chantant": Devotional Songs of the Trouvères. Ed. and transl. Marcia Epstein. Toronto: University of Toronto Press, 1997.

Richard of Bury. *The Love of Books: The* Philobiblon *of Richard of Bury.* Transl. Ernest Thomas. London: A. Moring, 1902. Reprinted with a foreword by Michael Maclagan, Oxford: Blackwell, 1960.

Le Roman de Fauvel. Clemencic Consort. Dir. René Clemencic. Harmonia Mundi, 1976; released on CD 1992.

Le Roman de Fauvel. Boston Camerata. Dir. Joel Cohen. Erato, 1995.

Le Roman de Fauvel in the Edition of Mesire Chaillou de Pesstain: A Reproduction in Facsimile of the Complete Manuscript, Paris, Bibliothèque Nationale, Fonds Français 146. Ed. Edward Roesner, François Avril, and Nancy Freeman Regalado. New York: Broude Brothers, 1990.

Le Roman de Fauvel par Gervais du Bus publié d'après tous les manuscrits connus. Ed. Arthur Långfors. Société des anciens textes français. Paris: Honoré Champion, 1914–19.

The Roman de Fauvel, The Works of Philippe de Vitry, French Cycles of the Ordinarium missae. Ed. Leo Schrade, Polyphonic Music of the Fourteenth Century 1, with a separate volume of commentary. Monaco: Editions de l'Oiseau-Lyre, 1956; repr. 1984 with a new introduction by Edward H. Roesner.

Le Roman de Renart. Ed. Armand Strubel with the collaboration of Robert Bellon, Dominique Boutet, and Sylvie Lefèvre. Paris: Gallimard, 1998.

Songs of the Troubadours and Trouvères: An Anthology of Poems and Melodies. Ed. Samuel Rosenberg, Margaret Switten, and Gérard Le Vot. New York: Garland Publishing, 1998.

Strunk's Source Readings in Music History, Revised Edition, vol. 2: *The Early Christian Period and the Latin Middle Ages.* Ed. James McKinnon. New York: Norton, 1998.

Die Stundenbuch der Jeanne d'Evreux/The Hours of Jeanne d'Evreux. With commentary by Barbara Drake Boehm, Abigail Quandt, and William Wixom. Lucerne: Faksimile Verlag; New York: Metropolitan Museum of Art, 1998.

The Teachings of Saint Louis: A Critical Text. Ed. David O'Connell. Chapel Hill: University of North Carolina Press, 1972.

Trouvère Lyrics with Melodies: Complete Comparative Edition. Ed. Hans Tischler. 15 vols. Corpus mensurabilis musicae 107. Neuhausen: American Institute of Musicology; Hänssler-Verlag, 1997.

Vincent of Beauvais. *De eruditione filiorum nobilium.* Ed. Arpad Steiner. Cambridge, MA: The Mediaeval Academy of America, 1938.

Women's Books of Hours in Medieval England: Selected Texts Translated from Latin, Anglo-Norman French and Middle English with Introduction and Interpretative Essay. Transl. Charity Scott-Stokes. Cambridge: D. S. Brewer, 2006.

Secondary Sources

Abbate, Carolyn. "Music—Drastic or Gnostic?" *Critical Inquiry* 30 (2004): 505–36.

Ainsworth, Peter, and Tom Scott, eds. *Regions and Landscapes: Reality and Imagination in Late Medieval and Early Modern Europe.* Oxford: Peter Lang, 1998.

Akehurst, Frank, and Judith Davis, eds. *A Handbook of the Troubadours.* Berkeley: University of California Press, 1995.

Alexander, Jonathan. "Dancing in the Streets." *Journal of the Walters Art Gallery* 54 (1996): 147–62.

Anderson, Gordon. "Notre Dame Bilingual Motets: A Study in the History of Music c. 1215–1245." *Miscellanea musicologica Australia* 3 (1968): 50–144.

——. "Notre-Dame Latin Double Motets ca. 1215–1250." *Musica Disciplina* 25 (1971): 35–92.

Angeli, Giovanna. " 'Mundus inversus' et 'perversus' de la fatrasie à la sottie." *Revue des langues romanes* 86 (1982): 117–32.

Ashley, Kathleen. "Introduction: The Moving Subjects of Processional Performance." In *Moving Subjects,* ed. Ashley and Hüsken, 7–34.

——, and Wim Hüsken, eds. *Moving Subjects: Processional Performance in the Middle Ages and Renaissance.* Amsterdam: Rodopi: 2001.

Atchison, Mary. "*Bien me sui aperceuz*: Monophonic Chanson and Motetus." *Plainsong and Medieval Music* 4 (1995): 1–12.

Attali, Jacques. *Noise: The Political Economy of Music*. Transl. Brian Massumi. Minneapolis: University of Minnesota Press, 1985.

Aubrey, Elizabeth. "Genre as a Determinant of Melody in the Songs of the Troubadours and Trouvères." In *Medieval Lyric: Genres in Historical Context*, ed. William Paden, 273–96. Urbana: University of Illinois Press, 2000.

Auslander, Philip. *Liveness: Performance in a Mediatized Culture*. London: Routledge, 1999.

——. *Performance: Critical Concepts in Literary and Cultural Studies*, 4 vols. London: Routledge, 2003.

——. *Theory for Performance Studies: A Student's Guide*. London: Routledge, 2008.

Austin, Greta. "Marvelous Peoples or Marvelous Races? Race and the Anglo-Saxon Wonders of the East." In *Marvels, Monsters, and Miracles*, ed. Jones and Sprunger, 25–51.

Backhouse, Janet. *Books of Hours*. London: British Library, 1985.

Bakhtin, Mikhail. *The Dialogic Imagination: Four Essays*. Ed. Michael Holquist, transl. Caryl Emerson and Michael Holquist. Austin: University of Texas Press, 1981, repr. 2004.

——. *Rabelais and his World*. Transl. Hélène Iswolsky. Bloomington: Indiana University Press, 1984.

Balogh, Josef. " 'Voces paginarum': Beiträge zur Geschichte des lauten Lesens und Schreibens." *Philologus* 82 (1927): 84–109 and 202–40.

Baltzer, Rebecca. "The Little Office of the Virgin and Mary's Role at Paris." In *The Divine Office*, ed. Fassler and Baltzer, 463–84.

Bardsley, Sandy. *Venomous Tongues: Speech and Gender in Late Medieval England*. The Middle Ages Series. Philadelphia: University of Pennsylvania Press, 2006.

Bec, Pierre. *La Lyrique française au Moyen Age (XIIe–XIIIe siècles): Contribution à une typologie des genres poétiques médiévaux. Études et textes*. 2 vols. Paris: A. and J. Picard, 1977–78.

Bell, Susan Groag. "Medieval Women Book Owners: Arbiters of Lay Piety and Ambassadors of Culture." *Signs* 7 (1982): 742–68.

Belmont, Nicole. "Fonction de la dérision et symbolisme du bruit dans le charivari." In *Le Charivari*, ed. Le Goff and Schmitt, 15–21.

Bennett, Adelaide. "Christ's Five Wounds in the *Aves* of the *Vita Christi* in a Book of Hours about 1300." In *Tributes in Honor of James H. Marrow*, ed. Hamburger and Korteweg, 75–84.

——. "A Thirteenth-Century French Book of Hours for Marie." *Journal of the Walters Art Gallery* 54 (1996): 21–49.

——. "A Woman's Power of Prayer Versus the Devil in a Book of Hours ca. 1300." In *Image and Belief*, ed. Hourihane, 89–108.

Benson, Marc. "L'Aspect musicale du *Jeu de la feuillée*." *Romania* 106 (1985): 510–18.

Bent, Margaret. "Polyphony of Texts and Music in the Fourteenth-Century Motet: *Tribum que non abhorruit/Quoniam secta latronum/Merito hec patimur* and its Quotations." In *Hearing the Motet*, ed. Pesce, 82–103.

——. "Reflections on Christopher Page's *Reflections*," *Early Music* 21 (1993): 625–33.

———, and Andrew Wathey, eds. *Fauvel Studies: Allegory, Chronicle, Music, and Image in Paris, Bibliothèque Nationale de France, MS Français 146*. Oxford: Clarendon Press, 1998.

Berger, Christian. "*... a li ne doit on nule autre comparer*: Musik und Text in der Motette des 13. Jahrhunderts am Beispiel der Motette *Lonc / Aucun / Annuntiantes* von Petrus de Cruce." In *Studien zur Musikgeschichte: Eine Festschrift für Ludwig Finscher*, ed. Annegrit Laubenthal, 49–57. Kassel: Bärenreiter, 1995.

Berger, Roger. "Le *Jeu de la feuillée*: Quelques notes." In *Arras au Moyen Age*, ed. Castellani and Martin, 221–27.

Berkhofer III, Robert. *Day of Reckoning: Power and Accountability in Medieval France*. Philadelphia: University of Pennsylvania Press, 2004.

Besseler, Heinrich. *Die Musik des Mittelalters und der Renaissance*. Handbuch der Musikwissenschaft. Potsdam: Akademische Verlagsgesellschaft Athenaion, 1931–34.

Bildhauer, Bettina. "Blood, Jews and Monsters in Medieval Culture." In *The Monstrous Middle Ages*, ed. Bildhauer and Mills, 75–96.

———, and Robert Mills. "Introduction: Conceptualizing the Monstrous." Ibid., 1–27.

———, eds. *The Monstrous Middle Ages*. Toronto: University of Toronto Press, 2003.

Binski, Paul. *Becket's Crown: Art and Imagination in Gothic England, 1170–1300*. New Haven: Yale University Press, 2004.

———. "Reflections on the 'Wonderful Height and Size' of Gothic Great Churches." In *Magnificence and the Sublime: The Aesthetics of Grandeur in Medieval Art, Architecture, Literature and Music*, ed. Stephen Jaeger, 129–56. New York: Palgrave Macmillan, 2010.

Bloch, R. Howard. *Etymologies and Genealogies: A Literary Anthropology of the French Middle Ages*. Chicago: University of Chicago Press, 1983.

Block, Elaine, and Kenneth Varty. "Choir-Stall Carvings of Reynard and Other Foxes." In *Reynard the Fox: Social Engagement and Cultural Metamorphoses*, ed. Varty, 125–62.

Bolduc, Michelle. "Fauvel's Wayward Wives." *Medievalia e humanistica* 32 (2007): 43–62.

Boogaard, Nico van den. *Rondeaux et refrains du XIIᵉ siècle au début du XIVᵉ: Collationnement, introduction et notes*. Bibliothèque française et romane, D.3. Paris: Klincksieck, 1969.

Bornstein, Diane. *The Lady in the Tower: Medieval Courtesy Literature for Women*. Hamden, CT: Archon Books, 1983.

Bowles, Edmund. "Musical Instruments in Civic Processions during the Middle Ages." *Acta Musicologica* 33 (1961): 147–61.

———. "Musical Instruments in the Medieval Corpus Christi Procession." *Journal of the American Musicological Society* 17 (1964): 251–60.

Boynton, Susan. "Prayer as Liturgical Performance in Eleventh- and Twelfth-Century Monastic Psalters." *Speculum* 82 (2007): 896–929.

Branner, Robert. *Manuscript Painting in Paris during the Reign of Saint Louis: A Study of Styles*. Berkeley: University of California Press, 1977.

Brantley, Jessica. *Reading in the Wilderness: Private Devotion and Public Performance in Late Medieval England*. Chicago: University of Chicago Press, 2007.

Briggs, Charles. *Giles of Rome's* De regimine principum: *Reading and Writing Politics at Court and University, c. 1275–c. 1525*. Cambridge Studies in Palaeography and Codicology 5. Cambridge: Cambridge University Press, 1999.

Brown, Elizabeth A. R., "The Chapels and Cult of Saint Louis at Saint–Denis."
Mediaevalia 10 (1988): 279–331.

——, and Nancy Freeman Regalado. " 'Universitas et communitas': The Parade of the
Parisians at the Pentecost Feast of 1313." In *Moving Subjects*, ed. Ashley and Hüsken,
117–54.

Brown, Michelle. *The World of the Luttrell Psalter.* London: British Library, 2006.

Brownlee, Kevin. "Authorial Self-Representation and Literary Models in the *Roman de
Fauvel.*" In *Fauvel Studies*, ed. Bent and Wathey, 73–103.

Bruce, Scott. *Silence and Sign Language in Medieval Monasticism: The Cluniac Tradition c.
900–1200.* Cambridge: Cambridge University Press, 2007.

Bryant, Lawrence. "The Medieval Entry Ceremony at Paris." In *Coronations: Medieval and
Early Modern Monarchic Ritual*, ed. János Bak, 88–118. Berkeley: University of
California Press, 1990.

Bull, Michael, and Les Back, eds. *The Auditory Culture Reader.* Oxford: Berg, 2003.

Burnett, Charles. "Perceiving Sound in the Middle Ages." In *Hearing History*, ed. Smith,
69–84.

——. "Sound and its Perception in the Middle Ages." In *The Second Sense: Studies in Hearing
and Musical Judgement from Antiquity to the Seventeenth Century*, ed. Charles Burnett,
Michael Fend, and Penelope Gouk, 43–69. London: The Warburg Institute, 1991.

Butterfield, Ardis. "*Enté*: A Survey and Reassessment of the Term in Thirteenth- and
Fourteenth-Century Music and Poetry," *Early Music History* 22 (2003): 67–101.

——. "The Language of Medieval Music: Two Thirteenth-Century Motets." *Plainsong
and Medieval Music* 2 (1993): 1–16.

——. *Poetry and Music in Medieval France: From Jean Renart to Guillaume de Machaut.*
Cambridge: Cambridge University Press, 2002.

——. "The Refrain and the Transformation of Genre in the *Roman de Fauvel.*" In *Fauvel
Studies*, ed. Bent and Wathey, 105–59.

Bynum, Caroline Walker. *Holy Feast and Holy Fast: The Religious Significance of Food to
Medieval Women.* Berkeley: University of California Press, 1987.

——. *Metamorphosis and Identity.* New York: Zone Books, 2001.

——. *Resurrection of the Body in Western Christianity, 200–1336.* New York: Columbia
University Press, 1995.

——. *Wonderful Blood: Theology and Practice in Late Medieval Northern Germany and
Beyond.* Philadelphia: University of Pennsylvania Press, 2007.

Camille, Michael. "Hybridity, Monstrosity, and Bestiality in the *Roman de Fauvel*," in
Fauvel Studies, ed. Bent and Wathey, 161–74.

——. *Image on the Edge: The Margins of Medieval Art.* London: Reaktion Books, 1992.

——. *Mirror in Parchment: The Luttrell Psalter and the Making of Medieval England.*
London: Reaktion Books, 1998.

——. "Seeing and Reading: Some Visual Implications of Medieval Literacy and
Illiteracy." *Art History* 8 (1985): 26–49.

Cannon, Christopher. "The Owl and the Nightingale and the Meaning of Life." *Journal
of Medieval and Early Modern Studies* 34 (2004): 251–78.

Carruthers, Mary. *The Book of Memory: A Study in Memory in Medieval Culture.* Cambridge
Studies in Medieval Literature 10. Cambridge: Cambridge University Press, 1990,
repr. 1996.

———. *The Craft of Thought: Meditation, Rhetoric, and the Making of Images, 400–1200*. Cambridge Studies in Medieval Literature 34. Cambridge: Cambridge University Press, 1998.

———. "Reading with Attitude, Remembering the Book." In *The Book and the Body*, ed. Dolores Warwick Frese and Katherine O'Brien O'Keeffe, 1–77. Notre Dame: University of Notre Dame Press, 1997.

———. "Sweetness." *Speculum* 81 (2006): 999–1013.

———, and Jan Ziolkowski, eds. *The Medieval Craft of Memory: An Anthology of Texts and Pictures*. Philadelphia: University of Pennsylvania Press, 2002.

Cassidy, Brendan, and Rosemary Muir Wright, eds. *Studies in the Illustration of the Psalter*. Stamford: Shaun Tyas, 2000.

Castellani, Marie-Madeleine, and Jean-Pierre Martin, eds. *Arras au Moyen Age: Histoire et littérature*. Arras: Artois Presses Université, 1994.

Caviness, Madeline. "Patron or Matron? A Capetian Bride and a *Vade mecum* for her Marriage Bed." *Speculum* 68 (1993): 333–62.

Cawsey, Kathy. "Tutivillus and the 'Kyrkchaterars': Strategies of Control in the Middle Ages." *Studies in Philology* 102 (2005): 434–51.

Cazelles, Raymond. *Nouvelle histoire de Paris: De la fin du règne de Philippe Auguste à la mort de Charles V, 1223–1380*. Paris: Hachette, 1972, repr. 1994.

Certeau, Michel de. "Walking in the City." In *The Practice of Everyday Life*, transl. Steven Rendall, 91–114. Berkeley: University of California Press, 1984.

Cheyette, Fredric. *Ermengard of Narbonne and the World of the Troubadours*. Ithaca: Cornell University Press, 2001.

———. "Women, Poets, and Politics in Occitania." In *Aristocratic Women in Medieval France*, ed. Theodore Evergates, 138–77. Philadelphia: University of Pennsylvania Press, 1999.

Chilcoat, Michelle. " 'Walking Rhetorics': Articulations of Daily Life in Paris in Some Thirteenth-Century Old French *dits*." http://www.georgetown.edu/labyrinth/e–center/chilcoat.html.

Clanchy, Michael. *From Memory to Written Record: England 1066–1307*. 2nd ed. Oxford: Blackwell, 1993.

———. "Images of Ladies with Prayer Books: What Do They Signify?" In *The Church and the Book: Papers Read at the 2000 Summer Meeting and the 2001 Winter Meeting of the Ecclesiastical History Society*, ed. Robert Swanson, 106–22. Studies in Church History 38. Woodbridge: Boydell and Brewer for the Ecclesiastical History Society, 2004.

Clark, Suzannah. " 'S'en dirai chançonete': Hearing Text and Music in a Medieval Motet." *Plainsong and Medieval Music* 16 (2007): 31–59.

Clifford, James, and George Marcus, eds. *Writing Culture: The Poetics and Politics of Ethnography*. Berkeley: University of California Press, 1986.

Cohen, Jeffrey. *Of Giants: Sex, Monsters, and the Middle Ages*. Medieval Cultures 17. Minneapolis: University of Minnesota Press, 1999.

Colton, Lisa. "The Articulation of Virginity in the Medieval *Chanson de nonne*." *Journal of the Royal Musical Association* 133 (2008): 159–88.

Corbin, Alain. *Village Bells: Sound and Meaning in the Nineteenth-Century French Countryside*. Transl. Martin Thom. New York: Columbia University Press, 1998.

Cottier, Jean-François, ed. *La Prière en latin de l'antiquité au XVIᵉ siècle: Formes, évolutions, significations*. Collections d'études médiévales de Nice 6. Turnhout: Brepols, 2006.

Coulet, Noël. "Processions, espace urbain, communauté civique." In *Liturgie et musique (IXᵉ–XIVᵉ siècles)*, ed. Marie-Humbert Vicaire, 381–97. Cahiers de Fanjeaux 17. Toulouse: Privat, 1982.

Crane, Susan. *The Performance of Self: Ritual, Clothing, and Identity During the Hundred Years War*. Philadelphia: University of Pennsylvania Press, 2002.

Crossley, Paul. "The Man from Inner Space: Architecture and Meditation in the Choir of St Laurence in Nuremberg." In *Medieval Art – Recent Perspectives: A Memorial Tribute to C. R. Dodwell*, ed. Gale Owen Crocker and Timothy Graham, 165–82. Manchester: St. Martin's Press, 1998.

Davis, Alva, and Raven McDavid. " 'Shivaree': An Example of Cultural Diffusion." *American Speech* 24 (1949): 249–55.

Davis, Michael. "*Desespoir, Esperance*, and *Douce France*: The New Palace, Paris, and the Royal State." In *Fauvel Studies*, Bent and Wathey, 187–213.

Davis, Natalie Zemon. *Society and Culture in Early Modern France*. Oxford: Polity Press, 1987.

Delisle, Léopold. "Durand de Champagne," *Histoire littéraire de la France*, 30: 302–33. Paris: Imprimerie nationale, 1888.

———. *Recherches sur la librairie de Charles V*. 3 vols. Paris: Honoré Champion, 1907.

Dessì, Rosa Maria. "Prière, chant et prédication: A propos de la *lauda*. De François d'Assise à Machiavel." In *La Prière en latin*, ed. Cottier, 245–72.

Dillon, Emma. *Medieval Music-Making and the* Roman de Fauvel. Cambridge: Cambridge University Press, 2002.

Doob, Penelope. *Nebuchadnezzar's Children: Conventions of Madness in Middle English Literature*. New Haven: Yale University Press, 1974.

Douët-d'Arcq, Louis. *Nouveau recueil de comptes de l'argenterie des rois de France* Paris: Librairie Renouard, 1874.

Dragonetti, Roger. "Le Dervé-roi dans le *Jeu de la feuillée* d'Adam de la Halle." *Revue des langues romanes* 95 (1991): 115–35.

———. *La Technique poétique des trouvères dans la chanson courtoise: Contribution à l'étude de la rhétorique médiévale*. Bruges: De Tempel, 1960.

Driesen, Otto. *Der Ursprung des Harlekin: Ein kulturgeschichtliches Problem*. Hildesheim: Gertsenberg, 1904, repr. 1977.

Dubois, Claude-Marel. "La Paramusique dans le charivari français contemporain." In *Le Charivari*, ed. Le Goff and Schmitt, 46–53.

DuBruck, Edelgard. "The 'Marvelous' Madman of the *Jeu de la feuillée*." *Neophilologus* 58 (1974): 180–86.

Duffy, Eamon. *Marking the Hours: English People and their Prayers, 1240–1570*. New Haven: Yale University Press, 2006.

———. *The Stripping of the Altars: Traditional Religion in England c.1400–c.1580*. New Haven: Yale University Press, 1992.

Dufournet, Jean. "Adam de la Halle et le *Jeu de la feuillée*." *Romania* 86 (1965): 199–245.

———. "Le *Jeu de la feuillée* et la fête carnavalesque." *L'information littéraire* 1 (1977): 7–13.

———. "Remarques sur la branche XII du *Roman de Renart*, les vêpres de Tibert." In *Homenaje a Alvaro Galmés de Fuentes*, 1: 431–46. Oviedo: Universidad de Oviedo, 1985.

———. *Sur le* Jeu de la feuillée: *Études complémentaires*. Paris: Société d'édition d'enseignement supérieur, 1977.

———. "Sur quatre mots du *Jeu de la feuillée*." *Romania* 94 (1973): 103–16.

Duggan, Anne, ed. *Queens and Queenship in Medieval Europe: Proceedings of a Conference Held at King's College London, April 1995*. Woodbridge: Boydell & Brewer, 1997.

Edson, Evelyn. *Mapping Time and Space: How Medieval Map-Makers Viewed their World*. London: British Library, 1997.

Egbert, Donald Drew. "The Grey-Fitzpayn Hours: An English Gothic Manuscript of the Early Fourteenth Century Now in the Fitzwilliam Museum, Cambridge, MS. 242." *Art Bulletin* 18 (1936): 527–39.

Egbert, Virginia Wylie. *On the Bridges of Mediaeval Paris: A Record of Early Fourteenth-Century Life*. Princeton: Princeton University Press, 1974.

Elwert, Wilhelm Theodor. *Traité de versification française des origines à nos jours*. Paris: Editions Klincksieck, 1965.

Erlmann, Veit. "But What of the Ethnographic Ear? Anthropology, Sound, and the Senses." In *Hearing Cultures*, ed. Erlmann, 1–20.

———, ed. *Hearing Cultures: Essays on Sound, Listening and Modernity*. Oxford: Berg, 2004.

Evans, Beverly Jean. "The Textual Function of the Refrain Cento in a Thirteenth-Century French Motet." *Music & Letters* 46 (1993): 295–305.

Everist, Mark. *French Motets in the Thirteenth Century: Music, Poetry and Genre*. Cambridge: Cambridge University Press, 1994.

———. "Motets, French Tenors, and the Polyphonic Chanson ca. 1300." *Journal of Musicology* 24 (2007): 365–406.

———. *Polyphonic Music in Thirteenth-Century France: Aspects of Sources and Distribution*. New York: Garland, 1989.

Farmer, Sharon. *Surviving Poverty in Medieval Paris: Gender, Ideology, and the Lives of the Poor*. Ithaca: Cornell University Press, 2002.

Fassler, Margot, and Rebecca Baltzer, eds. *The Divine Office in the Latin Middle Ages: Methodology and Source Studies, Regional Developments, Hagiography. Written in Honor of Professor Ruth Steiner*. New York and Oxford: Oxford University Press, 2000.

Favier, Jean. *Paris: Deux mille ans d'histoire*. Paris: Fayard, 1997.

Feld, Steven. "Waterfalls of Song: An Acoustemology of Place Resounding in Bosavi, Papua New Guinea." In *Senses of Place*, ed. Feld and Bassa, 91–135.

———, and Keith Basso, eds. *Senses of Place*. Santa Fe, NM: School of American Research Press, 1996.

Fiero, Gloria. "Prayer Imagery in a 14th-Century Franciscan Missal (Oxford, Bodleian Library, MS Douce 313)." *Franciscan Studies* 42 (1982): 21–47.

Flannigan, C. Clifford. "The Moving Subject: Medieval Liturgical Processions from a Semiotic and Cultural Perspective." In *Moving Subjects*, ed. Ashley and Hüsken, 35–51.

Foley, Edward. "Franciscan Liturgical Prayer." In *Franciscans at Prayer*, ed. Johnson, 385–412.

Fortier-Beaulieu, Paul. "Le Charivari dans le *Roman de Fauvel.*" *Revue de folklore français* 11 (1940): 1–16.

Foucault, Michel. *Madness and Civilization: A History of Insanity in the Age of Reason.* Transl. Richard Howard. London: Routledge, 2001; first published 1961.

Fournel, Victor. *Les Cris de Paris: Types et physiognomies d'autrefois.* Paris: Firmin-Didot, 1887.

Freedman, Paul, "The Medieval Other: The Middle Ages as Other." In *Marvels, Monsters, and Miracles*, ed. Jones and Sprunger, 1–24.

Freitas, Roger. "Towards a Verdian Ideal of Singing: Emancipation from Modern Orthodoxy." *Journal of the Royal Musical Association* 127 (2002): 226–57.

Friedman, John Block. *The Monstrous Races in Medieval Art and Thought.* Cambridge, MA: Harvard University Press, 1981.

Frugoni, Chiara. *A Day in a Medieval City.* Transl. William McCuaig with an introduction by Arsenio Frugoni. Chicago: University of Chicago Press, 2005.

Frye, Northrop. *The Great Code: The Bible and Literature.* New York: Harcourt Brace Jovanovich, 1982.

Fulton, Rachel. *From Judgment to Passion: Devotion to Christ and the Virgin Mary, 800–1200.* New York: Columbia University Press, 2002.

———. "Praying with Anselm at Admont: A Meditation of Practice." *Speculum* 81 (2006): 700–733.

———. " 'Taste and See that the Lord is Sweet' (Ps. 33:9): The Flavor of God in the Monastic West." *Journal of Religion* 86 (2006): 169–204.

———, and Bruce Holsinger, eds. *History in the Comic Mode: Medieval Communities and the Matter of Person.* New York: Columbia University Press, 2007.

Gally, Michèle. "Poésie en jeu: Des jeux-partis aux fatrasies." In *Arras au Moyen Age*, ed. Castellani and Martin, 71–80.

Gambero, Luigi. *Mary in the Middle Ages: The Blessed Virgin Mary in the Thought of Late Latin Theologians.* Transl. Thomas Buffer. San Francisco: Ignatius Press, 2000.

Gaposchkin, M. Cecilia. "Philip the Fair, the Dominicans, and the Liturgical Office for Louis IX: New Perspectives on *Ludovicus decus regnantium.*" *Plainsong and Medieval Music* 13 (2004): 33–61.

Gaunt, Simon. "Orality and Writing: The Text of the Troubadour Poem." In *The Troubadours*, ed. Gaunt and Kay, 228–45.

———, and Sarah Kay, eds. *The Troubadours: An Introduction.* Cambridge: Cambridge University Press, 1999.

———, eds. *The Cambridge Companion to Medieval French Literature.* Cambridge: Cambridge University Press, 2008.

Gauvard, Claude, and Altan Gokalp. "Les Conduites de bruit et leur signification à la fin du Moyen Age: Le charivari." *Annales: Economies, Sociétés, Civilisations* 29 (1974): 693–704.

Gehl, Paul. "Competens silentium: Varieties of Monastic Silence in the Medieval West." *Viator* 18 (1987): 125–60.

———. "Mystical Language Models in Monastic Educational Psychology." *Journal of Medieval and Renaissance Studies* 14 (1984): 219–43.

Geremek, Bronisław. *The Margins of Medieval Society in Late Medieval Paris.* Transl. Jean Birrell. Cambridge: Cambridge University Press, 1987.

Gies, Joseph, and Frances Gies. *Life in a Medieval City*. New York: Harper Row, 1981.

Gifford, Douglas. "Iconographical Notes towards a Definition of the Medieval Fool." In *The Fool and the Trickster*, ed. Williams, 18–35.

Gilman, Sander. *Disease and Representation: Images of Illness from Madness to AIDS*. Ithaca: Cornell University Press, 1988.

——. *Seeing the Insane*. New York: John Wiley and Sons, 1982.

Goldthwaite, Richard. *Wealth and the Demand for Art in Italy, 1300–1600*. Baltimore: Johns Hopkins University Press, 1993.

Gouk, Penelope. *Music, Science, and Natural Magic in Seventeenth-Century England*. New Haven: Yale University Press, 1999.

——, and Helen Hills, eds. *Representing Emotions: New Connections in the Histories of Art, Music and Medicine*. Aldershot: Ashgate, 2005.

Gould, Karen. *The Psalter and Hours of Yolande of Soissons*. Cambridge, MA: Mediaeval Academy of America, 1978.

Grewe, Cordula. *Painting the Sacred in the Age of Romanticism*. Farnham: Ashgate, 2009.

Gross, Angelika. "La Représentation de *l'insipiens* et la catégorisation esthétique et morale des parties corporelles dans le *Buch Der Natur* de Konrad von Megenberg." In *Le beau et le laid au Moyen Age*, Sénéfiance 43, 187–211. Aix-en-Provence: Centre universitaire d'études et de recherches médiévales d'Aix, 2000.

Guest, Gerald. "A Discourse on the Poor: The Hours of Jeanne d'Evreux." *Viator* 26 (1995): 153–80.

Gumbrecht, Hans Ulrich. *Production of Presence: What Meaning Cannot Convey*. Stanford: Stanford University Press, 2004.

Günther, Ursula. "Les Versions polyphoniques du *Deus in adiutorium*." *Cahiers de civilization médiévale* 31 (1988): 111–22.

Hahn, Cynthia. "The Voices of the Saints: Speaking Reliquaries." *Gesta* 36 (1997): 20–31.

Hamburger, Jeffrey, and Anne Korteweg, eds. *Tributes in Honor of James H. Marrow: Studies in Painting and Manuscript Illumination of the Late Middle Ages and Northern Renaissance*. Turnhout: Harvey Miller Publishers, 2006.

Hamesse, Jacqueline. "The Scholastic Model of Reading." In *A History of Reading in the West*, ed. Guglielmo Cavallo and Roger Chartier, transl. Lydia Cochrane, 103–19. Oxford: Polity, 1999.

Hamilton, Sarah, and Andrew Spicer. "Defining the Holy: The Delineation of Sacred Space." In *Defining the Holy*, ed. Spicer and Hamilton, 1–23.

Harper, Stephen. " 'So Euyl to Rewlyn': Madness and Authority in *The Book of Margery Kempe*." *Neuphilologische Mitteilungen* 98 (1997): 53–61.

Harvey, Paul. Mappa mundi: *The Hereford World Map*. Toronto: University of Toronto Press, 1996.

Harvey, Ruth. "Rhymes and 'Rusty Words' in Marcabru's Songs." *French Studies* 56 (2002): 1–14.

Hawkins, Anne Hunsaker. "Yvain's Madness." *Philological Quarterly* 71 (1992): 377–97.

Henriet, Patrick. *La Parole et la prière au Moyen Age: Le verbe efficace dans l'hagiographie monastique des XIᵉ et XIIᵉ siècles*. Brussels: De Boeck and Larcier, 2000.

—— "Prière, expérience et fonction au Moyen Age: Remarques introductives." In *La Prière en latin*, ed. Cottier, 197–207.

Henson, Karen. "Verdi, Victor Maurel and *Fin-de-siècle* Operatic Performance." *Cambridge Opera Journal* 19 (2007): 59–84.

Hentsch, Alice. *De la littérature didactique du Moyen Age s'adressant spécialement aux femmes.* Cahors: Conselant, 1903.

Hoekstra, Gerald. "The French Motet as Trope: Multiple Levels of Meaning in *Quant florist la violete/El mois de mai/Et gaudebit.*" *Speculum* 73 (1998): 32–57.

Hoepffner, Ernest. "Chansons françaises du XIIIᵉ siècle (*Ay Dex! ou porrey jen trouver*)." *Romania* 47 (1921): 367–80.

Holbert, Kelly. "The Vindication of a Controversial Early Thirteenth-Century *Vierge Ouvrante* in the Walters Art Gallery." *Journal of the Walters Art Gallery* 55–56 (1997–98): 101–21.

Holladay, Joan. "The Education of Jeanne d'Evreux: Personal Piety and Dynastic Salvation in her Book of Hours at the Cloisters." *Art History* 17 (1994): 585–611.

——. "Fourteenth-Century French Queens as Collectors and Readers of Books: Jeanne d'Evreux and her Contemporaries." *Journal of Medieval History* 32 (2006): 69–100.

Holmes, Olivia. *Assembling the Lyric Self: Authorship from Troubadour Song to Italian Poetry Books.* Minneapolis: University of Minnesota Press, 2000.

Holsinger, Bruce. *Music, Body, and Desire in Medieval Culture: Hildegard of Bingen to Chaucer.* Stanford: Stanford University Press, 2001.

Holtz, Louis. *Donat et la tradition de l'enseignement grammatical: Étude sur l'Ars Donati et sa diffusion (IVᵉ–IXᵉ siècle) et édition critique.* Paris: CNRS, 1981.

Horst, Koert van der, William Noel, and Wilhelmina Wüstefeld, eds. *The Utrecht Psalter in Medieval Art: Picturing the Psalms of David.* Tuurdijk: Hes Publishers, 1996.

Hourihane, Colum, ed. *Image and Belief: Studies in Celebration of the Eightieth Anniversary of the Index of Christian Art.* Princeton: Department of Art and Archaeology, Princeton University in Association with Princeton University Press, 1999.

Hughes, Andrew. *Medieval Manuscripts for the Mass and Offices: A Guide to their Use and Terminology.* Toronto: University of Toronto Press, 1982.

Huizinga, Johan. *The Autumn of the Middle Ages.* Transl. Rodney Payton and Ulrich Mammitzsch. Chicago: University of Chicago Press, 1996.

Huot, Sylvia. *Allegorical Play in the Old French Motet: The Sacred and the Profane in Thirteenth-Century Polyphony.* Stanford: Stanford University Press, 1997.

——. *From Song to Book: The Poetics of Writing in Old French Lyric and Lyrical Narrative Poetry.* Ithaca: Cornell University Press, 1987.

——. *Madness in Medieval French Literature: Identities Lost and Found.* Oxford: Oxford University Press, 2003.

——. "Others and Alterity." In *Cambridge Companion to Medieval French Literature,* ed. Gaunt and Kay, 239–50.

——. "Transformations of Lyric Voice in the Songs, Motets, and Plays of Adam de la Halle." *Romanic Review* 78 (1987): 148–64.

Hyde, John. "Medieval Descriptions of Cities." *Bulletin of the John Ryland Library* 48 (1966): 308–40.

Inglis, Erik. "Gothic Architecture and a Scholastic: Jean de Jandun's *Tractatus de laudibus Parisius* (1323)." *Gesta* 42 (2003): 63–85.

Ingram, Martin. "Ridings, Rough Music and Mocking Rhymes in Early Modern England." In *Popular Culture in Seventeenth-Century England*, ed. Barry Reay, 166–97. New York: St. Martin's Press, 1985.

Jacobsthal, Gustav. "Die Texte der Liederhandschrift von Montpellier H. 196." *Zeitschrift für romanische Philologie* 3 (1879): 526–56, and 4 (1880): 278–317.

Jackson, Stanley. "Unusual Mental States in Medieval Europe I. Medical Syndromes of Mental Disorder: 400–1100 A.D." *Journal of the History of Medicine and Allied Sciences* 27 (1972): 262–97.

Jaeger, Stephen. *The Envy of Angels: Cathedral Schools and Social Ideals in Medieval Europe, 950–1200*. Philadelphia: University of Pennsylvania Press, 1994.

——. *The Origins of Courtliness: Civilizing Trends and the Formation of Courtly Ideals, 939–1210*. Philadelphia: University of Pennsylvania Press, 1985.

——, ed. *Magnificence and the Sublime: The Aesthetics of Grandeur in Medieval Art, Architecture, Literature and Music*. New York: Palgrave Macmillan, 2010.

Jeanroy, Alfred. "Trois dits d'amour du XIIIe siècle." *Romania* 22 (1893): 45–70.

Jennings, Margaret. "Tutivillus: The Literary Career of the Recording Demon." *Studies in Philology: Texts and Studies* 74 (1977): 1–93.

Johnson, Timothy, ed. *Franciscans at Prayer*. The Medieval Franciscans 4. Leiden: Brill, 2007.

Jones, Timothy, and David Sprunger, eds. *Marvels, Monsters, and Miracles: Studies in the Medieval and Early Modern Imaginations*, Studies in Medieval Culture 42. Kalamazoo: Medieval Institute Publications, 2002.

Jordan, Mark. "Homosexuality, *Luxuria*, and Textual Abuse." In *Constructing Medieval Sexuality*, ed. Karma Lochrie, Peggy McCracken, and James Schultz, 24–39. Medieval Cultures 11. Minneapolis: University of Minnesota Press, 1997.

Karnoouh, Claude. "Le Charivari ou l'hypothèse de la monogamie." In *Le Charivari*, ed. Le Goff and Schmitt, 33–43.

Kastner, Georges. *Les Voix de Paris: Essai d'une histoire littéraire et musicale des cris populaires de la capitale depuis le Moyen Age jusqu'à nos jours*. Paris: Brandus, 1857.

Kay, Sarah. "Desire and Subjectivity." In *The Troubadours: An Introduction*, ed. Gaunt and Kay, 212–27.

——. "Occitan Grammar as a Science of Endings." *New Medieval Literatures* 11 (2009): 39–61.

——. *The Place of Thought: The Complexity of One in Late Medieval French Didactic Poetry*. Philadelphia: University of Pennsylvania Press, 2007.

——. "Rhetoric and Subjectivity in Troubadour Poetry." In *The Troubadours and the Epic: Essays in Memory of W. Mary Hackett*, ed. Linda Patterson and Simon Gaunt, 102–42. Warwick: University of Warwick Press, 1987.

——. *Subjectivity in Troubadour Poetry*. Cambridge: Cambridge University Press, 1990.

Kelly, Louis. *The Mirror of Grammar: Theology, Philosophy, and the* Modistae. Amsterdam: J. Benjamins, 2002.

Kidwell, Susan. "Elaboration through Exhortation: Troping Motets for the Common of Martyrs." *Plainsong and Medieval Music* 5 (1996): 153–73.

Kivy, Peter. *New Essays on Musical Understanding*. New York and Oxford: Oxford University Press, 2001.

Knuuttila, Simo. *Emotions in Ancient and Medieval Philosophy*. Oxford: Clarendon Press, 2004.

Kowaleski, Maryanne, ed. *Medieval Towns: A Reader*. Readings in Medieval Civilizations and Cultures 11. Toronto: Higher Education University of Toronto Press, 2008.

Krause, Kathy, and Alison Stones, eds. *Gautier de Coinci: Miracles, Music, and Manuscripts*. Medieval Texts and Cultures of Northern Europe 13. Turnhout: Brepols, 2006.

Kreitner, Kenneth. "Music in the Corpus Christi Procession of Fifteenth-Century Barcelona." *Early Music History* 14 (1995): 153–204.

Lacaze, Charlotte. "*Parisius–paradisus*: An Aspect of the *Vie de Saint Denis* Manuscript of 1317." *Marsyas* 16 (1972–73): 60–66.

Langley, Frederick. "Community Drama and Community Politics in Thirteenth-Century Arras: Adam de la Halle's *Jeu de la feuillée*." In *Drama and Community: People and Plays in Medieval Europe*, ed. Alan Hindley, 57–77. Turnhout: Brepols, 1999.

Lausberg, Heinrich. *Handbook of Literary Rhetoric: A Foundation for Literary Study*. Transl. Matthew Bliss et al., and ed. David Orton and R. Dean Anderson. Leiden: Brill, 1998.

Lavedan, Pierre. *Nouvelle histoire de Paris: Histoire de l'urbanisme à Paris*. Paris: Hachette, 1993.

Law, Vivian. *Grammar and the Grammarians in the Early Middle Ages*. London: Longman, 1997.

Leach, Elizabeth Eva. *Sung Birds: Music, Nature, and Poetry in the Later Middle Ages*. Ithaca: Cornell University Press, 2007.

Leber, Constant. *Collection des meilleurs dissertations, notices et traités particuliers relatifs à l'histoire de France*. 20 vols. Paris: G.-A. Dentu, 1838.

Lebrun, François. "Le Charivari à travers les condemnations des autorités ecclésiastiques en France du XIVᵉ au XVIIIᵉ siècle." In *Le Charivari*, ed. Le Goff and Schmitt, 221–28.

Lecco, Margherita. "Lo *charivari* del *Roman de Fauvel* e la tradizione della *Mesnie Hellequin*." *Mediaevistik* 13 (2000): 55–85.

Leclercq, Jean. *The Love of Learning and the Desire for God: A Study of Monastic Culture*. Transl. Catharine Misrahi. New York: Fordham University Press, 1961, 3rd ed. 1982. First published in French in 1957.

——. "Monasticism and Asceticism. II: Western Christianity." In *Christian Spirituality*, ed. McGinn and Meyendorff, 113–31.

——. "Ways of Prayer and Contemplation. II: Western." Ibid., 415–26.

Leech-Wilkinson, Daniel. *The Modern Invention of Medieval Music: Scholarship, Ideology, Performance*. Cambridge: Cambridge University Press, 2002.

Le Goff, Jacques. *Time, Work, and Culture in the Middle Ages*. Transl. Arthur Goldhammer. Chicago: University of Chicago Press, 1980.

——, and Jean-Claude Schmitt, eds. *Le Charivari: Actes de la table ronde organisée à Paris (25–27 avril 1977) par l'Ecole des Hautes Etudes en Sciences Sociales et le Centre National de la Recherche Scientifique*. Paris: Mouton, 1981.

Le Guin, Elisabeth. *Boccherini's Body: An Essay in Carnal Musicology*. Berkeley: University of California Press, 2006.

L'Engle, Susan, and Gerald Guest, eds. *Tributes to Jonathan J. G. Alexander: The Making and Meaning of Illuminated Medieval and Renaissance Manuscripts, Art and Architecture*. London: Harvey Miller, 2006.

Lilley, Keith. *Urban Life in the Middle Ages, 1000–1450.* Houndmills: Palgrave, 2002.

Logemann, Cornelia, *Heilige Ordungen: Die Bild-Räume der Vie de Saint Denis (1317) und die französische Buchmalerei des 14. Jahrhunderts* (Cologne: Böhlau, 2009).

Ludwig, Friedrich. "Musik des Mittelalters bis zum Anfang des 15. Jahrhunderts." In *Handbuch der Musikgeschichte*, ed. Guido Adler, 157–295. Frankfurt: Frankfurter Verlags-Anstalt, 1924.

——. "Die Quellen der Motette ältesten Stils," *Archiv für Musikwissenschaft*, 5 (1923): 185–222 and 273–315.

——. "Studien über die Geschichte der mehrstimmigen Musik in Mittelalter II: Die 50 Beispiele Coussemakers aus der Handschrift von Montpellier," *Sammelbände der Internationalen Musikgesellschaft* 5 (1903–1904): 200–203.

Madan, Falconer. "Hours of the Virgin (Tests for Localization)." *Bodleian Quarterly Record* 3 (1920): 40–44.

——. "The Localization of Manuscripts." In *Essays Presented to Reginald Lane Poole*, ed. Henry Davis, 5–29. Oxford: Clarendon Press, 1927.

Maillard, Jean. *Adam de la Halle: Perspective musicale.* Paris: Honoré Champion, 1982.

Marcel-Dubois, Claudie. "La Paramusique dans le charivari français contemporain." In *Le Charivari*, ed. Le Goff and Schmitt, 45–53.

McCulloch, Florence. "The Funeral of Renart the Fox in a Walters Book of Hours." *Journal of the Walters Art Gallery* 25–26 (1962–63): 8–27.

McDonald, William. "The Fool-Stick: Concerning Tristan's Club in the German Eilhart Tradition." *Euphorion* 82 (1988): 127–49.

McEntire, Sandra. *The Doctrine of Compunction in Medieval England: Holy Tears.* Studies in Mediaeval Literature 8. Lewiston, NY: The Edwin Mellen Press, 1990.

McGavin, John. "Robert III's 'Rough Music': Charivari and Diplomacy in a Medieval Scottish Court." *Scottish Historical Review* 74 (1995): 144–58.

McGee, Timothy. *The Sound of Medieval Song: Ornamentation and Vocal Style according to the Treatises.* Oxford: Clarendon Press, 1998.

McGinn, Bernard, and John Meyendorff, eds. *Christian Spirituality: Origins to the Twelfth Century.* In collaboration with Jean Leclercq. World Spirituality: An Encyclopedic History of the Religious Quest 16. New York: Crossroad, 1985.

McGregor, Gordon Douglas. *The Broken Pot Restored: Le Jeu de la feuillée of Adam de la Halle.* The Edward C. Armstrong Monographs on Medieval Literature 6. Lexington, KY: French Forum, 1991.

Menard, Philippe. "Les Emblèmes de la folie dans la littérature et dans l'art (XIIe–XIIIe siècles)." In *Hommage à Jean-Charles Payen. 'Farai chansoneta novele': Essais sur la liberté créatrice au Moyen Age*, 253–65. Caen: Centre de publications de l'Université de Caen, 1989.

——. "Le Sens du *Jeu de la feuillée.*" In *Travaux de linguistique et de littérature*, 16: Études romanes du Moyen Age et de la Renaissance, 381–93. Strasbourg: C. Klincksieck, 1978.

Meyer, Paul. "Le *Salut d'amour* dans les littératures provençale et française." *Bibliothèque de l'Ecole des chartes* 28 (1867): 24–170.

Michael, Michael. "Seeing In: The Macclesfield Psalter." In *Cambridge Illuminations*, ed. Panayotova, 115–28.

Millar, Eric. *The Luttrell Psalter* (London: British Museum, 1931).

Miner, Dorothy, ed. *Illuminated Books of the Middle Ages and Renaissance, Walters Art Gallery Exhibition Catalogue.* Baltimore: Johns Hopkins University Press, 1949.

Mittman, Asa Simon. "The Other Close at Hand: Gerald of Wales and the 'Marvels of the West.'" In *The Monstrous Middle Ages*, ed. Bildhauer and Mills, 97–112.

Moll, Richard. "Staging Disorder: Charivari in the *N-Town* Cycle." *Comparative Drama* 35 (2001): 145–61.

Morrison, Karl. *I Am You: The Hermeneutics of Empathy in Western Literature, Theology, and Art.* Princeton: Princeton University Press, 1988.

Muller, Carol Ann. *Musical Echoes: South African Women Thinking in Jazz.* With Sathima Sea Benjamin. Durham: Duke University Press, 2011.

Nathan, Hans. "The Function of Text in French 13th-Century Motets." *Musical Quarterly* 28 (1942): 445–62.

Neff, Amy. "The Pain of *Compassio*: Mary's Labor at the Foot of the Cross." *Art Bulletin* 80 (1998): 254–73.

Nelson, Janet. "Medieval Queenship." In *Women in Medieval Western Culture*, ed. Linda Mitchell, 179–207. New York: Garland Publishing, 1999.

Newhauser, Richard. "The Sin of Curiosity and the Cistercians." In *Erudition at God's Service*, ed. John Sommerfeldt, 71–95. Studies in Cistercian History 9. Kalamazoo: Cistercian Publications, 1987.

Noel, William. *The Harley Psalter.* Cambridge Studies in Palaeography and Codicology 4. Cambridge: Cambridge University Press, 1996.

———. "Medieval Charades and the Visual Syntax of the Utrecht Psalter." In *Studies in the Illustration of the Psalter*, ed. Cassidy and Wright, 34–41.

Norwood, Patricia. "Evidence Concerning the Provenance of the Bamberg Codex." *Journal of Musicology* 8 (1990): 491–504.

———. "Performance Manuscripts from the Thirteenth Century?" *College Music Symposium* 26 (1986), 92–96.

Oakes, Catherine. *Ora pro nobis: The Virgin as Intercessor in Medieval Art and Devotion.* Turnhout: Harvey Miller, 2008.

O'Neill, Mary. *Courtly Love Songs of Medieval France: Transmission and Style in the Trouvère Repertoire.* Oxford: Oxford University Press, 2006.

Page, Christopher. "Around the Performance of a 13th-Century Motet." *Early Music* 28 (2000): 343–57.

———. *Discarding Images: Reflections on Music and Culture in Medieval France.* Oxford: Clarendon Press, 1993.

———. "Johannes de Grocheio on Secular Music: A Corrected Text and a New Translation." *Plainsong and Medieval Music* 2 (1993): 17–41.

———. "Listening to the Trouvères." *Early Music* 24 (1997): 38–59.

———. *The Owl and the Nightingale: Musical Life and Ideas in France 1100–1300.* London: Dent, 1989.

———. "A Reply to Margaret Bent," *Early Music* 22 (1994): 127–32.

Panayotova, Stella, ed. *The Cambridge Illuminations: The Conference Papers.* London: Harvey Miller, 2007.

Parsoneault, Catherine. "The Montpellier Codex: Royal Influence and Musical Taste in Late Thirteenth-Century France." Ph.D. diss., University of Texas at Austin, 2001.

Parsons, John Carmi, ed. *Medieval Queenship*. New York: St. Martin's Press, 1993.

Payne, Thomas. "Poetry, Politics, and Polyphony: Philip the Chancellor's Contribution to the Music of the Notre Dame School." 3 vols. Ph.D. diss., University of Chicago, 1991.

Peden, Alison. "Medieval Concepts of the Antipodes." *History Today* 45 (1995): 27–33.

Peraino, Judith. "*Et pui conmencha a canter*: Refrains, Motets and Melody in the Thirteenth-Century Narrative *Renart le nouvel*." *Plainsong and Medieval Music* 6 (1997): 1–16.

———. "Monophonic Motets: Sampling and Grafting in the Middle Ages." *Musical Quarterly* 85 (2001): 644–80.

———. "Re-Placing Medieval Music." *Journal of the American Musicological Society* 54 (2001): 209–64.

Pesce, Dolores. "Beyond Glossing: The Old Made New in *Mout me fu grief/Robin m'aime/ Portare*." In Pesce, *Hearing the Motet*, 28–51.

———. "The Significance of Text in Thirteenth-Century Latin Motets." *Acta Musicologica* 58 (1986): 91–117.

———, ed. *Hearing the Motet: Essays on the Motet of the Middle Ages and Renaissance*. New York: Oxford University Press, 1997.

Pettit, Tom. "Protesting Inversions: Charivari as Folk Pageantry and Folk-Law." *Medieval English Theatre* 21 (1999): 21–51.

Poe, Elizabeth. Compilatio: *Lyric Texts and Prose Commentaries in Troubadour Manuscript H (Vat. Lat. 3207)*. Lexington, KY: French Forum, 2000.

Porter, Lambert. *La Fatrasie et le fatras: Essai sur la poésie irrationnelle en France au Moyen Age*. Geneva: Librairie E. Droz, 1960.

Porter, Roy. "Margery Kempe and the Meaning of Madness." *History Today* 38 (1988): 39–44.

Poulet, André. "Capetian Women and the Regency: The Genesis of a Vocation." In *Medieval Queenship*, ed. Carmi Parsons, 93–116.

Privat, Jean-Marie. "Sots, sotties, charivari." In *Atti del IV Colloquio della Société internationale pour l'étude du théâtre médiéval*, ed. Maria Chiabò, Frederico Doglio, and Marina Maymone, 331–47. Viterbo: Centro studi sul teatro medioevale e rinascimentale, 1984.

Randall, Lilian. "The Fieschi Psalter." *Journal of the Walters Art Gallery* 23 (1960): 26–47.

———. "Games and the Passion in Pucelle's Hours of Jeanne d'Evreux." *Speculum* 47 (1972): 246–57.

———. *Images in the Margins of Gothic Manuscripts*. Berkeley: University of California Press, 1966.

———. *Medieval and Renaissance Manuscripts in the Walters Art Gallery*. Vol. 1: *France, 875–1420*. With the assistance of Judith Oliver et al. Baltimore: Johns Hopkins University Press in Association with the Walters Art Gallery, 1989.

———. *Medieval and Renaissance Manuscripts in the Walters Art Gallery*. Vol. 3: *Belgium, 1250–1530*. With the assistance of Judith Oliver, Christopher Clarkson, and Claudia

Mark and consultants John Plummer and James Marrow. Baltimore: Johns Hopkins University Press in Association with the Walters Art Gallery, 1997.

Reddy, William. *The Navigation of Feeling: A Framework for the History of Emotions.* New York: Cambridge University Press, 2001.

Regalado, Nancy Freeman. "Masques réels dans le monde de l'imaginaire: Le rite et l'écrit dans le charivari du *Roman de Fauvel*, MS B.N. fr. 146." In *Masques et déguisements dans la littérature médiévale*, ed. Marie-Louise Ollier, 111–26. Montreal: University of Montreal Press, 1988.

——. "Staging the *Roman de Renart*: Medieval Theater and the Diffusion of Political Concerns into Popular Culture." *Mediaevalia* 18 (1995): 111–42.

Rézeau, Pierre. *Répertoire d'incipits des prières françaises à la fin du Moyen Age: Addenda et corrigenda aux répertoires de Sonet et Sinclair.* Geneva: Droz, 1986.

Robertson, Anne Walters. "Remembering the Annunciation in Medieval Polyphony." *Speculum* 70 (1995): 275–304.

——. *The Service-Books of the Royal Abbey of Saint-Denis: Images of Ritual and Music in the Middle Ages.* Oxford: Clarendon Press, 1991.

Rohloff, Ernest, ed. *Die Quellenhandschriften zum Musiktraktat des Johannes de Grocheio.* Leipzig: Deutscher Verlag für Musik, 1972.

Rosen, Charles. "From the Troubadours to Frank Sinatra." *New York Review of Books*, Part I in 53/3 (2006), 41–45 and Part II in 53/4 (2006), 44–49.

Rosenwein, Barbara. *Emotional Communities in the Early Middle Ages.* Ithaca: Cornell University Press, 2006.

——, ed. *Anger's Past: The Social Uses of an Emotion in the Middle Ages.* Ithaca: Cornell University Press, 1998.

Rothenberg, David. *Marian Devotion and Secular Song in Medieval and Renaissance Music* (New York: Oxford University Press, 2011).

——. "The Marian Symbolism of Spring, ca. 1200–ca. 1500: Two Case Studies." *Journal of the American Musicological Society* 59 (2006): 319–98.

Rouse, Edward Clive, and Kenneth Varty. "Medieval Paintings of Reynard the Fox in Gloucester Cathedral and Some Other Related Examples." *Archaeological Journal* 133 (1976): 104–17.

Rubin, Miri. *Corpus Christi: The Eucharist in Late Medieval Culture.* Cambridge: Cambridge University Press, 1991.

——. *Emotion and Devotion: The Meaning of Mary in Medieval Religious Cultures.* The Natalie Zemon Davis Annual Lectures. Budapest: Central European University Press, 2009.

——. *Mother of God: A History of the Virgin Mary.* London: Penguin, 2009.

Rudolph, Conrad. *The "Things of Greater Importance": Bernard of Clairvaux's "Apologia" and the Medieval Attitude toward Art.* Philadelphia: University of Pennsylvania Press, 1990.

Saenger, Paul. "Books of Hours and the Reading Habits of the Later Middle Ages." In *The Culture of Print: Power and the Uses of Print in Early Modern Europe*, ed. Roger Chartier, transl. Lydia Cochrane, 141–73. Princeton: Princeton University Press, 1989.

Said, Edward. *Humanism and Democratic Criticism.* New York: Columbia University Press, 2004.

Saltzstein, Jennifer. "Relocating the Thirteenth-Century Refrain: Intertextuality, Authority, and Origins." *Journal of the Royal Musical Association* 135 (2010): 245–79.

———. "Wandering Voices: Refrain Citation in Thirteenth-Century French Music and Poetry." Ph.D. diss., University of Pennsylvania, 2007.

Salusbury-Jones, Goronwy Tidy. *Street Life in Medieval England*. Oxford: Pen-in-Hand, 1948.

Sanders, Ernest. "The Medieval Motet." In *Gattungen der Musik in Einzeldarstellungen: Gedenkschrift Leo Schrade*, ed. Wulf Arlt et al., 497–573. Berne: Francke Verlag, 1973.

Sandler, Lucy Freeman. "The Images of Words in English Gothic Psalters." In *Studies in the Illustration of the Psalter*, ed. Cassidy and Wright, 67–86.

———. "In and Around the Text: The Question of Marginality in the Macclesfield Psalter." In *The Cambridge Illuminations*, ed. Panayotova, 105–14.

———. "Reflections on the Construction of Hybrids in English Gothic Marginal Illustration." In *Art, the Ape of Nature: Studies in Honor of H. W. Janson*, ed. Moshe Barasch and Lucy Freeman Sandler, 51–65. New York: Harry N. Abrams; Englewood Cliffs: Prentice Hall, 1981.

———. "The Word in the Text and the Image in the Margin: The Case of the Luttrell Psalter." *Journal of the Walters Art Gallery* 54 (1996): 87–99.

Saward, John. *Perfect Fools: Folly for Christ's Sake in Catholic and Orthodox Spirituality*. Oxford: Oxford University Press, 1980.

Schafer, R. Murray. *The Soundscape: Our Sonic Environment and the Tuning of the World*. Rochester: Inner Traditions International, 1993; reissue of New York: Knopf, 1977.

Schmitt, Jean-Claude. "Entre le texte et l'image: Les gestes de la prière de Saint Dominique." In *Persons in Groups: Social Behavior as Identity Formation in Medieval and Renaissance Europe*, ed. Richard Trexler, 195–214. Medieval and Renaissance Text Studies 36. Binghamton: Medieval and Renaissance Texts and Studies, 1985.

———. *Ghosts in the Middle Ages: The Living and the Dead in Medieval Society*. Transl. Teresa Fagan. Chicago: University of Chicago Press, 1998.

Schulze-Busacker, Elisabeth. "Topoi." In *A Handbook of the Troubadours*, ed. Frank Akehurst and Judith Davis. Berkeley, University of California Press, 1995.

Serchuk, Camille. "Paris and the Rhetoric of Town Praise in the *Vie de St. Denis* Manuscript (Paris, Bibliothèque nationale de France, ms fr. 2090–2)." *Journal of the Walters Art Gallery* 57 (1999): 35–47.

Sinclair, Keith Val. *Prières en ancien français: Nouvelles références, renseignements complémentaires, indications bibliographiques, corrections et tables des articles du Répertoire de Sonet*. Hamden: Archon Books, 1978.

Smart, Mary Ann. *Mimomania: Music and Gesture in Nineteenth-Century Opera*. Berkeley: University of California Press, 2004.

Smith, Bruce. *The Acoustic World of Early Modern England: Attending to the O-Factor*. Chicago: University of Chicago Press, 1999.

Smith, Mark. "Introduction: Onward to Audible Pasts." In *Hearing History*, ed. Smith, ix–xxii.

———, ed. *Hearing History: A Reader*. Athens: University of Georgia Press, 2004.

Smith, Norman. "The Earliest Motets: Music and Words." *Journal of the Royal Musical Association* 114 (1989): 141–63.

Smith, Robyn. *French Double and Triple Motets in the Montpellier Manuscript: Textual Edition, Translation and Commentary*. Musicological Studies 68. Ottawa: Institute of Mediaeval Music, 1997.

Sonet, Jean. *Répertoire d'incipit de prières en ancien français*. Geneva: Droz, 1956.

Spanke, Hans, *G. Raynauds Bibliographie des altfranzösischen Liedes, neu bearbeitet und ergänzt.* Leiden: E. J. Brill, 1955.

Spence, Sarah, "Rhetoric and Hermeneutics," in *The Troubadours*, ed. Gaunt and Kay, 164–80.

Spicer, Andrew, and Sarah Hamilton, eds. *Defining the Holy: Sacred Space in Medieval and Early Modern Europe.* Aldershot: Ashgate, 2005.

Sprunger, David. "Depicting the Insane: A Thirteenth-Century Case Study." In *Marvels, Monsters, and Miracles*, ed. Jones and Sprunger, 223–41.

—— "Introduction: The Marvelous Imagination." Ibid., xi–xxv.

Sterne, Jonathan. *The Audible Past: Cultural Origins of Sound Reproduction.* Durham, NC: Duke University Press, 2003.

Stevens, John. *Words and Music in the Middle Ages: Song, Narrative, Dance and Drama, 1050–1350.* Cambridge Studies in Music. Cambridge: Cambridge University Press, 1986.

Stones, Alison. "Les Manuscrits du Cardinal Jean Cholet et l'enluminure Beauvaisienne vers le fin du XIIIème siècle." In *L'Art gothique dans l'Oise et ses environs (XIIème–XIVème siècle): Architecture civile et religieuse, peinture murale, sculpture et arts précieux. Colloque international organisé à Beauvais les 10 et 11 octobre 1998 par le Groupe d'Étude des Monuments et Oeuvres d'Art de l'Oise et du Beauvais*, 230–68. Beauvais: GEMOB, 2001.

——. *Manuscripts Illuminated in France: Gothic Manuscripts, 1260–1320* (Turnhout: Brepols, forthcoming).

Strohm, Reinhard. "How to Make Medieval Music our Own: A Response to Christopher Page and Margaret Bent," *Early Music* 22 (1994): 715–92.

——. *Music in Late Medieval Bruges.* Oxford: Clarendon Press, 1985.

Swain, Barbara. *Fools and Folly during the Middle Ages and the Renaissance.* New York: Columbia University Press, 1932.

Symes, Carol. *A Common Stage: Theater and Public Life in Medieval Arras.* Ithaca: Cornell University Press, 2007.

Taruskin, Richard. *The Oxford History of Western Music*, 6 vols. New York and Oxford: Oxford University Press, 2005.

Teeuwen, Mariken. *The Vocabulary of Intellectual Life in the Middle Ages.* Turnhout: Brepols, 2003.

Thompson, Emily. *The Soundscape of Modernity: Architectural Acoustics and the Culture of Listening in America, 1900–1933.* Cambridge, MA: MIT Press, 2002.

Tischler, Hans. *The Style and Evolution of the Earliest Motets (to circa 1270).* 4 vols. Musicological Studies 40. Henryville: Institute of Mediaeval Music, 1985.

Tomasch, Sylvia. "Introduction." In *Text and Territory*, ed. Tomasch and Gilles, 1–12.

——, and Sealy Gilles, eds. *Text and Territory: Geographical Imagination in the European Middle Ages.* Philadelphia: University of Pennsylvania Press, 1998.

Tomlinson, Gary. "Monumental Musicology." *Journal of the Royal Musical Association* 132 (2007): 349–74.

Trexler, Richard. *The Christian at Prayer: An Illustrated Prayer Manual Attributed to Peter the Chanter (d. 1197).* Medieval and Renaissance Texts and Studies 44. Binghamton, NY: Medieval and Renaissance Texts and Studies, 1987.

Uhl, Patrice. "Non-sens et parodie dans la fatrasie: Contribution à la localization du champ interférentiel." *Archiv für das Studium der neueren Sprachen und Literaturen* 144 (1992): 71–97.

——. "Les 'Sotes chançons' du *Roman de Fauvel* (MS E): La symptomatique indécision du rubricateur." *French Studies* 45 (1991): 385–402.

Valesio, Paolo. "The Language of Madness in the Renaissance." *Yearbook of Italian Studies: An Annual Publication of the Italian Cultural Institute*, 199–234. Florence: Casalini Libri, 1971.

Van Buren, Anne Hagopian. Review of Otto Pächt and Dagmar Thoss, *Die illuminierten Handschriften und Inkunabeln der flämische Schule II*, in Speculum 68 (1993): 1187–90.

Vance, Eugene. "*Le Jeu de la feuillée* and the Poetics of Charivari." *Modern Language Notes* 100 (1985): 815–28.

Van Vleck, Amelia. *Memory and Re-Creation in Troubadour Lyric*. Berkeley: University of California Press, 1991.

Varty, Kenneth. "The Death and Resurrection of Reynard in Mediaeval Literature and Art." *Nottingham Mediaeval Studies* 10 (1966): 70–93.

——. "The Pursuit of Reynard in Mediaeval English Literature and Art." *Nottingham Mediaeval Studies* 8 (1964): 62–81.

——. *Reynard, Renart, Reinaert and Other Foxes in Medieval England: The Iconographic Evidence. A Study of the Illustrating of Fox Lore and Reynard the Fox Stories in England during the Middle Ages*. Amsterdam: Amsterdam University Press, 1999.

——. *Reynard the Fox: A Study of the Fox in Medieval English Art*. Leicester: Leicester University Press, 1967.

——, ed. *Reynard the Fox: Social Engagement and Cultural Metamorphoses in the Beast Epic of the Middle Ages to the Present*. New York: Berghahn Books, 2000.

Vaultier, Roger. *Le Folklore pendant la guerre de Cent Ans d'après les Lettres de Rémission du Trésor des Chartes*. Paris: Librairie Guénégaud, 1965.

Vettori, Alessandro. "Singing with Angels: Iacopone da Todi's Prayerful Rhetoric." In *Franciscans at Prayer*, ed. Johnson, 221–48.

Wallace, David. *Premodern Places: Calais to Surinam, Chaucer to Aphra Behn*. Malden, MA: Blackwell Publishing, 2004.

Ward, Graham. *Cities of God*. London: Routledge, 2000.

Webb, Diana. "Domestic Space and Devotion in the Middle Ages." In *Defining the Holy*, ed. Spicer and Hamilton, 27–47.

Wegman, Rob. "Reviewing Images." *Music & Letters* 76 (1995): 256–73.

Weller, Philip. "Frames and Images: Locating Music in Cultural Histories of the Middle Ages," *Journal of the American Musicological Society* 50 (1997): 7–54.

Welsford, Enid. *The Fool: His Social and Literary History*. London: Faber, 1968, first published 1935.

Werf, Hendrick van der. *The Extant Troubadour Melodies: Transcriptions and Essays for Performers and Scholars*. Rochester, NY: Author's Publication, 1984.

Wieck, Roger. *Time Sanctified: The Book of Hours in Medieval Art and Life*. With essays by Lawrence Poos, Virginia Reinburg, and John Plummer. New York: G. Braziller in Association with the Walters Art Gallery, 1988.

Williams, David. *Deformed Discourse: The Function of the Monster in Mediaeval Thought and Literature*. Montreal: McGill–Queen's University Press, 1996.

Williams, Paul, ed. *The Fool and the Trickster: Studies in Honour of Enid Welsford*. Cambridge: D. S. Brewer, 1979.

Williamson, Beth. "Altarpieces, Liturgy, and Devotion." *Speculum* 79 (2004): 341–406.

———. *The Madonna of Humility: Development, Dissemination and Reception, c. 1340–1400.* Bristol Studies in Medieval Culture. Woodbridge: Boydell & Brewer, 2009.

Wilson, Blake. *Music and Merchants: The Laudesi Companies of Republican Florence.* Oxford: Clarendon Press, 1992.

Wogan-Brown, Jocelyn. "Reading the World: The Hereford *Mappa mundi*." *Parergon* 9 (1991): 117–35.

Wolinski, Mary. "The Compilation of the Montpellier Codex," *Early Music History* 11 (1992): 263–301.

———. "The Montpellier Codex: Its Compilation, Notation, and Implications for the Chronology of the Thirteenth-Century Motet." Ph.D. diss., Brandeis University, 1988.

Wright, Craig. "The Palm Sunday Procession in Medieval Chartres." In *The Divine Office in the Latin Middle Ages*, ed. Fassler and Baltzer, 344–71.

Wright, Rosemary Muir. "Introducing the Medieval Psalter." In *Studies in the Illustration of the Psalter*, ed. Cassidy and Wright, 1–11.

Zieman, Katherine. *Singing the New Song: Literacy and Liturgy in Late Medieval England.* Philadelphia, University of Pennsylvania Press, 2008.

Zink, Michel. *Le Moyen Age et ses chansons, ou un Passé en trompe-d'oeil.* Paris: Editions de Fallois, 1996.

Ziolkowski, Jan. *Talking Animals: Medieval Latin Beast Poetry, 750–1150.* Philadelphia: University of Pennsylvania Press, 1993.

Zumthor, Paul. *Essai de poétique médiévale.* Paris: Seuil, 1972.

———. "Fatrasie et coq-à-l'âne (de Beaumanoir à Clément Marot)." In *Fin du Moyen Age et Renaissance: Mélanges de philologie française offerts à Robert Guiette*, 5–18. Antwerp: Nederlandsche Boekhandel, 1961.

———. "*Mappa mundi* et performance: La cartographie médiévale." In *Le Moyen Age dans la modernité: Mélanges offerts à Roger Dragonetti*, ed. Jean Scheidegger, Sabine Girardet, and Eric Hicks, 459–71. Paris: Honoré Champion, 1996.

———. *La Poésie et la voix dans la civilization médiévale.* Paris: Presses Universitaires de France, 1984.